THE IMAGINARY REVOLUTION

Parisian Students and Workers in 1968

Michael Seid.

Berghahn Books

NEW YORK • OXFORD

Published in 2004 by
Berghahn Books

www.berghahnbooks.com

© 2004 Michael Seidman
Reprinted in 2006

Library of Congress Cataloging-in-Publication Data

Seidman, Michael (Michael M.)
    The imaginary revolution : Parisian students and workers in 1968 /
by Michael Seidman.
        p. cm.
    Includes bibliographical references.
    ISBN 1-57181-675-5 (alk. paper) ISBN 1-57181-685-2 (pbk.)
      1. Riots—France—Paris—History—20th century. 2. College stu-
dents—France—Political activity—History—20th century. 3. Working
class—France—Paris—Political activity—History—20th century.
4. Radicalism—France—History—20th century. 5. Paris (France)—
History—1944– 6. France—Politics and government—1958– I. Title.

DC420.S44 2004
944'.3610836—dc22

                                                                  2003063940

British Library Cataloguing in Publication Data

A catalogue record for this book is available from
the British Library.

Printed in the United States on acid-free paper

Lovin' eyes can never see.

— Percy Sledge

CONTENTS

—◦◦◦—

Illustrations

—❦—

ACKNOWLEDGMENTS

—◈◈◈—

A number of individuals helped to bring this fifteen-year project to completion. Many thanks go to Marcel van der Linden, Jean-Claude Dumas, Jean-Paul Vilaine, Steve Leiber, Arthur Arrivant, Marc Tomsin, and Henri Simon. My colleagues at UNC-W—James McNab, P.-J. Lapaire, Pascale Barthe, Kathleen Berkeley, Susan McCaffray, and Bruce Kinzer—were extremely helpful. So were Parisian archivists Stéphanie Méchine, Edouard Vasseur, and Patrice Havard. Sophie Williams and Andrew Dutka performed selflessly in Randall Library. The copyeditor, Jaime Taber, exhibited impressive professionalism. The two referees improved the following pages immeasurably. All errors and omissions are unfortunately and undoubtedly my own.

ABBREVIATIONS

AERUA   Association des étudiants de la résidence universitaire
         d'Antony (Antony residents' association)
AFGEN   Association fédérative des groupes d'études de Nanterre
         (Nanterre-UNEF group)
ARCUN   Association des résidents de la cité universitaire de Nanterre
         (Nanterre residents' association)
ARLP   Alliance républicaine pour les libertés et le progrès (extreme-
         right political party)
CAL   Comités d'action lycéens (high-school action committees)
CFDT   Confédération française démocratique du travail (trade-
         union federation)
CFTC   Confédération française des travailleurs chrétiens (Catholic
         trade-union federation)
CGC   Confédération générale des cadres (executives' and man-
         agers' union)
CGPME   Confédération nationale des petites et moyennes entreprises
         (small and mid-sized employers' association)
CGT   Confédération générale du travail (PCF-oriented trade
         union federation)
CLER   Comité de liaison des étudiants révolutionnaires (Trotskyite
         student organization)
CNPF   Conseil national du patronat français (major employers'
         organization)
CNT   Confédération nationale du travail (anarchosyndicalist union)
CRAC   Comité révolutionnaire d'agitation culturelle (group for rev-
         olutionary culture)
CROUS   Centre régional des oeuvres universitaires et scolaires (offi-
         cial student affairs office)
CRS   Compagnies républicaines de sécurité (national riot police)
CVB   Comités Vietnam de base (Maoist pro-FLN organization)

CVN	Comité Vietnam national (Trotskyite pro-FLN organization)
EDF-GDF	Electricité de France, Gaz de France (nationalized gas and electricity company)
ESU	Etudiants socialistes unifiés (PSU student organization)
FEN	Fédération de l'éducation nationale (teachers' union)
FER	Fédération des étudiants révolutionnaires (Trotskyite student organization)
FGDS	Fédération de la gauche démocrate et socialiste (left-center political party)
FGEL	Fédération des groupes d'études de lettres (UNEF student group)
FLN	Front de libération nationale (Algerian independence organization or Vietnamese Communists' independence organization)
FNEF	Fédération nationale des étudiants de France (rightist student union)
FNSEA	Fédération nationale des syndicats d'exploitants agricoles (farmers' lobby)
FO	Force ouvrière (moderate trade-union federation)
GIM	Groupement des industries métallurgiques (Parisian metallurgical industrialists' association)
IFOP	Institut français d'opinion publique (polling organization)
JCR	Jeunesses communistes révolutionnaires (Trotskyite)
JOC	Jeunesse ouvrière chrétienne (Catholic youth organization)
LEA	Liaison des étudiants anarchistes (anarchist student group)
MAU	Mouvement d'action universitaire (militant student group)
MNEF	Mutuelle nationale des étudiants de France (student mutual-aid organization)
MOI	Main d'oeuvre immigré (Communist immigrant worker organization)
OAS	Organisation Armée Secrète (extreme-right terrorist organization)
ORTF	Office de radio et television française (state monopoly of radio and television)
PCF	Parti communiste français (French Communist Party)
PDM	Progrès et démocratie moderne (centrist party)
PSU	Parti socialiste unifié (leftist political party)
PTT	Postes, Télégraphes, Téléphones (state communications monopoly)
RATP	Régie autonome des transports parisiens (Parisian public transportation)
RTL	Radio, Télévision Luxembourg (Luxembourg radio and television)
SAC	Service d'action civique (Gaullist agents)
SDS	Students for a Democratic Society (American student group)

SDS	Sozialistische Deutsche Studentenbund (German student group)
SFIO	Section française de l'Internationale ouvrière (Socialist political party)
SGP	Syndicat général des personnels de la Préfecture de Police (Parisian police union)
SNCF	Société nationale des chemins de fer (nationalized railroad network)
SNESup	Syndicat national de l'enseignement supérieur (leftist university teachers' union)
SNI	Syndicat national des instituteurs (elementary-school teachers' union)
TSRF	Tendance syndicale révolutionnaire fédéraliste (anarchist student group)
UDCA	Union de défense des commerçants et artisans (Poujadist right-wing political organization)
UDR	Union pour la défense de la République (Gaullist Party)
UEC	Union des étudiants communistes (Communist student organization)
UNR	Union pour la nouvelle République (Gaullist Party)
UIMM	Union des industries métallurgiques et minières (heavy-industry employers' association)
UJCml	Union des jeunesses communistes marxistes-léninistes (Maoist youth organization)
UNEF	Union national des étudiants de France (leftist student union)

Abbreviations for Notes

ADHS	Archives départementales des Hauts-de-Seine, Nanterre
AN	Archives Nationales, Fontainebleau and Paris
APP	Archives de la Préfecture de Police, Paris
BN	Bibliothèque Nationale, Paris
GIM	Groupement des Industries Métallurgiques, Neuilly
BDIC	Bibliothèque de documentation internationale contemporaine, Nanterre

INTRODUCTION

May 1968—a Rupture?

—◦◦◦—

In 1968 worldwide revolutionary agitation was greater than at any time since the end of World War I. From Paris to Peking, governments were forced to deal with varieties of unrest. The global revolts of 1968 seemed to constitute an international revolutionary wave comparable to the Atlantic Revolutions at the end of the eighteenth century or to the continental European revolutions of 1848. As in 1789 and 1848, Paris was once again a center of revolt. Although this time Paris did not initiate the movement (German, Italian, and American upheavals preceded it), the French capital became the first major theater in which student and worker unrest coincided. Revolutionaries and radical reformers throughout the world believed that combined student and worker protests in France were nearly successful in overthrowing the government and creating a new society. Some argued that Paris had "surpassed" the other rebellions.[1] During and after the rebellions, the rebels were optimistic: "It is only a beginning," they chanted.

This vision of the French May (a word that often serves as shorthand for the "events" of May–June 1968) remains dominant. The events are still viewed as a rupture with the past and the beginning not of proletarian revolution (as many radicals thought at the time), but rather of a cultural rebellion that led to a more emancipated society. Almost all agree that the crisis of the spring of 1968 changed France profoundly. Given its perceived importance, it was not surprising that in the immediate aftermath of May and in subsequent years the events were, according to police, "overexploited by publishers" of books and even music.[2] The publishing explosion confirmed the judgment of Georges Pompidou, then prime minister, who remarked in the midst of the crisis: "The only historical precedent [of the May events] is the fifteenth century when the structures of the Middle Ages were collapsing and when students were revolting at

---

Notes for this section begin on page 13.

the Sorbonne. Right now, it is not the government which is being attacked, nor institutions nor even France. It is our own civilization."[3]

Pompidou's minister of culture, André Malraux, echoed his boss and labeled the events an epochal "crisis of civilization.... We are at the beginning of a drama."[4] For Malraux, "the unprecedented abdication of the world's young people from Mexico to Japan" unveiled "one of the deepest crises our civilization has known."[5] Both the Count of Paris and the capital's prefect of police, Maurice Grimaud, believed that the "deep meaning" of the movement was youth's "refusal ... of a society that is decomposing."[6] Even for those hostile to the May movement, the events were both dramatic and extremely significant.

Historians, sociologists, and, of course, journalists have followed this conception. Immediately after the events, two reporters provided a detailed history that viewed "the explosion of May" as altering France profoundly: "In several weeks everything—the old ways, habits, customs, and ideas—collapsed.... From now on, French history after World War II will be divided into pre- and post-1968."[7] Adrien Dansette's *Mai 1968* appeared three years after the events and provided a political history of the "crisis."[8] Dansette's approach followed that of a traditional political historian who competently chronicled the "great events" of French history. Convinced of the overriding significance of these events, Anglo-American journalists adopted a similar approach, even if they were more sympathetic than Dansette to the actions and vision of the radical actors.[9] Their histories equated 1968 with a revolutionary political, social, and cultural crisis.

The works of major French sociologists on May were also founded on the assumption that May was a seminal "crisis." Henri Lefebvre posited students, especially social science students at Nanterre, as major actors who challenged the civilization of a bureaucratic-consumer society and nearly succeeded in making a revolution.[10] According to Lefebvre, students politicized the streets and appropriated social space during the crisis. By proceeding "towards the re-conquest of urban space," protesters evoked the Paris Commune of 1871. In their widely disseminated volume, Edgar Morin, Claude Lefort, and Cornelius Castoriadis viewed the happening as a welcomed "rupture" (*une brèche*) with conformist consumer society.[11] This trio of French sociologists/philosophers found the rebellion anticipatory of a new social order.

Fellow sociologist Alain Touraine saw the movement in similar terms. May represented a crisis of the old regime, which—like most of his colleagues—he painted as rigidly repressive:[12] "The only response left to the regime by its *grandeur* was the police." The May Movement constituted a great turning point: "New class struggles are emerging and being organized in areas which a short time ago were considered outside the sphere of 'productive' activities: urban life, the management of needs and resources, education." May fostered the birth of a "new social movement," which would replace the old class struggle between bourgeois and workers.

According to Touraine, the workers—like peasants in the late nineteenth century—were a class in decline in the late twentieth century. Students and workers no longer battled the bourgeoisie but instead "reinvented the class struggle" by fighting the Fifth Republic's technocracy. Young people challenged the latter by demanding democratic decision-making and participation. Students of the mass university had developed into revolutionary actors since they were part of the productive apparatus of modern industrial society. They revolted not so much because they were socialist or even communist but rather because they were antitechnocratic. May 1968 "marked the birth of a new period in the social history of industrial societies." The movement was a healthy response against "authoritarian rationalism" and "an archaic society with a modern economy." The May and June events were "both so extraordinary and so important" that Touraine predicted they would initiate "new conflicts that will be as fundamental and as enduring as the worker movement was in the period of capitalist industrialization." Many Anglo-American historians of the 1960s have continued to focus on the transformative political/social projects of the decade. James Miller has identified the American New Left of the decade with "participatory democracy."[13] Paul Ginsborg calls the period from 1968 to 1973 in Italy "the era of collective action."[14]

Despite his hostility to the May movement and his maverick reputation, Raymond Aron agreed with much of the analysis of his fellow sociologists and historians. Like his colleagues, Aron saw *autogestion* (self-management or workers' control) as a key component of the revolt. However—unlike Touraine, Morin, Lefort, Lefebvre, Castoriadis et al.—Aron thought it an impossible and even a ridiculous goal.[15] He sensibly insisted that the universities and workplaces of an advanced industrial society could not be managed democratically. However, in accord with the Morin-Lefort-Castoriadis trio, Aron believed that the unfettering of speech defined the events of what he labeled the *révolution introuvable*. Instead of lauding this emancipation of the word, as did the trio and other observers (such as Michel de Certeau), Aron was bitterly critical of it.[16] He likened student rebels to members of the Club de l'Intelligence in 1848, whose utopian utterances and verbalized nonsense Flaubert humorously derided in *Sentimental Education*. Thus, the students engaged in what Aron called a "psychodrama" or a "symbolic revolt," not a real revolution. Yet, in the end, Aron shared his fellow sociologists' view that May was a crisis of civilization and a rupture with the past: "They [revolutionary students] deserve to be taken seriously. They will not be able to construct a new order but they have ruptured the old [*ouvert une brèche*]."[17] Even if illogical and irrational, "bourgeois students ... express a *malaise* of the entire Western Civilization." They demonstrated "the fragility of the modern order" and of "twentieth-century liberal France."

Newspapers, magazines, popular and learned works have repeatedly offered analysis, commentary, and reproductions on the tenth, fifteenth, twentieth, twenty-fifth, and thirtieth anniversaries of May. At the time of the first decennial celebration, French scholars and the mass media persisted in their view of May as the beginning of a new age. In 1978, Morin et al. reaffirmed the diagnosis of "crisis of civilization."[18] As critics of bureaucracy and technocracy, the trio welcomed May as a break with a sterile social order and a healthy step toward *autogestion*. Alain Delale and Gilles Ragache, in their *La France de 68* (1978), seconded this perspective by re-emphasizing the so-called revolutionary crisis, even as they abandoned the Paris-centric approach of most previous studies.

Also, in 1978 Régis Debray anticipated the presently dominant interpretation when he wrote that the events were "the cradle of a new bourgeois society."[19] In other words, the crisis remained revolutionary but the revolution was "bourgeois," not proletarian. For Debray, May 1968 carried the new-age culture of neocapitalism that changed "the peasant mentality" that tenaciously held sway over a newly industrialized France: "Capitalist development strategy required the cultural revolution of May." In 1978 the *tiersmondiste* Debray identified May as a stratagem of Western modernity.

Mai 68: Histoire des Evénements, by the journalist Laurent Joffrin, appeared on the twentieth anniversary and argued in a similar manner that "in this country which loves revolutions so much, we had to have one fail so that everything could change." The eminent sociologist Pierre Bourdieu concurred and posited that the events were "a visible break" with the past.[20] May was "the critical moment" "when all become possible." Three other sociologists argued that the May movement produced both "new values" and "a new form of sociability."[21] Concurrently, the political scientist (and ex-Trotskyite) Henri Weber agreed that "without the earthquake of May 68 and its aftershocks, France would have remained a blocked society."[22] Hamon and Rotman's *Génération*, the printed and audio-visual success of the twentieth anniversary, posited a polyvalent May that became a busy major interstate highway with a multitude of exits.[23] For these authors, May led to feminism, the brink of terrorism, and finally to a tolerant, pluralistic, and emancipated democratic consciousness. The historian Antoine Prost expressed doubts that *Génération* had made an original contribution to the literature on May and was skeptical concerning the representivity of the group of radicals who were the focus of the two-volume work.[24] *Génération* portrayed the history of relatively well-known militants, not anonymous students or workers. It remained within the boundaries of traditional political history, which was one of the reasons for its outstanding commercial success. Jean-Pierre Duteuil's *Nanterre 1965–66–67–68* also recounted the adventures of the militants, but its spotlight on their cultural activities and everyday existence makes his work indispensable to an understanding of the extreme left at that *faculté*.[25]

The demise during the 1980s of any hope of proletarian/social revolution and the revival of individualism stimulated interpretations by philosophers Luc Ferry, Alain Renaut, and Gilles Lipovetsky.[26] Ferry and Renaut analyzed the "revolution" of 1968 as another manifestation of what the pair called revolutionary individualism, which had first emerged during the French Revolution and progressed afterwards. Revolutionary individualism contained two essential aspects. First, individuals revolted against hierarchy in the name of equality. Second, liberty challenged tradition. The ultimate expression of revolutionary individualism came in 1968 when, according to Ferry and Renaut, large numbers revolted against hierarchies in the name of liberty and equality.[27] These philosophers posited that the essence of May was its antihierarchical nature and not its utopian political forms. May dramatically changed the traditions and customs of a stratified society and anticipated the rise of the narcissistic individualism of the 1980s. Therefore, 1968 was not a failed revolution. Instead, it inherited the revolutionary individualism of 1789 and transformed it in a more egotistical direction.

Gilles Lipovetsky offered a variant of this interpretation.[28] Although Lipovetsky was much more sympathetic to the movement, his analysis ironically confirmed not only hostile psychoanalytic interpretations of events but also certain Communist intellectuals' bitter charges that the students were too spontaneous, too libertarian, and too self-indulgent.[29] Unlike Ferry and Renaut, who regarded the individualism of May as "democratic" and "republican," Lipovetsky classified it as subversive and even anarchistic. To prove his point, he highlighted the radically individualist character of certain May graffiti: "It is forbidden to forbid." "Neither God nor Master." "God is me." May expressed the desire of the individual to be free from all collective constraints or what Lipovetsky labeled "utopian individualism." Radicals challenged university hierarchy, a repressive state, and traditional politics. Their utopian spirit had little in common with Fourierist or Owenite visions, i.e., "the great deductive and hyperlogical utopian philosophies which described in minute detail the administration and regulations of the Ideal City." Instead, May was about spontaneous humor and, even more, pleasure. The revolt merely reinforced the hedonism of 1960s consumer society.[30]

In important ways, Lipovetsky's view recalled the hostile psychoanalytic interpretation of events by André Stéphane, who saw May as an expression of the personal problems of a narcissistic generation.[31] Aron's "psychodrama" also hinted at a psychoanalytic interpretation of May. Expressions of oedipal tensions inevitably emerged from some of the literature.[32] According to Luisa Passerini, *soixante-huitards* in Europe and America "chose to be orphans."[33] Yet the psychoanalytic approach ultimately remains unsatisfactory since its ahistorical framework fails to explain the timing and content of protest movements.

Individualistic interpretations have naturally raised strong objections, particularly from the sociologist and psychoanalyst Cornelius Castoriadis: "The interpretation of May 68 in terms of the preparation (or acceleration) of contemporary individualism constitutes one of the most extreme examples that I know—given the incontestable good faith of the authors—to rewrite against all credibility the history which most of us have lived through and to alter the meaning of events even though they are fresh in our minds."[34] According to Castoriadis, May was not about individualism, but its opposite, "re-socialization." People "were looking for truth, justice, liberty, and community." Members of *groupuscules*—the Maoists, for example—admired China not because it was "a Nazi or even a Leninist society but because they dreamed that a real revolution was taking place, that the masses were eliminating the bureaucracy, that 'experts' were put in their place, etc. That this vision could produce virtually criminal illusions is *another* discussion." For Castoriadis, the essence of May was this powerful challenge to bureaucratic and technocratic elites.

The political scientist Bernard Lacroix echoed Castoriadis by making another incisive critique of the individualists. Lacroix argued that Ferry, Renaud, and Lipovetsky were not really interested in what happened in 1968. He accurately accused them of neglecting political and social history in favor of what intellectuals said about the events: "They have no desire to rediscover what people thought or what they wished to do. They completely ignore the meaning the actors gave to their own actions."[35] "In all of this, there is an assumed superiority of a philosopher's competence and a reaffirmation of his methods compared to any empirical investigation." Lacroix concluded that the methods of purely intellectual history were inadequate for comprehending May. Only by acknowledging the subjects' alleged revolutionary actions and intentions could the events be understood.

Castoriadis and Lacroix exposed the reductive nature of the interpretations of Lipovetsky, Ferry, and Renaut, who ignored much of what actually happened in 1968. The individualist school has forgotten the extent to which faith in the working class constrained individualism in 1968. For the radicals of that era, personal liberation was tied to justice for workers. Individual emancipation could not be severed from the class collectivity. Furthermore, Renaut and the others worked in the somewhat outmoded tradition of idealism and were too exclusively concerned with thought. They did not analyze the role of politics, class, and the state. The historian Jean-Pierre Rioux has perceptively remarked that their May 1968 was cool and hedonistic, without political goals and worker strikes.[36]

Yet despite their many apparent faults, individualist interpretations probed a central issue. Although Castoriadis and Lacroix correctly criticized the school's omissions and simplistic methodology, the individualists did incisively stress that May was not merely—as Castoriadis would have it—a collective political project oriented toward a self-managed society. Lipovetsky appropriately emphasized the truly radical nature of individualism in 1968. It is hard to imagine how the demands of radical students, such as the *Enragés* or even the March 22 Movement, could have been met by any society. Antiwork, antihierarchical, and generally antirepressive desires would ultimately subvert any social order. Castoriadis's *autoges-tionnaire* perspective, in which May represented the hope that the auton-omous individual would mesh with a self-managed society, is, to some degree, naive and wishful. The radical and hedonistic individualism of the 1960s was incompatible with student self-management or workers' control. Repression of subversive individualism proved necessary to get students and workers to perform their social roles, even if in his often Panglossian manner Lipovetsky has ignored this repression and posited the decline of "brute force" and the automatic rise of "participation."[37]

Both the individualist and anti-individualist interpretations have con-tinued to see May as a profound rupture in French society. Each has viewed the events as an intense challenge to an old regime of cultural and social conservatism. Ferry, Renaut, and Lipovetsky assumed a culturally repressive Gaullist society. Progressives such as Castoriadis and his fellow sociologists—Touraine, Morin, Lefort, Lefebvre, and even conservative Aron—perceived students and workers attempting to overcome the bureau-cratic, technocratic, and capitalist Fifth Republic. May was significant since it gave protesters the opportunity to begin emancipating themselves from a traditional and constraining Gaullist regime.

The thirtieth anniversary inspired another wave of publication fever. In 1998 Lefebvre's *L'Irruption*, Touraine's *Mouvement*, Hamon and Rot-man's *Génération*, and Joffrin's *Mai 68* were all reissued, along with sev-eral inexpensive histories of May.[38] Anarchist, Trotskyite, and other leftist *groupuscules* reproduced primary sources to show how May be-came their moment of glory in post–World War II France.[39] Specialized studies—on Jews, Daniel Cohn-Bendit, Catholics, Charles de Gaulle, and workers—also appeared.[40] Major periodicals such as *Le Monde, Paris Match,* and *Le Nouvel Observateur* printed special supplements or devoted many pages to recounting and analyzing the events of May and June. At the same time, the thirtieth anniversary also encouraged the publication of one of the largest and most serious books about May, Jean-Pierre Le Goff's *Mai 68, l'héritage impossible.* Le Goff, a sociologist, deepened *Génération*'s thesis of a polyvalent May. Indeed, the divergent tendencies of May con-stituted "an impossible heritage." May spawned two powerful but con-tradictory currents: first, the libertarian/countercultural (what Americans in the 1960s labeled the "freaks"), and second, the Leninist/neo-Marxist (or in American slang, the "rads"). The first tendency demanded personal and sexual freedoms, and libertarianism became the connecting theme of a number of famous and continually reproduced May graffiti: "Live with-out dead time." "Enjoy without obstacles." "Take your desires for reality." "Boredom is counter-revolutionary." "I came in the cobblestones." "The more I make revolution, the more I want to make love." The second cur-rent of 1968 has received comparatively less attention from scholars and the media. In France and in Italy, the *groupuscules* that provoked 1968 protests—whether anarchist, Trotskyite, pro-Situationist, or Maoist—were overwhelmingly *ouvriériste*, believing that the workers would and must make the revolution. The ideology of workers' control attempted to synthesize *ouvriérisme* and libertarianism.

Despite attempts by anarchists, Trotskyites, and other surviving *groupuscules* to revive the "workerist" perspective, by the 1990s it had been eclipsed by the individualist argument. If some conceded that May had failed to change society politically, a popular consensus formed that it had succeeded culturally. Instead of working-class revolution or a popular front, the events unleashed a torrent of hedonism, libertarianism, and individualism. Sexual mores relaxed, social relationships became less authoritarian, and society became more tolerant.[41] According to the special thirtieth anniversary issue of *Le Nouvel Observateur*, the events constituted "a false revolution that changed everything." The magazine devoted several pages to an interview with Lipovetsky, who—like Debray twenty years earlier—argued that May constituted a cultural revolution of considerable import: "May freed society from a matrix of conventions which were no longer in sync with neo-capitalism and yet persisted. Revolutionary violence eliminated outdated customs from consumer society. It helped to bring forth cultural liberalism."[42] The exchange between former prime minister Michel Rocard and ex-student leader Daniel Cohn-Bendit in the thirtieth-anniversary issue of *Paris Match* made a similar point.[43] Cohn-Bendit: "The movement wanted to change lifestyles more than to change a government." Rocard concurred that "student protest challenged authoritarianism and an excess of hierarchy." Cohn-Bendit: "You remarried twice and would have never become prime minister if May hadn't happened. May destroyed moral hypocrisy."

In the face of such media hype about May's legacy, skepticism is warranted. The connection between the events of the spring of 1968 and the social/cultural changes which were allegedly manifest years later remains unclear. Other societies—such as the British and German—experienced similar transformations and trends toward permissiveness without undergoing the conjuncture of puissant worker and student movements that France experienced in 1968.[44] The pre-1968 old regimes were not as repressive and monolithic as analysts of the French May have painted them.[45] In fact, there was a sociocultural continuity between pre- and post-May periods in Europe and America. Similarly, there was continuity in working-class demands and desires.[46] French workers continued to press for higher salaries and less work, as they had throughout the nineteenth and early twentieth century.

The student-worker juncture in 1968 France was exceptional. Certainly, in no major Western nation did the student and worker movements intersect as they did in France in May. Italy came closest to repeating the French precedent, but French centralization encouraged the simultaneity of its student and worker protests. The more decentralized Italian peninsula underwent a delayed and regionalized worker response to the student agitation.[47]

The zenith of the Italian workers' movement—the "hot autumn of 1969" —came more than a year after the French climax. The Italians refer to their events as the *maggio strisciante*, the drawn-out May, which—while significantly invoking the model of the French May—also included 1969 and even beyond.[48]

Ultimately, though, France became the exception that proved the rule. The paths of French students and workers repeated the American and German experiences of the 1960s. Student and worker trajectories only briefly merged. As in other countries, radicals supported revolutionary ideals; workers, practical gains. Young French radicals went beyond the quantitative demands of trade-union movements to challenge social hierarchy and property. They defied sexual, educational, and political constraints. The student movement wished to synthesize movements for personal liberation with social justice. This encounter gave the movement its force and is a major reason why the 1960s continue to fascinate. The split between the personal and the political provoked a crisis of the left, especially of Marxism. The works of Lefebvre, Herbert Marcuse, and prominent Situationists such as Guy Debord and Raoul Vaneigem responded to this crisis by offering tantalizing prospects of reconciliation of the personal with the political.

Young French revolutionaries of various sects believed fervently in working-class revolution.[49] Antihierarchical students had paradoxically accepted the authority of the "working class." May participants often espoused a radical but conventional leftism that was partially an outgrowth of opposition to the Algerian War and ensuing *tiersmondisme*.[50] The American fiasco in Vietnam followed the French failure in Algeria and resurrected a moral and political anti-imperialism that propelled protest. Anti-imperialists condemned the Vietnam War as immoral while *tiersmondistes* looked upon socialist governments in undeveloped countries—Algeria, Cuba, and China—as models for the future. They were projections of students' romantic thinking and reflected their earnest search for a revolutionary theory and agent. However, in contrast to the situation during the Algerian War, anti-imperialism never became the raison d'être of the movement. Instead, it served the function of pulling diverse *groupuscules* together. In the 1960s, anti-imperialism coalesced with antifascism, which had also had deep roots in the twentieth-century left. The *groupuscules* of the racist, xenophobic, and anti-Semitic right contested leftist students in educational institutions and on the streets of the capital. Antifascist and anti-imperialist legacies fleetingly meshed with a hatred of wage labor and a politicized hedonism to create the most powerful student movement in French history. Traditional leftism and a democratized libertinism motivated large numbers of young people.

Alexis de Tocqueville argued that Enlightenment ideas penetrated not just the bourgeoisie but also the educated classes before 1789. Tocqueville also stressed continuities between radical and conventional politics before and during the Revolution. The social/cultural historian Arthur Marwick has adopted a similar position on 1968 and has de-emphasized the ruptures between the pre- and post-68 periods.[51] He has downplayed the conflict between generations and between radical and mainstream politics. French scholars have begun to approximate this approach by using the era that they label "the '68 years" as shorthand for the years of protest that preceded and followed 1968.[52] This is undoubtedly a conceptual advance that permits historians to discuss longer-term cultural changes, but it also shows that French scholarship still remains wedded to a supposed *annus mirabilis* or what German historians have critically dubbed "a magical date."[53] The title of the collection by Geneviève Dreyfus-Armand et al., *Les Années 68* (The '68 Years), has once again highlighted 1968, a year that allegedly liberated "ideas, words, and bodies."[54] May–June is said to have "inaugurated an unceasing, multiform, and sometimes radical agitation."

Likewise, North American scholars of France have recently stressed the political significance of the May events and their militant legacy. According to Kristin Ross, May shattered the conventional "social identity" of both students and workers and thus allowed "politics to take place."[55] The month constituted "a pivotal if not founding moment." May was a political as well as an intellectual starting point: "A new renegade historical practice [labor history] could continue the desire of '68 to give voice to the 'voiceless.'" Similarly, Andrew Feenberg and Jim Freedman have asserted that "the May Events triumphed in the political culture of the society that defeated it in the streets.... The May Events were at once the last gasp of the old socialist tradition and the first signal of a new kind of opposition."[56]

The following pages will attempt to contribute to the debate on the French May by using old and new sources to narrate and analyze the events in Paris during 1968. That year can be better understood, not as "A World Transformed," as the title of a recent work has argued, but rather in the context of short- and long-term continuity.[57] The concern for Paris and its suburbs needs little justification. Internationally, the French capital has, as mentioned, played an essential role in the major revolutionary waves of the West. Within France itself, the capital has been the major pole around which French unity has been molded. Yet, as in 1848 or 1871, revolutionary Paris remained isolated from the countryside and ultimately even its own *banlieue*. This isolation reflected the urban nature of the "Revolution of '68" throughout France and much of the world.

Chapter 1, "Sex, Drugs, and Revolution," and chapter 2, "Making Desires Reality," explore student politics and life in Parisian universities through official university and police archives, which show cultural change and conflict in the early and mid 1960s. In dormitories at Antony and Nanterre, political freedom (usually in the form of Marxism and an unquestioned faith in the working class), libertarianism (sex and drugs), and disrespect for property (theft and vandalism) intensified from 1962 to 1967. Students were sleeping together, speaking out, and engaging in radical political and cultural activities well before May. The early 1960s should not be reduced to a period of pre-Revolution but must be considered a dynamic time of their own. Historians have often pointed out that the first decade of the Fifth Republic (1958–1968) witnessed the economic modernization of France. Just as significantly, *moeurs* (mores) also changed during this period. The Gaullist regime and French society were more tolerant than is generally acknowledged. The protection of property concerned authorities more than the defense of morality.

Chapter 3, "Incendiary Occupations," examines the student and youth movement's creation of defiant and violent communities that challenged police and property. The hatred of police drew together a coalition of libertarians, young and older Marxists who saw cops as representatives of the bourgeoisie, and—often forgotten—extreme rightists who viewed the Gaullist regime as their adversary. In the nineteenth century, priests were the object of popular distrust; in the twentieth, it was police. Violent events have often monopolized the iconography of May and are often featured in films, book covers, etc. They deserve a history that includes and evaluates the perspective of the forces of order. Newly opened police archives show that the barricades of May–June were not merely "symbolic," as some recent historiography has argued.[58] On the contrary, they produced a high level of nonlethal violence during which thousands of protesters, bystanders, and officers were injured. For more than a month, demonstrators struggled with police over space, time, and the elements. As in past revolutions, male and some female protesters sought control of urban spaces—including cultural and artistic institutions—and attempted to assert their domination of the night. Worker and especially student movements fought the state over possession of air, water, fuel, and fire. The hundreds of fires set by young rebels threatened to inflame much of the city, including the occupied universities and theaters.

As in other periods of French history (Popular Front, Liberation), the challenge to state power provoked a massive strike wave, the subject of chapter 4, "Workers Respond." Police and employer archives will clarify the age, nationality, and demands of the workers engaged in the greatest strike in French history. They were not as young or as interested in workers' control as many have argued.[59] The events of 1968 cannot be reduced to a youth revolt. Nearly all workers' strikes were intended to increase the value of labor and had little in common with either street protesters' idealism or their destruction. Wage earners' sit-downs (unlike the barricades and occupations of the students) were undertaken by militants rather than masses. Workers did not wish to take control of the means of production; instead, they were attracted by a large array of commodities—especially the automobile—offered by a productive, modern economy. They did not try to expand sexual and personal freedoms, as did youth. Their movement was more traditional and thus has been more neglected or distorted. The triangle of the state, employers' organizations, and trade unions bargained to redistribute wealth and end the strike wave. Those groups—whether of the extreme left or extreme right—that refused to cooperate with this triad were unable to win major concessions. They could battle police but could not come close to overthrowing the state. Unions delivered the bulk of their troops and generally avoided violence against property. A hesitant corporatism turned political parties into minor players.[60] In addition, the state proved capable of controlling the ethnic protests of blacks, Jews, and Arabs.

The final chapter, "The Spectacle of Order," will show how authorities were able to respond to the challenges to property and order. In contrast to 1789, 1848, and 1871, protests and strikes had weakened the state only momentarily. It was restoring normality even before General de Gaulle's 30 May address to the nation, which observers and historians have exaggerated as the turning point of the crisis.[61] Prior to that date, the corporatist triad of state, unions, and employers was powerful enough to win the cooperation of the lower middle classes. The collaboration of these groups of shopkeepers, independent truck owners, and farmers enabled the government to break the fuel and transportation strikes and to supply Paris with gasoline and thus food. The role of the *petits* has generally been ignored even though small property owners played an essential role in reestablishing everyday existence in May and June. In other branches of the economy further concessions by the state and employers helped to end strikes. Repression by an efficient and sporadically brutal police force encouraged a return to work.

The conclusion, "A Modest or Mythical May?" argues that the effects of 1968 were rather limited. Culturally, the events changed little that had not already been questioned and altered in the late 1950s and early 1960s. Of course, the May movement also failed in its main political goal. Despite the optimism of much of the extreme left, May was not the beginning of a workers' revolution. The strike wave led to fewer working hours and higher wages, but these changes reflected the secular and traditional demands of the French workers' movement. May was not a contemporary Bastille Day, an event that much of educated opinion in France views as the foundation of its supposedly hedonistic culture. If the May events were important, it is not because of what they altered. Instead, they are remarkable by virtue of the transformative power that much of the media, many scholars, and ordinary French people have attributed to them. Whatever the historical truth, they have become a symbol of a youthful, renewed, and freer France.

Notes

1. Ingrid Gilcher-Holtey, "May 1968 in France: The Rise and Fall of a New Social Movement," in Carole Fink, Philipp Gassert, and Detlef Junker, *1968: The World Transformed* (Cambridge, 1998), 260.
2. Direction générale de la Police nationale, renseignements généraux, Bulletin mensuel, November 1968, AN 820599/89. A British wit once said that the French had '68 so that they could write about it. Unless otherwise stated, all translations are my own.
3. Pompidou quoted in Adrien Dansette, *Mai 1968* (Paris, 1971), 413. See also his remarks in Georges Pompidou, *Pour rétablir une vérité* (Paris, 1982), 196–200, in which he sees May as a "crisis of regime" and a "crisis of the Republic."
4. Quoted in Philippe Labro, ed. *Ce n'est qu'un début* (Paris, 1968), 238; see also Jules Monneret, *Sociologie de la révolution* (Paris, 1969), 734.
5. Cited in Keith Reader, *The May 1968 Events in France: Reproductions and Interpretations* (New York, 1993), 35–36.
6. Count of Paris quoted in Maurice Grimaud, *En mai, fais ce qu'il te plaît* (Paris, 1977), 90.
7. Lucien Rioux and René Backmann, *L'Explosion de mai* (Paris, 1968), 594.
8. Dansette, *Mai*.
9. Daniel Singer, *Prelude to Revolution: France in May 1968* (New York, 1970); Patrick Seale and Maureen McConville, *Red Flag Black Flag: French Revolution 1968* (New York, 1968).
10. Henri Lefebvre, *The Explosion: Marxism and the French Revolution*, trans. Alfred Ehrenfeld (New York, 1969), 118.
11. Edgar Morin, Claude Lefort, Cornelius Castoriadis, *Mai 68: La brèche* (Paris, 1988), 185.
12. The following is from Alain Touraine, *The May Movement: Revolt and Reform*, trans. Leonard F. X. Mayhew (New York, 1979), 26–81.
13. James Miller, *Democracy Is in the Streets: From Port Huron to the Siege of Chicago* (New York, 1987).
14. Paul Ginsborg, *A History of Contemporary Italy: Society and Politics 1943–1988* (London, 1990), chap. 9.
15. Raymond Aron, *La révolution introuvable* (Paris, 1968).
16. Michel de Certeau, *La prise de parole: Pour une nouvelle culture* (Paris, 1968).
17. Aron, *La révolution*, 16.
18. Morin et al., *La brèche*, 160.
19. Régis Debray, "A Modest Contribution to the Rites and Ceremonies of the Tenth Anniversary," *New Left Review*, no. 115 (May–June 1979): 46.
20. Pierre Bourdieu, *Homo Academicus*, trans. Peter Collier (Stanford, 1988), 161, 182; Ingrid Gilcher-Holtey, *Die 68er Bewegung: Deutschland-Westeuropa-USA* (Munich, 2001), 72, 80, 83, employs Bourdieu's concept of the "critical event."
21. Daniel Bertaux, Danièle Linhart, and Beatrix Le Wita, "Mai 1968 et la formation de générations politiques en France," *Le Mouvement social*, no. 143 (April–June, 1988): 79, 84.
22. Henri Weber, *Vingt ans après: Que reste-t-il de 68?* (Paris, 1988), 153.
23. Hervé Hamon and Patrick Rotman, *Génération*, 2 vols. (Paris, 1987).
24. Antoine Prost, "Quoi de neuf sur le mai français," *Le Mouvement social*, no. 143 (April–June, 1988): 91–97.
25. Jean-Pierre Duteuil, *Nanterre 1965–66–67–68: Vers le Mouvement du 22 mars* (Paris, 1988).
26. Luc Ferry and Alain Renaut, *68–86: Itinéraires de l'individu* (Paris, 1987), chap. 2; Gilles Lipovetsky, "Changer la vie ou l'irruption de l'individualisme transpolitique," *Pouvoirs*, no. 39 (1986): 91–100.
27. Guy Michaud, *Révolution dans l'université* (Paris, 1968), has stressed the Proudhonian and federalist nature of the revolt.
28. Lipovetsky, "Changer la vie," 91–100.
29. Claude Prévost, *Les étudiants et le gauchisme* (Paris, 1969).

30. Paul Yonnet, in *Jeux, Modes et Masses: La société française et le moderne, 1945–1985* (Paris, 1985), argues that the postwar period saw the "proliferation of extremely individualistic leisure," which was both apolitical and antipolitical.

31. André Stéphane, *L'Univers contestationnaire* (Paris, 1969). On the limitations of psychoanalytic interpretations, see Hervé Savon, "Les événements de mai 1968 et leurs interprètes," *Guerres et Paix*, no. 14–15 (1969–1970): 84.

32. Claude Dejacques, *A toi l'angoisse, à moi la rage: Mai 68 Les fresques de Nanterre* (Paris, 1969).

33. *Autobiography of a Generation*, trans. Lisa Erdberg (Hanover and London, 1996), 29.

34. Morin et al., *La brèche*, 185.

35. Bernard Lacroix, "A contre-courant: le parti pris du réalisme," *Pouvoirs*, no. 39 (1986): 119.

36. Jean-Pierre Rioux, "A propos des célébrations décennales du mai français," *Vingtième siècle* (July–September, 1989): 49–58.

37. Gilles Lipovetsky, *L'Ere du vide: Essais sur l'individualisme contemporain* (Paris, 1983), 22.

38. Marie-Claire Lavabre and Henri Rey, *Les Mouvements de 1968* (Florence, 1998); Michel Gomez, *Mai 68 au jour le jour* (Paris, 1998). Reproductions and facsimiles of graffiti, music, and photo albums were also published during this year.

39. Liaison des Etudiants Anarchistes, *Anarchistes en 1968 à Nanterre* (Vauchrétien, 1998); Mouvement du 22 mars, *Mai 68 Tracts et Textes* (Vauchrétien, 1998); René Viénet, *Enragés et Situationnistes dans le mouvement des occupations* (Paris, 1998).

40. Yaïr Auron, *Les juifs d'extrême gauche en mai 68* (Paris, 1998); Laurent Lemire, *Cohn-Bendit* (Paris, 1998); Jacques Foccart, *Le Général en mai: Journal de l'Elysée – II 1968–1969* (Paris, 1998); Grégory Barrau, *Le mai 68 des catholiques* (Paris, 1998); Hervé Le Roux, *Reprise: Récit* (Paris, 1998).

41. See Reader, *May 1968*, 87.

42. *Le Nouvel Observateur*, 29 April 1998, 28. For a scholarly treatment that agrees with Lipovetsky's analysis, see Philippe Raynaud, "Mai 68," in Frédéric Bluche and Stéphane Rials, eds., *Les Révolutions françaises* (Paris, 1989), 450.

43. *Paris Match*, 23 April 1998, 62.

44. For the end of Victorianism in Britain, see Arthur Marwick, *British Society since 1945* (New York, 1982), chap. 9 and, more generally, Arthur Marwick, *The Sixties: Cultural Revolution in Britain, France, Italy, and the United States, c. 1958–1974* (New York, 1998).

45. Marwick, *The Sixties*, chaps. 3–7.

46. Cf. Serge Berstein, *La France de l'expansion: La République gaullienne, 1958–1969* (Paris, 1989), 310–311.

47. Ginsborg, *Contemporary Italy*, 312.

48. Robert Lumley, *States of Emergency: Cultures of Revolt in Italy from 1968 to 1978* (London and New York, 1990), 3.

49. Cf. George Katsiaficas, *The Imagination of the New Left* (Boston, 1987), 17, 23.

50. Cf. Alain Schnapp and Pierre Vidal-Naquet, *Journal de la commune étudiante* (Paris, 1969), 10–15.

51. Marwick, *The Sixties*.

52. Geneviève Dreyfus-Armand, Robert Frank, Marie-Françoise Lévy, Michelle Zancarini-Fournel, eds., *Les Années 68: Le temps de la contestation* (Brussels, 2000), 14; Michelle Zancarini-Fournel, "Genre et Politique: Les Années 1968," *Vingtième Siècle* (July–September, 2002): 133–143.

53. Axel Schildt, Detlef Siegfried, and Karl Christian Lammers, eds., *Dynamische Zeiten: Die 60er Jahre in den beiden deutschen Gesellshaften* (Hamburg, 2000), 11.

54. Michelle Zancarini-Fournel, "Conclusion," in Dreyfus-Armand et al., *Les Années 68*, 501.

55. Kristin Ross, *May '68 and Its Afterlives* (Chicago, 2002), 3, 7, 116.

56. Andrew Feenberg and Jim Freedman, *When Poetry Ruled the Streets: The French May Events of 1968* (Albany, NY, 2001), xxi–xxii, 68.

57. Fink et al., *1968*. Not all essays in this collection follow the periodization of the title.

58. Alain Corbin, "Préface," in Alain Corbin and Jean-Marie Mayeur, eds., *La barricade* (Paris, 1997), 21.

59. Cf. Touraine, *The May Movement*, chap. 5; David Caute, *The Year of the Barricades: A Journey through 1968* (New York, 1988), 235; Rioux and Backmann, *L'Explosion de mai*, 615.

60. Suzanne Berger, ed. *Organizing Interests in Western Europe* (Cambridge, 1981), 18.

61. Dansette, *Mai*, 328–329; Alain Delale and Gilles Ragache, *La France de 68* (Paris, 1978); Maurice Agulhon, *La République: Nouveaux drames et nouveaux espoirs (1932 à nos jours)*, 2 vols. (Paris, 1990), 2: 367.

Chapter One

SEX, DRUGS, AND REVOLUTION

The radical students who started the chain of events that led to the greatest strike wave in French history lashed out against capitalism, the state, and property. They extended their protests to what they considered the plea-sure-denying restraints of bourgeois society and desired "to liberate man from all the repressions of social life."[1] Repression meant not just police but a wide spectrum of social activities—wage labor, sexual restraint, industrial hierarchy, and academic discipline. As in other Western nations, universities became the launching pad of their assaults. The most liberal institution pro-vided cover for adversaries of the dominant social/political order and fos-tered those who wished to destroy it and revolutionize society.

Gauchistes—whether Maoists, Trotskyites, anarchists, or even Situation-ists—who sparked the revolts in the spring of 1968 did not believe that they could make revolution by themselves. As in other periods of French his-tory—for example, 1848—they desired unity with the people or, more specifically, with the workers. They had little faith in the revolutionary role of students or of any other sector of what they considered the petty bour-geoisie. Their movements contained not only *autogestion* but also what might be called *autocontestation* (self-criticism). They were heirs of the nine-teenth-century revolutionary legacy of Karl Marx and Mikhail Bakunin, and they attempted to create a dynamic that would lead to a classless soci-ety. These *trublions* (troublemakers), as one author called them, were over-whelmingly *ouvriériste*, trusting that the workers—and no one else—must and would make the revolution.[2] On this fundamental point *gauchistes* were in agreement. The symbols of student revolutionaries—red flag, black flag, the *Internationale*, and the clenched fist—were all taken from the work-ing-class movement. Some have argued that the anti-authoritarianism of the radicals made them "premature anti-Communists" who contributed to the demise of that ideology; however, their faith in the victory of the work-ers placed them squarely in the Marxist tradition.[3] A psychoanalyst has also contrasted the "utopian," "destructive," and "immature" student radicals

---

Notes for this chapter begin on page 47.

to the constructive and rational Communists.[4] Yet both Communists and radical students believed in the historical mission of wage earners. Throughout the crisis, the PCF (Parti Communiste Français) insisted that "the working class" was the "only truly revolutionary class."[5] Like the Communists, radicals were as scientific or as unscientific as the Marxist tradition itself.[6]

Their utopia, which envisaged a nonrepressive society of liberated workers, attracted the efforts of only a small number of students, but they were able to energize greater numbers of the usually apathetic when agitation centered on specific issues that addressed their needs. When activists could speak to immediate problems, they could involve a significant base. The struggles against sexual segregation, against government reforms of higher education, against examinations, and against police brutality built a mass student movement.

The base was potentially large. Students acted from a position of increasing demographic and biological strength. Youthful hormones provided the biological foundation of revolt. The massive numbers of baby boomers in higher education and their improving health, which made them sexually active at a younger age, created a powerful force for sexual liberalization. During the century the average age of menstruation had fallen from seventeen to twelve.[7] Throughout the same period, the marriage age was increasing. Youth was stronger and better fed, and I.Q. tests demonstrated increasing intelligence. In 1963 more than one-third of the population was under twenty, the largest percentage since the beginning of World War I.[8] Greater numbers and higher quality promoted a putatively cross-class category of youth.[9] Young people wanted more independence and expanded autonomy. Economic growth allowed them more purchasing power. Business, advertising, and the media encouraged a youth culture of music, records, and clothes. A few of these commodities—such as protest music—encouraged critical attitudes towards society. Even apolitical young people from various social classes could agree that the new consumption was considerably more amusing than working. A hedonistic generation seemed to resist labor and the responsibilities of the adult world. Students actively participated in a fun-loving lifestyle and became its propagandists.

By the 1960s, demographic change had bolstered student power. Numbers of students had increased from 3,000 during the First Empire (1804–1814) to over 600,000 in 1968 or one hundred fold relative to population growth.[10] In 1906 Paris had a student population of 15,000; in 1968 it was 160,000. Enrollment in institutions of higher education multiplied quickly in the twentieth century:

1938–1939	60,000
1955–1956	150,000
1962–1963	280,000
1967–1968	605,000

Between 1950 and 1964, France had the largest increase of any major European nation, but others, such as Italy, also had difficulty accommodating the baby boomers and experienced corresponding university unrest.[11]

Likewise, the number of professors grew rapidly. The 200 teachers employed in the French universities in 1808 increased to 2,000 at the end of World War II and 22,000 in 1967.[12] Most of the expansion of university teaching in the 1960s took place among lower-ranking instructors (*maîtres assistants* and *assistants*), who permitted the French university to become a mass university. Their percentage of the university teaching staff rose from 44 percent in 1956–1957 to 72 percent in 1967–1968. The *assistants* were generationally and politically close to their students. The growing disparity between the increasing numbers of junior faculty compared to the relative stability of senior faculty posts deepened tensions between younger and older teachers.

The French educational system required that a student pass a national, standardized *baccalauréat* examination to enter the university. The *bac* differed from the American high-school diploma in that it was considered the first diploma of higher education, not the last of secondary education.[13] This indicated the tight administrative connection between the *lycée* and the university. Indeed, teachers—like their students—could and did move from the *lycée* to the *faculté*. It was no accident that turbulence in 1968 would spread throughout both institutions.

Bloated university enrollment was especially severe in the humanities and sciences. Students in these areas increased from 32 percent in 1945 to 65 percent in 1962. In 1945, the more professional law, medicine, and pharmacy programs enrolled 57.8 percent of students, but by 1962–1967, their percentage had declined to 35 percent. Feminization accompanied massification. Only 6 percent of students were female in 1906, jumping to 33 percent in 1950, 42 percent in 1962, and nearly 50 percent in 1965–1966.[14] The less pragmatic disciplines in the humanities and sciences attracted proportionally more male and especially female students than the vocationally oriented options of law and medicine. In the 1960s, requirements for the scientific *baccalauréat* were toughened, but the *bac* remained comparatively easy in the humanities. Humanities students suffered overcrowded classrooms and inadequate facilities more often than students in other areas. The former were increasingly insecure economically and professionally and perhaps—as in the United States—more willing to revolt.

Demographic growth had paradoxical effects by increasing both the power and the anxieties of young people. Fears of unemployment may have affected students more than workers. Humanities graduates had traditionally found jobs in education, but this option was less certain in the late 1960s. Female students, many of whom were oriented towards a teaching career, were especially concerned by the specter of relatively fewer opportunities in this domain. Between 1962 and 1968, the number of unemployed persons under twenty-five increased threefold.[15] A math professor at the Faculty of Science in Paris reported that of 1,600 students participating in a degree program in 1968, only 200 had found employment as of June.[16] Even though many of those who participated in the May events were reportedly from families of high-level executives, 52 percent of participants feared joblessness.[17] The days when a university diploma meant easy access to respectable positions were over. Furthermore, both the length of time that it took to obtain a liberal arts degree and the dropout rate were growing.[18] Given the weight of their numbers and deepening economic/social insecurity, it is not surprising that students in the humanities and social sciences led the revolts.

The state made a huge but ultimately insufficient effort to accommodate the youthful influx. It expanded old universities and created new ones, such as Nanterre in the western suburbs of Paris. The budget devoted to higher education exploded sixfold from 605 million francs in 1958 to 3,790 billion in 1968, and the number of professors of all ranks jumped from 5,870 to 25,700.[19] During and after the electoral campaign of 1967, the prime minister, Georges Pompidou, boasted that more universities had been constructed since 1962 than were operating when he became prime minister that year. This expansion transformed higher education. The university of the Third Republic had offered the sons of a comfortable bourgeoisie knowledge of French culture and had provided them with skills to enter law, medicine, and higher education.[20] The goal had been to train an enlightened and republican elite. During the Fifth Republic, masses of students came from the less comfortable middle classes whose futures were much more insecure. In 1939, 34.8 percent of the fathers of students were business executives or practiced liberal professions, 16.4 percent were employees, artisans, or small shopkeepers, 1.6 were industrial workers.[21] The percentage of sons of employees, artisans, or small shopkeepers hardly varied from 1939 to 1950.[22] However, their percentage of the student population had risen from 17.2 percent in 1950 to 31.2 percent in 1960, whereas the percentage from the liberal professions had dropped from 17.4 percent in 1950 to 9.6 percent in 1965–1966. The ratio of the number of students from the middle and lower-middle classes to the number of students from the upper classes multiplied fourfold in fifteen years. Yet democratization had limits. Although the proportion of students from working-class families had risen from 1.9 percent in 1950–1951 to 5.5 percent in 1960–1961, it remained the lowest among major industrial nations.[23] By 1968, the minister of education, Alain Peyrefitte, claimed that 10 percent of students came from working-class families. PCF publications put the figure somewhat below that number.[24] By contrast, American institutions of higher learning—whose quality varied much more than their French counterparts—recruited roughly 30 percent of their student body from working-class families. Even in Italian universities, students from the working class constituted over 20 percent of the student body.[25]

Despite the achievement of a more socially diverse student body, the French university system remained solidly bourgeois. The son of a high-level executive was eighty times more likely to enter the university than the son of a rural wage earner and forty times more likely to enter than the son of a worker.[26] The student body was gradually becoming somewhat less bourgeois, but professors originated almost exclusively from that group, with seventy-two percent of them the sons of high-level *fonctionnaires* and only 2 percent from working-class backgrounds. French institutions of higher learning were bourgeois in more than social origin of personnel. In effect, the university perpetuated a bourgeois elite based putatively on achievement. It trained future executives who would run public and private bureaucracies, and it promoted high culture. The latter function gave students from upper layers of society a distinct advantage since they were more familiar with it than their peers from the lower-middle and lower classes.

Nanterre (see map 1) was one of the starting points for revolts against the bourgeois university. Henri Lefebvre, who taught and agitated there, aptly describes it:

> [Nanterre] is a Parisian faculty located outside of Paris … Right now it contains misery, shantytowns, excavations for an express subway line, low-income housing projects for workers, and industrial enterprises. This is a desolate and strange landscape. The university was conceived in terms of the concepts of industrial

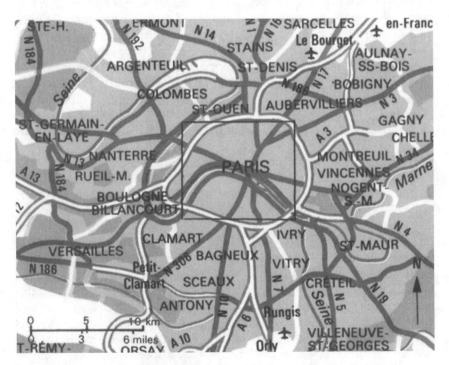

MAP 1: Paris and Its Suburbs

production and productivity of an advanced capitalist society…. The buildings and the environment reflect the real nature of the intended project. It is an enterprise designed to produce mediocre intellectuals and junior executives for the management of society. [In this suburb] unhappiness becomes concrete.[27]

This kind of criticism was not limited to leftist social observers, such as the author of the stimulating *Le droit á la ville*. Reflecting widespread ambivalence of the French towards the *banlieue*, almost all of those who wrote about Nanterre thought it ugly. Its dean, Pierre Grappin, found "no charm" in campus buildings and was shocked by their "absence of windows."[28] Students detested the anonymous and depersonalized university complexes.[29] The surrounding suburb was nearly always described as depressing. Authors of all stripes noticed gloomy subsidized public housing (HLM), industrial warehouses, and miserable shantytowns. According to one effusive journalist, the air was unbreathable, "full of smoke, fetid emanations, bacteria, slimy filth vomited continuously by factory chimneys."[30] The contrast with adjacent Neuilly, an upper-middle-class residential area, was scandalous to some but evident to all. The newly constructed campus lacked basic facilities or amenities—libraries, sporting equipment, flowers, and trees.

In 1963 a prize-winning (*prix de Rome*) architect had begun construction of the Faculté des Lettres et des Sciences humaines at Nanterre. The site was not chosen for its suitability (regal Versailles would have been much more appropriate) but for its availability and relative economy. The minister of education did not have the funds to purchase property in the real-estate marketplace but was able to use land once employed by the Ministry of Defense as an aviation supply depot.[31] One of the purposes of erecting the new institution in the *banlieue* was to attempt to emulate—for the first time in the history of the Paris region—the design and roominess of American campuses. The *faculté* was to be both a teaching and, because of its projected size, a research institution. It would be the first faculty of letters that would showcase the social sciences.[32]

The rapidly growing Nanterre student body reflected demographic and educational expansion: 4,600 in 1965, 8,500 in 1966, and 11,000 in 1967.[33] By the fall of 1966, Nanterre had become a mass university where the dean could walk the halls without any of the hundreds of students he passed recognizing him. Overcrowding became a problem. At the beginning of the 1967–1968 academic year, when the campus was suited to accept only 2,500 first-year students, a heterogeneous group of more than 5,000 enrolled.[34] French university administrators assigned students to a campus on the basis of geographical, not social, origin. The authorities wanted to limit the number of provincials who matriculated in Parisian institutions, which had about 30 percent of the nation's student population. Administrators were aware that students might prefer to be in the Latin Quarter rather than in new universities.[35] Given its proximity to the prosperous areas of the city, a large number of *fils à papa* (rich kids) or elegant *minettes* (fashionable young

women) from the *beaux quartiers* were assigned to Nanterre. Forty-five percent of Nanterre's students came from the 8th, 9th, 15th, 16th, and 17th
arrondissements, 8.5 percent of students were of working-class origin, and 17
percent were from families of *employés* (white-collar workers). Over 50 percent had fathers who were heads of enterprises, practiced a liberal profession, or occupied a high place in the administration. Others lived in the
working-class suburbs of Colombes, Argenteuil, Bezons, and Courbevoie.

According to the prominent Nanterre leftist Jean-Pierre Duteuil, most
agitators and militants were from working- or middle-class families.[36] Professor and post-1968 dean of Nanterre René Rémond did not entirely dis-
agree, but qualified this assertion by adding that students from wealthier
families were generally more receptive to certain *gauchiste* practices than
others from more modest backgrounds. Those with fewer resources were
less likely to strike over abstractions such as the "bourgeois" nature of the
institution and the culture it dispensed. They were reluctant to risk their
careers, for which their parents had heavily sacrificed, over such issues. A
delay of their studies for a semester or two because of strikes might mean
the end of their academic hopes. On the other hand, those from less prosperous families were militant about concrete issues, such as selective
admissions policies.[37] They regarded the university as one of the few
avenues that could offer social mobility in French society.

Whatever the class background, the history of devoted militancy at
Nanterre and other universities is, in large part, the history of a small
minority. A September 1968 survey concluded that only 12 percent of students wanted to change society radically, 31 percent were mainly concerned with passing their examinations, and 54 percent desired the reform
of the university.[38] Radical Marxists acknowledged that "the mass of students remain attached to their petty bourgeois privileges."[39] During the
1967–1968 academic year, a handful of *groupuscules* gathered between 130
and 140 students or a little over 1 percent of the student population, who
were mostly in the humanities and social sciences.[40] At their height in
1968, the activists never exceeded 12 percent of the student body. Their
minority status might seem a weakness, but at Nanterre it had the paradoxical effect of encouraging the transcendence of ideological divisions
among the various leftist organizations. As mentioned, in contrast to the
universities in the Latin Quarter, social spaces at Nanterre—cafes, bars,
parks, cinemas, and even bookstores—were rare, and public transportation inadequate. Students frequently complained of the lack of facilities.
Leftist undergraduates of whatever denomination found that they could
rely only on themselves for social sustenance. Camaraderie in an un-
sightly suburb replaced divisive ideological purity, and *groupuscules* served
as fraternities and sororities.

The activist minority was fragmented into a number of organizations
that recalled the clubs of the Revolution of 1848 or the Great Revolution
itself. Their development indicated the failure of the French Communist

Party (PCF) and especially its student organization, the Union des étudiants communistes (UEC), to attract some of the most energetic segments of activist youth. The PCF's failure was similar to that of other Communist and Socialist parties throughout the West. It was paralleled by the difficulties that the Catholic church in France and Italy encountered controlling the radicalism of their own youth movements. Mainstream labor—whether CGT in France or AFL-CIO in the U.S.—also proved unable to appeal successfully to youthful intellectuals.[41]

The PCF's increasing commitment to a parliamentary road to socialism and its reformist practices created a void for revolutionaries that the *groupuscules* gladly filled. The party seemed to have abandoned working-class revolution and to have become fully engaged in parliamentarianism. At the same time, its internal workings remained undemocratic. Young people of the UEC became divided ideologically. Some conformed to the party's norms, but others were repulsed by the purer forms of Stalinism that continued to reign unapologetically throughout the organization. As a result, the UEC became anemic in the early 1960s. The Nanterre campus was born during the UEC's decline, and it exercised little influence at the new university.

The PCF path of peaceful transition to socialism and its support for the presidential candidacy of François Mitterrand in 1965 further alienated student revolutionaries. Some reacted by joining or forming Trotskyite organizations. Leon Trotsky had always found a small number of talented and enthusiastic followers in France. By the 1960s those who were seduced by the Russian revolutionary and his doctrine had become divided into two tendencies—the Lambertists and the Frankists. The Lambertists were rigid disciples of Trotsky. They believed that capitalism could no longer develop the productive forces and had entered a period of crisis. Therefore, a truly revolutionary working-class party could take control and establish a workers' state. The Lambertists formed a student organization, the CLER (Comité de liaison des étudiants révolutionnaires), which would energize small numbers of militants at Nanterre and other universities. The CLER exercised some influence within the Nanterre UNEF chapter, where it oriented the fifteen students of what was known as the Tendance révolutionnaire. Nationwide, the CLER's approximately two thousand members had acquired a reputation for being extremely sectarian as well as foolishly violent.[42]

The other current of Trotskyism was known as Frankist, and its major theoretician was the Belgian Ernest Mandel. Mandel was less literal about Trotsky's writings and more flexible in his analysis. He recognized that capitalism had developed and continued to develop the productive forces. Misery by itself would not bring about the revolution. Instead, it would issue from a "mass strike" establishing a "dual power" that would eventually lead to a workers' state. Like all Trotskyites, Mandel believed that if only the correct revolutionary party—in other words, some sort of

Trotskyite group resembling his own instead of the PCF—were hege-
monic, then the workers would make the revolution.[43] Mandel and other
extreme leftists were ultimately unconvincing because they failed to answer
the question of why, if workers were revolutionary, the PCF and other
reformist parties maintained such influence on them.

The youth wing of the Mandel-influenced Frankists was the JCR
(Jeunesses Communistes Révolutionnaires), whose first congress was celebrated in Paris in April 1966. Its leader was Alain Krivine, whose sim-
plistically clear thinking and formidable verbal skills made him one of the
most prominent figures of the extreme left.[44] Krivine belonged to a left-wing
Jewish family that had fled the Russian pogroms of 1905. His four brothers were also active in revolutionary organizations. Alain had begun his
political career as a devoted Communist, and as a Trotskyist, he continued
to admire party discipline. Krivine's JCR was well organized and had a
formidable *service d'ordre* (non-uniformed paramilitary force) that sported
helmets and anti-gas equipment. It too was known for its courage or,
depending on one's perspective, folly in confrontations with police. Police
suggested that the organization had, at most, two thousand adherents
nationally, five hundred of whom were in the Paris region.[45]

At Nanterre in 1967, the JCR attracted between twenty-five and forty
persons. Independent of the Fourth International, it adopted as its symbolic
leader not Trotsky, whom it continued to admire, but rather Ché Guevara.
The JCR's attempt to reinvigorate Marxism led to an uncritical *tiersmondisme*
and total support for North Vietnam and Cuba.[46] The JCR attempted to constitute the avant-garde revolutionary party that Trotskyites were convinced
would lead workers to socialism. Its historical analysis was consequently
predictable. It criticized the PCF and the SFIO (Section française de l'Internationale ouvrière) for their failure to profit from the "objectively revolutionary situation" of the Popular Front strike wave in 1936 and the triumph
of the Resistance in 1945.[47] In addition, the JCR explored New Left themes.
A number of its members were interested in sexual issues, and its study
group read Wilhelm Reich, a theorist who had struggled to synthesize the
sexual and social revolutions. Students promoted discussion groups on his
thought by posting copies of a drawing by the cartoonist Siné, who depicted a girl in a short skirt being protected by barbed wire from a group
of concupiscent boys. Some JCR members joined anarchists in a campaign
for sexual liberation. Like their peers, Marxists in the 1960s were happy to
seek pleasure and explore personal liberation. In this context, it is not surprising that JCR militants would play an important role in the occupation
of the women's dormitory in the spring of 1967.[48] Not all JCR members
welcomed open discussion of sex. Many looked to their leader, Alain Krivine, as an example of a traditional father and loyal husband.[49]

Like Trotskyism, French Maoism was a reaction to the perceived parliamentarianism of the mainstream left. Revolutionaries who were critical
of Soviet "revisionism" were often receptive to Maoist thinking. In 1964,

when six hundred Maoists within the UEC were expelled, they established the UJCml (Union des jeunesses communistes marxistes-léninistes). It emphasized the working class as the only revolutionary force and consequently disdained "petty bourgeois" students. French Maoists concluded that the lesson of the Chinese Cultural Revolution was that students must desert *en masse* to the workers' side. In 1966 they established the Comités Vietnam de Base (CVB), which gathered some of the most active "anti-imperialists" and anti-Americans. The CVB opposed the PCF slogan of "Peace in Vietnam" in favor of a total North Vietnamese victory. Like the UJCml, the CVB had several thousand members.

Although all *gauchistes* condemned orthodox Communism and agreed that it had betrayed the working class, the anarchists were the most venerable left-wing anti-Communists. For them, the summits of history had first been reached during the councilist experiments following World War I and then in the collectives established by workers and peasants during the Spanish Civil War. Anarchists argued that Communists were guilty of treason by emasculating the Soviets—the councils of the Russian Revolution—and by destroying the agrarian and industrial collectives of the Spanish Revolution. Their critique of Bolshevism put anarchists at odds with Trotskyites and Maoists. Trotskyites lauded the role of the party in 1917–1921 and believed that only subsequently did Stalin and his bureaucracy betray the working class. Maoists thought the revolution was compromised not by Stalin, but by his revisionist successors.

At Nanterre, anarchist militants were few but made quite an impact. The Liaison des étudiants anarchistes (LEA) had only fifteen participants. It was founded at the beginning of the 1964–1965 academic year in the Parisian headquarters of the exiled Spanish Confederación Nacional de Trabajo (CNT) and brought together students who vociferously opposed the "individualist and non-violent" variety of anarchism that dominated some libertarian organizations.[50] The LEA advocated anarcho-syndicalism and believed that the class struggle was the "motor of history." Members read as much Georg Lukacs and Henri Lefebvre as Bakunin. Libertarians revived council communism by demanding *autogestion*. They proposed to abolish the separation between the producer and his product by eliminating the strict division of labor between those who commanded and those who executed orders.

Although the LEA believed that trade-union and political-party bureaucracies often betrayed those whom they supposedly represented, libertarians nevertheless thought it desirable to enter worker or student unions to raise proletarian and student consciousness. They struggled against narrow union corporatism by demanding broad social change. At the same time, anarchists refused to neglect student issues. They authored a critique of the "bourgeois" university, charging it with training managers committed to running capitalist society.[51] To fight for specific student goals and local autonomy, the LEA formed the Tendance syndicale révolutionnaire fédéraliste (TSRF). It maintained a revolutionary perspective while it fought against increasingly selective admissions policies, overcrowded courses, long lines and bad food in university cafeterias, and sexual segregation in dormitories. The forty Nanterre activists of the TSRF reached out to less politicized and non-anarchist students.

In 1965–1966, the anarchist militants included Dany Cohn-Bendit, who was to become the most prominent student radical in France. Cohn-Bendit was born in 1945 in Montauban (Tarn-et-Garonne). His parents were non-observant Jews who had fled Germany after the Nazis came to power in 1933. With much difficulty, they survived the war in the French Free Zone. When the conflict ended, the family moved to a small Parisian apartment where Dany would spend most of his childhood and adolescence. In 1959 he accompanied his sick father to Frankfurt, where he finished his last years of high school. In 1960 Dany became a German citizen to avoid French military service. Four years later, his orphan status enabled him to receive a German government scholarship to study sociology in France. By March 1967, his radicalism was so notorious that police investigators informed the Nanterre administration that the redheaded young man was out to destroy the university.[52]

Anars (anarchists), such as Cohn-Bendit and his friends, banded together both politically and socially. They did not confine themselves to espousing libertarian ideology but attempted to live according to their beliefs.[53] Libertarian influence distinguished Nanterre from the Sorbonne and focused attention on problems of everyday campus life. Students of anarchist sensibility reacted against what they considered to be common forms of repression by defying the ban on smoking in classrooms and by continually insulting the university ushers who tried to enforce it.[54] They defied property rights by demanding free meals from the university cafeteria and occasionally entering it to pilfer food. Although their call for sexual liberation often served as a transparent line to seduce females, some women did participate in their movement and spoke freely at their meetings. Anticareerist libertarians always addressed professors with the informal *tu*, and they made sure to take the elevators reserved for faculty and staff. At Nanterre, professed leftism did not exempt professors from insult and challenge. At the end of the 1966–1967 school year, anarchist activists distributed without charge in Henri Lefebvre's class copies of the notable Situationist pamphlet, *On the Misery of Student Life*. This was a particularly provocative act since the Situationists had accused the philosopher/sociologist of plagiarizing their ideas. At Nanterre, the classroom encouraged radicalism. The presence of Lefebvre and others in the Nanterre sociology department refuted the assertion that university teachers and classes were so uninteresting and irrelevant that radicals found their real university in the UEC and JCR headquarters.[55]

Anarchists had a symbiotic relationship with the Situationists and a larger group of pro-*situs*. The latter matched the sociological profile of the rebels of 1968. They were usually young, male, and if not formally enrolled students, at least intellectuals. Both Marxism and anarchism inspired anarchists and Situationists. In the fall and winter of 1966, the libertarians diffused the Situationist-inspired cartoon *The Return of the Durruti Column* and the pamphlet *On the Misery of Student Life. The Return of the Durruti Column* had appeared at the University of Strasbourg in October 1966. Significantly, one of the first major documents of the student revolt was a comic strip. Revolutionaries were creative and resourceful in using a variety of means to propagate their messages. Tracts, pamphlets, cartoons, songs, and graffiti were cheaply reproduced in a consumer economy where copying machines and spray paint cans were easily available. Indeed, one of the graffiti advocated "ne faites plus la bombe, bombez," which might be translated as "make graffiti, not war."[56] Although illegal since 1881, graffiti and other means of radical expression took on added importance in a society whose central government directly controlled the sole television channel and most of the radio stations. Rebels were willing to risk arrest to paint their messages on walls since they had, to say the least, limited access to mass-circulation newspapers and magazines. With bold ingenuity, they overcame disadvantages by placing their messages in public arenas and distributing provocative literature without charge.

Like the anarchists, the Situationists synthesized personal rebellion with class struggle and articulated the desire to change everyday life. In the oft-quoted words of Raoul Vaneigem, "those who speak of revolution and class struggle without changing everyday life and without understanding what is subversive about love and beneficial about the refusal of constraints have a corpse in their mouth."[57] Dramatic changes in everyday existence implied social and individual rebirth: "Revolutionary moments are festivals in which individuals celebrate their union with a regenerated society." According to Vaneigem, revolutions became reactionary when they demanded individual sacrifice. Revolutionaries must seize the moment and act as though there were no personal future.

The Situationists sought to overcome tension between the pleasure-seeking individual and the social revolutionary. In the end, the *situs,* like the rest of the left and its social movements, favored the collectivity.[58] While demanding a different daily existence, they condemned the isolated individual. The realization of the personal had to be collective. Workers' councils would be the foundation of a truly libertarian communist society. The working class would create a social utopia: "Without a doubt, the proletariat brings forth the project of human fulfillment and complete existence." Only exploited workers had sufficient creativity to break bourgeois constraints, and only they would know how to live. This proletarian and communitarian project of the Situationist International has been relatively obscured in recent years by authors who have emphasized its countercultural orientation.[59] Although not as focused on the proletariat as the French *situs* and *gauchistes,* the American SDS likewise criticized the "isolation of the individual" from "community" as the great failure of American democracy.[60] In the mid 1960s the SDS became obsessed with "community organizing."[61]

To spread their message, the Situationists practiced what they called *détournement*, or employing art for subversive ends. In Arthur Rimbaud's words, *détournement* was a *rencontre surprenante* (astonishing encounter), or a reversal of conventional associations. *Détournement* wrestled an image or form from its original context and literally re-presented it.[62] The banal comic strip, which was used to sell newspapers and other commodities, was transformed into revolutionary propaganda tinged with irony. A handful of pro-Situationists at Strasbourg, who were able to take control of the local chapter of the UNEF because of the apathy of their classmates, distributed *The Return of the Durruti Column*.[63] This comic *détourné* lacks a certain coherence, but its bold novelty succeeded in presenting a number of Situationist messages that resonated in the 1960s. It defended theft and approved the shoplifting of *blousons noirs* (young delinquents) by arguing that pilfering was a positive act in consumer society. By stealing commodities and giving them away, the *blousons noirs* began to transcend the exchange relationship that dominated late capitalism. They attempted to make the so-called society of abundance into what it claimed to be. *The Return of the Durruti Column* invited students to pick up "the most scandalous brochure of the century," *On the Misery of Student Life Considered in its Economic, Psychological, Political, and Notably Intellectual Aspects, and Some Means to Correct It*. This pamphlet had appeared in Strasbourg in 1966 and was probably (and may continue to be) the most widely read and translated French tract produced in the 1960s.[64] By 1969, 250,000 to 300,000 copies of *Misery* had been printed, and the pamphlet had been translated into numerous languages. One of the most accessible examples of Situationist thinking, it elaborated their most important concepts in a lively and polemical style. Its sarcastic humor alternated between childishness and sophistication.

The brochure offered a critique of the university and the students' position within it. The authors complained that the academic analysts of the student condition were superficial. "Bourderon's and Passedieu's," (a deliberate spoonerism that confused the names of co-authors Pierre Bourdieu and J.-C. Passeron) *Les Héritiers: les étudiants et la culture* offered only a partial critique of the university. Bourdieu and Passeron called for a mere democratization of educational institutions rather than a critique of the university's role in perpetuating what the Situationists called the spectacle, i.e., the vast parade of material and cultural commodities that constituted contemporary consumer society. The university rendered the students passive and trained them to play roles as junior executives in the continuation of the spectacle.

Misery disdained students, who, it claimed, were happy to harvest the crumbs of prestige of the university but too stupid to realize that their education was becoming increasingly mechanical and specialized.[65] The contemporary economy no longer needed intellectuals but rather junior executives. The *sorboniqueurs* had replaced the *encyclopédistes*. Nor did students understand that the economic system demanded the massive production of degree holders who were incapable of original thinking. For the Situationists, the much-discussed "Crisis of the University" of the 1960s was merely a detail in a larger crisis of capitalism. The bourgeois and liberal university of the nineteenth century had given way to the modern and technocratic counterpart of the twentieth. The nineteenth-century university had provided a ruling elite with a general culture. Its twentieth-century successor trained prospective white-collar workers for jobs in offices and factories. Hence, professors had lost their previous role as watchdogs for the ruling class and instead had become sheep dogs who "herded the flock of future white-collar workers towards their workplaces." Some instructors complained nostalgically but continued gutlessly to throw out a smattering of knowledge to future *cadres* who did not know what to do with it. Students exhibited "menopause of the spirit" when they continued to listen respectfully to teachers: "Everything which happens today in higher education will be condemned in the future revolutionary society as socially pernicious noise. Students are laughable."

Students sought relief from their misery by spontaneously and willingly consulting the "para-police," or, in common language, psychiatrists and psychologists. Students needed only to know that asylum-outposts were open in their ghettos, whereupon so many rushed to consult these policemen of the mind that they had to be given numbers to keep their places in line. Student misery found even quicker relief with its preferred drug, the cultural commodity. Students were respectful disciples of the cultural spectacle. They filled up the movies and theaters in an era when, according to the *situs*, art was dead. They were generally the most avid consumers of art's corpse, which had been frozen and distributed in cellophane wrap to cultural supermarkets, those *maisons de culture* that the then minister of culture, André Malraux, had promoted during the 1960s. Students crowded into auditoriums where clerics of different churches multiplied their discussions with Marxist "intellectuals." The typical student cultural consumer read *L'Express* and *L'Observateur* and believed that *Le Monde*, even though its style was too difficult for him, was truly "objective."

Misery asserted that politicized students remained unaware that their politics were those of the spectacle. They adopted the ridiculous fragments of a revolutionary left that had been wiped out more than forty years ago by both socialist reformism and the Stalinist counterrevolution. When students wanted to be really "independent," they joined the falsely advertised Jeunesse Communiste Révolutionnaire, which was not young, not communist, and certainly not revolutionary. They adhered to that pontifical slogan, "Peace in Vietnam." They usually believed that de Gaulle was archaic, but—on the contrary, *Misery* argued prophetically—his government had all the tools to administer modern society. It was the student who was out of step, which was why the churches and their rubbish often seduced them. Students adored the rotting and smelly corpse of God along with the decayed fragments of prehistoric religions. The student milieu was, along with that of provincial old ladies, the terrain where religious belief was strongest. Whereas other sectors of the population had rejected or expelled priests, the student ghettos remained the most fruitful arena for missionary work. Student-priests continued "shamelessly to sodomize thousands of students in their spiritual outhouses."

The Situationists considered only a few students intelligent. Among them were those who despised the educational system but succeeded because they understood it. They got the best thing it had to offer—grants and scholarships. They profited from its weaknesses, especially the need that forced it to encourage some research. However, to be truly intelligent, these students had to transcend rebellion against their studies. Since students were, like Coca-Cola, products of modern society, their alienation could only be overcome by making a total critique of the spectacle. The solution to their problems was the abolition of the commodity system and its replacement by a worldwide network of workers' councils. The reification of commodities constituted the essential obstacle preventing liberation. Creation had escaped the control of its creators. The overcoming of the commodity system implied the end of work and its replacement by a new type of activity. In the councils the distinction between work and leisure would dissolve, and real desires that the spectacle suppressed would return. The proletarian revolution promised to be a festival with play as its ultimate rationality: "To live without dead time and to *jouir* (enjoy) without inhibitions were its only rules."

Misery had a powerful effect among revolutionary student groups throughout France and perhaps in Italy, where students authored a similar critique of the university.[66] At Nanterre anarchists considered it "well done and original."[67] At the beginning of 1967, it may have helped inspire anarchists grouped in the Tendance syndicale révolutionnaire fédéraliste (TSRF) to take control of the Philosophy-Sociology-Psychology section of the UNEF. As had occurred at Strasbourg, the TSRF won the elections largely because of the apathy of the vast majority. It planned to use its position to wage war against examinations and invited students, professors, and the dean (whom it deliberately confused with Maurice Papon, Parisian Prefect of Police, 1958–1967) to a meeting to discuss the question. The anarchists expected a low turnout of not more than 50 persons; yet, to their surprise, over 200 attended the debate. The critique of examinations would remain a key issue in the student movement. This was hardly surprising since the French university system placed great, if not exclusive, weight on finals. *Misery* had already called exams into question, but Nanterre's students took their criticisms a step further. Exams, they claimed, were not learning experiences. They generated anxiety and, perhaps worst of all, sexual abstinence. Exams also discriminated against part-time students, who were forced to work for wages and had less time for study.

A few were energized by the Situationist-inspired critique of art. Art, they felt, should not remain separate from the revolution but merge with it. Lefebvre had invited to the campus Jean-Jacques Lebel, a disciple of the Living Theater, who was famous for having introduced the happening to France. On 10 February 1967, Lebel—who would later play a key role in the occupation of the Odéon theater—planned an American-style happening for the student body. A large number of spectators arrived, but the public quickly became confused by a growing number of interruptions from the audience. It rapidly lost the sense of what was disruption or what was part of the performance. Libertarians interrupted one "beautiful black actor" to ask whether he "screwed."[68] They continued their provocation by throwing yogurts, which had been pilfered from the university restaurant, at Lebel and his troupe. Post-performance glasses of beer in the university cafeteria reconciled agitators and actors.

The avant-garde was soon given another lesson that it was hazardous to enter Nanterre. Shortly after the Lebel counterhappening, "student-poets" were scheduled to read their own "Happ[ening] Poems." Several Situationist-inspired students objected to what they considered to be another example of "the artistic spectacle" and decided to disrupt the proceedings. Scuffles erupted during the reading, and the following day, those responsible for the disorder issued a tract:

> On Monday December 11, a troop of student poets, "the majority of whom had been published," presented their spectacle entitled "Happ poems." It was a happening. It finished badly with police officers on stage....
>
> Two naughty students yelled out, "Tomorrow's cops and priests will also be poets."... They should have spoken to us of Nanterre, model city, shantytowns … North Africans, subway, Stalinist municipality, future prefecture, future barracks of the Garde Républicaine. They should have also talked about the University of Nanterre, a university ghetto in the process of cybernetization, sexual repression, police repression, black list for troublemakers, Christian community, young UNEF bureaucrats …
>
> "We sure will be bored there," said Breton in 1932. BOREDOM IS COUNTER-REVOLUTIONARY.
>
> The struggle against cops, priests, cyberneticians, professors, and future sociologists begins today.
>
> No mercy for show-business amateurs and professionals.
>
> Against boredom, play.
>
> Against "poets," life....
>
> "From every authentic poem escapes a breath of freedom."[69]

This Dadaist and Surrealist revival continued to scandalize the uninitiated. The disciplinary hearing of one the pamphlet's authors, René Riesel, would later help to spark student riots in Paris in early May.

Those who were less extreme than the Situationists and more interested in student politics *per se* could join one of the *situs'* most derided targets, the UNEF, the major student organization in France. The UNEF had a distinguished background in postwar left-wing politics. As early as 1948, it had condemned the French war in Vietnam.[70] Its reputation among progressives was further enhanced by its very vigorous stand against the Algerian War. In the late 1950s and early 1960s, the UNEF, along with left-wing Catholic movements, espoused the cause of Algerian independence. It provided aid to the FLN (Front de Libération Nationale), an activity that some French nationalists and patriots considered treasonous. During the Algerian conflict, as it would again in 1968, the UNEF transgressed the conventional politics of the left, including, of course, the PCF and the CGT.[71] For the first time, it established the practice of regularly using university classrooms as meeting places for antiwar activities. Between 1958 and 1962, the UNEF participated in eleven national strikes and demonstrations against the war and in defense of republican institutions. By 1961, these initiatives had led to the "unions' front," or *intersyndicalisme*, in which the UNEF and even mainstream unions—such as the CGT, CFTC (Confédération française des travailleurs chrétiens), and FO (Force ouvrière)—demanded a negotiated settlement of the war and self-determination for the Algerian people. Under different circumstances, this united front of students, teachers, and workers would re-emerge in May 1968.

At the end of the Algerian War, the "fascism" and terrorism of the OAS (Organisation Armée Secrète), which fought ruthlessly to keep Algeria French, especially worried progressives. On 8 February 1962 the FEN (Fédération de l'éducation nationale), CGT, CFTC, and UNEF organized an anti-OAS demonstration that gathered ten thousand protesters. Police charged demonstrators at the Charonne *métro* station. One hundred fifty were injured and nine, including three women and a child, were killed.[72] On 13 February, the antifascist reflex culminated in a demonstration massing hundreds of thousands at the funeral of the victims of what became known to many as the Charonne Massacre. The UNEF's militancy during the Algerian conflict led the government to cut off its subsidy, but it was able to obtain funds from the CGT, FEN, SNI (Syndicat national des instituteurs), and the Ligue française de l'enseignement.[73] In the early 1960s, the UNEF's newfound prominence reflected the increasing demographic power and growing political autonomy of youth.

After the Algerian War ended, the organization increasingly focused on student needs and protested against government educational policies that it claimed had led to overcrowding and inadequate facilities. A strike over such issues in November 1963 caused a shutdown of a number of Parisian and provincial institutions. The left-leaning faculty union, the SNESup (Syndicat national de l'enseignement supérieur), supported the protest. Its members were often younger faculty who were becoming increasingly numerous as higher education expanded. The SNESup backed the UNEF in February 1964 when the latter used the occasion of a visit to the Sorbonne by the president of the Italian republic to embarrass the government. The UNEF wanted to focus public attention on the lack of teachers, insufficient classroom space, and inadequate scholarship funding. Prefiguring its actions in 1968, in February 1964 the government closed the Sorbonne and ordered five thousand policemen, mobile gendarmes, and CRS (Compagnies républicaines de sécurité)—a highly trained corps of riot police with an often-deserved reputation for brutality—to occupy the Latin Quarter, including the Sorbonne. Activists responded by demonstrating at Right Bank train stations, where a student was arrested. Shortly afterward, five to six thousand persons rallied to demand his release. An antirepressive coalition of the UNEF, CFTC, and the PSU (Parti socialiste unifié) united to free the arrested. However, in contrast to 1968, the government refused concessions. Indeed, at the end of 1964, when a new UNEF Bureau called for a march from the Mutualité to the Sorbonne, the government prohibited it and deployed thousands of police and CRS, who intimidated demonstrators by openly displaying their rifles and machine guns. Police actions did not provoke the massive negative reaction that they would in early May 1968. The Gaullist regime had won a round but at the cost of turning the UNEF into an even more resolute enemy. From 1964 to 1966, those who wanted to transform the organization into the "anti-[Gaullist] regime vanguard of the working class" were successful. The UNEF became the *bête noire* of Christian Fouchet, education minister from 1962 to 1967.

The UNEF's main rival was the FNEF (Fédération nationale des étudiants de France), which was born in 1961 in reaction to the "political" and antiwar positions of the UNEF. The regime favored the more conservative FNEF and provided it with subsidies denied to the UNEF. Police reported that "very rapidly" the right and the extreme right, especially partisans of *Algérie Française*, dominated the organization.[74] Over the next few years, a more moderate line came to prevail. The secretary general of the FNEF had close ties to the FO and the CFTC. He was at pains to project a centrist image and claimed that his union supported "universal suffrage, political pluralism, and both private and state initiatives."[75] The FNEF had a presence at Nanterre, but it was handicapped by its identification with the regime and its sometimes exaggerated anti-Marxism. The latter led the FNEF to condemn as "Marxist" a popular proposal for government subsidies to students.[76] The bulk of FNEF support came from those who enrolled in professional schools, and it was weak in humanities, letters, and sciences. Officials concluded that it exercised little influence in Paris.[77] Before May, the UNEF remained the most popular student organization and possessed about forty to fifty thousand members, only about one-third of whom paid their dues.[78] The dominance of the UNEF and the minority status of the FNEF showed that the right continued to be discredited among students long after the Vichy regime. Not all members of the UNEF or FNEF agreed with their unions' political positions. Unknown numbers of apolitical and pragmatic students joined a union—whether the UNEF or FNEF—to benefit from its range of services, which included publishing lecture notes, managing scholarships, and formulating student demands.

As in other French universities, the Nanterre chapter of the UNEF would become less of a union and more of a club where diverse tendencies—UEC factions, Trotskyites, anarchists—would fight to control the organization.[79] Of 2,000 Nanterre students enrolled in the academic year 1964–1965, 600 joined the student union, a remarkably large percentage. Of these, only 150–200 attended assemblies, even during crises, and just 50 were willing to devote themselves to the work and organizational needs of the union. At Nanterre, which was founded in the post-heroic period of student opposition to the Algerian War, the UNEF lost influence after 1966. Nanterre students may have identified the UNEF with the Sorbonne and felt that the organization did not speak to the needs of their new university.[80] Although 600 students still remained in 1967, the fivefold increase in the student body signified a percentage drop of membership from 30 to 6 percent. Fifty devoted militants from various *groupuscules* composed the heart of the organization. These activists were usually male, reflecting the national reluctance of female students to join student unions or interest groups.

Many UNEF radicals devoted themselves less to the student union's traditional tasks of providing student services than to larger issues that linked student, worker, and Third World concerns. The most active among them also struggled against imperialism, especially the Vietnam War, which was responsible for energizing numerous militants.[81] French anti-imperialism was transformed in the twentieth century. It shifted to an internationalist view and shed its nationalist orientation of the nineteenth century when right-wing students attacked the architect of empire, Jules Ferry, and praised the fanatical patriot Paul Déroulède. Internationalist anti-imperialism merged with the antifascism inherited from the Popular Front of the late 1930s when the Ligue d'action universitaire républicaine et socialiste demanded that "young French intellectuals support the legitimate demands of the working class."[82] In terms that anticipated the 1960s' radicals, the Ligue asked that "intellectual workers" refuse to exploit manual workers in the interests of big capital.

From 1965 to 1967 sporadic fascist raids on Nanterre galvanized the unity of anti-imperialist and antifascist students. The most prominent of the extreme-right *groupuscules* was Occident, which had five to six hundred members, most of whom inhabited the Paris region. The organization was born at the beginning of 1964 as a result of the fracturing of the Fédération des Etudiants Nationalistes. Originally, its members backed the rabid nationalist Pierre Sidos, who advocated violent combat against the left. Authorities frowned upon these activities and as a result, Occident became semiclandestine and obsessed with security. It changed its headquarters frequently and engaged in paramilitary training. In 1966, Sidos was removed from his leadership post. Among the new directors was the 23-year-old Alain Madelein, the future leader of the liberal right. Occident followed the rightist intellectual tradition of Maurice Barrès, Charles Maurras, Pierre Drieu la Rochelle, and Robert Brasillach. It did not consider itself fascist since it opposed a powerful centralized state and favored a decentralized but hierarchical and "syndicalist" France. A police report referred to its small number of militants whose "untiring dynamism" compensated for numerical weakness: "The [Occident] commandos are well-led and armed with iron bars and ax handles. They attack precise objectives—theaters, [left] party headquarters, bookstores, black and leftist students—and usually win small battles which have a significant impact." Commandos were active at Nanterre and the Latin Quarter and attempted to infiltrate and dominate "certain apolitical organizations," such as the FNEF.[83]

Despite its disclaimers that it was not fascist, racist, or anti-Semitic, *gauchistes* perceived it as such.[84] They were seconded by African, Jewish, and Arab students who refused to tolerate the repeated and aggressive incursions of the extreme right. Confrontations between the extreme right and extreme left at Nanterre differed from those in the Latin Quarter. In the latter, they were ritualized and localized in habitual spaces of confrontation, thereby leaving the majority of students unaffected. At Nanterre the battles took place just outside of campus dormitories, the social center of student life. Many apolitical residents became outraged by the commando tactics of the French *nazillons* [little Nazis] who descended from Paris without warning, shouting "Occident will win," screaming against "red vermin," and leaving behind their symbol of the Celtic cross.[85] These groups of twenty to forty young people affected a "skinhead" style *avant la lettre*. On 17 October 1966, seven Occident activists, armed with iron clubs, attacked JCR members who were distributing their propaganda at Nanterre. Leftists quickly counterattacked and nearly lynched the rightists. The following day, twenty-five Occident militants, armed with clubs and helmeted, descended *squadristi*-like from their van to confront several hundred *gauchistes*. The latter, who also sported helmets and clubs, had added stones and gas-filled bottles to their arsenal. The ensuing battle caused several injuries. In a subsequent confrontation on 2 November, underequipped Occident raiders met "total defeat."[86] To combat fascist incursions, all extreme-left groups agreed to peddle their newspapers simultaneously. Coordination of this sort anticipated future antifascist coalitions. By the academic year 1967–1968, fascist raids on Nanterre had nearly ended. As shall be seen, extreme-right wing commandos would henceforth concentrate on the properly Parisian front. In France, as in Italy, youthful leftists reacted to the aggressive stimuli of their rightist counterparts.

The antifascist and anti-imperialist struggles remained essential to the UNEF because both provided a basis upon which members of various leftist tendencies could construct a working unity. Antifascism and anti-imperialism offered common ground among *groupuscules* sparring over leadership and ideological dominance of the future working-class revolution. Even Communists were able to participate in the anti-American and pro-Vietcong campaigns.[87] At the same time, anti-imperialism and antifascism did not monopolize the theory and practice of the UNEF. Unlike the period of the Algerian War when anticolonialism had become its political raison d'être, the UNEF devoted its energies to a critique of the bourgeois university and bourgeois society. *Gauchiste*-inspired tracts aimed to show how the university meshed with a "capitalist social formation," which, they argued, only a working-class revolution could overcome.[88]

Anticapitalism could pull activists together, but it was less effective in rallying masses of students who were concerned with their own concrete grievances, one of which involved sex. Restrictions on visitation rights provoked massive discontent throughout the Paris region. Demonstrating the power of the libertarian current in the mid 1960s, young people attacked the *ordre moral* (traditional morality) of the Gaullist university administration. University students rejected the *internat* (disciplinary regime) of the *lycée* when imposed in college dormitories.

Nanterre *enragés* are often seen as creating the movement, but an equally logical starting point might be Antony, where students were protesting against dormitory restrictions as early as 1962.[89] Between 1955 and 1957 eight dormitory buildings of four, five, or eight floors were erected on eleven hectares in this *banlieue*, which was located about twelve kilometers southwest of Paris.[90] The dorms housed students who commuted to their classes and jobs in Paris by public transport or with their own automobiles. The complex included dining halls, three daycare centers, a kindergarten, athletic fields, and a library. Indeed, the intention of Jean Zay, the minister of education during the Popular Front after whom the dormitory complex was named, was to provide decent living conditions for low-income students. During his ministry, Zay had established the Centre Régional des Oeuvres Universitaires et Scolaires (CROUS), a student affairs office that organized material and social life for its charges. In the 1960s the Préfecture de Police began to take a keen interest in the Antony dorms and reported that they hosted nearly three thousand baby boomers and a large number of foreign students. Many were from modest families, were working their way through school, and could not afford the higher rents in Paris proper. In 1967 the population included 1,513 single men, 310 single women, and 488 married couples. Students majored in roughly equal numbers in sciences, law, and the humanities, although women tended to favor the last area of study. Foreign students, who totaled 658 or nearly 23 percent of dormitory residents, were overwhelmingly African. This reflected both the twilight of the French Empire and the beginnings of a new multicultural society. Three hundred thirty-eight came from western and central Africa (*Afrique noire*). One hundred thirty were Algerian, 78 Tunisian, and 44 Moroccan.

Three hundred sixty-three (62 percent) were single men; 172 were married, and only 55 (9 percent) were single females.

In 1962 Antony residents had destroyed a lodge that enabled a concierge or guard to control visits to a female dorm. They therefore defied an official policy that prohibited mingling of sexes in dormitory rooms and, for an unspecified period of time, practiced de facto open visitation, which, according to the housing director, bordered on the indecent: "This experiment [of liberalization in 1962] failed. Students were incapable of following the rules. The difficulties of enforcing them and the lack of sanctions encouraged so much licentiousness that the authorities had to act to preserve simple decency."[91] In 1963–1964, Antony residents initiated a successful, national rent strike.[92] The strike resulted in reduced rents, establishment of daycare centers, and the allocation of meeting places and social centers.[93]

In September 1964, prior to the beginning of the academic year, a series of issues sparked agitation. Foreign students demanded the opening of a restaurant: "On 4 September 1964 … one hundred students, led by Miss C., surrounded the apartment of the housing administrator. They withdrew before the arrival of police. The goal of the demonstration was to advance the date of the opening of the restaurant…. The majority of the demonstrators were foreign or African."[94]

Student unionists protested against the removal of the posters of the Association des étudiants de la résidence universitaire d'Antony. AERUA was born in 1957 during protests against the Algerian War. At that time the association had attracted large numbers of African and antiwar French students close to the UNEF. By 1964 the antiwar platform had been replaced by the demand for the right of men and women to visit each other with fewer restrictions. The 1964 movement showed how much higher education had changed since the early nineteenth century, when students and even professors were expected to be single and chaste.[95] The former insisted upon the right of men and women to visit each other without constraint.

Much of the battle for sexual freedom seems to have been fought and often won prior to 1968. Brigitte Bardot's *God Created Women* (1956) was a cultural milestone. The sensuality of Bardot's performance "revealed to the French that they had changed, that the old moral codes no longer held."[96] The film initiated a youthful cinematic wave that dethroned the venerable male stars Jean Gabin and Pierre Fresnay.[97] Also in 1956, the first family planning agency, Association Maternité Heureuse, opened. Traditional Catholic sexual morality was on the defensive well before the 1960s. French women continued to practice illegal abortions, which were estimated at 800,000 per year in the late 1950s.[98] Even more telling, on the eve of May 1968, 65 percent of Catholic women employed contraceptive techniques prohibited by the Church.[99] Many who did not use birth control devices, which the Neuwirth legislation of 1967 legalized, had recourse to clandestine abortion.[100] The student mutual aid organization

MNEF crusaded against "old ideologies of sexual morality" and for "the right of youth to love." Protestants of the Mouvement Français pour le Planning Familial (MFPF) often manned the family-planning bureaus, which maintained that women were an "oppressed 'minority.'"[101]

In January 1965, 1,500 Antony residents signed petitions in support of liberal—if not liberated—lower rents and visitation rights: "[We demand] adoption of a new set of rules that understands that the student is an adult and responsible individual."[102] They insisted upon "an immediate halt" of projects to construct lodges that would enable concierges and guards to control visits to men's and women's dorms. In effect, they wanted to maintain the de facto status quo that, despite the official restrictions, allowed them easy access to dorms of the opposite sex. For example, one female dorm had three entrances, two of which had no lodge for the concierge. Protesters knew that the construction of "*loges de concierge* has the precise goal of reducing nocturnal comings and goings."[103] Protesters' rearguard resistance was effective: "Only one [observation post]—most importantly in a girls' dorm—has been able to be built ... It could not have been [constructed] without police protection."[104]

The administration responded to protest with a certain amount of tolerance. Despite the rules' absolute prohibition on "any political or religious propaganda," it allowed party and union publications. For example, the PCF newspaper *L'Humanité* was posted. At Antony, French students had no need to stage massive demonstrations and sit-ins to ensure their right to engage in political activity, as the Berkeley Free Speech Movement had done in 1964.[105] However, French authorities remained intransigent on the completion of construction projects designed to control residents' movements. The director voiced his wish that "every visitor to a dorm be seen by a concierge." Men would have "limited freedom," and women, many of whom were minors, would remain under closer supervision in their dorms. In the night of 16–17 February 1965, unknown residents took matters into their own hands and destroyed a wall separating dormitories B and D.[106] A general assembly of students opposed its reconstruction. Building activity nevertheless continued in the spring of 1965 but was stopped temporarily in June, in response to student complaints of noise during the exam period. In July, construction restarted; however, students sabotaged bulldozers, causing two to three thousand francs worth of damages. The beginning of workers' August vacations further delayed completion of the project. In the fall of 1965, administrators—believing that the discontent was limited to a "minority"—continued to refuse student-union demands for liberalized visiting rights and lower rents. Militants warned the administration that there was a strong possibility that students might sabotage the lodges of concierges. Authorities suspected that the ultimate goal of the AERUA was the establishment of "a regime of liberty" at Antony, which, they worried, would serve as a model for other university dormitory complexes throughout the nation.[107] Consequently, the Antony director adopted a hard line. He refused to allow continued violations of rules and insisted on safeguarding the status quo by making students understand that "direct-action methods, [which are] characterized by systematic lies and ceaseless agitation, are not compatible with cogestion or simple collaboration."[108] Thus, at the beginning of the 1965 academic year, confrontations continued between an administration *in loco parentis* and students who considered themselves responsible adults in sexual matters.

The administration weakened its credibility by conflating security, morality, and racial purity. Night watchmen had sporadic conflict with unauthorized visitors in female dorms. Incidents erupted when strangers or disgruntled boyfriends invaded women's rooms. Watchmen were on the lookout for foreign, especially African, men. One guard claimed that "Africans make up 80 percent of those committing infractions in the dorm." Yet his own statistics refuted his accusation. Of thirty-three men questioned by this night watchman between 30 November 1964 and 6 June 1965, only six were African. The watchman's unfounded assertions lent credence to charges by local UNEF members that the housing director insisted upon a literal reading of dormitory rules because of his desire to stop miscegenation: "Mr. X ... justifies the strict application of the rules by the necessity of preventing young girls from mixing with African and Algerian students."[109]

The massive student resistance to the construction of lodges culminated in October 1965. Demonstrations and occupations "spontaneously" occurred on Friday, 1 October, both before and after a meeting of residents opposed to the building of observation posts. Young women were particularly active in the struggle, but their opposition to the project was nuanced. They did not oppose the building of the lodge *per se* because, they reasoned, it was needed for security reasons. "The young girls of the *pavillon* (dorm) know very well that for reasons of security lodges are necessary, but they also know that the current rules limit our freedom and our residential life too much."[110] Indeed, large numbers of thefts occurred in the rooms and parking lots during the daylight hours when many residents were working or studying in Paris. Although women agreed in principle to enhanced security, they nonetheless objected to the use of the lodge to impose what they considered to be outdated regulations that restricted their choices. On Saturday, 2 October, forty to fifty protesters continued to occupy the construction site. They claimed to have won the support of hundreds of their male and female comrades. Agitation was deep and broad enough to impel the administration and the chancellor himself, who was "informed that a certain number of students opposed with violence and threats the execution of work ordered by the administration," to authorize police penetration into the area to stop any sit-down strike.[111] Students reported that the "repressive state apparatus" in the form of six to eight hundred policemen was given the green light to occupy the site.[112] Graffiti denounced the presence of the forces of order.

The widespread revulsion that police repression of students provoked throughout the mid and late 1960s began in France at Antony. Other Western nations—especially the U.S. and Italy—would experience similar negative reactions to the forces of order on campus.

The administration prosecuted protesters in a controversial manner. From dozens of demonstrators, it picked out prominent student-union militants and pressed charges against them at the university discipline council. Even the director of the dormitory complex doubted the wisdom of his own decision "to make a few students bear the weight of a collective error."[113] However, he too was determined to domesticate the residents' association, whose energetic challenge—"by methods of direct action"— to rules and to official morality risked spreading to other universities. The decision to haul eight activists—four male and four female—before the university disciplinary council had the immediate effect of heightening tensions. Nearly six hundred residents signed a petition defending their persecuted comrades.[114] On 14 October, another petition endorsed by one hundred female residents protested against the police presence at the complex. On 16 October, the disciplinary council met to decide the fates of the militants. The council was composed of one representative of the chancellor, a housing director, a professor, and three students who—the accused claimed—were members of the Fédération des Etudiants de Paris (FEP), an organization hostile to the UNEF. The accused were supported by their attorney and Marc Kravetz, UNEF vice-president. The council decided to expel indefinitely from all university residences three men and two women. Another woman and another man were punished with exclusion for one year. No sanctions were taken against one male student.[115] The punishments were relatively severe and unwisely ignored widespread support for the accused. Fellow residents had written in solidarity 610 letters in which they claimed that they too had committed the same infractions as those who had been sanctioned.

News of the seven expulsions aroused more acts and declarations of solidarity. Fellow militants lauded the sanctioned as "hostages of *l'ordre moral*."[116] Activists linked the persecution of their union organization and its militants with the government's attempt to smash resistance to the implementation of the Fouchet plan, which intended to modernize higher education and to alter the universities "according to the needs of capital."[117] The UNEF feared that the expulsions and the accompanying prohibition forbidding the punished from eating at university restaurants would create financial problems for the seven and force them to quit the university. The supposedly puritanical left came to the defense of the sanctioned seven, prefiguring its support for students in the second half of May 1968. The PCF deputy of the Seine, Marie-Claude Vaillant-Couturier, declared her solidarity. The Communist group in the Conseil général de la Seine objected to "police repression" and demanded "the immediate lifting of sanctions against the seven."[118] Socialist, Protestant, and Jewish student groups objected to expulsions of UNEF activists when "notorious" "fascists" were allowed to attack their opponents with impunity in the Latin Quarter.[119]

The execution of the expulsions aggravated troubles. The date of eviction was set for Tuesday, 23 November, but the offenders resisted leaving their rooms. A picket line was established, and a flimsy furniture barricade obstructed the evictors: "Tables were positioned in front of the doors and those concerned [sanctioned students] refused to leave their rooms until they received orders from the Association [AERUA]."[120] Foot dragging convinced the administration to call in police (including the CRS) once again. Defying the forces of order, four to five hundred students continued their protests. Police reported that 18 students were arrested and 7 policemen injured, some in fights with members of the PCF and the UEC.[121] A number of students were also injured, and at least 5 had to be treated at the dispensary. One married female resident was seriously hurt when a sadistic policeman jammed a long (eight-centimeter) veterinary needle into her thigh.[122] The physician who treated her at the dispensary confirmed that she "had been a victim today of police brutality."[123] This cruel act signaled a struggle between the state and the student movement to control women's bodies and provoked new protests the following day.

Solidarity with students spread. The mayors of Arcueil and Choisy-le-Roi challenged the expulsions, which they considered highly unjust. The UNEF branch at the University of Strasbourg objected to police brutality and "repression" of "union rights."[124] Other organizations—the PSU, the Ligue française pour la défense des droits de l'homme et du citoyen—also defended the students. In the dormitory complex itself, some of the most prominent student militants were elected by overwhelming margins to the administrative council.[125] A solid front against repression had been created. In the spring of 1968, police repression would once again backfire, but in that year brutality would not be limited to the *banlieue* but would spread into the heart of Paris itself. Although the Antony incidents of 1965 gained some national media coverage, the movement failed to expand into the provinces or even into the capital.

One of the sanctioned female students appealed her sentence, but the upper court paternalistically justified the right of the administration to construct lodges to protect "young girls."[126] It ruled that the director was absolutely correct to request police intervention to ensure that construction could continue. By occupying the construction site, students were guilty of creating a "grave and intolerable disorder." The court rejected the defendants' argument, which claimed that the punished were victims of unfair discrimination since they had been arbitrarily selected from large numbers who had participated in demonstrations and had obstructed construction but were not prosecuted. It also refused to accept the reasoning that the sanctioned were persecuted because they were student unionists. The court judged that the AERUA did not qualify as a *syndicat* (union) but rather as an association, since students and dormitory residents did not exercise a profession or engage in regular salaried labor.

The condemnations of students continued to provoke troubles. The emotionally exhausted director of the housing complex resigned to protect his large family (he had six children) from the "consequences of events."[127] He asked for a transfer to the quieter provinces and was appointed headmaster of a provincial *lycée*. His resignation was reluctantly accepted by superiors who correctly predicted that students, who had "acted violently and nastily," would enjoy gloating over it. The resignation did indeed bolster the morale of activists who concluded that the *démission* represented "the failure of coercive policies," and it demoralized the already "traumatized" staff who "seriously needed to be supported in order to rebuild their confidence."[128] The housing director was among the first university officials—ranging from security personnel to presidents—whom student protests throughout the West would force to step down. In January 1966, the 36-year-old Jacques Balland was named the new director. Balland, a SFIO member and a professor *agrégé* of history, was no reactionary. His appointment revealed a little-appreciated liberalism or at least flexibility at the Gaullist Ministry of Education. As president of the UNEF in 1955, Balland had organized the first visit since 1947 of Chinese and Soviet students to France.

The new director quickly and wisely decided to tolerate practices of cohabitation and frequently voiced a desire to work harmoniously with students.[129] His surrender ended what became known as "The Love War" at Antony. Balland reached out to improve relations with activist students by dining with them in the university restaurant. He was undoubtedly successful in lowering tensions, but he failed to protect certain property rights and to enforce a rent increase. Indeed, students welcomed the new housing director with a rent strike. Foreign students continued to pay, if at all, at the former, lower rates. Many African students skipped payments entirely and defied the regulations by lodging their friends either in their own rooms or on cots and mattresses at the local UNEF offices. The AERUA supported them by demanding successfully that doors remain open all night. Students rendered watchmen powerless, and their "surveillance … purely theoretical."[130]

In November 1967, the directors of the various university dormitory complexes of the Paris region approved the de facto liberalization that had occurred at Antony and in other dorms.[131] Balland continued to allow nearly total visitation rights—with the exception of female minors (under 21) who did not have their parents' permission to receive male visitors. He argued that freedom of visitation had functioned smoothly and that complaints (including rape) were few. The director considered that his post no longer obligated him to impose an old-fashioned morality but rather to ensure the smooth operation of the housing complex. He also thought it wise to authorize political discussions, the distribution of propaganda, and exposure to contrasting opinions. By 1967 these freedoms had the effect of weakening the PCF and increasing support for other leftist groups, such as the SFIO, PSU, and CLER. Whatever their politics, Antony residents exercised so much de facto power that they were able—contrary to the wishes of administrators—to participate in decisions concerning the readmission of residents. Likewise, at Grenoble university dorms, "there were no regulations, men and women mixed without problems."[132] Officials were flexible, not repressive, and wanted to formalize the existing tolerance.

Nanterre continued what Antony had begun. It showed the limits and finally the progress of permissiveness. Cultural life surrounding the new university was minimal. In this context, dormitory issues became immediate concerns for the relatively isolated residents. In 1964 students inaugurated the first dorms, although the UNEF had challenged the construction of residences in the *banlieue* and preferred a downtown location. The buildings, constructed in the functionalist style of the 1960s, would house about 1,400 residents.[133] As at Antony, those who inhabited them were often from moderate-income provincial families. The dorms and the campus in general offered few facilities or amenities. In this pre-RER (Parisian rapid transit) age, transportation to the center of Paris was infrequent. Buses stopped at 9:00 P.M., and trains from the Gare Saint-Lazare at midnight. Only a few students had cars and thus residents were dependent on themselves for amusement. The diverse backgrounds and religions of inhabitants did not prevent the formation of a student community in the crucible of the suburbs. Several male students turned an abandoned blockhouse into a primitive nightclub. Consumption of alcohol and even hashish encouraged socializing. Hedonistic *Gemeinschaft* overcame the isolation, solitude, and anonymity that characterized student life in Paris.[134] Unlike their German or American counterparts, French universities had no system of fraternities or sororities, and the dorms would provide a base for future political action at Nanterre since their residents were the most likely to belong to student associations and to the leftist group which controlled organized cultural life.[135]

Official dormitory regulations were a mix of rational and irrational prohibitions. Students were forbidden to move furniture, put thumbtacks in walls, cook in rooms, and engage in political activities. Most importantly, although females were able to enter male dormitories, visits by male students to female dormitories were severely restricted.[136] In March 1967, to protest against the restrictions on visits by males to female dorms, dozens of male students decided to stage a sleep-in and occupied the female dormitory. The occupation tactic, like strikes, was modular or transferable. It had originally been associated with worker protests, which served as the model for politicized French youth, and became a part of the repertory of student movements in Europe and America.[137] Its use by students in a new context made it a particularly effective form of protest: "The power of protest thus lies neither in its numbers nor in its level of violence, but in its threat to burst through the boundaries of accepted limits of social behavior."[138] In this case, activists had broken down the barrier between public and private in their search for freedom and pleasure.

The dean had authorized the police to enter and seal off the dormitory in the event of an occupation.[139] As at Antony, the arrival of the forces of order created sympathy for the male invaders and revealed, at least for activists, the repressive nature of the university and its dean, Pierre Grappin. A sensationalist journalist reported that male invaders were "surrounded and coddled by a multitude of admiring females who touched them, flattered them, and ogled them."[140] Female reactions were undoubtedly more complex. Whatever the case, libertarian university students provided an example for the *lycéens* who protested their *lycées casernes* (barracks).[141] Administrative centralization confused lines of authority and complicated negotiations between Nanterre officials and the central Parisian authorities. An agreement was reached in which occupiers vacated the building with the understanding that they would not be subject to sanctions. Several days later, however, twenty-nine students—five of whom, activists claimed, had never taken part in the occupation—received letters from the housing office that suspended sanctions against them while warning them not to repeat their actions. Activists claimed with some credibility that authorities reneged on the deal. Many on campus believed those menaced with sanctions were being punished for their political activities, not for the dormitory occupation.[142] The threatened disciplinary measures reinforced hatred of the bourgeois university. Radicals thought they had revealed its "repressive structures," even if at Nanterre, unlike Antony, these did not include institutional racism and police brutality.

Protesters also believed that the administration possessed informants who supplied it with the names of activists who were then inscribed on infamous "black lists."[143] Most historians, including those with leftist sympathies, believe the existence of black lists to be a myth, but activists did not doubt that the lists were real. Anarchists jokingly suggested that Dean Grappin, who was known to be sympathetic to the political parties of the left, was attempting to demonstrate that he was a candidate for the post of minister of interior in a Gaullist government. Grappin seemed to be an unlikely target of leftist students.[144] A former Resistance fighter who had escaped from the train deporting him to a concentration camp, Grappin had firmly opposed the Algerian War and complemented his left-wing politics with progressive educational policies. At Nanterre, he wanted to replace the top-down monologue that characterized student-teacher relations in traditional French universities with a dialogue that would encourage student participation. He intended to modernize instruction of the social sciences (sociology, philosophy, psychology, ethnology, demography, and linguistics), which occupied a third of Nanterre professors, the highest percentage ever attained in a *faculté des lettres*.[145] Nevertheless, for many students he was the establishment and therefore responsible for sexual repression and the persecution of militants.

Militants embellished their allegations of a Grappin-inspired "repression." No evidence exists that he revealed the names of occupiers to police, who undoubtedly had their own sources of information. Indeed, at the beginning of the year, traditionalists criticized the dean for his "deplorable tolerance" because he permitted the distribution of tracts and pamphlets near university buildings.[146] The Nanterre faculty assembly categorically and unanimously denied the existence of black lists at its 27 January meeting and labeled the story "a defamatory rumor."[147] Grappin himself was decidedly conciliatory towards student demands even before the occupation.[148] In a letter to his superior, he recognized that students had gained total autonomy in dormitory matters. Student power was strong enough to force administrators of residence halls to tolerate violations of rules. Grappin accommodated students and favored residents' desires to be treated as adults, not high-school students. Following the path blazed by the new Antony housing director, he advised a liberalization of the rules and more local (not Parisian) control of decisions concerning Nanterre dormitories. He and other high-level administrators requested more funding for student housing.[149] During the 22 March 1968 occupation of the Nanterre administrative building, a vital event leading to the May unrest, the Nanterre dean and his associate would reject the police raid that the minister of education, Alain Peyrefitte, ordered to empty the building.[150]

It is hardly surprising that the police intervention at the March 1967 sit-in did not restore moral order in the dorms. If some consumed drugs (hashish, ether), many more ignored the restrictions on mixing.[151] Girls roamed the boys' dorms freely and vice-versa. One month after the beginning of the fall 1967 semester, "the situation has become so depraved.... Everyone knows that no set of rules worthy of the name is being applied. The most total anarchy is the rule."[152] Trash and noise were ubiquitous at all hours. About half of the residents housed at least one "clandestine" (a friend sharing a room who was not an official resident), and some lodged several. These illegal squatters were often brazen enough to use a dormitory address to get their mail. Several future *Enragés*, as campus pro-Situationists came to be known, gained reputations for imbibing drugs and for refusals to pay rent. Their actions anticipated the squatters' movement of the 1970s. Students were aware that the administration—even though it had the right to call police into dormitories (only buildings devoted to teaching were exempt from common law)—was reluctant to use force for fear of provoking more incidents.

The March 1967 dormitory occupation left regulations unchanged. The minister of education categorically rejected visitation rights for men.[153] In response, the libertarians produced a highly scatological leaflet, which opened with a direct quotation from *Misery*: "When people don't shit in his [the student's] face, they piss on his ass."[154] With tongue in cheek, the anarchists stated that students were eternally grateful to the French state for giving them such a beautiful and highly functional university. They were happy that they were able to live in such close proximity to their classrooms and workplaces and argued that their situation was even better than at suburban Sarcelles (a planned commuter development known, like Nanterre, for its ugliness). How marvelous it was that no one wasted time commuting or developing relationships! Whereas in the Latin Quarter left-wing students indulged in dating and discussions, at Nanterre students devoted themselves to their studies. They made love for only hygienic reasons and approved the prohibition on men entering female dormitories. In its eternal wisdom, the French state understood correctly that youth needed work. It knew that political, cultural, and sexual concerns merely diminished student productivity. All students agreed that instinctive individual desires must be restrained so that France could become strong and healthy. They were glad that the minister of youth, who had published a white paper on the problems of young people, wanted to establish a "dialogue" with them, and they urged him to consider ideas which would prepare them for adult life:

1. The wearing of a uniform for all young people.
2. The introduction of ranks for the most meritorious and dunce caps for those with persistently negative attitudes.
3. Corporal punishment for those who desecrate love.

By the end of the 1966–1967 academic year, an influential number of students believed that Nanterre was intolerably repressive. Examinations, restrictions on cohabitation, and, most annoyingly, police intervention had demonstrated to them that the university was an integral—but a very vulnerable—part of a highly authoritarian society.

Notes

1. *Quelle université? Quelle société?* (Paris, 1968), 84.
2. Nicole de Maupeou-Abboud, *Ouverture du ghetto étudiant: La gauche étudiante à la recherche d'un nouveau mode d'intervention politique (1960–1970)* (Paris, 1974), 207, 260, 289, limits the definition of *ouvriérisme* to those, such as Maoists, who excluded students from playing any revolutionary role whatsoever. Jean Bertolino, *Les Trublions* (Paris, 1969).
3. Cf. Hervé Hamon and Patrick Rotman, *Génération*, 2 vols. (Paris, 1987–1988), 2: 640, which claims that the *gauchistes* contributed significantly to the ideological decline of Communism.
4. André Stéphane, *L'Univers contestationnaire* (Paris, 1969), 294 and *passim*. See also Marc Kravetz, ed., *L'Insurrection étudiante* (Paris, 1968), 32, which denies the movement was "anti-communist."

5. Marc Goldstein, "Le Parti communiste du 3 mai au 6 juin 1968," *Les Temps modernes*, no. 269 (November, 1968): 831.

6. Cf. Gianni Statera, *Death of a Utopia: The Development of Student Movements in Europe* (Oxford, 1975), 201, which contrasts the "prescientific" and "chiliastic" utopia of the students with the presumably more "scientific" Marxist-Leninism.

7. Jérôme Ferrand, *La jeunesse nouveau tiers état* (Paris, 1968), 50. Jean Fourastié, *Les 40,000 heures* (Paris, 1965), 196.

8. Michel Winock, "Années 60: La poussée des jeunes," in *Etudes sur la France de 1939 à nos jours* (Paris, 1985), 304–322.

9. John R. Gillis, *Youth and History* (New York and London, 1974), 185–209.

10. Adrien Dansette, *Mai 1968* (Paris, 1971), 25; Alain Monchablon, *Histoire de l'UNEF de 1956 à 1968* (Paris, 1983), 14, 185; see also see statistics in Theodore Roszak, *The Making of a Counter Culture* (New York, 1968), 28.

11. Paul Ginsborg, *A History of Contemporary Italy: Society and Politics 1943–1988* (London, 1990), 299.

12. Philippe Labro, ed. *Ce n'est qu'un début* (Paris, 1968), 260; Statera, *Death*, 213; "L'Origine et sens du mouvement," *Esprit*, no. 372 (June–July, 1968): 1057.

13. François Bourricaud, *Universités à la dérive* (Paris, 1971), 44–48.

14. Pierre Bourdieu and Jean-Claude Passeron, *Les Héritiers: Les étudiants et la culture* (Paris, 1964), 129–131; Raymond Boudon, "Quelques causes de la révolte estudiantine," *La Table ronde*, no. 251–252 (December–January, 1968–1969): 178; Bertolino, *Trublions*, 212; A. Belden Fields, *Student Politics in France: A Study of the Union Nationale des Etudiants de France* (New York, 1970), 144.

15. Mattei Dogan, "Causes of the French Student Revolt in May 1968," in Stephen D. Kertesz, ed. *The Task of Universities in a Changing World* (Notre Dame, Ind., 1971), 313.

16. Fields, *Student Politics*, 86.

17. Louise Weiss, "Télémaque 1969," *Guerres et Paix*, no. 14–15 (1969–1970): 50. Cf. the statement by Jacques Chirac, state secretary in charge of employment, quoted in Kravetz, *L'Insurrection étudiante*, 311: "I don't believe that fear of unemployment is the cause of student discontent."

18. Bourricaud, *Universités*, 67.

19. Dansette, *Mai*, 31; Bourricaud, *Universités*, 69.

20. Dansette, *Mai*, 32; Bourricaud, *Universités*, 43–64.

21. Dansette, *Mai*, 32. See George Weisz, *The Emergence of Modern Universities in France, 1863–1914* (Princeton, 1983), 248, for 1939 tables.

22. Raymond Boudon, "La crise universitaire française: Essai de diagnostic sociologique," *Annales E.S.C.*, vol. 24, no. 3 (May–June, 1969): 747.

23. Fields, *Student Politics*, 74.

24. See Kravetz, *L'Insurrection étudiante*, 153; F. G. Dreyfus, "Problems in the French University," in Kertesz, *The Task of Universities*, 288, places the figure at nearly 10 percent.

25. Robert Lumley, *States of Emergency: Cultures of Revolt in Italy from 1968 to 1978* (London and New York, 1990), 55.

26. Bourdieu and Passeron, *Les héritiers*, 14; Labro, *Début*, 264.

27. Henri Lefebvre, *The Explosion: Marxism and the French Revolution*, trans. Alfred Ehrenfeld (New York, 1969), 104.

28. Pierre Grappin, *L'Ile aux peupliers* (Nancy, 1993), 237. Builders replied that windows disturbed student concentration.

29. *Le Mnefomane: Mutuelle Nationale des Etudiants de France Information*, special issue 4 A, September 1967. On the extreme right, François Duprat, *Les journées de mai 68: Les dessous d'une révolution* (Paris, 1968), 66, calls it "a horrid shantytown."

30. Bertolino, *Trublions*, 225.

31. René Rémond, *La règle et le consentement* (Paris, 1979), 58.

32. Aristede and Vera Zolberg, "The Meanings of May (Paris, 1968)," *Midway*, no. 3 (Winter, 1969): 96.

33. Dansette, *Mai*, 58; Grappin, *L'Ile*, 241.

34. Jean-Raymond Tournoux, *Le mois de mai du général* (Paris, 1969), 36.

35. Rémond, *Règle*, 85–87; Jean-Pierre Duteuil, *Nanterre 1965–1968: Vers le Mouvement du 22 mars* (Paris, 1988), 11.

36. Duteuil, *Nanterre*, 12. Cf. Boudon, "Crise," 761, who states without much evidence that most radicals at Nanterre were from the comfortable classes. Stéphane, *L'Univers contestationnaire*, 46, declares without citing references that "investigations have demonstrated that radicals were mostly recruited from the *haute bourgeoisie*."

37. Rémond, *Règle*, 88.

38. Three percent did not respond. See Dansette, *Mai*, 190.

39. Alain Schnapp and Pierre Vidal-Naquet, *Journal de la commune étudiante* (Paris, 1969), 387.

40. Duteuil, *Nanterre*, 11, 21.

41. James Miller, *Democracy Is in the Streets: From Port Huron to the Siege of Chicago* (New York, 1987).

42. Dansette, *Mai*, 52.

43. Ernest Mandel, "The Lessons of May 1968," *New Left Review* (November–December, 1968): 9–31.

44. Roland Biard, *Dictionnaire de l'extrême gauche de 1945 à nos jours* (Paris, 1978), 199; Dansette, *Mai*, 46. Krivine would remain head of the JCR's successor, the Ligue communiste révolutionnaire.

45. Direction générale de la Police nationale, renseignements généraux, bulletins hebdomadaires, 15 May 1968, AN 820599/75.

46. This may lead Maupeou-Abboud, *Ouverture*, 197, to assert that for the JCR the class struggle had become primarily international, i.e., between imperialist powers and the Third World.

47. JCR pamphlet quoted in Duteuil, *Nanterre*, 28.

48. Cf. Statera, *Death*, 196: "These groups [JCR and UJCml] were minority fringes of the student movement until the summer of 1968."

49. Duteuil, *Nanterre*, 26; Jean-Pierre Duteuil, "Les groupes politiques d'extrême-gauche à Nanterre," in Geneviève Dreyfus-Armand and Laurent Gervereau, eds., *Mai 68: Les mouvements étudiants en France et dans le monde* (Nanterre, 1988), 110.

50. Duteuil, *Nanterre*, 42.

51. Cited in Duteuil, *Nanterre*, 55.

52. Grappin, *L'Ile*, 244.

53. Duteuil, *Nanterre*, 48.

54. Mouvement du 22 Mars, *Ce n'est qu'un début, continuons le combat* (Paris, 1968), 14.

55. Cf. Hervé Hamon, "68: The Rise and Fall of a Generation," in D. L. Hanley and A. P. Kerr, eds., *May 68: The Coming of Age* (London, 1989), 15. For relations between Lefebvre and the Situationists, see Henri Lefebvre, *Le temps des méprises* (Paris, 1975).

56. Alain Delale and Gilles Ragache, *La France de 68* (Paris, 1978), 162.

57. The following paragraphs are based on Raoul Vaneigem, *Traité de savoir vivre à l'usage des jeunes générations* (Paris, 1967), 19–250.

58. Cf. Ingrid Gilcher-Holtey, *Die 68er Bewegung: Deutschland-Westeuropa-USA* (Munich, 2001), 15.

59. Greil Marcus, *Lipstick Traces: A Secret History of the Twentieth Century* (Cambridge, Mass., 1989).

60. Miller, *Democracy*, 124.

61. Ibid., 270; Edward Shils, "Dreams of Plentitude, Nightmares of Scarcity," in Seymour Martin Lipset and Philip G. Altbach, eds., *Students in Revolt* (Boston, 1970), 12.

62. Elisabeth Sussman, "Introduction," in Elisabeth Sussman, ed. *On the Passage of a Few People through a Rather Brief Moment in Time: The Situationist International, 1957–72* (Cambridge and London, 1989), 13; Pascal Dumontier, *Les Situationnistes et mai 68: Théorie et pratique de la révolution (1966–1972)* (Paris, 1990), 74–75; Jean-François Martos, *Histoire de l'Internationale Situationniste* (Paris, 1989), 24–25.

63. *L'Internationale situationniste*, [hereafter *IS*], no. 11 (October, 1967): 25; *IS*, no. 10 (March 1966): 40; see also Marcus, *Lipstick*, 416–425.

64. *IS*, no. 12 (September, 1969): 103; *Misery* is reproduced in René Viénet, *Enragés et Situationnistes dans le mouvement des occupations* (Paris, 1968), 219–243.

65. Here the argument resembles that of one of the Situationists' most derided targets, Alain Touraine. See his *The May Movement: Revolt and Reform*, trans. Leonard F. X. Mayhew (New York, 1979).

66. Guido Martinotti, "Notes on Italian Students in Periods of Political Mobilization," in Lipset and Altbach, *Students*, 191.

67. Schnapp and Vidal-Naquet, *Journal*, 111–157.

68. On Lebel, see Laurence Bertrand Dorléac, "Les artistes et la révolution," in Geneviève Dreyfus-Armand, Robert Frank, Marie-Françoise Lévy, and Michelle Zancarini-Fournel, eds., *Les Années 68: Le temps de la contestation* (Brussels, 2000), 230–232; on multiculturalism, Arthur Marwick, *The Sixties: Cultural Revolution in Britain, France, Italy, and the United States, c. 1958–c. 1974* (New York, 1998), 417.

69. "Le déshonneur des poètes," quoted in Duteuil, *Nanterre*, 108.

70. Fields, *Student Politics*, 28.

71. Patrick Seale and Maureen McConville, *Red Flag Black Flag: French Revolution 1968* (New York, 1968), 43; Maupeou-Abboud, *Ouverture*, 27–36; Fields, *Student Politics*, 36.

72. Bernard Droz and Evelyne Lever, *Histoire de la guerre d'Algérie* (Paris, 1982), 326. Apparently, police responsible for the deaths were never punished.

73. Fields, *Student Politics*, is the source of the following paragraphs.

74. Direction générale de la Police nationale, renseignements généraux, bulletin mensuel, April 1968, AN 820599/89.

75. Bertolino, *Trublions*, 153; Duprat, *Les journées*, 158, noted its moderation.

76. Fields, *Student Politics*, 105.

77. La crise de mai, 24 June 1968, AN 800273/61.

78. Alain Monchablon, "L'UNEF et mai 1968," paper presented to Colloque: Acteurs et terrains du mouvement social de 1968, Paris, 24–25 November 1988; Dansette, *Mai*, 93.

79. Monchablon, *UNEF*, 176.

80. Maupeou-Abboud, *Ouverture*, 253; Fields, *Student Politics*, 150.

81. Alain Geismar, Serge July, Erlyne Morane, *Vers la guerre civile* (Paris, 1969), 20.

82. Quoted in André Coutin, *Huit siècles de violence au Quartier latin* (Paris, 1969), 339.

83. Direction générale de la Police nationale, renseignements généraux, 15 May 1968, AN 820599/75.

84. Bertolino, *Trublions*, 126.

85. Duteuil, *Nanterre*, 74.

86. Duprat, *Les journées*, 68.

87. On the importance of Vietnam for PCF militants, see "Bilan d'une adhésion au PCF," *Informations Correspondance Ouvrières* (hereafter *ICO*), no. 91 (March–April, 1970); for the "movement" in general, see "Origine et sens du Mouvement," *Esprit*, no. 372 (June–July 1968): 1046–1079.

88. "La structure de l'Université et sa position dans la formation sociale capitaliste," cited in Duteuil, *Nanterre*, 17.

89. On Nanterre as starting point, see Touraine, *The May Movement*, 271, or A. Belden Fields, "The Revolution Betrayed: The French Student Revolt of May–June 1968," in Lipset and Altbach, *Students*, 128.

90. La résidence universitaire d'Antony, May 1967, Ga Brochure 42, APP [Archives de la Préfecture de Police].

91. Le directeur à ministre, 29 October 1965, Versement 5 [hereafter v. 5], Rectorat de Paris.

92. Pour le front, not dated [hereafter n.d.], v. 5, Rectorat de Paris.

93. Tuchman à M. le Recteur, 5 November 1965, v. 5, Rectorat de Paris.

94. Annexe no. 2, La méthode de l'action directe, 29 October 1965, v. 5, Rectorat de Paris.

95. John C. Gallaher, *The Students of Paris and the Revolution of 1848* (Carbondale and Edwardsville, Ill., 1980), 3–4.

96. Jean-Pierre Rioux, *La France de la Quatrième République: L'Expansion et l'impuissance, 1952–1958* (Paris, 1983), 335.

97. Antoine de Baecque, *La nouvelle vague: Portrait d'une jeunesse* (Paris, 1998), 20.

98. Rioux, *Quatrième République*, 217.

99. "Contraception, Amour, Sexualité et Planning familial," March 1968, MNEF, BDIC [Nanterre].

100. Dominique Veillon, "Corps, beauté, mode et modes de vie," in Dreyfus-Armand et al., *Les Années 68*, 173

101. *Planning Familial* (December 1967).

102. Annexe no. 2, La méthode de l'action directe, 29 October 1965, v. 5, Rectorat de Paris. It should be noted that it was forbidden to cook in dormitory rooms.

103. Rapport de M. Caron, September 1965, v. 5, Rectorat de Paris.

104. Ibid.

105. Seymour Martin Lipset and Sheldon S. Wolin, eds., *The Berkeley Student Revolt: Facts and Interpretations* (New York, 1965), xii.

106. Annexe no. 2, La méthode de l'action directe, 29 October 1965, v. 5, Rectorat de Paris.

107. Le directeur à Ministre, 29 October 1965, v. 5, Rectorat de Paris.

108. Ibid.

109. 7 Expulsions, n.d., v. 5, Rectorat de Paris.

110. Letter from Mlle. P. to M. le Recteur, 5 November 1965, v. 5, Rectorat de Paris.

111. Le recteur, 6 October 1965, v. 5, Rectorat de Paris.

112. Pour le front, n.d., v. 5, Rectorat de Paris.

113. Le directeur à ministre, 29 October 1965, v. 5, Rectorat de Paris.

114. Letter from Mlle. P. to M. le Recteur, 5 November 1965, v. 5, Rectorat de Paris.

115. Conseil de discipline, 16 October 1965, v. 5, Rectorat de Paris.

116. Des otages pour l'ordre moral, n.d., v. 5, Rectorat de Paris.

117. Pour le front unique, n.d., v. 5, Rectorat de Paris.

118. Préfet de la Seine, 28 October 1965, v. 5, Rectorat de Paris.

119. Il y a quelques jours, n.d., v. 5, Rectorat de Paris.

120. B. à M. le directeur, 25 November 1965, v. 5, Rectorat de Paris.

121. La résidence universitaire d'Antony, May 1967, Ga Brochure 42 APP.

122. Docteur C., Dispensaire de la résidence universitaire, 23 November 1965, v. 5, Rectorat de Paris.

123. Ibid.

124. UNEF, 30 November 1965, v. 5, Rectorat de Paris.

125. Liste des membres, 7 December 1965, v. 5, Rectorat de Paris.

126. Tribunal, 21 March 1966, v. 5, Rectorat de Paris.

127. Antony, 29 November 1965, v. 5, Rectorat de Paris.

128. Passage intérieur, 11 January 1966 and Le directeur, 6 January 1966, v. 5, Rectorat de Paris.

129. Dansette, *Mai*, 60.

130. La résidence universitaire d'Antony, May 1967, Ga Brochure 42 APP.

131. CROUS, 14 November 1967, 1208W, articles 115–117, ADHS [Archives départementales des Hauts-de-Seine].

132. *Le Mnefomane*, special issue 4 A, September 1967.

133. Bertolino, *Trublions*, 228; Dansette, *Mai*, 57.

134. Bourdieu and Passeron, *Héritiers*, 61; Raymond Aron, *La révolution introuvable* (Paris, 1968), 31; Fields, *Student Politics*, 151; Frank A. Pinner, "Western European Student Movements through Changing Times," in Lipset and Altbach, *Students*, 69–70.

135. René Rémond, "Nanterre: Vingt ans après," in Dreyfus-Armand and Gervereau, *Mai 68*, 9.

136. Hamon and Rotman, *Génération*, 1: 387.

137. Sidney Tarrow, "Modular Collective Action and the Rise of the Social Movement," *Politics and Society*, vol. 21, no. 1 (March, 1993): 82.

138. Sidney Tarrow, *Struggle, Politics, and Reform: Collective Action, Social Movements, and Cycles of Protest* (Ithaca, 1991), 7.

139. Grappin, *L'Ile*, 243.

140. Bertolino, *Trublions*, 238.

141. See Didier Leschi, "Mai 68 et le mouvement lycéen," in Dreyfus-Armand, *Mai 68*, 260.

142. Alain Touraine in Philippe Labro, *Début*, 43, confirms that the administration broke the spirit of its agreement with the occupiers; Mouvement du 22 Mars, *Ce n'est qu'un début*, 12; Bertolino, *Trublions*, 241, wrongly reports that twenty-five students were disciplined.

143. Schnapp and Vidal-Naquet, *Journal*, 103, 122.

144. Dansette, *Mai*, 62.

145. Epistémon (Didier Anzieu), *Ces idées qui ont ébranlé la France* (Paris, 1968), 22.

146. Letter, J. B., 23 January 1968, 1208W, art. 180, ADHS.

147. Assemblée de la Faculté, 27 January 1968, 1208W, arts. 1–2, ADHS.

148. Grappin au Recteur Roche, 20 March 1967, 1208W, art. 180, ADHS.

149. Grappin au Recteur Roche, 17 April 1967, 1208W, art. 180, ADHS.

150. M. B. à M. le recteur, 27 March 1968, 1208W, art. 180, ADHS. See Tournoux, *Le mois*, 347–348; Dansette, *Mai*, 73; Duteuil, *Nanterre*, 74.

151. L'Inspecteur Général, 4 July 1967, 1208W art. 180, ADHS; Rapport, 31 December 1968, 1208W, art. 180, ADHS.

152. Le directeur, 22[?] November 1967, 1208W, art. 180, ADHS.

153. Christian Charrière, *Le Printemps des enragés* (Paris, 1968), 25.

154. Reproduced in Duteuil, *Nanterre*, 73.

Chapter Two

MAKING DESIRES REALITY

—◦◦◦◦—

Contrary to Francis Fukuyama's denigration of the Paris students of 1968 as "pampered offspring," lacking any "rational reason to rebel," they had real educational grievances.[1] Compared with other nations, the French universities were considerably overenrolled. In 1967 the number of students was between 700,000 and 750,000; whereas in Great Britain and also in Germany, whose economy was larger than the French, enrollment was between 300,000 and 350,000.[2] Moreover, there was a much less satisfactory instructor per student ratio in France than in other major Western European nations with the exception of Italy. Great Britain and Germany had, compared with France, more than twice as many teachers per hundred students.[3] The poor faculty/student ratio explains, at least in part, the high failure rate of French students compared with their European counterparts. In addition, unlike some foreign systems that selected students at the beginning of their university career, the French system permitted anyone with a *baccalauréat* to enter the university. All were admitted, but few finished. Only 53 percent of pre-medical students, 42 percent of humanities' students, and 36 percent of law students advanced to the second year of study.[4] Twenty-five percent did not even take the first year's examinations. Ultimately, merely 30 to 40 percent of those with advanced high-school degrees who were candidates for the *licence* (a French B.A.) in the humanities or law received their degree. The rest were eliminated, and in the 1960s the dropout and failure rates were increasing. In Great Britain, in contrast, the failure rate was 10 percent.[5]

The government wanted to reform a system that wasted considerable resources and led to frustrations among unsuccessful students. At the opening of the 1967–1968 academic year, it decided to impose a series of reforms that had been formulated by Christian Fouchet, who had served as minister of education from 1962 to 1967, the longest tenure at Education since Victor Duruy during the Second Empire and Jules Ferry in the early Third Republic.[6] The reforms were among the most important in

---

Notes for this chapter begin on page 85.

the history of French higher education and reflected both the coming of age of the baby boomers and Gaullist desires for modernization. Though Fouchet created the plan, it was to be implemented by his successor, Alain Peyrefitte. The 42-year-old Peyrefitte, an alumnus of the elite Ecole Normale Supérieure, had served as minister of information and his transfer to the head of education in 1967 marked him as one of the rising young men of the Fifth Republic. Like General de Gaulle himself, Peyrefitte was a firm believer in selective admissions and wanted to change the old system radically. In November 1967, he declared, "It is as if the university were organizing a shipwreck to pick up the swimmers who have escaped drowning."[7] The Ministry of Education aimed to make the universities better adapted to a marketplace where, as Situationists and others pointed out, twentieth-century technicians were replacing nineteenth-century *diplômés*. The regime, in keeping with its desires to render the French economy more competitive, wanted to reform the university so that its graduates would fit into available jobs.[8] Thus, it was the government's desire for reforms, not its immobility, that fostered student discontent. Its reforms nevertheless did not address what students considered some of their most pressing problems—the overcrowding of classes, impersonal lecture courses, and lack of funding for scholarships. Italian students would articulate similar complaints against a government that also wanted to modernize its institutions of higher education.[9]

Officials attempted to change procedures so that a *baccalauréat* would be more difficult to acquire or would no longer automatically guarantee admission. It would become, as a high-school diploma was for most American universities, merely one admissions factor among others. Peyrefitte wanted each institution of higher education to determine its own entrance policies, thus encouraging less centralization and more autonomy.[10] The minister's measures were to be put into effect by decree, thereby avoiding parliamentary debate. This procedure reinforced the government's reputation for authoritarianism and recalled the traditions of the Third Republic's democratically dubious decree-laws, which had allowed the government to bypass the legislature.

The proposed changes aroused opposition among many students, parents, and even professors. A majority of Nanterre professors (87 versus 62) who responded to a questionnaire rejected any selection (beyond the *baccalauréat*) to enter the university.[11] De Gaulle himself realized that it would have been much easier to establish more rigorous selection in 1962–1963, when 280,000 were enrolled, than in 1967–1968 with 600,000 students. *Lycéens* from modest social strata were outraged by threats to educational egalitarianism, and university students feared the perspective of endless cramming to remain enrolled. The prospect of the elimination of their offspring frightened parents who knew that higher education was increasingly the path to upward social mobility. Students rejected policies of selection for social and economic reasons. They argued that the winnowing system favored children of the bourgeoisie, whose financial means and cultural inheritance gave them more opportunity to succeed in their studies.[12] The university, it seemed, would now be reserved primarily for an elite with an uncertain destiny as high-level civil servants or executives. Students and their families felt betrayed by a system that had promised them opportunity if they could pass the *baccalauréat*.

In 1967 the increased controls and immediate constraints of the plan were more annoying to students than the principle of selection. The reforms prevented them from switching majors without losing a year's credit, limited the number of times an exam could be repeated, and made attendance obligatory in certain seminars or discussion sections.[13] The government wanted to reform inexpensively and did not provide the resources—especially teaching personnel—to achieve a successful transition.[14] Pierre Grappin, Nanterre's dean, thought the reforms were academically ill advised and did not command sufficient teaching personnel to staff the necessary seminars.[15] Nor was the number of administrators adequate to register five thousand first-year students. Assembled professors "protested vigorously against the failure to build the university library, promised since the opening of the university in 1964." One faculty advisor became so distressed by his inability to help students arrange their schedules to meet the new requirements that he broke down in tears.[16]

The plan also created problems for students in arts and sciences who had begun their *licence* under the old system (*propédeutique-licence-doctorat* or *agrégation*) and now had to transfer credits into the new system (three *cycles* of two years each). Advanced students found that the new requirements delayed the completion of their diplomas.[17] For example, students who had never taken Latin might be required to pass an exam in that language and thus be forced to enroll in a class for which they lacked the necessary preparation. Many were compelled to take new courses that were often overenrolled due to lack of resources.[18] Those who had failed exams found that meeting requirements was now more time-consuming and more expensive. The perception that the reforms discriminated against lower-income students with part-time jobs became widespread.

The plan, its disorganized and underfunded implementation, and the prospect of more work sparked immediate opposition in Paris, where growing numbers of students aggravated already overcrowded living and working conditions. On 17 October 1967, four hundred students and teachers demonstrated against selective admission procedures at the Faculté des Sciences (Halle aux vins). On 7 November, four to five hundred Nanterre students protested against selection.[19] On 9 November, five thousand students—the largest number of student demonstrators since the 1963 protest against insufficient funding and overcrowding—came together in Paris to contest the government's reforms. Although only a small minority of the 160,000 Parisian university students, they showed their militancy by fighting with police in the Latin Quarter and by shouting slogans: "Down with selection," "Professors, not cops," and "The Sorbonne for students."[20] In the aftermath of the demonstration, UNEF militants formed two new organizations, Mouvement d'action universitaire (MAU), and the Comité la Sorbonne aux étudiants.[21] The latter published a tract in which it ridiculed the "planners" who wished to integrate students into the capitalist economy. It also called for the end of "dusty courses, stumbling *bergsonades*, examinations for those with a talent for repetition, and repressive lecture courses."[22] In 1968 both the MAU and the Comité la Sorbonne aux étudiants would catalyze action at the Sorbonne. As other right-wing governments would learn in later decades, making French universities more selective was no easy task. On 17 November in Paris, five hundred students staged a sit-in at the office of the dean, Marc Zamansky, a proponent of selection who, for many radical students, was quite representative of the Gaullist regime's arrogance, elitism, authoritarianism, and demand for effort.[23]

Simultaneously at Nanterre, sociology students initiated the largest strike in the history of the new university. This was bad news for the authorities since sociology was a growing and popular major, enrolling 700 to 750 students.[24] Across Europe, radicals majoring in that discipline were accustomed to thinking critically about society and seeking collective solutions for its problems.[25] Not only Lefebvre, whose connections to Communism and Situationism were well known, but also other Nanterre sociologists, such as Alain Touraine, encouraged radical critiques. Indeed, in essential ways and despite mutual animosity, Touraine's analysis of the role of the university resembled that of the Situationists. Both argued—as did some American and Italian radicals—that the aim of the institution was to produce *petits cadres* (middle management) who could fill the slots of the new bureaucratic/capitalist economy.[26] The late nineteenth-century university had prepared a well-educated elite, whereas its twentieth-century counterpart trained a specialized mass.

Hostile reaction to the minister's reforms dissolved the barrier between political and classroom activity. After sociology students—with the approval of some faculty members—voted to strike against the principles and consequences of the Fouchet Plan, protest spread to other disciplines.[27] On Tuesday, 21 November 1967, 2,500 students gathered for a meeting of the strike committee, and approximately 9,000 to 10,000 boycotted classes. Left-wing Catholics, UNEF activists, JCR members, and nonaffiliated students composed a massive and heterogeneous student movement.[28] *Gauchiste* coercion contributed partially to the movement's success since a number of radicals used threats and physical force to empty classrooms.[29] The protest copied workers' strikes by its refusal to work and intimidation of scabs. The withdrawal of effort anticipated the giant work stoppages of May. The weekend did not calm militancy, and on Saturday morning, 25 November, approximately one thousand demonstrated.

Student demands were essentially corporatist. Many wanted some form of *comités paritaires* (student participation) in the functioning of their departments and throughout the university in general. They insisted on smaller seminar classes and more professors. In the view of students, reduced class size was not merely a pedagogical improvement but also an opportunity for them to work in a group and thus "not to engage in individual competition concerning exams."[30] The demand for smaller classes reflected the inability of the French state, despite considerable efforts, to improve university teaching that was too frequently based on the *cours magistral*, in which a senior professor lectured to a student audience of hundreds.[31] This demand for more individualized instruction would persist at Nanterre.

Other strike demands were less concerned with pedagogy and more focused on students with academic and financial difficulties. Protesters argued for voluntary, not mandatory, attendance and advocated that classmates who failed their examinations—often those with jobs—should be allowed to repeat them. Students were determined to avoid "overwork" and argued that failing classes was insufficient reason to eject them from the university. The government was ultimately unable to convince students that its reforms were desirable or practical. Even if its plan had been successfully implemented, it remained unclear whether graduates would be able to sell their skills in the marketplace. Some *ouvriériste* students wanted to extend the strike beyond educational issues and ally with the CGT and the CFDT to block other government reforms, including those that involved making workers pay more for social security.

Anarchists supported the November strike (Cohn-Bendit was a member of the strike committee), but found a number of strikers' demands, such as smaller class size and more professors, "laughable."[32] The radicals' goal was to make the strike less corporatist and more political, but they did insist upon one corporatist demand—"an immediate end of compulsory [classroom] attendance." When this was rejected, radicals blamed "those, who not satisfied with being good students, want to force others to be like them." As with restrictive dormitory rules, obligatory attendance reminded revolutionaries of their experience in the disciplinarian French *lycée*. They also wished to defend part-time students, who would be the most adversely affected by the government's desire to trim the rolls of the university. Part-timers needed the social benefits, including the health plan, conferred by their status as students. Insurrectionaries rhetorically asked their fellows, "Why should we fight against the *étudiants-fantômes* [absent students]? They don't disturb the studies of others but are rather the ones who have the most fun." Anarchists urged half-seriously that in preparation for the next demonstration, students should learn karate "so that they would not appear ridiculous in front of the CRS or in comparison with the revolutionary Japanese students [of the radical Zengakuren]."

The anarchists viewed the work stoppage as a model of libertarian democracy since the strike committee had been responsible to the rank and file, but they were disappointed with its results. It might be expected that libertarian-inspired demands for the end of obligatory attendance would not be accepted by an administration that suspected many anarchists—along with the CLER and the JCR—of wanting to tear down the university. Indeed, one libertarian frankly told a reporter, "We anarchists wanted the destruction of the bourgeois university."[33]

Nonrevolutionary students were encouraged by several significant reforms that did emerge from the November strike. For the first time, students were able to attend faculty meetings (which had been a long-standing UNEF demand) and also to participate on joint departmental student-faculty committees.[34] In certain cases, transfers of credit that had been refused under the new system were awarded. Yet observers of various orientations have nearly unanimously regarded the gains of November strike as illusory and disappointing.[35] They have not acknowledged that administrators once again responded to student demands with flexibility, as they had during dormitory protests. In retrospect, the dean's concessions were inadequate, but Nanterre officials were by no means intransigent.

Divisions among the student left over participation in university affairs immediately surfaced. Despite the acceptance of the principle of *comités paritaires* by the national UNEF and the SNESup, the UNEF section at Nanterre rejected *paritarisme* as a capitalist "illusion," designed to trick both student and worker unionists.[36] The committees, it claimed, were virtually powerless. In addition, the refusal or delay in implementing what many considered to be justified and feasible reforms—such as seminars limited to twenty-five students, assignment of more teachers, and the establishment of libraries—alienated a number of activists in the humanities.[37] They became convinced of the necessity of building a combative student union. To realize their goals, some joined the UNEF in December 1967. Anarchist and Situationist analyses became more persuasive to others, who were radicalized by the national administration's failure to respond quickly and positively to many of their demands. The ministry's short-sighted refusal to concede further politicized many students and a good number of professors who now saw that their struggle had to be conducted on a national level, i.e., against the Ministry of Education itself. Given perceived government obduracy, a coalition of diverse radical groups was able to encourage solidarity against the state.

The strike's outcome reinforced libertarian and Situationist skepticism over the revolutionary role of students. At the end of November, the TSRF concluded gloomily that "at this moment any mass student movement results in only ... a more sophisticated alienation."[38] They thought that the class struggle divided students who ultimately could not possess any common interests. There could be no revolutionary student organization simply because most students were not revolutionary. *Anars* and pro-*situs* criticized wishfully thinking leftists who predicted that failure to climb the professional ladder would embitter these potential junior executives, who would then react by joining revolutionary movements. On the contrary, according to anarchists and *situs*, the modern capitalism of the Fifth Republic was adapting students and the university to its needs. Blind to this accommodation, student unionists mistakenly believed that their constituents were natural allies of the proletariat, not future bourgeois or petty bourgeois. For example, students attempted to protect the discipline of psychologists and their professional status. In contrast, libertarians and *situs* considered mental-health professionals "alternatively prison guards for delinquent youth, mediators between workers and employers, and destroyers of the revolutionary desires of protesters."[39] True revolutionaries must denounce the capitalist nature of the psychological profession, not defend it. In their own bit of wishful thinking, libertarians concluded that workers who had to deal with industrial psychologists would eventually show their gratitude by struggling against old and new forms of domination.

Situationists and anarchists assumed that a successful revolutionary movement must win the support of workers. Yet the student movement remained isolated from wage earners until the middle of May 1968. Provocation helped to sustain it. At Nanterre, the trickster Daniel Cohn-Bendit was partially responsible for keeping agitation alive. Cohn-Bendit has often been viewed as a celebrity whose importance was exaggerated by media hype, but this explanation of his role is unsatisfactory because it fails to ask why, among the hundreds of radicals, he became so prominent. First, Dany was able to bridge gaps between anarchism and Marxism and between violence and nonviolence. He could mesh subversives and moderates. Although a mediocre theoretician (his books are derivative and unoriginal), he conveyed a libertarian but ecumenical leftist ideology that brought together a variety of *groupuscules*. Second, Dany was quick-witted and propagandized cleverly. His audience listened with "amusement because his harangues were a festival of hilarity, of making faces, of jokes, of little comedies."[40] He could put, as the French say, "those who laugh on his side."[41] The filmmaker François Truffaut recounted his first exposure to the young anarchist:

> For me the *Affaire de la Cinémathèque* [January-March 1968] was a prologue of the May events.... Intellectuals were protesting against the government's decision to fire Henri Langlois, the founder and soul of the Cinémathèque.... During this demonstration, I was beaten with a club.... At the next demonstration ... I saw Cohn-Bendit for the first time.... Honestly I had a poor impression. Several of us wanted to keep our fight "apolitical" because we thought that if it became politicized, Langlois would never return as head of the Cinémathèque.
>
> I saw a red-headed boy who had climbed a street lamp.... We all asked what this guy was doing there.... The police had arrested a young demonstrator, and we were getting ready to leave peacefully and at that moment Cohn-Bendit addressed us: "We shall not leave until our comrade is freed." I thought the arrested boy was somewhere in a police station.... Cohn-Bendit continued, "In Brittany, the peasants waited six hours so that they would free one of their comrades. How long will Parisians wait?" He was very effective. Because of

him, several directors went to speak with the police and obtained the boy's liberation.… I learned that you can sometimes beat city hall. I asked who that redhead was, and someone said, "It's a guy from Nanterre."[42]

The Parisian prefect of police, Maurice Grimaud, had a different history of that event that unsurprisingly was more favorable to the forces of order.[43] Grimaud, who had earned an advanced degree in history, had been promoted during the Fourth Republic by François Mitterrand, minister of interior (1954–1955). The new prefect proved skillful adapting himself to the needs of both right and left politicians. He had won the trust of Prime Minister Pierre Mendès-France but then advanced his career under the Gaullists.[44] Grimaud asserted that in the evening of 18 March at 7:00 P.M. five hundred persons gathered for a demonstration to support Langlois. Some carried rocks, and police blocked their path to the Cinémathèque. Demonstrators near the movie directors François Truffaut and Claude Chabrol were well behaved, but others, "incited by a more violent orator" (presumably Dany), insulted officers. When they attacked an officer and hit him with a banner, police arrested the aggressor. Two other policemen were injured in scuffles. Chabrol asked the crowd to disperse, but 250 remained at the request of the "troublemaker," who sought to provoke more violence. Of course, the police—according to the prefect—retained their calm. The protest finally disassembled at 9:15 P.M.

Cohn-Bendit's major media breakthrough had occurred when he confronted François Missoffe, the minister of youth and sports, at Nanterre on 8 January 1968.[45] Students had just returned from Christmas vacation and learned that the minister, accompanied by the dean and other prominent academics, was scheduled to visit the newly constructed swimming pool. A number of radicals, including Trotskyites and anarchists, decided to use the occasion to amuse themselves. The minister was a particularly attractive target since he was a key figure in the Gaullist government's somewhat fruitless attempts to depoliticize the student body.[46] Missoffe had recently issued a white paper that painted a Boy or Girl Scout image of French youth and concluded that the greatest concern of young people was their own careers: "French youth dream about marrying young but remain concerned about having children without having the means to raise them. Thus, their first priority is professional success. While waiting, he saves money to buy a car and she for her dowry."[47]

As Missoffe inaugurated the pool, Cohn-Bendit, backed by several dozen students, questioned—probably not in the most respectful tone—the minister concerning his white paper's lack of information on sexuality. Missoffe replied sharply that if his questioner had sexual problems, he should jump in the pool. The extreme-right weekly *Minute* offered another version of the retort and asserted that the minister countered quickly: "With your looks, I'm not surprised that you have those kinds of problems."[48] Whatever the case, Cohn-Bendit responded by charging that the minister was reacting like a Nazi. The exchange of insults inaugurated Cohn-Bendit's celebrity as verbal *provocateur*. Throughout May in person or on television and radio, Dany would amply demonstrate his talent as an entertainer and his ability to amuse an audience. Even his adversaries admitted that he made them laugh.[49] It is not surprising that in the 1990s he would become, like a number of political personalities, a television talk show host.[50]

The verbal confrontation with the minister took on mythic proportions, which revealed that many from different bands of the political spectrum would identify "anti-authoritarian" student rebels with sexual liberation. Concerning Dany himself, the Ministry of the Interior began a procedure that was intended to expel the foreign radical who had chosen German nationality. In February and March, the anarchist remained in France and, with other libertarians, continued agitation at Nanterre. *L'Humanité* became alarmed at the growing celebrity of the extreme leftists and suggested that Cohn-Bendit was secretly collaborating with the minister. Rumors circulated that the reason for the government's failure to expel Dany was that he had slept with Missoffe's daughter.[51] At the end of January, the Nanterre *trublions*—Cohn-Bendit and two pro-Situationists—were subject to disciplinary action because they had disturbed courses or violated dormitory rules. According to one of their defenders, these *Enragés* "intended to disrupt systematically an intolerable order, beginning with the university."[52]

Nanterre was a particularly fitting target for Situationists. They were revolted by both its physical appearance and its mission as the flagship of modernity in French higher education. Furthermore, two of their favorite targets—Henri Lefebvre and Alain Touraine—taught sociology there. Lefebvre had once been a companion of the Situationist theoretician Guy Debord who had broken with him in the usual fissiparous manner of the Situationist International. Alain Touraine annoyed many *gauchistes* by insisting that the proletariat was no longer revolutionary. At the end of January, an *Enragé* was expelled from the dormitories for one month. He had been lodging a squatter who had refused to leave and, in addition, had acquired a record of involvement with drugs.[53] This exclusion and the punishment of others became causes célèbres for campus radicals.

The expulsion of the *Enragé* helped to spark a demonstration on Friday, 26 January. Radicals viewed this *manif* as a protest against repression. Despite professors' "categorical and unanimous" denial of black lists, rumors persisted concerning the existence of these confidential records intended to persecute subversives.[54] Notwithstanding little hard evidence, extreme leftists continued to give great credence to the specter of black lists.[55] Radicals believed these legends because of their profound distrust of the state and the established elites that they thought were plotting against students and workers. Furthermore, legends are ways of mobilizing people when a new social movement occurs.[56] The more verifiable presence of plainclothes policemen and informers on campus angered students and led to the anarchist-initiated demonstration on Friday. Demonstrators protested against proposed disciplinary measures against Dany and another student accused of drug dealing.

This defiant agitation by anarchists, Situationists, and some Trotskyites led the administration to call in police and thereby break a century-old tradition of sanctuary that kept the forces of order outside university walls to preserve academic independence in order to guarantee freedom of research and teaching. Nineteenth-century legislation had specified that only with the dean's permission could police enter classroom buildings. Most teachers and students were attached to the idea of sanctuary and hostile to uniformed coercion in an institution that was devoted to free expression of ideas. Revolutionaries were aware of the negative effects of police presence on university opinion and were more than willing to provoke it to show the coercive nature of capitalist society in one of its least repressive institutions. They knew that antipolice feeling was endemic among students and that a movement against repression could always find support among scholars. For example, in February in the twelfth *arrondissement* officials reported that a group of medical students inhabiting the upper floors of a residence threw unidentified liquids on several policemen issuing parking tickets and insulted them as "a bunch of lazy good-for-nothings, butt-fuckers, and assassins."[57]

Some prominent intellectuals have argued that Nanterre began the movement to liberate the French from restrictions on speech inherited from the relatively uptight society of the 1950s, a movement that reached its high point in the May uprising.[58] Radicals believed that the January demonstration at Nanterre and then the May revolt in Paris were spurred by their refusal to accept the traditional ban on political activity on campus.[59] At the 26 January protest, university ushers warned thirty protesters, who were carrying signs with photos of the plainclothes officers who were allegedly observing the campus, to stop their "political" demonstration.[60] When ushers attempted to confiscate the protesters' signs, the revolutionaries fought back determinedly and were quickly joined by approximately thirty more students who found scuffles more interesting than their studies. Disregarding the tradition of sanctuary, the administration called in the forces of order to end the protest, but students—newly reinforced by their more studious mates, who had just finished attending classes—responded by throwing tables, chairs, and stones at the uniformed officers, who then retreated to their vehicles. The vigor, spontaneity, and unanimity of the student reactions against police intervention astonished their professors.[61] The CLER estimated—with some exaggeration—the number of students "who chased the forces of order" to be 500 to 1,000.[62]

Both the Nanterre administration and faculty representatives tell a different story.[63] They claim that police were called in not to repress political expression (it had already existed for several years at Antony and was largely tolerated at Nanterre) but rather to protect people and, just as importantly, property. The associate dean, Professor Beaujeu, reminded the faculty assembly of 27 January that the forces of order were and would be requested only when "people or property were directly threatened." Both conditions had occurred on 26 January. The police had been summoned but, faced with stiff student resistance, had retreated "without making any arrests." The assembled professors unanimously approved a resolution authored by department heads that accused student demonstrators of having committed "acts of violence" and "treating the Dean as a 'Nazi'" despite his well-known record in the Resistance and his Communist and then PSU affiliation.[64] The professors concluded that police had been convoked not to repress dissent but to protect university personnel who had been "roughed up and injured" while trying to prevent "violence and the destruction of material": "The appearance of violent and provocative groups at Nanterre University poses a new problem of order and safety in an institution traditionally disarmed and whose functioning depends upon the refusal of violence."[65]

The assembled professors unanimously pledged to read the following statement to their classes: "The serious damage caused by the demonstrators to the furniture of the university and to several automobiles clearly demonstrate the reprehensible nature of their actions. They confuse the exercise of their freedom with calumny, insult, and vandalism."[66] Accounts by those sympathetic to the movement often omit its hard, intolerant, and revolutionary edges and ignore its violence to persons and destruction of university property.[67]

The Nanterre administration had unwittingly confirmed the radicals' diagnosis that the university was an appendage of the police state, even if students disregarded the fact that a police retreat in the face of angry students hardly characterized an authoritarian regime and sharply contrasted with police brutality at Antony several years previously. In some ways, the actions of the French revolutionaries recalled the Free Speech Movement in Berkeley, which also showed the vulnerability of the liberal university's restrictions on political activity. Although the movements of Nanterre and Berkeley were parallel, they were by no means identical. Characteristically, the French students protested against not only the (unenforced) ban on political activity but also a repressive national government willing to protect property. The French radicals denied the legitimacy of the authorities' defense of property. They were not liberals but revolutionaries for whom the university was to be put at the disposal of the proletarian social revolution. Pro-*situs* and anarchists repeatedly argued that the university was an institution good only for producing various kinds of policemen, who called themselves executives, psychologists, or sociologists. Radicals, many of whom would later join the 22 March Movement, conceived of the university not as an oasis of freedom or an ivory tower but as a class institution, i.e., a bourgeois body where professors took the place of capitalists.[68] On the other side, senior professors could not stomach revolutionary intolerance.[69]

Dialogue between liberals and class-conscious revolutionaries was not possible. May and its aftermath resolved the issue by force.

Pro-Situationist students or *Enragés* profited from the confrontation with police by issuing the leaflet "While waiting for the cybernetic [society], the cops," which accused the Dean ("Grappin-la-matraque") of placing the university under the protection of the gendarmerie and thereby revealing the bogus and violent nature of the "dialogue" between students and the administration. The leaflet, whose stylistic and graphic quality impressed even ideological adversaries, produced a rupture between anarchists and pro-*situs* that would culminate in a clash during the formation of the 22 March Movement. The unilateral decision of the pro-*situs* to replace the periods and commas of the text with swastikas offended anarchists who believed in maintaining the distinction between the capitalist police state of Gaullist France and a fascist or Nazi regime. The critique of 1960s radicals by the German philosopher Jürgen Habermas is apt: "Those who have had success with new demonstration techniques fancy themselves revolutionary fighters against fascist oppression while they are actually doing nothing but polemically exploiting the unexpected latitude granted by liberal institutions."[70] The elite police intelligence unit, the Deuxième Brigade, was unwittingly Habermasian when it recognized that the university was the most vulnerable institution of French society.[71] Higher education's liberal nature rendered it incapable of combating violent protest without renouncing its own liberalism. Police intelligence officers realized that calling the forces of order to campus only deepened the dilemma. Yet the state could not tolerate the destruction of the university since it played the essential role of integrating and promoting a new generation.

The physical and political victory of the students over police on 26 January did not end the threat to expel Cohn-Bendit from France or to discipline other revolutionaries. On 6 February, the AFGEN-UNEF (Association fédérative des groupes d'études de Nanterre) organized a demonstration against the repressive measures of the administration.[72] Almost simultaneously, the Nanterre sociology department protested against the proposed expulsion of Dany but remained silent concerning the disciplinary measures taken against other students close to the Situationists. Not fully appreciating the revival of Dadaist and Surrealist traditions, the faculty was understandably upset with the anarchist and Situationist disruptions of their courses. Troublemakers threatened the professors' function as teachers by cleverly bringing public derision upon them. According to the Italian historian Luisa Passerini, students made fun of their *profs* for political purposes:

> The resumption of that mocking tone is indicative precisely because of its tastelessness, because of its coarse guffaw. It re-proposes in public the crass jokes that students have always made about their professors.... Patrimony of generations of frustrated students, it maintains their giggle and their amusement,

infantile and for this reason sharp, irritating, capable of truly annoying professors. The transition to the public sphere, by means of the spoken and written
word, instills a sense of liberation, of relief, of power.[73]

Once again, 1960s radicals made public what had previously been private.

In October 1966, shortly before the appearance of the *Return of the Durruti Column*, the cybernetician Abraham Moles had experienced the first
disruption when he gave his inaugural lecture at the University of Strasbourg.[74] At that time, Situationist-inspired students had bombarded him
with tomatoes to protest against what they considered his support of the
technocratic university and of hideous Sarcelles-like urbanism. In the winter and spring of 1968, a favorite target of both Situationists and anarchists
was Alain Touraine. Young hecklers in his class so angered the sociologist
that, quivering with rage, he reportedly responded: "If this is the revolution, I am a counter-revolutionary.… I'm fed up with anarchists and even
more with Situationists. I'm the boss here. If you were, I'd leave for a place
where people know the meaning of work."[75] One heckler, known as Big
Richard because of his size, approached Touraine. Snapping his fingers, he
hummed "Cool man, do you know where the blues come from?" Another
distinguished sociologist, Edgar Morin, was also fair game. Undeterred
by disruptions, he confronted his tormentors, "The other day you told me
that I belonged to the trash can of history." Undismayed, a heckler shot
back: "How did you get out?"

Students moved easily from personal confrontation to global issues. The
Vietnam War was the international event that most concerned them.[76] Antiwar sentiment extended to professors and *lycéens*. The Vietcong's Tet Offensive at the end of January 1968 boosted February's "Anti-imperialist Days,"
organized by the UNEF and SNESup. In Paris on 7 February, the Maoist
CVB (Comité Vietnam de base) decided to disrupt a pro-American and
pro-South Vietnamese meeting sponsored by Occident. As hundreds of helmeted CVB members moved toward the Mutualité meeting hall, police
charged and street battles erupted.[77] Several days later, a larger and less violent demonstration assembled. Eighty thousand marched from the Place de
la République to the Place de la Bastille, the traditional route of the left. PCF
and CGT sympathizers composed the bulk of the crowd. Demonstrators
shouted "Peace in Vietnam," instead of the more aggressive Trotskyite or
Maoist slogan, "The NLF will win." Despite the divisions, sympathy for the
NLF and corresponding anti-Americanism provided a pillar of unity for
the entire left. The success of the Vietnamese against the United States led
a significant number of militants to believe that other "imperialist" powers—in this case, France—were also vulnerable.[78] Many French radicals
identified themselves with struggling Third World underdogs. For Maoists,
Trotskyites, and others, the Vietnamese cause was an integral part of the
worldwide socialist revolution for which they were fighting.

Some Nanterre students adhered to the revolutionaries' internationalism. Approximately 15 *nanterrois*, including Cohn-Bendit, participated in a

trip to Berlin sponsored by the JCR and its affiliate, the Comité Vietnam national (CVN). In Berlin, they joined 30,000 protesters and heard speeches from Alain Krivine and Ernest Mandel. The French delegation was introduced to the rhythmic chants of "Ho-Ho, Ho Chi-Minh" and "Ché, Ché Guevara," which would later be adopted as slogans in Parisian anti-imperialist demonstrations.[79] Nanterre anarchists came to admire the dedicated and intelligent German student leader Rudi Dutschke, even though he was close to the Trotskyite Fourth International. Dutschke had fled Stalinist East Germany, and his search for a new form of socialism appealed to libertarians. Internationalism and an uncritical Third Worldism informed his personal life. He had married an American, and the couple named their son Ché. Dutschke's organization, the SDS (Sozialistischer deutscher Studentenbund) impressed the *nanterrois*.[80] In addition to left-wing thinkers such as Guevara, Karl Liebknecht, Rosa Luxemburg, and Marx himself, German SDS members read Herbert Marcuse.

Although the SDS was a presence on most German campuses, it lacked support outside universities. The unions and, of course, the Social Democratic Party were hostile to it. Most of its adherents realized the need to link up with workers, but German workers, if not antagonistic, were indifferent to its politics. Many, but perhaps not a majority, of the approximately two thousand in the organization became convinced that the working class in advanced Western nations was no longer revolutionary. The adoption of the Marcusian skepticism on workers' revolution established an important barrier between German and French student radicals.[81] The powerful influence of the New Left among students in West Germany during the 1960s may have been a consequence of the destruction of traditional Marxism during the Third Reich and the subsequent conservative intellectual domination of the Federal Republic during the 1950s. In contrast, the established left in France remained vibrant throughout the postwar period and circumscribed the appeal of the New Left.

In France, Marcuse was less influential than in West Germany or the U.S. *One-Dimensional Man* had just been translated at the end of May 1968, but *Eros and Civilization* and *Soviet Marxism* were widely available before May.[82] Nevertheless, all factions of the movement at Nanterre continued to insist that the working class could and would make revolution. As in Italy, *ouvriérisme* dominated among French student radicals. In contrast, Dutschke praised Marcuse's essay "Repressive Tolerance," which doubted workers' revolutionary potential. So did most radicals in the U.S., where the influence of orthodox Marxism was much weaker than on the continent.[83] Their revolutionary subjects were students, blacks, and the poor throughout the world. Whether *ouvriériste* or not, radicals throughout America and Europe lauded the socialisms of Cuba and China. Apologies for both regimes were fashionable amongst much of the left in the 1960s.[84] Ho, Ché, and Mao became heroes of a new generation of young revolutionaries.[85]

The German SDS's four-point program influenced many Nanterre radicals: first, open admissions of candidates of working-class origins to democratize the university; second, student control of higher education through cogestion or co-determination; third, encouragement of political activity in the university; fourth, replacement of the ivory-tower tradition with radical community service.[86] After an anti-imperialist demonstration against the Shah of Iran on 2 June 1967 during which a student, Benno Ohnesorg, was shot and killed, SDS members founded the "Critical University," which would become a model for members of Nanterre's 22 March Movement. The critical university would establish commissions to study curriculum, politics, sexual denial, and bourgeois science. For its French admirers, the critical university held the promise of bridging the gap between the radical student movement and other progressive forces, especially the working class, by allowing students to venture forth from their academic ghetto. Some suggested that by following the model of the Cuban or Chinese universities, the critical university could help transform society by abolishing the distinction between manual and intellectual work.

At Nanterre in February 1968, *Enragés* went well beyond the critical university. They published two texts to spread protest and to poke fun at those whom they considered insufficiently radical.[87] The first was the "Chant de guerre des Polonais de Nanterre," known more popularly as the "Grappignole" and modeled on the revolutionary songs "La Carmagnole" and "Ça ira." The offensive parody, which derived its name from Nanterre's dean, derided the political, religious, and even sexual orientations of various campus mandarins. The *Enragés*' second text was a comic strip that attacked the UNEF, which had condemned the "excesses" of some radicals and had refused to defend those who were threatened with expulsion from the university. The cartoon showed a priest offering the use of a chapel to clean-cut UNEF militants. The UNEF activists then warned the hirsute *Enragés* against creating a scandal. The *Enragés* replied that they wanted to have fun and labeled the division between politics and pleasure counterrevolutionary. UNEF members countered by asking the *Enragés* from whom they derived their authority. The latter replied that they empowered themselves "as soon as they take their desires for reality."

Radical youth in the 1960s distinguished itself by its ability to move from the international to the intimate and from the self-denying to the hedonistic. The UNEF considered Valentine's Day an appropriate occasion to organize a national day of protest against restrictions on visiting rights and other dormitory rules that students considered ridiculous. In the afternoon of Valentine's Day (14 February) 1968, six hundred students gathered to discuss the modalities of the proposed occupation of the girls' dormitory at Nanterre.[88] The large turnout surprised observers, who did not suspect that the issue would activate the reserve army of protest. Even the FNEF realized *ex post facto* that it had underestimated the dormitory issue and had granted the UNEF an uncontested political opportunity.[89]

Organizers of the protest wanted to avoid the "folkloric" interpretation that the press had given their movement in March 1967. At that time, the media had stamped their occupation as "a student springtime," i.e., college kids just letting off steam or the equivalent of an American "panty raid" of the 1950s.[90] Also, like their U.S. counterparts in the 1960s, French students were determined to call into question the fundamentals of sexual morality and control.[91] Militants wanted not a short-term or symbolic victory but a permanent change of the regulations: "We don't wish to invade or to occupy dorms, but instead to establish the right of everyone to receive anyone they wish." They urged both male and female activists to act as responsible adults. That night, 450 persons occupied the women's dormitory without police interference and imposed a regime of open visitation that would remain in effect for the rest of the year. In 1968 the support for the expansion of sexual freedom had become a national phenomenon. UNEF dormitory residents officially designated 13–14 February as "days of action to abolish the interior regulations." At Nantes fifty students invaded the office of the chancellor and "tore down curtains, tore up paper, and dirtied rugs."[92] Nanterre militancy served as a model for students in other provincial universities, such as Nancy, Montpellier, and Nice. More universities abroad would follow.

The education minister's decree of 22–23 February attempted unsuccessfully to limit the progress of permissiveness. It sought to prevent males from entering women's dorms and prohibited females from visiting males after 11:00 P.M. The minister, Alain Peyrefitte, admitted the need to "liberalize" and alter "an outdated system of rules … which were now in part ignored."[93] He also conceded an expansion of visitation rights and noted that "society has evolved and no longer treats university students as *lycéens*." Ultimately though, he drew the line: "We cannot permit *mineures* (young girls) to visit young men," and we cannot "be less strict than our hotel regulations." Nevertheless, he offered parents of female minors the option to request an *dérogation* (exemption) for their daughters. Peyrefitte insisted upon maintaining the ban on male visits to female dorms: "This does not mean that we are opposed to female equality. On the contrary, we support it. But the risks for males and females are not the same…. A female student who enters a boy's room knows the risk; however, to let men enter girl's dormitories will expose all female residents…. In addition, according to polls, the great majority of female students do not wish that men enter their dormitories." Students challenged Peyrefitte's decree by claiming that it violated the constitution of the Fifth Republic, whose preamble stipulated equal rights for women and men. Student protest did not focus on the right to sleep together since women had been allowed to visit men's dormitories. Instead, as at Antony, it defied restrictions widely regarded as repressive.[94] The UNEF considered "hypocritical" a policy that allowed women to visit male dorms and forbade men from passing the night in a female residence.

Not all female students agreed. Some of their delegates told Peyrefitte that even though they wanted the right to spend the night in the men's dormitory, they did not wish to have men, whose presence they regarded as intimidating, as permanent residents in their dorms.[95] In general, female students were less politicized and less unionized than males even though, compared to other French women, they were less traditional.[96] A poll confirmed that 83 percent of students believed that sexual freedom before marriage was desirable for men, whereas 67 percent thought it desirable for women.[97] Curiously, female students were more patriotic and sympathetic to performing military service than men. They were also more inclined than males to live with their parents while attending the university. At Nanterre they were less mobile than their male counterparts.[98] The overwhelming majority of young women (447 of 523) who lived in the Nanterre dorms were enrolled at that campus, while a slight majority of male residents (315 of 609) studied in other institutions. Whether for or against male visitation rights, the conflict increased female politicization, an important result in a university whose Faculté des lettres had a female majority.

A number of members of the administrative council of the housing administration, which included the chancellors and deans of some of the most important Parisian institutions of higher education, objected to Peyrefitte's position. Echoing UNEF supporters, several recalled that the law guaranteed equality between men and women. Dr. Dubas, the chancellor's medical consultant, said he could not support "any segregation of the sexes and of adults and minors," who constituted over 60 percent of female residents and 43 percent of males.[99] One member thought that the minister's rules were inapplicable and unreasonable since they went against "social trends." Another, while agreeing with Peyrefitte concerning the desirability of limitations on visitation rights, nevertheless felt that the minister's decree was too complicated to execute and might lead to a "collective explosion." Instead, he wanted to compose "a simple system of rules that would be accepted."

Those in charge of setting and executing policy in the residences of Parisian institutions of higher education did their utmost to circumvent what they regarded as the rigidities of Peyrefitte's instructions. The director of Parisian housing warned the minister and the chancellor that the prohibition on men visiting female dorms that housed women over twenty-one would be totally ignored or would lead to "a showdown" at Nanterre and other housing complexes in the Paris region.[100] If the minister asked the administrative council to alter its liberalized policy, it would refuse. Furthermore, the Parisian housing director cautioned his superior that public opinion endorsed more freedom. He recommended that Peyrefitte accept visitation rights so that officials could concentrate their efforts on fighting squatters. Immediately prior to the Valentine's Day occupation, the housing commission had recommended substantial modifications of the rules to allow them to fit "the general mentality and *moeurs* (mores)."[101]

Although the commission predicted that some might find the changes "revolutionary" and "too liberal," it felt that the new regulations were "realistic." Each dormitory would be permitted to apply the new rules in its own way. The diffusion of all sorts of information, including political, would be tolerated. Cohabitation and visitation were considered less important than preventing *l'hébergement clandestine* (illegal squatting), which remained "by far, the most serious difficulty in our dormitory complexes."[102]

Nanterre dormitory and university officials in 1967–1968 were more tolerant and solicitous of student opinion than those at Antony in 1964–1965. In March 1968, they did not oppose the lecture sponsored by the student resident association (ARCUN) on "Sexuality and Repression" or its distribution of a 1936 manifesto authored by Wilhelm Reich.[103] In April 1967 housing administrators reported that several female occupants had circulated a questionnaire and received 97 responses, despite the "certain dishonest opposition" of ARCUN, which was partially successful in obstructing the questionnaire's circulation. Twenty-seven females opted to maintain the old rules, which prohibited visits by the opposite sex; 14 chose total freedom of visitation; 56 wanted a modification of the rules and limited freedom of movement. The option of limited freedom did not indicate that residents were prudish or conservative. On the contrary, it often meant that they wanted to be informed before either their parents or young men were able to enter their rooms.[104] Officials thought that any changes concerning visitation should not apply to minors.[105] Yet by 1967 even parents of minors were surprisingly favorable to liberalization of visitation rights.[106] The Commission du Logment of the CROUS, led by Dr. Dubas, undertook a poll among these parents of minors and established that 58 percent of them did not wish to apply the existing rules strictly, 30 percent were for controlled freedom, and 12 percent for unlimited freedom.[107] The liberality of parents, very few of whom demanded tight restrictions, astonished officials who had wrongly assumed a great generation gap.

The students close to ARCUN were even more insistent on liberalization of visitation rights. Authorities distrusted those who demanded complete freedom of visitation but worried that a publicly reactionary stance might lead to open rebellion in the dorms. By September 1967, an official inspector recorded "facts and practices which were very deplorable: uncontrolled comings and goings of strangers during the day and night creating nightly disturbances, debauchery, wild partying, use and trafficking of drugs."[108] Administrators were concerned to ensure peace and "general tranquility" since "the overwhelming majority demanded it." They also felt a paternal responsibility to prevent the emotional and physical collapse of the most decadent or pleasure-loving students. They agreed to beautify the barren grounds, offer the services of a nurse and social workers, open a bar (alcohol was preferred to illegal drugs), construct a cultural center, and improve the library. New electric doors would be installed to terminate unauthorized visits and to end illegal trafficking. In addition, visitors and residents would be required to show appropriate identification. All violations would be recorded, and suitable sanctions levied. Officials planned to close the dorms at 11:00 P.M. The elimination of "clandestines" was administrators' gravest problem and highest priority. Once again, as they would be throughout May and June, authorities were much more concerned with the protection of property, not morality.

At Nanterre following the Valentine's Day occupation of the women's dormitory, threats to expel the *Enragés* perpetuated tensions. At Parisian and provincial universities, student strikes persisted over issues such as visitation rights and selection. In this atmosphere, four anarchist students, including Cohn-Bendit, collaborated on the pamphlet *Why Sociologists?* which offered a variation on the theory of state monopoly capitalism.[109] It argued that competitive capitalism of the nineteenth century had been superseded by the organized version of the twentieth century. In other words, a laissez-faire state, Darwinian struggles among competing businessmen, and the suppression of organized labor no longer characterized contemporary capitalism. Instead, corporatist cooperation among big business, big government, and big labor distinguished the current economy. The U.S. had pioneered this model, and consequently, American sociologists adapted to organized capitalism by putting themselves in the service of profit and the maintenance of order. American industrial sociology sought to adjust the worker to his workplace, not the reverse. After 1958, Gaullism's authoritarian modernization encouraged French capitalism and the French system of higher education to catch up with the Americans. Gaullist modernization had inevitably affected the university and made it an integral part of organized capitalism. As a result, the overwhelming majority of professors and students were unable to form an oppositional mass movement. On the contrary, the fate of members of the university community was to work for "various authoritarian bureaucracies," whether public or private. The young sociologists' conclusion, which differed from that of some German or American SDS members, approached Situationist analysis by arguing that only workers, not students, could make revolution. It is difficult to judge which conclusions were more fanciful.

The Nanterre radicals' critique helped create a climate that encouraged some students in sociology and psychology to boycott exams during March. Denouncing the absurdity of the system, they prevented more compliant students from turning in their tests.[110] Professors challenged strikers' coercive tactics and questioned their devotion to their studies.[111] One recounted his experience with *meneurs*.[112] On 14 March, twenty students invaded his introductory psychology class, seized the microphone, and propagated a text of a resolution approved by "sociology and psychology students." Another thirty students then entered the classroom carrying picket signs. One of them read aloud a statement that complained of poor grades that certain students had received on the last exam.

Reflecting sentiment concerning black lists, students attributed the low marks to administration pressure on teaching assistants. The instructor sharply denied this: "If grades are low, it is because of the extreme passivity of some students who surprised me by never taking notes in class. They relied on lecture notes which were printed without my knowledge. These notes were not only ridiculously schematic but also full of serious errors, the same errors that I found on about one hundred tests."[113]

The professor's explanation did not satisfy the protesters, who then tried, without much success, "to shake up the other lethargic students." The invaders distributed the tract "Nanterre or the Fattening of the Geese," in which they demanded that lecture courses whose exams were based on regurgitation of information be replaced by small-group seminars centered around analysis and debate.[114] The instructor resisted the proposed changes, calling his introductory course an "an indispensable step" toward the mastery of the discipline. The classroom invasion and protest coincided with the UNEF-sponsored demonstration in Paris on 14 March that gathered six to seven thousand protesters against government reforms of higher education.

In addition, the Vietnam War continued to fuel already powerful internationalist and anti-imperialist sentiment. On 20 March several pro-Vietcong militants from Nanterre were arrested for having participated in a violent anti-American demonstration at the Parisian offices of American Express, whose windows they smashed. To protest against the "arbitrary" arrests of their "imprisoned anti-imperialist comrades," especially one JCR member who had won the sympathy and friendship of adherents of other *groupuscules*, radicals decided to occupy a campus building at Nanterre. Six years after the end of the Algerian War, the defense of those who destroyed "imperialist" property was the glue that bound together various political factions. The choice of the administration building, which had been off limits to most students, revealed both boldness and shrewdness. The conquest of this space offered a tactical goal that promoted an ephemeral unity. The takeover of the administrative edifice (and not, for example, the easier prey of social science departments) demonstrated that the movement now included students in disciplines other than the typically militant sociology and psychology. Furthermore, the administration building—a phallic tower twice as tall as other buildings—was a symbol, according to Cohn-Bendit and others, of omnipresent "repression."[115] In the afternoon of 22 March, twenty students invaded the administration building and forced the staff to allow them to use a loudspeaker to announce a meeting at 5:00 P.M.[116] A petty theft that occurred as students abandoned the building suggested a subversive intention: "When the students left, one of the employees discovered that he was missing his gold-plated pen." A short time later, at 5:00 P.M., several hundred students arrived at the ground floor of the building. Despite the active opposition of the associate dean, they decided to occupy the ninth floor where "they talked, ate, drank, and sang until 1:30." Top-level Nanterre administrators decided not to call in police. Illegality was tolerated.

Occupiers assumed some risk. Although hundreds in the UNEF general assembly had voted for the occupation, fear and ideological misgivings reduced the number of initial occupiers to sixty. Once inside the administrative building, protesters quickly became divided. The three *Enragés* who were present argued for looting and pillaging the offices in imitation, they believed, of African-Americans during the Watts riot.[117] They had no respect for either private or state property. *Enragés* showed little interest in participating in debates among those they considered less revolutionary than themselves. Instead, they wanted to put their theories into practice and imbibe the excellent bottles of Scotch whiskey that the dean had reserved for entertaining more academically and socially distinguished visitors.[118] *Enragés* were undoubtedly influenced by Sade, whose thought they considered "a critique of everyday life": "Permissible pleasures cannot compare to stronger pleasures which break with social constraints and overthrow all laws."[119] Anticipating one of the most famous May graffiti, the pro-*situs* opined that "Obstacles obstructing pleasures arouse the desire to enjoy pleasures without obstacles." A few anarchists sought to ransack desks and file cabinets to find the supposed black lists, which, predictably, they could not locate. Their existence nevertheless remained a bedrock of faith among almost all of the Movement of 142. The latter took its original name from the number of students who voted for its resolution condemning American imperialism and black lists; however, it soon became better known as the Movement of 22 March, an allusion to Fidel Castro's Movement of 26 July.[120] The 142 planned a special teach-in on student and especially worker struggles. As at Columbia University in New York a month later, agitation over a potent combination of international, national, and local issues would foment a spectacular sit-in.[121]

Most occupiers were not as daring as pillaging anarchists and pro-*situs* and wished to remain within respectable limits. The overwhelming majority refused to follow the *Enragés'* suggestions to expel several "Stalinists" of the UEC. They considered that beginning the occupation with a purge was an equally reprehensible "Stalinist" act. The *Enragés* then departed, but not before insulting their ex-comrades by calling them *petits cons*. The *Enragés* nonetheless proved capable of transcending this level of abuse and leaving behind the most memorable cultural artifacts of the 22 March occupation. They painted their Situationist-inspired graffiti on the walls: "Take your desires for reality," "Boredom is counter-revolutionary," and the in/famous "Never Work." Other scribblings included "Professors, you are old and your culture is too," "Knowledge is in pieces, let's create," and "Culture is not creative." New Leftists at Columbia University would shortly employ the wide-ranging formula "Up against the wall, motherfucker," whereas Nanterre *Enragés* invented the equally improper but more precise, "Unions are whorehouses. The UNEF is a whore."

The angry exit of the *Enragés* allowed the occupation to become more relaxed and even festive. One hundred fifty persons remained in the building, and many of them wanted to discuss the construction of a critical university, modeled on the vision of the German SDS. Occupiers were fortunate to have ended their sit-in at 1:30 A.M., less than an hour prior to the arrival of police whom the minister of education, Alain Peyrefitte, had ordered to empty the building, despite Grappin's and his associate's opposition.[122] Peyrefitte wanted to expel Cohn-Bendit immediately, but Interior Minister Fouchet restrained him. Fouchet warned that the expulsion of a foreign-exchange student would be a violation of traditional university privilege. Instead, Cohn-Bendit would be subject to a disciplinary hearing. This vacillation between toleration and repression anticipated another round of government indecisiveness in May.

Commemoratory accounts nostalgically obscure the fury of May. The Nanterre and Sorbonne radicals' guerrilla war against university property is largely omitted.[123] Some radicals never hid that their revolution aimed to destroy "the bourgeois university." Militants associated with the Movement of 22 March invaded the administrative building for political and symbolic reasons, but some also stole and damaged about 15,000 francs' worth of university property.[124] Of course, damages could have been much worse, and the associate dean called them "minimal" and "unsystematic." Other professors were more shocked by the destruction.[125] Activists of 22 March and other Nanterre students displayed their disdain for the campus. Doors were forced open, furniture vandalized, telephone wires ripped, keys pilfered, carpets seared by cigarettes, glassware smashed, a curtain charred, food looted, and vending machines vandalized. The dean reported that it had cost 20,000 francs to repair the destruction.[126] The university lodged a criminal complaint against those responsible.[127] Various organizations—ARCUN, the Nanterre UNEF and CGT branches—condemned "pillaging, theft, and vandalism," even if they were very critical of police and quite supportive of students who had protested against the intervention, however tardy and ineffective, of the forces of order.[128]

When the occupation ended, 142 participants approved a statement that became the foundation of the 22 March Movement. More than anything else it targeted the centralized state. The Manifesto of the 142 attacked "police repression of all forms of political action."[129] The repressive state, the 142 claimed, was arresting militants in their own homes. French capitalism in its effort to modernize and rationalize itself had to employ coercion on every level. Militants vowed to "retaliate with increasing force … to every act of repression." Their defiance overcame the divisions among the various *groupuscules* and the unorganized. The latter constituted half of the 142, and their participation helped to forge its working unity. Thus, the 22 March Movement was not a *groupuscule* but rather an ad hoc coalition.[130] Throughout the spring of 1968, especially in the second half of May, protest against the state's sometimes aggressive protection of the property of the universities and the streets would come to be a unifying theme of the left.

Following the occupation of the administration building, agitation intensified at Nanterre. Radicals and *Enragés* continually disrupted classes and boycotted exams. Cohn-Bendit and others justified the refusal to take exams and the denial of speech to certain professors by arguing that revolutionaries should reject "the terrain of the adversary: examinations and the normal functioning of the university."[131] Student radicals stole books, cut telephone lines, and vandalized university property. In response, an overwhelming majority of professors (including senior and many junior faculty) voted (46 for, 14 against, and 5 abstentions) for a brief but immediate suspension of classes. An anarchist militant claimed that some instructors, whom radicals considered among the most reactionary, considered arming themselves.[132] At a faculty meeting at the end of March, a substantial number of teachers thought that Nanterre should adopt the American model of an independent campus police who would be able to act effectively inside the university. In addition, they asked for an autonomous and decentralized disciplinary council that could impose penalties on disruptive students.[133] UNEF members who were sympathetic to the 22 March Movement defended it by arguing with a certain degree of credibility that "any spontaneous movement" would produce its share of "minor incidents."[134] Less convincingly, the students attributed these incidents to the "de-politicization of university life" and the "collusion of reactionary elements (extreme right, Occident, FNEF … [and the] sensationalist press)."[135]

On Thursday afternoon, 28 March, Dean Grappin announced his decision to close the university until Monday because of "repeated incidents during classes, examinations, and in administrative buildings. [These are] sparked by small groups of individuals who attempt to impose their will by violence." Administrators also considered closing the dorms. The housing director informed the chancellor that "the dormitories are a hotbed of protest. They are detonators in an explosive situation." However, the authorities could not shut them down because they lodged not only Nanterre revolutionaries but also foreign students and others enrolled in off-campus institutions.[136] Additionally, Grappin may have feared the intervention of an Occident commando. Leftist students certainly did and wanted to "stop the neo-Nazis of Occident from disturbing the Friday [meeting]."[137] At any rate, the decision to shut down the institution from Friday, 29 March until Monday, 1 April received support from the zealously *ouvriériste* UCJml. It endorsed the view of a group of non-teaching staff who put the blame for the closing of the library "on anarchist bands that stand out as much for their indiscipline as for their acts of vandalism." The Maoists condemned as "anti-worker" those "irresponsible [students]" of the 22 March Movement who made the librarian lose two days' pay.

Relations between Nanterre radicals and the PCF were just as tense. Like the Maoists, the Nanterre Communist cell also censored "a handful of agitators." The party withdrew the support that it had given in 1965 to Antony students who had fought for sexual liberty. The expansion of *gauchisme*, the escalation of student demands, and the destruction of property alienated and frightened some PCF militants. Their solution for the problems of the university was not more agitation but more funding. Of course, *gauchistes* distrusted Stalinists. They were convinced that *L'Humanité* was full of lies and fabrications. When a reporter from the PCF daily dared to venture onto the campus, he was harassed with hostile questions on Kronstadt, the Hitler-Stalin Pact, the Gulag, the Hungarian uprising of 1956, and current unrest in Poland. In one notorious *L'Humanité* article, Georges Marchais, future head of the PCF, blamed the troubles on the "German anarchist, Cohn-Bendit": "A group of anarchists and Situationists have dirtied the walls of the university with the giant letters of their slogan, 'NEVER WORK.' For these forty or so students, action means disrupting lectures, classes, jazz shows, theatrical events, occupying buildings, and covering the walls with graffiti."[138] Echoing the PCF, the right/centrist FNEF, which claimed to have won the electoral support of almost one-third of the students, denounced the acts of the radicals as behavior of the "mentally ill."[139]

On 29 March, four to five hundred students arrived to protest against the administration's closure of the *faculté* and to demand the right to express themselves politically on the campus. Busloads of riot police surrounded their meeting on the university lawn. The slogan of the Berlin demonstration, "One, Two, Three Vietnams," was replaced by the more modest and realist, "One, Two, Three Nanterres." This chant did not remain entirely rhetorical. In imitation of the Nanterre model, students at Toulouse would occupy a university auditorium and constitute their Movement of 25 April. More immediately, on the evening of 29 March, a number of Nanterre students journeyed to Paris to participate in the MAU, whose members included future journalists Marc Kravetz and Jean-Louis Peninou and future ecologist politician and minister Brice Lalonde. Like many others, the MAU linked the success of the student movement to "a society where workers have power."[140] Its militants— some of whom had been politically active since the movement against the Algerian War—scheduled a political meeting at the Sorbonne, which the chancellor, Jean Roche, prohibited.[141] Nanterre radicals, accustomed to defying interdictions, helped to convince their Sorbonne comrades to occupy an auditorium. Protesters forced the chancellor to tolerate the gathering. He decided—in contrast to his decision a month later—that calling in police would be counterproductive.

At Nanterre itself on Saturday, 30 March, another meeting of junior and senior professors endorsed the concept of a university police force. The dean recognized that the tradition of sanctuary was necessary for the preservation of academic freedom, but he asserted that the university was not an institution where the law could be violated with impunity. The assembled supported the proposals of its administration, which, it believed, had correctly insisted upon normal enforcement of the law, a policy that campus radicals had inaccurately termed "police repression." The historian François Crouzet affirmed that the university was a workplace and professors retained their own version of the right to work, i.e., the right to teach their courses. Didier Anzieu—a social psychologist who would later write a book on Nanterre in 1968 under the pseudonym Epistémon—declared that in every society a fundamental and inevitable law correctly posited that students must be judged by professors. Dean Grappin stressed the antisocial aspects of the Nanterre movement by pointing out that most students "were unaware of the constraints and conventions of the social order."[142] Hoping to isolate the radicals, the faculty made known its desire "to cooperate with all students who act in the interests of the university community."[143] The assembly agreed unanimously to support Dean Grappin, who issued a solemn statement that amounted to an endorsement of the "bourgeois" university: "Teachers and students will return to work in order to demonstrate that the fundamental social task of the university is teaching and research. Anything that disrupts a course is a violation of our work rules and of everyone's freedom. Students must be able to prepare for their examinations which fulfill the essential social functions of the university: To train students and to grant degrees and diplomas."[144]

The dean's words and actions had little effect as boycotts of classes and examinations persisted after the reopening of the university on Monday, 1 April. On 2 April (which became known as "Talking Tuesday") 1,500 students participated in the general assembly of the 22 March Movement. The number of participants was considerable, given that on an average day approximately 4,000 students frequented the campus. The numerical force of the movement enabled it to commandeer auditoriums without the administration's approval. Simultaneously, vocal opposition to radicals intensified not just among faculty but also among centrist and right-wing students. The FNEF held its own countermeeting and accused revolutionaries of preventing students from studying.[145] The *trublions*, they said, were engaging in practices that would eventually lead to, in its formula, "intolerant totalitarianism."[146]

The administration hoped and activists feared that the Easter vacation (4–18 April) would dampen political enthusiasms.[147] Events abroad, though, sharpened tensions and lessened the appeal of nonviolence. On 4 April, Martin Luther King was murdered, and the American ghettos erupted spontaneously. The Situationists had praised the Watts riot of 1965 as a revolutionary anticipation of the end of commodity fetishism, and the looting of the April 1968 rioters in the urban ghettos revived their analysis. On 11 April, Rudi Dutschke, the best-known figure of the German SDS, was shot and seriously wounded by a fascist who was inspired by the ferociously anti-Communist Springer press. SDS sympathizers attacked Springer offices in every major German city. In solidarity with their German comrades, the UNEF, JCR, CVN, and, for the first time, the Movement of 22 March organized a Parisian demonstration, which police attempted unsuccessfully to disperse.

The violence against King and Dutschke helped keep agitation alive by reinvigorating antifascist and internationalist sentiment among *groupuscules*, especially the JCR, which played a key role in protesting against the attempted assassination of Dutschke.[148] When students returned to the campus on Thursday 18 April, they were greeted by new slogans proffered by the JCR and the 22 March Movement: "Springer, Assassin" and "Long live the struggle of the German students." To demonstrate solidarity with the German SDS, Cohn-Bendit planned to spread the anti-Springer agitation beyond Nanterre.[149] Lacking a Springer office to attack, a small commando, who included a number of activists from Nanterre, went out to shatter the windows of the Institute of American Studies in Paris. The following day, Cohn-Bendit addressed two thousand anti-Springer students assembled in the Latin Quarter.

Dany and others developed the Movement of 22 March in an innovative fashion. They went beyond predictable street demonstrations with their mantra-like slogans and published a *Bulletin du 22 Mars*, which they mockingly numbered 5494 bis (supplement to number 5,494). The *Bulletin* synthesized contributions from the German SDS with homegrown French libertarianism and reflected an intense distrust of the traditional university.[150] It repeated the critique that higher education produced cops and junior executives who were trained to maintain order. Examinations were indispensable in this process by promoting those who were willing to conform and by eliminating students of working-class origin who had not had access to bourgeois culture. Exams also promoted bourgeois individualism, competition, and social Darwinism. Other groups—for instance, the MAU—propagated similar criticism of the capitalist individualism fostered by the examination system.[151] The *Bulletin* argued that the "dialogue" proposed by university administrators masked repression. The Movement wanted to raise the "consciousness" of students by provoking "the latent authoritarianism" of the power structure. Oppressed students were justified in using revolutionary violence: "The only possible protest against the university was violence." Authoritarian reactions to revolutionary acts induced students and professors to denounce the repressive apparatus. At the same time, revolutionary agitation revealed the bankruptcy of so-called "Marxists," such as the UEC and certain "left-wing" instructors, who supported the system by demanding the smooth functioning of the university. By renouncing the slogan "Defend the common interests of all the students" in favor of the notion of a "critical university," the *Bulletin* placed political demands before corporatist ones.

By admitting that at most it represented only 1,000 of 12,000 students, the Movement of 22 March broke with the inflated numbers and the customary triumphalism of the radical tradition. An enemy of bureaucracy, its only structure was the general assembly. This made 22 March somewhat impervious to control by a single *groupuscule*. The Nanterre section of the UNEF rallied to its side. It viewed the Movement as constituting a united front of the extreme left that was capable of resisting, through violence if necessary, the repression of the bourgeois state.[152] Even the Maoists, although believing that militants must devote their energies exclusively to the working class, appreciated the 22 March Movement for its rejection of "the reactionary system of the university," which—they concurred—was dedicated to reproducing the ruling class. They applauded the refusal of "1,200 Nanterre students" to "become the ideologues and agents of capitalist exploitation."[153]

The 22 March Movement added a critique of work to its trashing of the bourgeois university. Violations of property rights and destruction of property itself manifested its hatred of labor. Work, 22 March argued, was the central aspect of a repressive society. The French word, *travail*, came from the Latin *tripalum* [*sic*] or instrument of torture. Christianity, Communism, and capitalism all glorified work and lied about its nature so that workers would accept it. All these ideologies revealed their vileness by stressing the morality of labor. The future society must terminate the centrality of work and institute *autogestion*, where the producer could become creative. After the revolution, work must become play. On this point, 22 March agreed with the *Enragés*, who declared: "Work is a disgrace.... Its elimination is a prerequisite of the transcendence of the society of commodities."[154] The critique of labor—the *situs'* "Never Work" was one of their most popular graffiti—continued a long tradition that could be traced back to the Surrealists, Paul Lafargue, and even the libertines of the Old Regime. The movements of the 1960s may have been the first time that antiwork sloganeering attracted a large and public mass of followers, who included extreme leftists, hippies, and a few workers.[155]

Social and economic factors help to explain why the critique of work emerged in the 1960s. The weight of young people in the population, their increasing years of schooling, and their consequent delayed entry into wage labor provided a large potential constituency for the spread of antiwork ideology. Of course, the traditional juvenile dislike of the classroom continued. In addition, the expansion of education during the "thirty glorious years" of unparalleled economic expansion in postwar Europe and North America offered adolescents and young adults more time to avoid working for wages. The rapid development of machinery that was replacing human power promoted a vision of a prosperous cybernetic utopia where machines would replace the labor of men and women.[156] Western societies were becoming more urbanized, and the service sector was growing rapidly. Thus, the connection between wage labor and production was less obvious than in any previous historical period. Much output came to be seen as senseless and even destructive. The Situationists and others critiqued the "spectacle" whose parasitism was paradoxically necessary to maintain a consumer society that constantly manufactured "false" needs. Many contemporary commodities or services served only to perpetuate an irrational world.

Debord, Lefebvre, and Marcuse authored antiwork attitudes. They became popular because they seemed to be able to synthesize the New Left's desire for simultaneous personal and social liberation. Debord's and Lefebvre's appeal for a revolution in everyday life and Marcuse's endorsement of a "Great Refusal" of the consumerist and "repressive" society combined individual emancipation with a desire for profound social change. All three situated themselves in the Marxist tradition. Debord and Marcuse believed that the bourgeoisie had developed the means of production to a level where it became possible to abolish work.[157] The advanced productive forces had the potential to render wage labor superfluous. The critique of labor spread throughout the West to radicals and their organizations, such as the American SDS, which asked themselves, "Why meaningless work?"[158] In Berkeley, the defenders of People's Park identified "labor with oppression."[159] Radical Italian theorists went further and celebrated workers' struggles against work (absenteeism, sabotage, theft, etc.) as the most potentially emancipatory aspects of the class struggle.[160]

It seemed to a number of full professors—such as René Rémond, Jean Bastié, Crouzet, and Anzieu—that destructive, antiwork revolutionaries had succeeded in capturing control of Nanterre. On Monday, 22 April, they once again gathered to consider steps that would guarantee order at the university. Professorial disgust resulted in hard-line attitudes. Instructors deplored the "inefficiency of the authorities" and demanded the punishment of agitators.[161] By an overwhelming majority (25 for, 5 against, 6 abstentions), they finally voted for the creation of a university police force. The dean believed that an autonomous university corps of twenty officers was needed to patrol the campus. By an even larger margin (32 for, 1 against, 8 abstentions), professors approved a campus disciplinary council. Courses were suspended for two days and police mobilized. The faculty was willing to abandon the university's tradition of sanctuary and permit police to occupy the campus.

Maître-assistants and *assistants* (junior faculty), who were closest to the students both in age and spirit, were more doubtful about the virtues of repression.[162] They sought to avoid confronting dilemmas, insisting upon freedom of expression and the right to teach, and, at the same time, opposing any police presence on the campus. On 29 March, twenty-seven *assistants* and *maître-assistants* of French literature, acting collectively for the first time, demanded respect for the right of free political discussion and the maintenance of the traditional prohibition on police entry on campus.[163] They did, however, recognize the necessity of a smoothly functioning university. In a similar manner, the SNESup wanted students to engage in a "critical and constructive" dialogue that would transform the university, but it also urged "freely holding classes, seminars, and examinations." On

29 April, after the Movement of 22 March made clear its intention to boycott exams, the general assembly of junior faculty seconded student objections to "technocratic selection" and opposed police presence on campus. They nonetheless inconsistently exhorted that "examinations proceed normally without any attempt at sabotage."[164] In contrast to Italy, a significant sector of the teaching faculty in France supported student protesters.[165]

The PCF took the side of full professors and opposed radical domination of the campus. The party decided to send Pierre Juquin—deputy, *normalien*, and specialist on questions of higher education—to Nanterre to bolster the faltering UEC.[166] On 25 April, Juquin appeared before a diverse audience of 100 persons. Before he was able to speak, the Maoists began to heckle him by chanting the *Internationale* and waving Mao's little red book. Cohn-Bendit intervened to try to permit Juquin to talk and told the Maoists to *arrêter leur cirque* (stop their nonsense). His words had no effect, and Maoists attempted to assault Juquin, who fled through the back door. After his departure, Maoists ridiculed the PCF leader by formulating the memorable and catchy slogan *Juquin-Lapin* (Juquin-the-missed-appointment).

Dany generally fought for free speech for leftists but had a backhanded way of defending it. "Let him speak," he would reply to hecklers and hooters in the audience, "the quicker he finishes his foolishness, the sooner we'll be done."[167] If grudgingly tolerant of the left, he was sharply intolerant of the right and center. When on 25 April he attempted to persuade his "student-comrades" in a humanities seminar to join the movement, one FNEF activist, a certain Hubert Jouan de Kervenoaël, interrupted him, and the redhead responded by threatening the "fascist."[168] Several minutes later, forty people attacked the right-winger and thrashed him severely. That evening the injured FNEF militant lodged a complaint with the police against Cohn-Bendit. The antileftist Comité étudiant pour les libertés universitaires protested against the incident. It claimed that on 26 April, Dany had "condemned to death" a student who did not share his views.[169] Police confirmed that Dany had indeed threatened a student who was later assaulted and injured.[170] The supposed victim filed a complaint accusing Cohn-Bendit "of death threats and injuries."[171] He also claimed that "Dany hit him, threw him on the ground, and threatened to kill him if he returned to the campus." In retaliation, graffiti painted on the wall of the humanities building announced, "After the heinous attack on a French militant of Occident at Nanterre, Occident sentences the *israélite* (Jew) Cohn-Bendit to death."

Violence against supposed "fascists" revealed revolutionary resolve but also intolerant and undemocratic aspects of a movement divided between libertarian and authoritarian tendencies. In theory, everyone had a chance to speak, but for many, including sympathizers, general assemblies were alienating and intimidating. According to one Italian participant, "the absence of any institutional acknowledgment of forms of authority highlighted the role of charismatic figures. The idea of democracy as participation with equal rights of speech was called into question by a certain movement elitism, by the conviction of being different, of opposing consensus, the broad majorities, the established order, and social hypocrisy."[172]

Like Tom Hayden in the U.S., Dany provided a good example of such charisma. He was skillful at handling crowds and countering the intrigues of *gauchiste* organizations that wanted to control the movement. A Situationist reluctantly gave him some stinting respect:

> Cohn-Bendit belonged to the independent anarchist group and magazine, *Noir et Rouge*.... He was in the most radical wing of the Movement of 22 March. He was more revolutionary than the rest.... Although insufficiently intelligent ... he was talented enough to amuse a student audience, honest enough not to be sucked into the maneuvers of the *gauchistes*, and yet flexible enough to deal with their leaders. He was an honest revolutionary but lacked genius.... Since he accepted his role as a media star without any real analysis of the spectacle, his speeches—which were always a combination of lucidity and stupidity—were naturally distorted in the latter sense by the media.[173]

His media ascendancy touched off a debate about the role of the press at Nanterre. Student radicals generally distrusted reporters. As mentioned, they understandably detested *L'Humanité*. The supposedly left-wing *Combat* was also resented because it had promoted sensationalist stories that downplayed politics and focused on drugs, sex, and partying at Nanterre. In its pages, Dany had been called "a walking pile of manure."[174] *Combat* also denigrated the women of the movement, an attitude that may have increased their political commitment. In the provocative words of Christian Charrière, a *Combat* editor: "At Nanterre, women are abundant. Inside the university ... perfumed game is available. As you walk down the long passageways, their walls covered with bombastic graffiti, you see sweet constellations of flesh, bosoms in which innumerable sighs have accumulated. Fifteen thousand jutting breasts, ready for wicked love-making, hot grenades unavailable to the CRS.... At Nanterre, there was no life without love."[175] Regarding the small harem of the star, Cohn-Bendit:

> Two young girls continually followed him and smothered him with loving admiration. Isabelle Saint-Saëns, 19 years old, went directly from the sad evening parties of the fancy sixteenth *arrondissement* to the disheveled boasting of the protesters.... A body in full bloom, a calm beauty, she provides some order. Danielle Schulman, 21 years old, like Dany a sociology student, is the Pasionaria of the 22 March Movement. She goads on the red hair, pushes him into storms, and encourages him to face danger. A thin body, an adolescent chest, hair in a boyish bob, somber eyes, there is something satanic about her.

The distinguished historian Adrien Dansette shared similar attitudes towards female radicals. When Cohn-Bendit spoke to a Parisian crowd on 10 May, he "was greeted enthusiastically. Female students, among whom were Nanterre girls ... became hysterical and shouted, 'Vive Dany. He is really good-looking. It's our Dany.'"[176] In fact, many female students had strong reservations about their male counterparts. As has been seen, a number objected to the occupations of female dorms. Others were reluctant to spend time in the university's public spaces, such as the cafeteria, which they regarded as a kind of *dragodrome* (singles' bar) where it was impossible to engage in serious conversation with males.[177]

Typical of the media's relations with student radicals was the bizarre tale of Cohn-Bendit's radio interview. It was scheduled for Saturday, 27 April at 7:00 A.M. on the major station France-Inter. Dany recounted his misadventure:

> I wasn't yet a media celebrity, but I was considered a troublemaker because of the Missoffe Affair [at the swimming pool]. The announcer was scared that I wouldn't show up, and he had scheduled me for an hour interview. I told him not to worry. I would be there. At 7:00 the show began without me. He said, "Anarchists come late. It's normal." He played a little music. I still wasn't there. "It's normal. Anarchists never take anything seriously. Now you see what the Nanterre movement is all about." A half-hour later, he was furious ... "It's disgraceful. You see how he treats our listeners."
>
> We had left the house but as we departed, some guys jumped on us.[178]

Dany soon discovered that they were police officers whose mission was to arrest him. They were responding to the assault complaint of the FNEF militant and to a rather crude and fanciful recipe for making Molotov cocktails that the *Bulletin du 22 mars* had published. The recipe, as could be expected of apprentice sociologists and philosophers, would not have worked, but it uncannily anticipated a fiery May. His arrest created more media attention, and the press began to label him "Dany the Red," much to his chagrin since the anarchist color is also black. Police quickly released him, but his brief detention became another occasion for the formation of a coalition against repression. The Trotskyite FER protested against the government's brief custody of "Cohen-Bendit [*sic*]."[179] The group believed the arrest revealed that "the bourgeois state" planned a "massive elimination of students [from the university]."

In late April, attention turned to preparations for the traditional May Day parade and the newer celebration of Anti-Imperialist Day on 2 May. On 30 April, the struggle against imperialism inspired a handful of Nanterre students to agitate at their former *lycée*. As they were distributing leaflets, police arrived and arrested the unlucky few who were unable to escape. The news spread to the campus, and an assembly of thousands gathered to protest against the detentions. University students issued an ultimatum to the Nanterre prefecture: Free our comrades or we shall massively demonstrate at police headquarters. Vacillating local authorities quickly relented and released the arrested students. As it would in May, the authorities' capitulation raised radical morale and showed that victory against "repression" was possible.

On Anti-Imperialist Day, Thursday, 2 May, rumors circulated that Occident would retaliate at Nanterre. Several weeks earlier, on Sunday, 28 March, in the sixth *arrondissement*, Maoists had attacked and destroyed an exhibition mounted by the United Front for South Vietnam, an Occident front group.[180] The Maoist assault won the approval of Nanterre radicals and reflected the increasing integration of the followers of Chairman Mao into the Movement of 22 March. Anti-imperialists praised "the beautiful thrashing" given to Occident and its allies. Occident responded by circulating at Nanterre a tract that threatened to "oppose red terror and to reestablish order by any means."[181] Leftists feared that it would not be the usual rightist student contingent that would descend upon the campus but rather professional fighters, ex-paratroopers, or the bodyguards of Jean-Louis Tixier-Vignancourt, who had been the candidate of the extreme right during the presidential elections of 1965. The increase of tensions among political street fighters of the Paris region produced a run on broomsticks and other items used as weapons. Dozens of Maoists, led by Robert Linhart, a student at the Ecole Normale Supérieure, came to Nanterre to take control of its defense. The would-be leader of the French Long March spoke to the crowd for a half-hour, citing Mao and offering his grand vision of international politics. Some in the crowd were impressed by his charisma, fluency, and the coherency of his vision. Others, especially anarchists, were disgusted by the know-it-all nature of the talk and the arrogance of the Maoist movement, which, although largely ignorant of the Nanterre situation, presumed to take charge of local preparations for antifascist defense.

The fascist assault never occurred, but students continued to disrupt classes, challenge instructors, and even throw eggs at professors.[182] The dorms remained a radical recruiting base.[183] Housing officials reported "clubs, iron bars, and stones stockpiled in the dormitory rooms of both male and female students."[184] On 2 May, a group again invaded the administration building, this time to show a film on the Black Panthers. They were ejected but found an auditorium where René Rémond was scheduled to teach. They insulted Rémond and expelled him and his students from the room. The ensuing faculty protests against *gauchiste* coercion convinced Dean Grappin to suspend classes until further notice. Interior Minister Fouchet, whom de Gaulle had told on 1 May "to put an end to those incidents at Nanterre," also encouraged the shutdown.[185] Grappin may have needed little insistence from his superiors since he was the victim of night-time telephone harassment and was forced to disconnect his home line from 11:00 P.M. to 8:00 A.M.[186] To justify his closure of the university, the dean cited student threats, intimidation of teaching personnel and administrators, disregard for the right to work, and violation of freedom of expression. He might have added attacks on property.

The University of Nanterre would not reopen until the fall semester. Radicals whose goal was to shut down, if not destroy, the bourgeois university were more successful than they could have ever imagined.

Notes

1. Cf. Francis Fukuyama, *The End of History and the Last Man* (New York, 1992), 330.
2. Adrien Dansette, *Mai 1968* (Paris, 1971), 35; Raymond Boudon, "La crise universitaire française: Essai de diagnostic sociologique," *Annales E.S.C.*, vol. 24, no. 3 (May–June, 1969): 740.
3. A. Belden Fields, *Student Politics in France: A Study of the Union Nationale des Etudiants de France* (New York, 1970), 84.
4. F. G. Dreyfus, "Problems of the French University," in Stephen D. Kertesz, ed., *The Task of Universities in a Changing World* (Notre Dame, Ind., 1971), 290; Jean-Raymond Tournoux, *Le mois de mai du général* (Paris, 1969), 36.
5. Alain Schnapp and Pierre Vidal-Naquet, *Journal de la commune étudiante* (Paris, 1969), 33.
6. On Duruy, see Sandra Horvath-Peterson, *Victor Duruy and French Education* (Baton Rouge and London, 1984). A similar treatment awaits Fouchet.
7. Peyrefitte quoted in Jean Lacouture, *De Gaulle: The Ruler 1945–1970*, trans. Alan Sheridan (New York and London, 1992), 530.
8. Tournoux, *Mois*, 23; Jacques Perret, *Inquiète Sorbonne* (Paris, 1968), 56–57.
9. Robert Lumley, *States of Emergency: Cultures of Revolt in Italy from 1968 to 1978* (London and New York, 1990), 59.
10. Tournoux, *Mois*, 44–45.
11. Conseil de la Faculté, 15 January 1968, 1208W, art. 1, Archives départementales des Hauts-de-Seine [hereafter ADHS].
12. This argument might have been influenced by the work of sociologists P. Bourdieu and J.-C. Passeron. See Dansette, *Mai*, 37; François Bourricaud, *Universités à la dérive* (Paris, 1971), 63–66; Jean-Pierre Duteuil, *Nanterre 1965–1968: Vers le mouvement du 22 mars* (Paris, 1988), 111.
13. Boudon, "Crise," 759; Pierre Grappin, *L'Ile aux peupliers* (Nancy, 1993), 241; Nicolas Daum, *Des révolutionnaires dans un village parisien* (Paris, 1988), 129; 19 May 1968, Fa 259, APP.
14. Jean-Philippe Legois, *La Sorbonne avant mai 68* (Mémoire de maîtrise, Paris I, 1993), 163; Jean Bertolino, *Les Trublions* (Paris, 1969), 245.
15. Conseil de Faculté, 25 November 1967, 1208W, art. 1, ADHS. The following information comes from this meeting.
16. Dansette, *Mai*, 62; Perret, *Sorbonne*, 21.
17. Alain Touraine, *The May Movement: Revolt and Reform*, trans. Leonard F. X. Mayhew, (New York, 1979), 131.
18. Alain Monchablon, *Histoire de l'UNEF de 1956 à 1968* (Paris, 1983), 185; Perret, *Sorbonne*, 21; Fields, *Student Politics*, 87.
19. Schnapp and Vidal-Naquet, *Journal*, 106–113; Duteuil, *Nanterre*, 95–107.
20. Monchablon, *L'UNEF*, 185. Police estimated the number of demonstrators to be three thousand. See Direction générale de la Police nationale, renseignements généraux, Bulletin mensuel, May–July 1968, AN 820599/89.
21. Monchablon, *L'UNEF*, 186. Cf. Jean-Claude and Michelle Perrot, Madeleine Rebérioux, and Jean Maitron, eds., *La Sorbonne par elle-même*, special issue of *Le Mouvement social*, no. 64 (July–September, 1968): 10, which claims that the MAU was created in March 1968 as does Dansette, *Mai*, 88, and Geneviève Dreyfus-Armand, "D'un mouvement étudiant à

l'autre: La Sorbonne à la veille du 3 mai 1968," in Geneviève Dreyfus-Armand and Laurent Gervereau, eds., *Mai 68: Les mouvements étudiants en France et dans le monde* (Nanterre, 1988), 143; Marc Kravetz, ed., *L'Insurrection étudiante* (Paris, 1968), 462; Patrick Seale and Maureen McConville, *Red Flag Black Flag: French Revolution 1968* (New York, 1968), 62.

22. Schnapp and Vidal-Naquet, *Journal*, 115.
23. Duteuil, *Nanterre*, 95–96.
24. René Rémond, *La règle et le consentement* (Paris, 1979), 190; Philippe Labro, ed., *Ce n'est qu'un début* (Paris, 1968), 43.
25. On radical German sociological students, see David Caute, *The Year of the Barricades: A Journey through 1968* (New York, 1988); on their English counterparts, Arthur Marwick, *The Sixties: Cultural Revolution in Britain, France, Italy, and the United States, c. 1958–c. 1974* (New York, 1998).
26. On the American argument, see Todd Gitlin, *The Sixties: Years of Hope, Days of Rage* (New York, 1987), 383; on Italy, Guido Martinotti, "The Positive Marginality: Notes on Italian Students in Periods of Political Mobilization," in Seymour Martin Lipset and Philip G. Altbach, eds., *Students in Revolt* (Boston, 1970), 167–201.
27. Duteuil, *Nanterre*, 96–110; Monchablon, *L'UNEF*, 186.
28. La Nature, n.d., 1208W, art. 256, ADHS, gives figures of 10,000 to 12,000 students.
29. Bertolino, *Trublions*, 253; Monique Suzzoni, "Chronologie des événements à Nanterre en 1967–1968," in Dreyfus-Armand and Gervereau, *Mai 68*, 133.
30. Schnapp and Vidal-Naquet, *Journal*, 109.
31. For a critique of lecture courses, see Guy Michaud, *Révolution dans l'université* (Paris, 1968), 102. For Nanterre, see *Quelle université? Quelle société?* (Paris, 1968), 110.
32. The following citations are from "La grève modèle," quoted in Duteuil, *Nanterre*, 107.
33. Jean-Pierre Duteuil quoted in Bertolino, *Trublions*, 250.
34. Monchablon, *UNEF*, 186.
35. Duteuil, *Nanterre*, 102; Dansette, *Mai*, 64; Bertolino, *Trublions*, 258; Touraine, *The May Movement*, 134.
36. Schnapp and Vidal-Naquet, *Journal*, 116–122; Duteuil, *Nanterre*, 102; Dansette, *Mai*, 63–64.
37. Duteuil, *Nanterre*, 102; Dansette, *Mai*, 64; Bertolino, *Trublions*, 258; Bourricaud, *Universités*, 68.
38. TSRF quoted in Duteuil, *Nanterre*, 109.
39. *Extraits de la plate-forme des « étudiants » révolutionnaires de Nantes, au début de l'année 1968*, reproduced in René Viénet, *Enragés et Situationnistes dans le mouvement des occupations* (Paris, 1968), 252–258.
40. Bertolino, *Trublions*, 238.
41. Pierre Peuchmaurd, *Plus vivants que jamais* (Paris, 1968), 130; Daniel Cohn-Bendit, *Le Grand Bazar* (Paris, 1975), 29.
42. Quoted in Labro, *Début*, 148–149.
43. 12 April 1968, Direction générale du travail et de l'emploi, Ministère du Travail, AN 860581/25. The incident is not mentioned in Maurice Grimaud, *En mai, fais ce qu'il te plaît* (Paris, 1977).
44. Bertolino, *Trublions*, 24–25.
45. Incident related in numerous works, including Schnapp and Vidal-Naquet, *Journal*, 115. See also Dansette, *Mai*, 66–67.
46. Nicole de Maupeou Abboud, *Ouverture du ghetto étudiant: La gauche étudiante à la recherche d'un nouveau mode d'intervention politique (1960–1970)* (Paris, 1974), 174.
47. White paper quoted in Hervé Hamon and Patrick Rotman, *Génération*, 2 vols. (Paris, 1987), 1: 401.
48. *Minute*, 4–10 April 1968.
49. Grappin, *L'Ile*, 268.
50. Laurent Lemire, *Cohn-Bendit* (Paris, 1998), 85.

51. Duteuil, *Nanterre*, 117. The unverified story had a long life, at least among members of the extreme right. In 1987 during a debate in the National Assembly, Roger Holeindre, ex-OAS and deputy of the National Front, blasted a certain neo-Gaullist Parisian deputy, Mme. de Panafieux, for having slept with Dany in 1968. Mme. de Panafieux is the daughter of François Missoffe.

52. Viénet, *Enragés*, 29.

53. 23 January 1968, 1208W, art. 180, ADHS. The student's father supported the expulsion and labeled his son "an imbecile."

54. For the denial, Assemblée de la Faculté, 27 January 1968, 1208W, art. 1, ADHS.

55. Suzzoni, "Chronologie," in Dreyfus-Armand and Gervereau, *Mai 68*, 134.

56. Véronique Campion-Vincent, *La légende des vols d'organes* (Paris, 1997), 220.

57. 12 February 1968, Fa 265, APP.

58. For example, Michel de Certeau, *La prise de parole: Pour une nouvelle culture* (Paris, 1968), 22–27 and Laurent Joffrin, *Mai 68: Histoire des événements* (Paris, 1988), 36. For a repetition of this argument, which contradicts several of the contributions in the collection, see Michelle Zancarini-Fournel, "Conclusion," in Geneviève Dreyfus-Armand, Robert Frank, Marie-Françoise Lévy, and Michelle Zancarini-Fournel, eds., *Les Années 68: Le Temps de la contestation* (Brussels, 2000), 502.

59. Duteuil, *Nanterre*, 120; Seale and McConville, *Red Flag*, 34.

60. Protesters claimed that all political demonstrations on campus were banned. See Duteuil, *Nanterre*, 118–120; The description of the incident in Seale and McConville, *Red Flag*, 35 differs slightly; cf. also Grappin, *L'Ile*, 248–249.

61. Epistémon [Didier Anzieu], *Ces idées qui ont ébranlé la France* (Paris, 1968), 98.

62. CLER, 29 March 1968, 1208W, art. 256, ADHS.

63. Assemblée de la Faculté, 27 January 1968, 1208W, arts. 1–2, ADHS.

64. Touraine, *The May Movement*, 129.

65. Assemblée de la Faculté, 27 January 1968, 1208W, arts. 1–2, ADHS.

66. Ibid.

67. Cf. Angelo Quattrocchi and Tom Nairn, *The Beginning of the End: France, May 1968* (London and New York, 1998), 6: "[Nanterre students'] minds are policed by discipline, patrolled by examinations. Their hearts frozen by authority." See La Nature, n.d., 1208W, art. 256, ADHS.

68. Mouvement du 22 mars, *Ce n'est pas qu'un début, continuons le combat* (Paris, 1968), 65.

69. Duteuil, *Nanterre*, 124.

70. Jürgen Habermas, *Toward a Rational Society: Student Protest, Science, and Politics*, trans. Jeremy J. Shapiro (Boston, 1971), 41.

71. Direction générale de la Police nationale, renseignements généraux, Bulletins quotidiens d'information, 30 May 1968, AN 820599/40.

72. Suzzoni, "Chronologie," in Dreyfus-Armand and Gervereau, *Mai 68*, 134.

73. Luisa Passerini, *Autobiography of a Generation*, trans. Lisa Erdberg (Hanover and London, 1996), 78.

74. *L'Internationale Situationniste*, no. 11 (October, 1967): 25, 44–48.

75. Ibid., no. 12 (September, 1969): 20–21; Duteuil, *Nanterre*, 126. Situationists claimed that *gauchistes* organized the defense of insulted professors.

76. "Enquête: Télémaque 1969," *Guerres et Paix*, no. 14–15 (1969/4–1970/1): 19.

77. Hamon and Rotman, *Génération*, 1: 413–418.

78. Jean-Marie Vincent, "Pour continuer mai 1968," *Les Temps modernes*, no. 266–267, (August–September, 1968): 279; R. Gregoire and F. Perlman, *Worker-Student Action Committees: France May '68* (Detroit, 1991), 37.

79. See Schnapp and Vidal-Naquet, *Journal*, 72–83.

80. Dansette, *Mai*, 17; Serge Bosc and Jean-Marcel Bouguereau, "Le mouvement des étudiants berlinois," *Les Temps modernes*, no. 265 (July, 1968): 1–69; Ulrich K. Preuss, "The Legacy of 1968 in Domestic Politics," paper presented to the conference of the German Historical Institute, "1968: The World Transformed," Berlin, May 1996; Ingrid Gilcher-

Holtey, *Die 68er Bewegung: Deutschland-Westeuropa-USA* (Munich, 2001), 40, 69. For the influence—sometimes exaggerated—of the SDS on other European student movements, see Gianni Statera, *Death of a Utopia: The Development of Student Movements in Europe* (Oxford, 1975), 50: "From Frankfort the 'critical theory of society' crossed the Atlantic, helped to shape the American student protest and then came back to West Berlin. There it matured into an impassioned utopia, crossed the borders of West Germany and provided theoretical roots for the French revolutionary May and the Italian 'hot autumn.'"

81. Claus-Dieter Krohn, "Die westdeutsche Studentenbewegung und das 'andere Deutschland,'" in Axel Schildt, Detlef Siegfried, and Karl Christian Lammers, eds., *Dynamische Zeiten: Die 60er Jahre in den beiden deutschen Gesellshaften* (Hamburg, 2000), 714–715.

82. For a view of Marcuse's influence before and during 1968, see Michel Trebitsch, "Voyages autour de la révolution: Les circulations de la pensée critique de 1956 à 1968," in Dreyfus-Armand et al., *Les Années 68*, 69–87. Cf. Kristin Ross, *May '68 and Its Afterlives* (Chicago, 2002), 193: Marcuse's "works were unread in France until after May."

83. James Miller, *Democracy Is in the Streets: From Port Huron to the Siege of Chicago* (New York, 1987), 16–23, 78.

84. Schnapp and Vidal-Naquet, *Journal*, 20.

85. Gitlin, *The Sixties*, 263.

86. Dansette, *Mai*, 17–18; Bertolino, *Trublions*, 78; Maupeou-Abboud, *Ouverture*, 249; Tournoux, *Mois*, 166; Kravetz, *L'Insurrection étudiante*, 21.

87. Texts reproduced in Viénet, *Enragés*, 31–36. "La Grappignole" is also found in Dansette, *Mai*, 375–376.

88. Duteuil, *Nanterre*, 136–144.

89. Direction générale de la Police nationale, renseignements généraux, Bulletin mensuel, April 1968, AN 820599/89.

90. Modalités, n.d., 1208W, art. 256, ADHS. On "panty raids," Seymour Martin Lipset and Sheldon S. Wolin, eds., *The Berkeley Student Revolt: Facts and Interpretations* (New York, 1965), 11.

91. Beth Bailey, "Sexual Revolution(s)," in David Farber, ed., *The Sixties: From Memory to History* (Chapel Hill and London, 1994), 245.

92. 10 May 1968, AN 820599/40.

93. Quoted in Centre Régional des Oeuvres Universitaires, 26 February 1968, 1208W, ADHS.

94. Bertolino, *Trublions*, 235; Suzzoni, "Chronologie," in Dreyfus-Armand and Gervereau, *Mai 68*, 134.

95. Dansette, *Mai*, 70.

96. Bourdieu and Passeron, *Héritiers*, 96.

97. "Télémaque," *Guerres et Paix*, 26–27, 56; Fields, *Student Politics*, 79; Epistémon, *Ces idées*, 41.

98. Résidence, 19 December 1967, 1208W, art. 115–117, ADHS.

99. Procès-Verbal, 11 March 1968, 1208W, art. 115–117, ADHS; Résidence, 19 December 1967, 1208W, art. 115–117, ADHS.

100. Le Directeur, 28 March 1968, 1208W, art. 115–117, ADHS.

101. CROUS, 7 February 1968, ADHS.

102. Le Directeur, 28 March 1968, 1208W, art. 115–117, ADHS.

103. Pamphlet reproduced in Duteuil, *Nanterre*, 147.

104. Nanterre, 11 April 1967, 1208W, art. 115–117, ADHS.

105. Résidence, 19 December 1967, 1208W, art. 115–117, ADHS.

106. "La Grande Fronde des Etudiants," *L'Express*, 3–9 April 1967. Cf. Lucien Rioux and René Backmann, *L'Explosion de mai* (Paris, 1968), 212, who, like many authors who emphasize the importance of 1968 events, often exaggerate pre-May traditionalism.

107. "Disons que 58% des parents considèrent le règlement actuel comme valable, mais qu'il ne doit pas être appliqué *strictement*! 30% sont pour un régime de liberté, mais contrôlée! et enfin 12% estiment, à quelques nuances près, qu'aucune entrave ne doit être établie. 12%!" [italics in original] Conseil, 7 December 1967, 1208W, art. 115–117, ADHS.

108. Le Directeur, 14 September 1967, 1208W, art. 115–117, ADHS.

109. Reproduced in Duteuil, *Nanterre*, 187–190.

110. Epistémon, *Ces idées*, 24; Assemblée de la Faculté, 26 March 1968, 1208W, art. 1, ADHS.

111. Schnapp and Vidal-Naquet, *Journal*, 134; Geneviève Dreyfus-Armand, "D'un mouvement étudiant à l'autre: La Sorbonne à la veille du 3 mai 1968," in Dreyfus-Armand and Gervereau, *Mai 68*, 138.

112. The following is based on a letter from Prof. Francès, Dépt. de Psychologie, 14 March 1968, 1208W, art. 180, ADHS; cf. Duteuil, *Nanterre*, 148, who criticizes the reaction of the professor.

113. CROUS, 7 February 1968, ADHS.

114. Reproduced in Duteuil, *Nanterre*, 150–151.

115. Cited in Labro, *Début*, 57.

116. The following citations are from M.B. à M. le recteur, 27 March 1968, 1208W, art. 180, ADHS.

117. For the Situationist interpretation of the Watts riot as a model of urban protest in consumer society, see *L'Internationale Situationniste*, no. 10, (March 1966): 1–11.

118. Duteuil, *Nanterre*, 158.

119. Quoted in Partout, 19 March 1968, 1208W, art. 256, ADHS.

120. A la suite, 25 March 1968, 1208W, art. 256, ADHS; Lemire, *Cohn-Bendit*, 35.

121. Robert V. Daniels, *Year of the Heroic Guerrilla: World Revolution and Counterrevolution in 1968* (New York, 1989), 142; Caute, *The Year of the Barricades*, 165.

122. Tournoux, *Mois*, 347–348; Dansette, *Mai*, 73; M.B. à M. le recteur, 27 March 1968, 1208W, art. 180, ADHS, on administrators' reluctance to call in police.

123. *Le Monde*'s thirtieth-anniversary Web site on the 22 March Movement, http://homer.span.ch/~spaw2154.

124. B. à Recteur, 27 March 1968, 1208W, art. 180, ADHS.

125. See also Assemblée de la Faculté, 26 March 1968, 1208W, art. 1, ADHS.

126. Note sur la police intérieure, 4 April 1968, 1208W, art. 180, ADHS.

127. Assemblée de la Faculté, 30 March 1968, 1208W, art. 1, ADHS.

128. ARCUN, 28 March 1968, 1208W, art. 256, ADHS.

129. Manifesto reproduced in Duteuil, *Nanterre*, 165.

130. See Schnapp and Vidal-Naquet, *Journal*, 314–315. On the unorganized in the 22 March Movement, see J.-P. Duteuil, "Les groupes," in Dreyfus-Armand and Gervereau, *Mai 68*, 113.

131. Cohn-Bendit, *Le Grand Bazar*, 47.

132. Duteuil, *Nanterre*, 168.

133. Schnapp and Vidal-Naquet, *Journal*, 136.

134. Documents reproduced in Duteuil, *Nanterre*, 170–173 and in Schnapp and Vidal-Naquet, *Journal*, 139–145.

135. Tract de l'UNEF et de l'ARCUN, reproduced in Duteuil, *Nanterre*, 173.

136. D. to R., 28 March 1968, 1208W, art. 180, ADHS. Most of the 145 foreign students were males from former French colonies in North and West Africa.

137. La ligne de partage, 28 March 1968, 1208W, art. 256, ADHS.

138. Marchais quoted in Hamon and Rotman, *Génération*, 1: 448 and in Duteuil, *Nanterre*, 172.

139. Duteuil, *Nanterre*, 168.

140. MAU quoted in Kravetz, *L'Insurrection étudiante*, 492.

141. Seale and McConville, *Red Flag*, 62; Duteuil, *Nanterre*, 182; Dansette, *Mai*, 79.

142. Schnapp and Vidal-Naquet, *Journal*, 143.

143. Quoted in Duteuil, *Nanterre*, 180.

144. Cited in Schnapp and Vidal-Naquet, *Journal*, 145.

145. Suzzoni, "Chronologie," in Dreyfus-Armand and Gervereau, *Mai 68*, 135.

146. Schnapp and Vidal-Naquet, *Journal*, 166.

147. "La Faculté de Nanterre de 1964–1969: Entretien avec Pierre Grappin," in Dreyfus-Armand and Gervereau, *Mai 68*, 103.

148. 15 May 1968, AN 820599/75.

149. Duteuil, *Nanterre*, 191; Bertolino, *Trublions*, 365.

150. Reproduced in Duteuil, *Nanterre*, 225–237.
151. Perrot et al., *Sorbonne par elle-même*, 21–23.
152. Duteuil, *Nanterre*, 193.
153. Allemagne, Italie, France (UJC-ML) and Etudiants, levée en masse (*Cause du Peuple*), quoted in Schnapp and Vidal-Naquet, *Journal*, 84, 100.
154. Partout, 19 March 1968, 1208W, art. 256, ADHS.
155. Nanni Balestrini, *Vogliamo tutto* (Milan, 1988); Nanni Balestrini, *Queremos todo*, trans. Herman Mario Cueva (Buenos Aires, 1974).
156. Therefore, most feminists—who believed that the path to women's emancipation involved engaging in salaried labor—did not share the critique of labor.
157. Herbert Marcuse, *An Essay on Liberation* (Boston, 1969), 5, 21; Anselm Jappe, *Guy Debord*, trans. Donald Nicholson-Smith (Berkeley, 1999), 151.
158. Miller, *Democracy*, 39.
159. Quoted in Marwick, *The Sixties*, 673.
160. Lumley, *States of Emergency*, 37–38.
161. Schnapp and Vidal-Naquet, *Journal*, 158; Duteuil, *Nanterre*, 198; Dansette, *Mai*, 81
162. Michaud, *Révolution*, 10; Schnapp and Vidal-Naquet, *Journal*, 139.
163. Touraine, *The May Movement*, 146.
164. Motion de l'Assemblée des assistants et maîtres-assistants, 29 April 1968, reproduced in Duteuil, *Nanterre*, 200, and in Schnapp and Vidal-Naquet, *Journal*, 163.
165. Paul Ginsborg, *A History of Contemporary Italy: Society and Politics 1943–1988* (London, 1990), 303.
166. Duteuil, *Nanterre*, 194–196.
167. Quoted in Peuchmaurd, *Vivants*, 86.
168. Grimaud, *En mai*, 75. Cf. Bertolino, *Trublions*, 369, who is skeptical that Kervenoaël [or Kervendael] was a fascist. The historian of France Bertram Gordon can find no reference to him among the Occident members he has interviewed. However, François Duprat, *Les journées de mai 68: Les dessous d'une révolution* (Paris, 1968), 68, notes a significant Occident influence in the Nanterre FNEF.
169. See Comité étudiant pour les libertés universitaires, *Pour rebâtir l'université* (Paris, 1969), 31.
170. Direction générale de la Police nationale, renseignements généraux, bulletins quotidiens d'information, 2 May 1968, AN 820599/40. See also UNEF and SNESup, *Le livre noir des journées de mai* (Paris, 1968), 8.
171. 9 May 1968, Fa 252, APP. Cf. Andrew Feenberg and Jim Freedman, *When Poetry Ruled the Streets: The French May Events of 1968* (Albany, 2001), 7: "[At Nanterre] everyone spoke as inspired, and no adherence to a doctrine was required."
172. Passerini, *Autobiography*, 63.
173. Viénet, *Enragés*, 39.
174. Duteuil, *Nanterre*, 170. See also Christian Charrière, *Le Printemps des enragés* (Paris, 1968), 29–30; Cohn-Bendit performs his *autocritique* in his *Le Grand Bazar*, 35.
175. Charrière, *Printemps*, 22, 44–45.
176. Quoted in Dansette, *Mai*, 117.
177. Bertolino, *Trublions*, 229.
178. Cohn-Bendit, *Le Grand Bazar*, 31.
179. Perrot et al., *La Sorbonne par elle-même*, 34.
180. Hamon and Rotman, *Génération*, 1: 438–439; Duteuil, *Nanterre*, 202; 15 May 1968, AN 820599/75.
181. Quoted in Dansette, *Mai*, 84; Bertolino, *Trublions*, 132.
182. Epistémon, *Ces idées*, 41; Duteuil, *Nanterre*, 210; Rémond, *Règle*, 10–31.
183. 19 April 1968, 1208W, art. 180, ADHS.
184. 3 May 1968, 1208W, art. 180, ADHS.
185. De Gaulle quoted in Lacouture, *De Gaulle*, 529.
186. Epistémon, *Ces idées*, 85; Tournoux, *Mois*, 94.

Chapter Three

INCENDIARY OCCUPATIONS

With Nanterre's doors locked, the hub of the student movement shifted from the *banlieue* to Paris. Those who had ventured from outlying areas occupied the heart of the city, whose reconquest recalled the Paris Commune.[1] Youth radicalism found the terrain welcoming. Even though Parisian universities contained the largest proportion of students of bourgeois origin, Parisian students—who constituted approximately one-fourth of the French total— were more leftist and more inclined to join *groupuscules* or the UNEF than their provincial counterparts.[2] Seventy-nine percent of Parisian students in humanities considered themselves on the left, compared to 56 percent of provincial humanities students. Exposure to political and cultural activities in the capital encouraged students to exhibit an urbane disdain for their studies, a distaste for convention, and a desire to break with their past. Furthermore, the Sorbonne suffered from material deficiencies nearly as acute as Nanterre's. Students complained of overcrowding, lack of teaching staff, insufficient classroom space, and an impersonal atmosphere.[3]

Student prominence in revolution was new. In 1830, only a few students had joined workers on the barricades. In 1848, students had helped to spark the revolution in February but had been frightened by workers' revolts in June.[4] They supported bourgeois reform but not proletarian revolution.[5] They were happy to toast "the indissoluble fraternity of the sons of the proletariat and the bourgeoisie" until the former began demanding a social republic, which students—true *fils a papa* (spoiled kids)—rejected.[6] Later in the nineteenth century, university youth played a minor role during the Commune of 1871, and many, if not most, were hostile to the insurrection.[7] Artisans and shopkeepers—not students—dominated nineteenth-century revolts.

The Dreyfus Affair politicized and polarized students of both right (the overwhelming majority) and left. Polarization continued during the interwar period and reached its zenith during the Popular Front when bands of rightists clashed with leftists in the Latin Quarter. After World War II, the left in France—as in other Western nations—gained increasing ascendancy among students that was to last until 1968 and beyond. In the postwar period, the UNEF, probably the oldest student organization in the world, was captured by progressives and came to symbolize left-wing dominance of the student body. Throughout Europe, mass established left parties—British Labour, German Social Democratic, and French Communist—thought it prudent to dissolve their student organizations and expel radicals who rejected social democracy, business unionism, and Stalinism. By 1968 students would initiate rebellions and constitute their most radical force. Perhaps one of the major effects of the development of consumer society in the West was to place the revolutionary current outside the working class as it had not been in the nineteenth century or after World War I or even during the Popular Fronts.

Following the closing of Nanterre on Thursday, 2 May, the Movement of 22 March and the UNEF called for demonstrations in the courtyard of the Sorbonne on Friday, 3 May.[8] Leftists were outraged by a fire set by Occident on the morning of 2 May at the Sorbonne office of FGEL (Fédération des Groupes d'Etudes de Lettres). Three companies of firemen took thirty minutes to extinguish the blaze.[9] The right-wingers' arson left 10,000 francs' worth of damages along with their insignia of the Celtic cross.[10] The UNEF participated in the Friday protests to show its opposition to "fascist terror and police repression." Its strike call spread the movement from Paris to the provinces.[11] Thus, fire literally sparked the May events in Paris. In any civilization, the quest to dominate fire is a quest for power.[12] May was a battle to control conflagrations. As shall be seen, throughout that month incendiary protesters put the city at risk.

On Friday afternoon, several hundred gathered in the Sorbonne courtyard as dozens of members of Occident counterdemonstrated on the boulevard Saint-Michel (see map 2). The right-wingers screamed, "Vietcong Assassins," "Bolshies to Peking," and "Clean up the Sorbonne."[13] Fifty extreme right-wingers sporting helmets and billyclubs marched down the boulevard Saint-Michel, and one of them tossed a smoke bomb at police.[14] Their newspaper, *Minute*, had goaded Occident to attack Cohn-Bendit, accused leftists of wanting to "destroy Western Civilization," and pledged "never to surrender the streets to the *chienlit* (disorder, literally *chier en lit* or shit in bed) of the *Enragés*."[15] Students attributed de Gaulle's later characterization of the student movement as *chienlit* to the influence of extreme-right journalism. At the Sorbonne, a few *Enragés* suggested organizing a defense against an apparently imminent Occident assault. Once again, as in Italy during the late 1960s, antifascism served to provoke and then unite the disparate factions of the extreme left. Throughout May, police remarked that rumors and realities of Occident attacks would cement radical forces.[16]

Like their Italian counterparts, leftist protesters suspected that police tolerated Occident, but the French forces of order seemed to have little

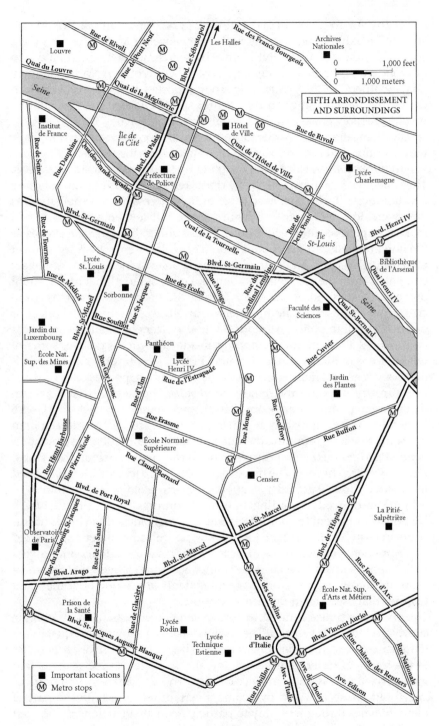

MAP 2: Fifth *arrondissement* and Surroundings

sympathy for these particular right-wingers. The Criminal Brigade responded to complaints filed by both the chancellor and FGEL after the 2 May attack on the FGEL-UNEF office by searching the homes of a dozen of Occident's principal leaders.[17] Paris police informers were routinely unsympathetic to the *groupuscule*. They reported that after one of Occident's regular meetings in the eighteenth *arrondissement*, "[militants] would probably engage in their usual night-time havoc."[18]

The chancellor, Jean Roche, asked the anti-Occident students to leave the Sorbonne, but they refused.[19] Once again showing no respect for university property, radicals began breaking up furniture for use as weapons. The collective violation of property rights reinforced their group cohesion and boldness. Roche "believed it absolutely necessary to expel students who were occupying parts of the university" since their activities would make it impossible for the Sorbonne to host either the *agrégation* classes or the university disciplinary council, both of which were scheduled to meet on 6 May. Radicals had planned to protest against the appearance of six students before the disciplinary council. Police asserted that at a meeting of the MAU at the Sorbonne, Cohn-Bendit had promised to stop the council's proceedings.[20] As he had years earlier at Antony, the chancellor decided to call in police. Around 3:00 P.M., officers blocked the entrances and exits of the Sorbonne, trapping inside 150 young people, some of whom were militants of the JCR and FER.[21] Twenty of them wore helmets, and some carried clubs.[22] In the late afternoon, police received word to occupy the building and remove protesters. They then arrested 300 students, among whom were Cohn-Bendit and Jacques Sauvageot, a UNEF leader. In the sociology classroom, police discovered several dozen light arms. In streets surrounding the university, thirteen students were apprehended and charged with possession of illegal weapons (slingshots, clubs) found in their vehicles.[23] The first convoy of buses packed with the arrested left without trouble at 5:10 P.M., but the departure of the second convoy at 5:15 P.M. provoked, according to official sources, "violent incidents."[24] Demonstrators from the boulevard Saint-Michel blocked the buses of students in custody and flattened a tire. The police commander emphasized that opponents of the forces of order were radical students who mixed with "passers-by and the curious." Other accounts claimed that arrests of students so outraged the ordinary inhabitants and workers of the Latin Quarter that they joined the demonstrators.[25]

Chivalrous police refused to throw female activists in the Sorbonne courtyard into their vehicles. The Italian *carabinieri* showed an equal reluctance to arrest women demonstrators.[26] The traditional sexist generosity of the forces of order allowed 150 females to surround the wagons that were ferrying away their male comrades. These women were a particularly bold group that had overcome a certain reluctance on the part of many females throughout May to participate in street actions.[27] They felt insulted by the discriminatory practices of the police, and they originated cries of "Liberate our comrades," "End repression," "CRS = SS."[28] Although the CRS did not participate on Friday, students confused them with police officers and *gendarmes mobiles* because of the similarity of battle uniforms.[29] Even before their mobilization, the CRS quickly became the symbol of the "total repression" of the bourgeois state. By late Friday afternoon, some demonstrators were digging up streets, and others were throwing cobblestones at the forces of order. They attempted to build barricades, but police quickly routed them.[30] Diverse objects thrown at police lines provoked a tear gas response. The battle for the air and earth of the Latin Quarter had begun. A flying object smashed the windshield of a police vehicle and "severely hurt" an officer. Police charged the crowd, and demonstrators displaced vehicles to obstruct the assaults. The anger of protesters was such that one officer declared "that for the first time in my career, police were forced to retreat because of the volley of cobblestones."[31]

Repression in the heart of Paris constituted a major political error for which the government was to pay from the beginning of May throughout much of June. The police invasion of one of the oldest universities in the world and the subsequent arrest of hundreds of students immediately shocked the public. The state's reaction to student unrest appeared excessive. Parisians believed students had been detained for merely expressing opinions. Many felt that the police invasion of the campus was unprecedented, but the forces of order had been called into the university several times since World War II. As late as February 1964, they had occupied its interior.[32] If, in the context of widespread student resentment of government reforms, the police intervention was unwise, it was perhaps inevitable given youth destruction and disruption. Predictably, police sources do not confirm their supposed "treachery," i.e., the breaking of their alleged agreement not to arrest students inside the university. On the contrary, police stressed their cooperation with the university administration on Friday. On Monday, prior to the meeting of the disciplinary council, that collaboration continued, and "sixty plainclothes officers patrolled the Sorbonne with the agreement of the chancellor."[33]

The intervention of the forces of order reinforced the identification of the centralized university with the repressive state apparatus. It also showed the authorities' shortsighted disdain of intermediate organizations (such as the UNEF), which, under other circumstances and as it had done in the past, might have played a greater role in calming violent agitation or conducting negotiations.[34] Furthermore, the police intervention occurred at the Sorbonne, which remained the symbol of the French university system. A revolt there could not be dismissed as *nanterrorisme*, a rising of rebels from a peripheral, marginal, and upstart campus. The Nanterre model nevertheless replicated itself in the capital. Henceforth, the Parisian student revolt closely resembled the rebellion in the suburban *faculté* where the administration had found it difficult to find "responsible" student representatives.

The mass arrests led to an immediate politicization of students in the Latin Quarter. Militants had expected a fascist invasion of the university, not a police assault. If the government had counted on pre-exam anxiety to depoliticize French students, it had miscalculated. Youth felt unprecedented solidarity with its persecuted peers.[35] Many considered the mass arrests illegal since they thought—somewhat erroneously—that those detained had not committed any infractions.[36] A broadening and spontaneous antirepressive coalition replaced the original antifascist alliance. News of hundreds of arrests mobilized activists from *lycées* in the Latin Quarter and elsewhere in the capital. Their own disciplinary institutions frustrated them, and they welcomed the chance to protest at the Sorbonne. Maoists awarded their ultimate accolade to the detained students by identifying them with oppressed workers. Strikers at Caen, Redon, Le Mans, and other areas of France had also been victims of government, or what Maoists dubbed "fascist," repression.[37] That night at the Ecole Normale Supérieure, they quickly formed "Defense Committees against Repression," which attracted a fair number of young people.[38]

Of the estimated 1,500–2,000 demonstrators (only 50 of whom were extreme rightists), police arrested 574 (including around 300 from the Sorbonne courtyard). All university students taken into custody were enrolled in Parisian universities.[39] Those with previous police records were usually militants of some *groupuscule* or association (UNEF, JCR, CVN, CAL, PSU, anti-Algerian or anti-Vietnam war committees). Approximately 12 percent of those with arrest records had been poster hangers, usually for the UNEF. Thus, a good number were street-smart and skilled in combating or avoiding the forces of order. The incidents of 3 May were largely a product of the militants, including a few from extreme-right groups that had been responsible either directly or indirectly for some of the violence and destruction. According to official statistics, 544 of those arrested or questioned were released. Of those, 179 were minors (33 percent), 58 foreigners (11 percent), and 45 women (8 percent).[40] Of the 45 females, 17 were adults and 27 minors; one was foreign. At the beginning of May, demonstrations remained overwhelmingly French, student, and male affairs. Thirty were placed in the hands of the *police judiciaire*, among whom were 13 from Nanterre arrested for carrying weapons (clubs, Molotov cocktails). Eighty-four policemen were injured.[41] Five were hospitalized, and 20 officers were hurt enough to require sick leave. Flying objects produced most injuries, but their own tear gas blowing back unpredictably upon police put some of them out of action. No deaths occurred since the Municipal Police and the Gendarmerie Mobile were tightly controlled and authorized to use only rubber batons and tear gas.[42] However, as at Antony and Nanterre, students continued to destroy property. Thirteen police vehicles, including three ambulances of *police-secours*, were damaged. Usually protesters shattered the headlights, windows, and windshields. Street signs and grills protecting trees were trashed, and shop windows smashed.

Reacting to the injuries in their own ranks, the forces of order began indiscriminately beating young people. That evening, the Movement of 22 March condemned "the general mobilization of police" and the "thousands of armed cops who have transformed Paris into an armed camp."[43] Repression pulled these *groupuscules* and unions together as the UNEF, 22 March Movement, PSU, JCR, FER, UJCml, and SNESup met to attempt to coordinate actions. Friday, 3 May, began the tradition of "red Friday nights." Nights aroused the most subversive behavior, and the cover of darkness emboldened both protesters and police. The first great night of the barricades on 10 May would renew the revolutionary traditions of 1830, 1848, and 1871.[44] The most violent Friday of the month would be 24 May. Students and *gauchistes* were often aggressively active at night and on Fridays, whereas, as shall be seen, workers protested peacefully during daylight hours on Mondays.

During the relatively calm weekend, the justice system processed between three and four hundred of the arrested.[45] On Saturday, 4 May, and even Sunday, 5 May, emergency courts examined the accused and issued a number of draconian sentences that gave a dozen demonstrators two to three months of prison. As a result, those sympathetic to protesters accused judges—and by implication, the government—of running a weekend kangaroo court. The Sunday sentencing of a Catholic student to several months in jail shocked the Nobel prize-winning physicist Alfred Kastler.[46] The UNEF, SNESup, Movement of 22 March, and *gauchiste* organizations united around the pro-tolerance slogan "Liberate our Comrades." Police brutality repulsed Socialist (SFIO) and Communist students who supported the *trublions*. Two hundred *lycéens* from the ninth *arrondissement* shouted "Down with Cops" at a Saturday demonstration.[47] Criticism of the forces of order came from seemingly unexpected quarters. The anti-*gauchiste* FNEF protested against their "brutality."[48] Police officials themselves noted that the weekend sentences levied against thirteen students arrested on 3 May "hardened the position of the troublemakers…. Numerous students who do not belong to any *groupuscules* have now joined the demonstrations."[49]

Antirepression acted in May 1968 as antifascism had in the 1930s: both pulled reformist and revolutionary forces together tactically but could not bridge their strategic differences. In the 1930s, revolutionary antifascists (Trotskyites and anarchists) had argued that the best way to prevent fascism was to make revolution, whereas nonrevolutionary antifascists wanted to build a broad-based coalition that included moderates. Likewise in the 1960s, reformists (Socialists and Communists), whose Popular Front-style coalition had won over 46 percent of the vote in the second round of the 1967 legislative elections, believed that an antirepressive alliance could end police brutality and, more importantly for them, might bring down the regime. They suggested that protest be directed against Gaullist rule, not bourgeois society. French revolutionaries of the 1960s believed that "fascist" or authoritarian repression was intrinsic to bourgeois society. They imagined that the only path to liberation was proletarian revolution. The reformist Communist/Socialist position condemned the government's police brutality and broadened the movement to include the tolerant middle classes. Front-line policemen did indeed perpetuate brutal and cruel acts; however, no archival evidence supports the charge that in 1968 police composed a "state within a state" beyond the control of their commanders and civilian authorities.

Public animosity toward the forces of order had a long history. In the 1930s Parisian police were thought to have favored the extreme right. World War II found them rounding up tens of thousands of Jews for shipment to Nazi death camps. During the Cold and Algerian wars, various units of the security forces had won an often-deserved reputation for racism and fanatical anti-Communism. They were plausibly accused of murdering "hundreds of Algerians (a conservative estimate)" and injuring thousands during and after the demonstration of 17 October 1961.[50] In February 1962 at the Charonne *métro* station, police and/or OAS agents killed eight CGT members during an unauthorized "anti-fascist" and anti-OAS demonstration. In response, massive numbers of CGT members and sympathizers turned out to challenge Gaullist repression.

On Monday, 6 May, the UNEF called for an unlimited strike in higher education that was unanimously backed by the leadership of the SNESup, which was willing to support an "insurrectional" strike that ignored the law requiring unions to notify the government of work stoppages. The support of the SNESup was consequential because it was an important component of the FEN, the major teachers' union. SNESup represented 20 to 25 percent of faculty members, usually younger teachers at the lower ranks, whose numbers had grown rapidly during the 1960s.[51] Radical Marxists in the union equated police with the detested "bourgeois state," and others blamed disorder on a government that had dispatched the forces of order into the Sorbonne. Sympathy for demonstrators reflected generational solidarity among students and young instructors. The movement had begun in the humanities and social sciences but quickly won broad support among those in the physical and natural sciences. At the Orsay science *faculté*, 70 percent of professors and students joined the strike.[52] Given these official statistics, the comment of the leader of the SNESup—Alain Geismar, a 29-year-old physicist—is credible: "Never had there been such a movement of solidarity of teachers for students."[53]

Geismar, like Cohn-Bendit, would become a media-recognized leader of the movement. Both were especially disliked targets of reactionaries. Born in 1939, Geismar was a child of the bourgeoisie. His father had been a bank inspector who was killed during the invasion of France in June 1940. The son had trained as an engineer and scientist. Politically, he had supported the PSU of former Prime Minister Pierre Mendès-France and had led that party's youth wing. In 1966 Geismar quit the PSU, and soon he was elected to head the SNESup on the strength of his reputation as a cultural radical.[54] He had authored a tract, *For a Cultural Revolution in the University*, which recommended a strong dose of Maoist leveling in the French academy. The events of May pushed him even further toward the "Chinese." Geismar opposed moderate union colleagues who wanted to change the university from within, and he advocated street actions to obtain reforms.

On Monday, 6 May, eight Nanterre students, including Cohn-Bendit, were scheduled to appear before the university disciplinary council. Police informers related that prior to his arrest on Friday, Dany had promised an audience at the Sorbonne that the council would not be able to render its judgment in peace.[55] The FGEL seconded him and warned, "not one student will be excluded from the university for political or union activities," conveniently neglecting that some of the defendants were officially accused of threats and violence against both property and people, including professors in their classrooms.[56] It is therefore not surprising that the chancellor had approved of sixty plainclothes officers patrolling the halls of the university.[57] The centralization of the French system (an autonomous disciplinary council did not yet exist at Nanterre although some professors had requested it in March) immediately encouraged the spread of unrest to the capital itself. The minister of education directly nationalized the issue by pushing for sanctions against the French-German anarchist.[58] The deans of each faculty composed the disciplinary council, whose presiding officer was the head of the Ecole Normale Supérieure. Radicals were charged with violating university rules by occupying buildings and ignoring the student "right to work."[59] Some prominent *profs*—Paul Ricoeur, Touraine, and Lefebvre—came prepared to defend the victims of their own institution's "repression." Thus, the "bourgeois" university hardly presented an intransigent front against the accused. Of the eight on trial, one—René Riesel—was an *Enragé* (pro-*situ*), two—Cohn-Bendit and Jean-Pierre Duteuil—were in the LEA; two were CVB; one had been in charge of the cultural commission of the Movement of 22 March; another was in the FER (Trotskyite). The sole female activist had been a member of the JCR but was moving toward the "Chinese." University authorities might have thought that prosecuting individual members of many *groupuscules* would make their actions seem evenhanded, but the effect of their attempt at impartiality was to unite a variety of *gauchistes* against them.

A number of the accused began singing the *Internationale* as they approached the Sorbonne.[60] One of the eight, René Riesel, wanted to distinguish himself from the others, just as his group, the *Enragés*, had detached itself from the mass during the 22 March occupation. Riesel's friends distributed a tract, "La Rage au ventre," which commended students for fighting the police: "Where violence begins, reformism ends."[61] The leaflet castigated cataclysmically the futility of student activism: "Protest against the university is insignificant when the entire society must be destroyed." Predictably, Riesel showed little respect for his judges. Nor was he impressed by the magnificent chamber of the Sorbonne where the disciplinary council met. To display his disdain, he took off his leather jacket and used it as a pillow as he reclined on the floor. Another of the accused, Michel Pourny, a UNEF and FER militant, refused to respond to questions because, he claimed, his judges had accepted selective admissions policies and were performing the work of the CRS. Transforming his modest social origins into a badge of honor, Pourny told the council that he was "proud of the sacrifices" that his father, "a metallurgical worker," had made for his education but that he would not cooperate with a state whose universities eliminated two-thirds of those enrolled.[62]

Several days later, Riesel issued the communiqué, "The Burning Chateau: Address to the [Disciplinary] Council of the University of Paris," an assemblage of Situationist insults directed at the liberal university and its professors:

> Vestiges,
>
> Your crude ignorance of life strips you of any authority. Do you want proof of it? If you are able to judge me today, it is only because there is a police cordon behind you. In fact, no one respects you any more. You ought to be crying about your antiquated Sorbonne.
>
> The fact that certain stupid modernizers intend to defend me—mistakenly imagining that after spitting on me I might become respectable enough for them to defend me—makes me laugh. In spite of their masochistic persistence, these opportunists do not even know how to save the university. Mr. [Henri] Lefebvre, go to hell....
>
> Seigniorial justice is menaced when the chateau is burning.[63]

The Sorbonne's MAU omitted the historical reference to the Great Fear of 1789, but made the similar point that "eminent professors ... [who] have been insulted, criticized, and routed" deserved it because they were "pillars of a bourgeois university."[64] The MAU backed a demonstration against the disciplinary council.[65]

Many protesters linked the attempt to discipline or expel the eight with the national problem of selection and retention.[66] For them, discipline and selection were two unattractive sides of the bourgeois university. Demonstrators shouted, "Free the students," "Profs, not cops," and "Down with repression." On Monday, 6 May, the SNESup urged its members to join the students, marking the first time since the Algerian War that professors had demonstrated *en masse* in the streets. The crowd of thousands shouted inventive slogans, which displayed both irony ("We are a *groupuscule*") and the rhetorical excess so characteristic of the 1960s ("We are all German Jews").[67] In the afternoon, three to four thousand students engaged in an "extremely violent" demonstration that police said "rapidly ... degenerated into street combat" and became "a riot." Protesters were said to have committed "numerous damages."[68] They "dug up streets, vandalized cars, and smashed shop windows." Officers blocked their path at various points.[69] The UNEF countercharged that police "savagery" recalled "the hateful regime of Pétain."[70] In a vain attempt to protect their image, police illegally confiscated a photographer's film.[71]

The vociferous protests of thousands of students outside the Sorbonne cowed the judges of the disciplinary council, who, according to Pierre Grappin, "vanished one by one" until only two maintained the courage to remain in the chamber.[72] Some judges had already experienced adolescent terrorism.[73] Officials were aware of a tract that encouraged the hounding of council members by informing extreme left militants of their names, addresses, and phone numbers.[74] Police reported that a few antagonists frequently harassed their enemies by telephone.[75] Professor Micha, who planned to attend the council's hearings, had received anonymous phone calls; officials posted officers to watch his home and eventually the residences of the other fourteen members of the council.[76] The council decided that the protests did not permit the impartial administration of justice, and on Thursday, 9 May, the chancellor postponed indefinitely its decision.

The UNEF did not possess sufficient unity or influence to absorb the shock of the student movement or to keep it within "respectable" limits. The Ministry of Interior was disappointed that "it [the UNEF] was incapable of playing the customary role of a traditional organization.... It is divided into clans.... Its leaders are incapable of dominating the chaos. It has become a cover for extremist groups."[77] Whatever the accuracy of this analysis, the state's policies and actions towards student demonstrators created a climate of sympathy for them. Christian democrats—such as Jean-Marie Lustiger, the future archbishop of Paris—and progressives of various stripes rallied to the student side.[78] Liberal Protestant and Catholic churchmen joined in sympathy with protesters. As in Italy, some Christian progressives desperately dreamed of reconciling Mao, Lenin, and Jesus. Police reported that the Secours Catholique donated 5,000 francs for student needs.[79] Later in the month, opposition from numerous students foiled Occident's attempt to occupy the Institut Catholique (see map 3).[80] At the same time, Jewish students occupied the Consistoire israélite on the rue de la Victoire to protest against the "lack of democracy" of official Jewish organizations.[81] The events of May and June 1968 manifested activists' declining anticlericalism (except among pro-*situs* and, curiously enough, among radical Catholics) as well as believers' relatively new sympathy for the left.

At the beginning of May, groups of militants quickly formed action committees and hoped to transform them into the soviets of the new revolution. Committees formulated the immediate demands of the student movement—liberation of those arrested, an end to the police lockout of the Sorbonne, and freedom of political expression in the university.[82] Additional demands included the resignation of Roche, who, the JCR charged, had acted like an official of "Franco's Spain."[83] Some of these demands were

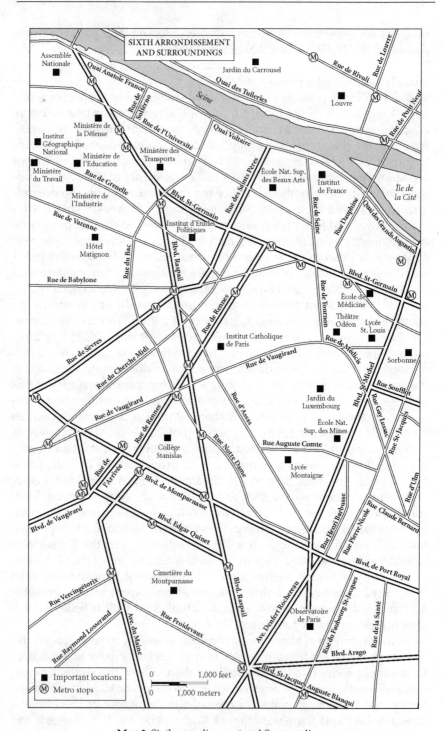

MAP 3: Sixth *arrondissement* and Surroundings

highly polemical, if not demagogic. The university largely permitted freedom of expression, and academic authorities—not police—had instituted the "lockout" of the university. Indeed, officials of the forces of order noted that the Sorbonne's closure had aggravated protests by causing "a spontaneous reaction … that had left too many students with nothing to do."[84]

The major student demand—amnesty and the reopening of the Sorbonne—won the support of four-fifths of Parisians, according to an IFOP (Institut français d'opinion publique) poll of 8 May.[85] The sympathy of the public and the dynamism of the left's unity against the state and government affected important sectors of the PCF.[86] As early as 3 and 4 May, its Paris Federation and the UEC lambasted police brutality but maintained their criticisms of "phony revolutionaries," the PCF code words for *gauchistes*.[87] On 4 May, Communist professors of the Sorbonne condemned "the brutality of police repression" and insisted on a coalition of "all progressive and democratic forces," Communist jargon for a coalition of the left. The condemnation of the forces of order showed that the antirepressive impulse briefly overcame the antagonism between Communist instructors and some protesters who doubly disdained them as professors and party members.

By Monday evening, the number of protesters had grown to twenty thousand, including some *blousons noirs* that Situationists imagined as a potential revolutionary force. The Maoists suggested tactics that stemmed from their fixation on the class struggle. The "Chinese" urged students to march into workers' neighborhoods, particularly Saint-Denis in the northern suburbs, and join proletarians who were supposedly protesting against capitalism. The UJCml's "Defense Committees against Repression" identified repression with capitalism's "fascist" state and preached that wage earners were the principal force against the latter.[88] Maoists were mistaken since throughout May and June the movement did not have to go to the *banlieue*. Instead, the *banlieue* would come to it. In fact, after the first few days of Parisian protests, police asserted that most demonstrators were no longer students but young delinquents.[89]

Authorities characterized the Monday protests as "extremely violent. Demonstrators systematically provoked police. Demonstrations degenerated into street fighting. In the provinces, incidents are rare and not on the same scale as Paris."[90] The forces of order reported that protests by the UNEF and *gauchistes* on 6 May "were characterized by incidents of exceptional violence."[91] On the other hand, an RATP (public transport) committee unanimously condemned police "abuses" after several employees of the Luxembourg *métro* station were manhandled on 6 May.[92] In the late afternoon, demonstrators set a construction trailer ablaze and then used the arriving fire trucks as protective barriers against police attacks.[93] At the rue Bonaparte, protesters climbed on roofs and threw cobblestones and bottles down on *flics*. According to the prefecture, they launched a driverless Citroën at a group of three policemen, dragging two of them twenty meters.[94] Some of the most violent confrontations occurred as darkness descended. At 8:00 P.M. three to four thousand demonstrators attacked police lines at the boulevard Saint-Germain.[95] Barricades—which had not been erected in Paris since the Liberation—were thrown up quickly and initially without much expertise. According to *Action*, the paper closest to the student movement, the construction of barricades in the Latin Quarter was the best way to celebrate the 150th birthday of Marx.[96] Protesters dug up a portion of the street, tore gratings from the road, and placed cars in the path of police. From one of their barricades, they "intensely bombarded [our men] with an incredible number of cobblestones."[97] Officers suffered numerous injuries in their attempt to remove a structure that demonstrators aggressively defended. A commissioner reported that "at the Blvd. Saint-Germain and the rue du Four … despite [our] massive use of tear-gas grenades and several successive charges, the demonstrators did not fall back since they were numerous and extremely virulent. At their head was a young girl, who, recalling La Pasionaria, encouraged them to assault the police."[98] Inspired by this leftist Joan, these protesters downed several CRS.

Another police superintendent found it hard to believe that his adversaries, some of whom waved the anarchist black flag, were students. Their effectiveness in battle convinced him that they were "groups organized for street fighting," and he called for the use of armored vehicles to combat them. The *flics* "extensively used" tear gas and fire hoses to disperse protesters. Poisoned air and sturdy streams of water were their weapons of choice. Students sometimes responded with their own homemade gas bombs, even though the wind was strong enough to make the circulation of vapors unpredictable. A commissioner declared that in the early morning of 7 May (1:35–2:00 A.M.), *blousons noirs* vandalized parts of the boulevard du Montparnasse.[99] Several hundred protesters built a bonfire from wooden street signs.[100]

Student-police confrontations on Monday produced 462 arrests.[101] Forty-six (10 percent) were foreign students and 155 were French students from all disciplines, not just the traditionally radical fields of the social sciences and humanities. Significantly, among the arrested were 199 French non-students from a wide variety of professions, as well as 36 foreign non-students. The forces of order publicized the surprisingly high proportion of non-students—51 percent. After holding them in custody, police released 422 detainees, of whom 9 percent were women, 82 percent French, 37 percent minors. Once again, despite exceptions, official statistics indicated that the demonstrations remained male, French, and youthful affairs. The violence left 481 police injured, including—for the first time—53 CRS.[102] The Red Cross aided 460 hurt students. Streets were uprooted throughout the city, and stores pillaged. Although a distinct minority, girls displayed as much reckless courage as boys.[103] A 26-year-old dressmaker was renowned for her ability to inflict damage on police with her slingshot.[104] *Lycéens* too proved to be excellent street fighters.

Approximately forty cars and ten buses were overturned and set on fire. The arson of May expressed the most radical tendency of the movement. Fire's immediate effect is destructive, but, as Gaston Bachelard has noted, it is also a "symbol of purity," emitting light as well as heat.[105] Even if their defenders and apologists never proclaimed arson as a legitimate weapon, incendiaries may have believed that they were purifying and enlightening a city that was threatened by the CRS and other forces of darkness.[106] Political arson had a long history in France. The Great Fear saw peasants putting to flame the castles of their lords. The Commune's *pétroleuses* are enveloped in myth, but the effects of the blazes of 1870–1871 were enormous in symbolic and real terms. Major monuments—Tuileries, Palais Royal, Hôtel de Ville—smoldered, and female arsonists became the negative representation of the Paris revolt.[107] May was more fortunate in reality and memory. Since—despite appearances—the state retained its strength, May's blazes were not nearly as destructive as the Commune's, and its image—unlike that of its revolutionary predecessor—does not remain tied to arsonists. Nonetheless, as shall be seen, the potential for devastation in 1968 was enormous.

Although much revolutionary action recalled previous revolts in Paris, newer and more specifically 1960s elements emerged. Most students and demonstrators either owned or had access to a transistor.[108] An astounding 400,000 transistors per week were reportedly sold during the May crisis. Protesters and barricade builders listened to the news, which boosted their spirits by showing that they were part of a mass movement that was rattling state power. The mass-media spectacle could help propagate the revolt, but as Gaullists were to show at the end of the month, it could also promote the restoration of order. In any event, throughout May and June, the radio proved its communicative flexibility and rapidity.

On Tuesday, 7 May, an increase in numbers elated protesters. Major *lycées*—Buffon, Voltaire, Michelet (of Vanves) and Condorcet—held their own gatherings of 300 to 500 in the morning. Later, 25,000 to 50,000 students and numerous teachers joined a protest march. The path of the demonstration passed by the National Assembly and the Elysée Palace, but marchers—scorning conventional politics—tried to ignore the official power centers of the Fifth Republic. "Power," they chanted as though to convince themselves, "is in the street."[109] Slogans reflected antirepressive sentiment ("Free our comrades"), antimedia feelings ("*Le Figaro* [a conservative daily] is fascist"), and internationalism ("Rome, Berlin, Warsaw, Paris").[110] Upon reaching the Arc de Triomphe, a few of the unorganized may have tried to defile in some manner or to urinate on the flame of the Tomb of the Unknown Soldier, but UNEF and JCR parade marshals tried to stop them. So did several policemen who, it was claimed, were able to protect the tomb and rescue the flame.[111] The supposed attempt at scatological sabotage showed the desire of some revolutionaries to desecrate the most cherished national symbols and to *épater les bourgeois* politically and sexually. Patriots did not forget the sacrilege. Some of them reacted to the incident by libeling Dany in the National Assembly. They asserted that Cohn-Bendit had encouraged his followers to profane monuments dedicated to World War I and II veterans who had fought against Dany's "friends."

During the demonstration, UNEF parade marshals found themselves helpless to control incidents of violence against police and property. Marshals complained to a police administrator that they had been forced to exchange blows with anarchists carrying black flags.[112] After midnight, the UNEF lost all authority, and riots broke out on the boulevard Raspail and the rue d'Assas. Police related that protected by darkness, protesters launched homemade gas grenades, dug up streets, and overturned vehicles.[113] They damaged police cars, flattened bus tires, and lit several fires. At the rue de Vaugirard and rue d'Assas, "uncontrollable" demonstrators erected a barricade and stoned an isolated CRS unit, which suffered thirteen injuries and six damaged vehicles. Isolated policemen in hostile areas risked beatings, and superiors warned officers to remain within their group.[114] The Vaugirard/Assas attackers escaped without arrest. At the Port Royal-Montparnasse-Saint-Michel intersection, property destruction seemed either Bakuninist or gratuitous. Three hundred demonstrators "burned wooden signs ... voluntarily damaged unlocked cars, and destroyed road and gas station signs." A police commissioner declared that "four UNEF parade marshals" became "so disturbed and frightened by the destruction (one was even crying)" that they felt compelled to inform him that the vandals "did not belong to their organization but were instead pro-Chinese." They begged him to put a stop to these acts of pillaging and havoc. In the sixth *arrondissement* alone, twenty-eight cars and twelve storefronts were damaged.[115] During these "bitter confrontations," police arrested 86, only half of whom—they claimed—were students.[116] Some were carrying light weapons, but no deadly firearms. Two students from the Ecole Polytechnique, an elite military academy where one could have presumed hatred of authority to be absent, were charged with destruction of street signs. Eighty-seven policemen were injured, three of whom were hospitalized.[117] The three had apparently received slivers of glass in their eyes when a demonstrator tossed a cobblestone through the window of their vehicle.[118] Another two suffered from the effects of a tear gas grenade hurled by demonstrators. Most injured officers had been struck by various kinds of missiles, especially cobblestones. Nighttime unleashed police fury. Parisian councilors D. Weill and C. Bourdet asserted that on 8 May at 1:15 A.M., officers invaded a café, filled it with tear gas, evacuated its clients, broke its windows, and arrested innocent bystanders. After dark, the streets belonged to the angry.

The extreme right contested the dominance of the left and of police. Although it could not match the left's numerical force, it prevailed in the western, bourgeois parts of the capital. Initially rightist demonstrations were essentially symbolic, but by the end of the month they would lend force to the government's strikebreaking and its anti-Communism. Police reported that on 7 May at the corner of the boulevards Saint-Michel and Saint-Germain, 500 to 600 extreme-right demonstrators, probably from Occident, shouted its simplistic slogan, "CRS take power."[119] In the evening of 15 May, 600–1,000 extreme rightists protested against the profanation of the Arc de Triomphe's Tomb of the Unknown Soldier.[120] Throughout the week, Occident and ARLP (Alliance républicaine pour les libertés et le progrès) militants continued to assemble in the evenings at the Tomb to guard its flame.[121] Indeed, by the week's end, attendance of extreme rightists at the relighting had nearly tripled to 2,500–3,000 persons.[122] On 20 May, Interior officials claimed that an Occident commando armed with batons and trashcan covers attacked the Institut d'études politiques where it fought with UNEF members, injuring one person and causing some damage.[123] An Occident sympathizer characterized the raid as a failure.[124] On 21 May, police intervened when 500–600 Occident demonstrators entered the occupied conservatory of music in the eighth *arrondissement*. At the school, they "went on a rampage and physically confronted student occupiers," injuring one.[125]

The extreme right made the PCF its main target, with de Gaulle a distant second. The Party became so worried about attacks from either the extreme right or extreme left that it posted more than one hundred militants to shield its offices throughout the Paris region. These precautions did not prevent confrontations, and police reported that four extreme rightists threw stones and then lobbed a firebomb at the PCF office in the seventeenth *arrondissement*.[126] On 21 May, a crowd of nearly one thousand, spearheaded by followers of Occident and supporters of Tixier-Vignancourt, marched to the offices of *L'Humanité*. The newspaper's employees responded by tossing beer bottles, metal objects, and cobblestones at the crowd from the windows of their offices.[127] Rightists retaliated by returning the makeshift missiles and, as leftist demonstrators had done in the Latin Quarter, by setting fire to trashcans that were located in front of the newspaper's offices. Several demonstrators were injured. Police then dispersed the crowd and were roundly booed by both Communists and Occident. The latter may have regretted as misguided its previous shouts of "CRS to power." Occident remained the dominant extreme-right force in May and outclassed its rivals, such as the minuscule Restauration Nationale, in violence and numbers of militants.[128]

The extreme right had to wait until the end of May to become at least partially respectable. In early May, the left displayed much more momentum. Reacting against virtually the entire left, the government had attacked not just *gauchistes* but the university itself. On Tuesday, 7 May, the CFDT teachers' union condemned the arrests of demonstrators.[129] Georges Séguy, the head of the CGT, demanded the liberation of arrested students.[130] Gaston Defferre and François Mitterrand of the Fédération de la gauche démocrate et socialiste (FGDS) disregarded their initial reservations about student methods and expressed "their indignation at the violence of police repression that has been employed since last Friday against the students. After ten years in power, this is how Gaullists respond."[131] Claude Estier, a *fédéré* deputy who was close to Mitterrand, advocated the liberation of arrested students, removing police from the Latin Quarter, and the reopening of the Sorbonne. The PCF deputy Louis Baillot accused the government of "savage repression," and a PCF tract condemned "police repression" while omitting its ritual condemnation of *gauchisme*. Communist students formulated demands for an "end to repression," amnesty for those arrested, and withdrawal of police from the university.[132] Although opposed to *gauchisme*, the parliamentary left was in basic agreement with student demands, at least as formulated by Geismar and Jacques Sauvageot, who were quickly becoming nationally recognized figures. The latter, twenty-five, was vice-president of the UNEF and linked to the PSU. He and Geismar insisted that the state drop all charges against those arrested, re-station police outside of the Latin Quarter, and reopen the university.[133] The political center also joined the chorus of critics. Its 1965 presidential candidate, Jean Lecanuet, leader of the Centre démocrate, declared that the government had used excessive force against students.[134]

On Wednesday, 8 May, the CGT, CFDT, FEN, and UNEF came together for the first time since the Algerian War and the miners' strike of 1963 to organize a demonstration to protest against "methods of police repression which violated democratic and trade-union freedoms."[135] The forging of an alliance with the CGT and the CFDT showed that the UNEF had successfully renewed its tradition of cooperating with major working-class organizations. May's developments reinvigorated the student union both politically and financially. During that month, police concluded that the UNEF increased its membership by three thousand and raised enough money to pay off its debts.[136] CGT locals praised young protesters, and non-militant workers were reported to be "shocked by the repression."[137]

A broad-based disgust at unnecessary police violence convinced moderates to join radicals. Five Nobel Prize winners—the physicist Alfred Kastler; biologists Jacques Monod, André Lwoff, and François Jacob; and author François Mauriac—appealed without success to the president of the republic to reopen the universities and to grant amnesty to students who had been sentenced. That François Mauriac—a columnist for *Le Figaro* and a devoted Gaullist—would publicly protest showed the profound unpopularity of the government's actions. Just as significantly, left-wing Gaullists—David Rousset (whose son had been arrested), Joseph Kessel, Philippe de Saint-Robert, and Emmanuel d'Astier de la Vigerie—supported the major student demands articulated by the UNEF. Mainstream journalists joined them. Jean-François Kahn and Jacques Dérogy of *L'Express*, Frédéric Gaussen of *Le Monde*, and René Backmann of *Le Nouvel Observateur* were among the founding members of the Committee of

Journalists against Repression established on 8 May. Other intellectuals took sides and, unsurprisingly, supported protesters. Maurice Nadeau, Marguerite Duras, Michel Leiris, Claude Roy, Nathalie Sarraute, André Gorz, Jean-Paul Sartre, Jacques Lacan, Marthe Robert, François Châtelet, and Henri Lefebvre condemned "police savagery," which revealed "the immense violence upon which contemporary societies are founded."[138]

Thousands of *lycéens* protested in the morning of 8 May, and perhaps 10,000 to 12,000 others demonstrated in the evening. At 7:30 P.M., they assembled at the Faculté des Sciences to hear Cohn-Bendit and then marched together with their professors.[139] Favorite slogans were "Stop repression" and "De Gaulle responsible."[140] Although street fights erupted in the Latin Quarter, few arrests or injuries occurred, with the exception of distributors of tracts and pamphlets, easy targets for police.[141] This lull may have encouraged a UNEF parade marshal to hand over to a police superintendent a 177-caliber Marksman repeater that he had confiscated from a demonstrator approximately thirty-five years old and of "Spanish" appearance.[142] Both the UNEF marshals and police agreed to avoid using firearms, and both sides were largely successful in restraining themselves.

In vocational high schools (*lycées techniques*), the "first incidents" occurred on Thursday, 9 May.[143] High-school protest took the form of strikes, demonstrations, and picket lines. Students challenged the authority of teachers and were especially concerned with expanding sexual freedoms.[144] *Lycéens* agitated for curricular and pedagogical reform and began to discuss sexuality much more openly than their teachers did. They also wanted to abolish restrictions on their right to smoke, dress, and leave the classroom. In addition, the strikes offered teenagers a welcome respite from homework. On 9 May, police estimated that 800 Parisian high-school students gathered around the Gare Saint-Lazare, 200 at the Gare de Lyon, and 4,000 at the Place de la Sorbonne.[145] The JCR assembled 3,200 at the Mutualité.

Coinciding with the *lycée* agitation, Georges Séguy of the CGT and Eugène Descamps of the CFDT met on Thursday at the UNEF headquarters to plan a unified demonstration.[146] According to a police analysis of the meeting, "the CGT's immediate goal is to turn the student revolt into a larger movement involving workers and to launch a widespread protest against the social and economic policies of the government. The CGT can count on the support of the CFDT which will not let the CGT upstage it."[147] Séguy and Descamps reaffirmed their commitment to the UNEF. James Marangé of the FEN, who opposed the Trotskyite tendency of Ecole Emancipée, which represented about 10 percent of the FEN membership, was—according to police—"more reluctant to support the UNEF but is being pressured by the SNESup."[148]

Faced with a broad and dynamic coalition and widespread revulsion against attacks on students, the authorities vacillated. On Wednesday, 8 May, Minister of Education Peyrefitte was reportedly ready to reopen the Sorbonne.[149] On Thursday, 9 May, a day without police injuries, Roche issued a communiqué that lifted the suspension of classes at the Sorbonne and Nanterre. On that day, however, Peyrefitte had come under strong pressure from de Gaulle, who had severely admonished him for his conciliatory gestures.[150] The government exhibited its hard line by preventing a group of German students and SDS members from entering Paris. On 10 May, in the absence of Prime Minister Pompidou, who was in Afghanistan, negotiations ensued between the government and the UNEF but collapsed when the UNEF insisted upon the liberation of four demonstrators condemned to prison sentences and twelve in preventive detention. Although the Ministry of Education had officially reopened Nanterre, Movement of 22 March militants disrupted the only two courses that met and made sure that the strike meetings continued at the *faculté*.[151] The authorities noted that the student council "proclaimed the autonomy of the University of Strasbourg with regard to the present government which is solely and uniquely responsible for the total deterioration of the situation."[152] The UNEF and *groupuscules* coalesced on Friday, 10 May, for another major demonstration against police and government repression. The continued backing of public opinion bolstered protesters' morale. Polls indicated that 80 percent of Parisians supported the students.[153]

If students were favored, police were hated. By the late twentieth century the police had replaced priests as targets of popular distrust. Protesters talked of *manger du flic* just as in the nineteenth century anticlericals had discussed *manger du curé*. Priests and police shared a number of features. Both sought domination of mind and body, and both served as concrete and imagined scapegoats. A broad unity surpassing class and political divisions could construct an anti-*flic* coalition, as it had earlier for anticlericals. Police and priests were uniformed and easily identifiable. Uniformed police were, of course, objects of demonstrators' projectiles and occasionally of drunken drivers who deliberately tried to run them over.[154] Police officers and police stations became central targets; in contrast, churches and convents suffered very little damage during the events. Reports by insulted officers revealed that police were stuck with the parasitical image that the *curé* had borne in the nineteenth century. When one 40-year-old divorcée was issued a parking ticket in the seventeenth *arrondissement*, she exploded: "You *bande de cons* [idiots], we're sick of your fines.... You're only good for bothering decent people."[155] Others labeled cops *trop payés* (overpaid). The favorite epithets "SS" and "assassin" had political overtones that identified the forces of order with the right. According to the reigning Marxist ideology, the police were errand boys of the rapacious bourgeoisie. Renewing the tradition of the Great Revolution, some radicals threatened to hang members of each from trees and lampposts.[156] The Church in the nineteenth century reflected and encouraged anti-Semitism; racist police in the late twentieth harassed Asians and Africans.[157] Like priests during an earlier period, police had attempted to impose "moral order" at Antony and Nanterre. Common insults leveled at them were *enculé* (dirty butt-fucker), which evoked sexual perversities that anticleri-cals had often identified with *curés*.

Widespread anti-*flic* hostility demoralized officers. A commissioner recounted that on 9 May, 200 students and 70 professors from the Sor-bonne's Institut d'Anglais pleaded with him, in the presence of Europe One reporters, to allow them to enter the university. He replied: "I sug-gested ... in a courteous and measured tone that should be used with such distinguished professors and excitable young people that it was the chancellor—not the police—who shut down the Sorbonne."[158] Indeed, Roche allowed the Sorbonne to reopen on the morning of Friday, 10 May, to receive two hundred candidates for the *agrégation*.[159] On that day, a few hours before the first Night of the Barricades, a policeman entered a Parisian-area *lycée* to inform a professor about an accident that had injured one of his students: "The students misdirected me to the principal's office and made me walk throughout the *lycée*. Finally, he [the principal] re-ceived me coldly. As I left, about five hundred students who were around twelve years old whistled, booed, and made me the object of many un-pleasant jeers."[160]

An officer assigned to duty as a school crossing guard in the sixth *arrondissement* found himself threatened and insulted by young people.[161] Immediately following the massive CGT-UNEF demonstration of 13 May against police brutality, the commissioner of the first *arrondissement* re-ported: "The criticisms and assaults on them by the press and other media greatly distress our personnel. A large number of uniformed officers have told me about the threats, attacks, and harassment that they have suffered these last few days in the subway, on the street, and even in their apart-ment houses."[162]

Many individual officers were themselves of working- or lower-middle-class background—often the sons of shopkeepers, artisans, white-collar workers, and foremen—and could not remain isolated from popular mis-trust. The commissioner of the nineteenth *arrondissement* perceived "certain bitterness and a definite weariness among my personnel."[163] Among the many complaints of insults and attacks, the story of one officer was typical. He related that schoolmates at Clichy had punched his 13-year-old son and scorned him as "cop's son, assassin's son, and SS's son."[164] Parents sent their children on anti-*flic* missions. At the intersection of the rue de Rennes and the rue de Vaugirard, a 5-year-old emerged from a group of approxi-mately fifteen persons and hit several policemen while insulting them as "dirty cops."[165] A policeman assigned to the Hôpital Cochin, which bor-dered the Latin Quarter, was forced to confront doctors who admonished him: "Look at what you've done. How can you be a cop?" Another physi-cian exploded: "I've had enough. They keep bringing me people that you've messed up. My job is to repair what you've done."[166] Other physi-cians' reports confirmed allegations of police brutality. To bolster faltering morale, on 15 May Interior Minister Fouchet and Police Prefect Maurice

Grimaud gave public pep talks to their men.[167] At the end of May in a letter addressed to the homes of 26,000 policemen, Grimaud confessed that a number of policemen had used "excessive force."[168]

The official theme of the 10 May demonstration repeated the spontaneous protest of 3 May—"Liberate our comrades," including arrested foreigners.[169] The ESU (Etudiants Socialistes Unifiés), the student organization of the PSU, officially joined the fray and congratulated students for combating "the bourgeois university." PSU youth praised the protesters for having "forced the PCF and the unions not to oppose them." A number of workers from the *banlieue* once again joined the march, and police estimated the crowd of demonstrators to be twelve thousand persons.[170] Some of them targeted the Santé prison (fourteenth *arrondissement*), at whose gates they demanded freedom for their confined comrades.[171] Other protesters wanted to show their anger at distorted reporting by demonstrating against the state-run media organization, the ORTF (Office de la Radio, Télévision française). The reassertion of violent community was itself an objective. On Friday evening barricades were erected, an act that evoked memories of the Paris Commune and energized demonstrators.[172] To obstruct police advances, protesters overturned parked cars and cut down trees, despite objections from more moderate UNEF and UEC militants. One demonstrator recalled: "A few of us objected—without much energy— to barricades built from newly cut trees. We were then mocked and insulted by those who believed that a tree on a barricade might save the life of a man. Imbeciles! The contrary would have been nobler."[173]

Less ecologically or aesthetically concerned participants argued the *ouvriériste* position that confiscated vehicles might belong to a member of the proletariat. The argument had some plausibility since proletarian cars, such as the Deux Chevaux or the Renault Dauphine, were more easily overturned than bourgeois BMWs or Mercedes. Radical demonstrators were nevertheless determined to show their disrespect for the "sacrosanct car," the most vaunted object of consumer society and the commodity whose utility and symbolism appealed most to wage earners.[174]

Yet no one wanted to alienate the workers. A broad spectrum of protesters—Maoists, Trotskyites, Christian progressives, 22 March activists— fervently desired that proletarians join them. *Ouvriérisme*—not hatred of orthodox Communism—united them.[175] During the first Night of the Barricades (10 May) rumors circulated that "20,000 workers" were about to arrive from working-class neighborhoods to rescue the besieged demonstrators in the Latin Quarter.[176] An older worker who was present responded coldly to this bit of dreaming with mature skepticism and common sense: "The workers," he informed the young radicals, "are sleeping."[177] Georges Séguy would correctly point out that workers are not mobilized in the middle of the night. Nevertheless, the bulk of protesters, including "reformists," found it absolutely necessary "to ally with the working class," even if some demonstrators were skeptical of the *ouvriérisme à la con* (idiotic workerism) of the Maoists. The latter advocated a university admissions quota of 50 percent for the sons of wage earners and peasants and several months per year of hard agricultural and industrial labor for each student.[178] The "Chinese" saw their primary task as explaining to workers that the movement was against the bourgeoisie. There is, however, little evidence that the "Chinese" were influential among proletarians of the *banlieue*, despite the Maoists' triumphant claims that workers in the suburbs greeted their message enthusiastically. Police estimated that their demonstration at Saint-Denis in the afternoon of 9 May drew only three hundred persons.[179] Maoists did not understand that the youth who gravitated to the Latin Quarter were attracted less by their pleasure-denying workerist ideology than by participation in the violent community that fought police and property with fire and stone.

On the night of 10–11 May, police assaulted barricades in the Latin Quarter. In the ensuing street battles, at least 400 (including 274 police) were injured and over 500 arrested. Two hundred cars were scorched or vandalized. Police were particularly brutal to young people of both sexes and recognizable foreigners. Officers savagely undressed a young girl and tossed her unclothed into the street.[180] Helmeted and inventive street fighters responded by downing well-equipped CRS with cobblestones. They occasionally pushed an unmanned automobile down a hill into a congregation of the forces of order. Police continued to restrain their use of firearms but were generous with beatings and tear gas. The noxious fumes suggested to protesters a bond between their antirepressive struggle and worldwide anti-imperialism. Indeed, the UNEF claimed that the Americans had previously tested in Vietnam the varieties of gas that French police were using for the first time against Parisian demonstrators. On 14 May in the National Assembly, leftist and centrist deputies—including Mendès-France—demanded a parliamentary inquiry into police usage of gas. Yet the employment of gas, however toxic, may have avoided needless fatalities. Throughout May and June, police continued to hold their fire, thereby minimizing the death toll.[181] Plainclothes inspectors monitored their colleagues to make sure that they did not violate the order not to use guns.[182]

Neither students nor police believed their battles to be "symbolic" or "imaginary," as analysts have claimed.[183] After all, demonstrations and demonstrators could—and often did—make symbolic points peacefully. For example, on Wednesday, 8 May, police estimated that ten thousand persons marched from the Faculté des Sciences (Halle aux vins) to the Place Edmond-Rostand and dispersed without incident or arrest.[184] The barricades of 1968 shared with their nineteenth-century predecessors a lack of military effectiveness. In June 1848, despite the monumentality of certain barricades, an ineffective localism prevailed when "the insurgents barricaded their own quarters and attempted to defend them."[185] Unlike the rebels of 1968, who occasionally undertook a local offensive, those of

1848 remained almost exclusively on the defensive. Nor was the Commune more efficient. Its barricades "were thrown up in a pell-mell and panicky fashion, often to the detriment of their own lines of communication, patched out of the urban detritus of upturned vehicles and old furniture as well as paving stones."[186] By 1871 barricades had a representational and symbolic aspect that linked revolutionaries to previous revolts.[187]

Certainly compared to other milestones of the revolutionary tradition—1789, 1848, 1871—violence was minimal in 1968. The relatively low death toll can be partially attributed to the fact that unlike 1848 and 1871, protesters were not armed members of the National Guard. Furthermore, by the 1960s the French state's monopoly over firearms was virtually complete. Demonstrators' (and counterdemonstrators') access to guns was severely limited, and they resorted to more primitive and less dangerous weapons. Parade marshals, informers, and ordinary citizens would immediately report firearms' possession, whether by protesters or counterprotesters, to police.[188] Sometimes their information, often derived from café or restaurant conversations, was false. For instance, a 21-year-old informer, an employee of the Saclay nuclear facility, overheard a conversation in a restaurant among three students who said that they were planning a bazooka attack on the Elysée Palace.[189] In addition to a weapons monopoly, by 1968 the French state had forged a professional force of riot police—CRS and Gendarmerie Mobile—who, unlike the regular and amateur soldiers of the Second Republic and the Paris Commune, were trained in techniques of crowd control without recourse to firearms.[190]

On Monday, 6 May, "barricade building" was "novel" yet amateurish, but by 10–11 May police deemed that "barricade construction was much more methodical."[191] The percentage of non-students involved rose from 5 percent on 3 May to 60 percent during 10–11 May, the "First Night of the Barricades."[192] The forces of order in the line of fire requested more protection for their men and machines.[193] Protesters' repeated launchings of Molotov cocktails created "a true terrorism" for them.[194] Activists congregated at night, when the police presence was lightest, to build the most formidable barricades. For example, during the afternoon of 10 May, 3,865 policemen (including 1,200 CRS) were on duty; at night only 446 (including 120 CRS) were officially scheduled to patrol. Several initial barricades were built with burning automobiles.[195] The barricade at the rue R. Collard turned "six vehicles into a blazing mass ... to obstruct our [police] access."[196] The noise of a jackhammer uprooting the pavement disrupted the silence of the darkness. Between 10:00 P.M. on 10 May and 2:00 A.M. on 11 May "important barricades" were built at the intersection of the rue Gay-Lussac and the rue d'Ulm.[197] A commissioner learned that "they were composed of the most heterogeneous materials which had been taken from a nearby construction site.... Sharp objects were dispersed on the streets along with boards with nails protruding. Wires were stretched across the road ... and gasoline was spread over the ground immediately in front of the barricade on rue Gay-Lussac. A very large number of demonstrators, most of whom wore helmets, manned the barricades."

The commissioner estimated that 400 "young people" garrisoned these fortifications. At 1:15 A.M. he and his men, composed of two companies of CRS (approximately 240 men), attempted to reach the Place du Panthéon by the rue d'Ulm but were blocked by a "very solid, well-manned, and well-organized barricade. An apartment house in front of the barricade harbored numerous demonstrators who possessed all types of primitive projectiles. At the same time, we risked being taken from behind by the young people of the first barricade." That night during his peregrinations through the Latin Quarter, he encountered more barricades composed of cars jumbled together at the intersection of the rue Cardinal Lemoine and the rue Monge. At the rue Thouin and the rue Descartes, his men assaulted the fortification with tear gas but were met "by a rain of cobblestones and pieces of scrap-iron coming from both street fighters and neighboring buildings." Police could not detain these mobile fighters, who had planned their escape well by retreating to another barricade at the rue Thouin and the rue de l'Estrapade. *Flics* who tried to capture it from behind found their access stymied by other barricades and their path obstructed by cars that crammed the narrow and steep streets. Advancing police became targets of Molotov cocktails "which burned along the side of the buildings." Firemen had difficulty entering the area. A police official plausibly contended: "There was a danger that the whole neighborhood might go up in flames." At other barricades in the Latin Quarter, "cars were burning ... everywhere firemen had difficulty approaching and extinguishing the flames that were threatening to burn down everything in the neighborhood."[198] Finally, at 5:30 A.M. CRS captured the rue Thouin barricade, but most of its defenders had already scattered into surrounding buildings. Only 25 arrests were made, and the commissioner admitted: "It is impossible to swear that these [arrested] individuals were really manning the barricades." Only one of the 25 possessed weapons (a Molotov cocktail and bolts). However, two boxes of Molotov cocktails were found at the barricade. At another fortification, police confiscated a rifle used to smoke out foxes and badgers.[199] The majority of those apprehended were between 20 and 25 years old, and only 9 of the 20 whose identity cards were checked acknowledged being a *lycéen* or university student. The police commissioner believed that some escaped fighters had disguised themselves as Red Cross "medics," who "immediately invaded the barricades once they were taken. These *secouristes* (volunteers) wore a makeshift armband with 'Red Cross' hastily sketched. They were certainly protesters, but ... to avoid incidents, I let them go."

Their escape made the CRS more furious. They had worked all night, exhausted their supply of tear gas grenades, and requested as yet unavailable bulldozers to level the barricades. Other police and fire vehicles lacked sufficient protection against objects and makeshift missiles.[200] At

4:15 A.M. on 11 May, a police official urgently requested a "shipment of grenades. We had depleted our supply ... and unfortunately we could not be re-supplied.... This demonstration was really a riot whose chief characteristic was hatred of the police."[201] The forces of order suffered high casualties. In one company alone (approximately 120 men) 28 were injured, and 4 were hospitalized. Especially significant was the wounding of Commandant Journiac, who was admitted to the hospital in a "very serious state." In another company, 46 were injured, and 3 of them hospitalized. This unit admitted it was "rancorous," but improbably denied that it had committed acts of brutality. Police were especially embittered over the fact that between 10:00 P.M. and 2:00 A.M., when the strategy of the forces of order was solely defensive (i.e., to protect the Sorbonne), they were told not to halt ongoing barricade building. During this period, as Cohn-Bendit and others were negotiating with the chancellor, the forces of order could not attack. After 2:00 A.M. they were ordered to tear down the already well-fortified positions.

Authorities claimed that the results of the First Night of the Barricades were grave.[202] Twenty-two barricades were built, between 60 and 63 vehicles burned, and 125 to 128 damaged. Thousands of square meters of pavement were unearthed. Most of the destruction occurred in the fifth *arrondissement*, and protesters proved unable to extend the movement beyond the Latin Quarter. In the early morning of 11 May, police informers infiltrated Maoists on the right bank who were attempting to build a barricade at the boulevard Saint-Denis and the boulevard de Sébastopol. They were quickly stopped and arrested.[203] Official statistics established that a total of 521 arrests occurred during that night. Three hundred ninety-eight (76 percent) were French, of whom 184 (46 percent) were students and 214 (54 percent) not. Seventy-one foreigners, of whom only 20 were students, were apprehended. Fifty-two were placed in custody.[204] Two hundred seventy-four policemen were injured, including 114 CRS, 12 of whom were hospitalized. This corps suffered proportionally more casualties than the Municipal Police or the Gendarmerie Mobile, indicating that its members were either especially aggressive and/or particularly hated.

During the First Night of the Barricades (10–11 May) demonstrators received unconditional support from residents of the fifth *arrondissement*, who supplied them with food, drink, and building materials for barricades.[205] A few offered the protesters free use of their automobiles. Those who were holding the fortifications on the rue Gay-Lussac obtained wet rags or buckets of water to protect them from tear gas. This sympathy for the movement did not always coincide with practical knowledge since humidity apparently aggravated the toxic effects of certain kinds of gas. Café owners, not usually reputed for their generosity or solidarity, aided the protesters. In fact, a number of them proposed a Monday, 13 May strike of merchants and shopkeepers.[206] Polls revealed the extent of public support for students: 61 percent of Parisians felt that student demands were justified, and 71 percent favored leniency towards those arrested.[207]

The violent notoriety of the CRS (even if this corps constituted only a minority of forces on the streets) was a factor in the public's condemnation of the Pompidou government. Distrust of police momentarily overcame fear for property. Given the CRS's tarnished reputation, previous governments had been reluctant to employ them in the Paris region.[208]

Criticism of the government emerged even from members of its own majority. The Gaullist deputy of the Latin Quarter, René Capitant, thought that the government had violated academic freedom.[209] Capitant had started his political career as a member of Léon Blum's private staff during the Popular Front. A courageous *résistant*, he entered the provisional government of 1945 and introduced educational reforms promoting more student participation. After World War II, he earned a reputation as a left-wing Gaullist. In the 1960s, he pushed for legislation that aimed to establish worker participation in enterprises and promoted policies that would encourage a more equitable distribution of wealth. His plans were blocked by Prime Minister Georges Pompidou, whom Capitant—like the Communists—considered a one-time servant of the Rothschilds and a lackey of big capital. Capitant contended that the political crisis of May could be resolved if the Pompidou government resigned and de Gaulle appointed new ministers.[210] This option was seconded by the centrist Lecanuet, who intensified his criticism of the government on 11 May, the day of Pompidou's return from Afghanistan. Lecanuet demanded the immediate dismissal "of those ministers who, since they are incapable of tackling the problems to which they are assigned, resort to repression."[211] Unlike Capitant, though, he attributed the crisis to de Gaulle's "excess of personal power."[212] The Independent Republicans, represented by Michel Poniatowski—the right-hand man of Valéry Giscard d'Estaing—and four other deputies of the Paris region, condemned the "brutal police repression unworthy of a democracy." Rebuke from the Independent Republicans was particularly noteworthy since the government's parliamentary majority rested upon their support. Even the FNEF denounced the government and demanded the liberation of arrested students.

Although most major Parisian dailies—with the partial exception of *Le Monde*—had been critical of the students from 2 May to 11 May, they unanimously condemned police brutality after the First Night of the Barricades.[213] Police authorities considered *Le Monde*'s stance in favor of students particularly influential on opinion.[214] Certain university administrators also broke ranks with the government. The dean and assistant deans of the rather staid Faculté de droit et des sciences économiques "denounced the unacceptable police repression which was not in line with the need to maintain order."[215] Most importantly, the major unions—the CGT, CFDT, FO, and various teachers' unions, including the SNESup and the FEN, and even the usually conservative Confédération générale de cadres (CGC)— reacted by briefly overcoming their long-standing differences to organize not merely a street demonstration but a twenty-four-hour general strike.

The CGC had its own interpretation of events and wanted to show its solidarity with the *"cadres* of tomorrow," a position that—however prophetic—must have then embarrassed many committed students.[216] The main goal of the general strike was to protest against government repression and to demonstrate solidarity with students. The courage or boldness of protesters—combined with the excesses of police—had effectively defied the state and sparked broad unity among many sectors of the population. While the CGC, CGT, and CFDT condemned "police brutality," the unions denounced *meneurs* who engaged in gratuitous violence.[217] In particular, CGT representatives objected to the proposed presence of Cohn-Bendit at the head of the demonstration. Yet the SNESup—which had already questioned hierarchy a few days before by demanding, for the first time in the history of the Sorbonne, a general assembly of instructors of all ranks—insisted in the face of CGT opposition that no victim of repression be excluded from participation.[218]

In its dealings with other labor unions, the SNESup benefited from the favorable image of French teaching personnel. Working-class militants were often raised with special respect for teachers and professors, who, in their eyes, represented the progressive republican tradition. The teachers' union of the 1930s, the Syndicat national des instituteurs, had been conspicuously left socialist. As has been seen, many Communist students and teachers endorsed the march and the principal student demands.[219] On 11 May, *L'Humanité* ceased blaming Cohn-Bendit and *gauchistes* for the unrest and attributed to the government "total responsibility for the dramatic events" in the Latin Quarter.[220] Culpability for police repression rested on the "despotic regime of the monopolies."[221]

On the night of 11 May, Pompidou returned from his official visit to Afghanistan. Unlike de Gaulle, who favored toughness, Pompidou attempted to calm the agitation and resolve the student-state conflict by ceding to the demands of student and faculty demonstrators. He was aware that the public favored protesters and feared a bloodbath for which he might pay politically. Such was the extent of police unpopularity that he distanced himself from his own forces of order and was willing to make a deal with official student and faculty organizations. His strategy was to give into student demands and thereby eliminate all ostensible reasons for protest. If violent demonstrations continued, he calculated that even the tolerant public would eventually turn against students. Therefore, the prime minister ordered the reopening of the Sorbonne and amnesty for arrested students. The amnesty revealed the lack of independence of the French judiciary, which—like higher education and television—was almost totally dependent upon the central government. The prime minister's reversal showed his desire to compromise and the calculated tolerance of high officialdom.

Pompidou's concessions upset the police, who interpreted them as a disavowal.[222] Particularly disturbed was the Union Interfédérale des syndicats de police, one of whose components was the Syndicat général des personnels de la Préfecture de Police (SGP), which represented 80 percent of those in uniform in the Paris region. Its 13 May statement reminded the government that the chancellor of the Sorbonne had ordered police into the university with government approval. The union viewed "the declaration of the prime minister as an endorsement of the students and a total repudiation of the behavior of the government's own police."[223] In a letter to Grimaud, the secretary general of the Syndicat des Gradés de la Police nationale appealed for a declaration of support from the prime minister and the minister of interior.[224] Like General de Gaulle himself, policemen felt that they were enforcing legitimate republican order even if much of the public disagreed.

Popular animosity aggravated the *flics'* material grievances. In previous years their unions had made unsatisfied demands for pay raises, and policemen sensed that May might be a propitious time to strike. Thus, police were among the first salaried personnel to take advantage of government weakness to advance their own corporatist demands. On 16 May the minister of interior received a delegation from the Union Interfédérale des syndicats de police, which had threatened to strike if its demands for salary increases and work-rule changes were not met. Certain officers' refusal to direct traffic (thus contributing to immense traffic jams) showed that threats of a police work stoppage were not entirely idle. A week later, the Union des syndicats de police warned the government that its members might be unable to carry out their duties if authorities unwisely "pitted police against workers."[225] The right-wing proclivities of many of the rank and file did not stop police from anticipating the actions of other salaried workers. Police unions operated as opportunistically as those of the left, the CGT and CFDT.

The government quickly conceded material gains to its forces of order as it called up more of them. Police alienation declined, and the regime's resources always remained formidable.[226] Nationally, it could count on 13,500 CRS, 14,700 plainclothes officers, 54,900 uniformed policemen, and 61,000 gendarmes.[227] In Paris, 25,000 police officers were on hand. If these proved inadequate, the armed forces possessed well over 500,000 men, most of whom could be mobilized to reinforce police. On 8 May the Fédération Syndicale de la Préfecture de Police exacted reinforcements to relieve tired Parisian officers, and on 10 May CRS and Gendarmerie Mobile units arrived from Brittany.[228] Seven to eight thousand *gendarmes mobiles*—a section of the Gendarmerie, a special branch of the French military dependent upon the Ministry of Defense—were ordered to the capital in mid May. Their arrival bolstered 3,500 CRS and the 7,000 municipal police whom the national government, or more specifically its Ministry of Interior and the Paris prefect of police, paid and controlled.[229]

It is difficult to know to what degree the new lenient phase, which was characterized by Pompidou's political concessions to students and his material compromises with police, furthered participation in the general strike of Monday, 13 May. The president of the Republic envisaged the use of the army on 11 May.[230] The general did not wish to compromise with street fighters, and his commitment to the maintenance of order was well known: "A riot is like a fire. You fight it at the beginning." A few months after May, he reflected regretfully: "Nobody thinks about the state, except me.... The state must be respected and must enforce respect ... We should have arrested 500 students per day."[231] Conservative professors and other state employees concurred. Certain ministers feared that concessions to students would unleash demands by other groups. They were not surprised when the "contagion" spread.

Pompidou's concessions failed to mollify the UNEF, which insisted on a continuing struggle against the "police state" while simultaneously advocating a "radical critique of the university."[232] In general, the right and in particular, a major Parisian employers' organization—the Groupement des Industries Métallurgiques (GIM)—attributed the success of the general strike of 13 May to the *faiblesse* (weakness) of the government.[233] Whatever the verdict on the consequences of government concessions, the general strike of 13 May manifested union strength and popular distrust of police. Estimates of the crowd varied between 200,000 and 800,000, though the police repeatedly insisted that the lower figure was correct or possibly inflated.[234] One police official reported that the number of demonstrators at the Place de la République was only 70,000 but conceded that he might have underestimated the figure.[235] The demonstration—although massive—had limits. White-collar workers seem to have participated less than others. At the Assurances Générales de France, one of the largest French insurance companies, which employed over 4,000 workers at its Parisian headquarters, the march went nearly unnoticed even though the unions had a potent presence in the firm.[236] Only a few young employees—who were recent graduates from *lycées* and universities—seemed concerned with the confrontation between students and authorities.

The strike of 13 May was not, as many thought, the beginning of worker-student unity but marked its zenith. As the CGT and other mass organizations became more involved in the agitation, the influence of *gauchistes* declined. The tens of thousands of wage earners who marched reflected the modest growth of the union movement, especially the CGT, which had expanded from 1,700,000 members in 1963 to 1,900,000 in 1967.[237] Twenty thousand students, many of whom were members or sympathizers of the UNEF, FER, JCR, or CVB, attended the march. After the demonstration formally dispersed, 10,000 paraded down the boulevard de Montparnasse. Scores of these young people, whose average age was 20 to 22, brandished the black and red flags of anarchy. Police tracked their movements to the Champs de Mars, where they heard Cohn-Bendit demand the resignations of Fouchet and Grimaud.[238] The march was the biggest and most dynamic demonstration since the funeral of the victims of the Charonne demonstration in 1962.

The legend of protesters massacred by police permeated and united the marchers into a credulous community. Protesters chanted, "De Gaulle, Assassin," and "Fouchet, Assassin," and "Where have the disappeared and the dead gone?" Persistent rumors of deaths had precedents in legends in which the powerful (including, among others, priests, military, and police) murder the weak and innocent.[239] According to authorities, the Movement of 22 March propagated a 10 May tract asserting that three people had been killed during demonstrations.[240] Before the marchers of 10 May journeyed to the Santé prison, a police superintendent reported that Dany "did not hesitate to speak of blindness caused by poison gas."[241] Authorities quoted Geismar: "There have been deaths. It is impossible that there is no one dead given that so many were injured."[242] According to a police informant, Dany claimed in Berlin on 21 May that "several persons (five to eleven) were killed during Parisian demonstrations, but the French government has ordered that their deaths be kept secret."[243] At the Sorbonne, police were aware that students had initiated an investigation to determine the "identities of seven demonstrators killed during the events."[244] The tale of the seven deceased was later shown to be a fabrication. In early June, the Comité d'Action révolutionnaire distributed a tract on the boulevard Saint-Michel that claimed that "cops have introduced to the Latin Quarter and in the universities LSD, hashish, and kif [a powdery form of hash]. They are giving it out in large quantities and for free." The committee asserted that the regime wanted to promote the image of students as irresponsible druggies, not antibourgeois and anti-Gaullist revolutionaries.[245] Radicals subscribed to these legends because of their profound distrust of the state.[246]

The route of the Monday afternoon march was intended to symbolize unity of workers and students against "savage police repression."[247] It began at the Place de la République, the center of neighborhoods of the modest classes identified with the progressive tradition of the French left, and ended in the Latin Quarter of students. As the demonstration passed in front of the Palais de Justice, a few of the "hundreds of helmeted young people, some armed with cudgels … seized several tricolor flags which they burned after they tore off the red third." In the Latin Quarter an emergency vehicle carrying seven police officers, a mother, and a sick child rashly sliced through the crowd with its sirens blasting and lights flashing. It struck an unfortunate pedestrian at the Place Denfert-Rochereau.[248] Interior officials asserted that angry demonstrators surrounded the vehicle and broke its windows. Several frightened police trapped inside fired their pistols into the air. The crowd attacked them and almost lynched one policeman, who was lucky enough to be saved by the parade marshals' quick intervention. Officials were grateful to the CGT marshals for rescuing their men, and police would treat the union *manifs* gingerly throughout

May and June. Not all demonstrators were as forgiving as the CGT marshals. A crowd rendered furious by reckless driving disarmed several officers and mutilated their uniforms. Six policemen were injured and placed on sick leave. Superiors reprimanded their men: "Given the tense situation, it was unwise for the vehicle to cut through the crowd of demonstrators."[249] After the incident, police in the fourteenth *arrondissement* felt "anger" and "insecurity."[250] Authorities asserted that at the Gare d'Austerlitz, an unknown individual emerged from a group of demonstrators, tapped a police officer on the shoulder, gave him a knockout punch, and escaped into the throng.[251]

Despite these incidents, the day passed peacefully for the hundreds of thousands of demonstrators and several thousand police. Few, if any, arrests were made since union demonstrators generally respected property. Indeed, both the CGT and UNEF *services d'ordre* cooperated to limit stone throwing and to control protesters.[252] Major demonstrations were held during daylight hours, a reliable formula for avoiding violence. Violence during the day was restrained and often symbolic; at night it was unchecked and destructive. Daylight saw cooperation between police and protesters. At the occupied Faculté des Sciences (quai Saint-Bernard) police responded to a student summons to transport a mentally ill person to the hospital.[253] Until the middle of June, police refused to invade the occupied universities, where protesters could retreat, rest, eat, and make Molotov cocktails and explosives without official interference.[254] The concession of sanctuaries for protesters revealed the reluctance of the government to engage in a massive repression that might once again have united its enemies and reconsolidated a hostile public opinion. The government's tolerance of sanctuaries in May and June 1968 continued its policy of forbearance regarding radical political activity in the universities and dormitories during the early 1960s.

In addition to the presence of hundreds of thousands of anonymous trade unionists and students, elite political participation was also quite significant in the 13 May protest. François Mitterrand, Guy Mollet, and Charles Hernu represented the Socialist Fédération; Mendès-France the PSU; Waldeck Rochet, Georges Marchais, and Roland Leroy the Communist Party. Signs and banners urged "Down with De Gaulle" and demanded a vaguely defined "Popular Government" that promised a potential basis of unity for the parliamentary left. One effect of extensive political and popular participation was to convince state-controlled television—whose middle and lower-ranking personnel supported the strike in varying degrees—to cover the agitation. After 13 May, Mitterrand, Sauvageot, Geismar, and Cohn-Bendit had access to the airwaves.[255]

Police reported that although the Communists privately referred to students as *"ces cons,"* unity against "repression" obligated the PCF to accept student demands for amnesty and reopening of the Sorbonne.[256] Official Communist discourse did not deceive students, who greeted Louis Aragon with boos when he visited the Sorbonne.[257] Communists wanted to represent themselves as a (or rather the) party of order. The PCF had to consider that its long-term interests would suffer if the Party and organizations close to it became identified with disorderly students. Apparently, the CGT never displayed in any of its publications the group photo of Cohn-Bendit, Sauvageot, Geismar, Descamps, and Séguy in the front lines of demonstrators. Communists preferred to ignore that Cohn-Bendit's position at the head of the march reflected the ultra-left spark that had ignited the events. Dany called this to public attention provocatively and polemically when he stated that nothing had given him more pleasure than leading a march in which the "Stalinist scum" were relegated to the second rank. During the demonstration the PCF and an unlikely ally, the UJCml, tried to veto the unfurling of the anarchist black flag, but red and black flags nonetheless mingled for the first time in many years. Throughout May and June, both flew atop academic institutions in the Latin Quarter and other places throughout the capital. Firemen sometimes countered the symbolic challenge to the established order by taking down the subversive standards.[258]

The Monday demonstration reflected and provoked political and social unrest but did not change the plans of the president of the Republic who left on Tuesday, 14 May, for his scheduled visit to Rumania. De Gaulle's voyage demonstrated the high priority he placed on foreign affairs even, in this case, at the risk of neglecting and aggravating domestic disorder. The general's absence from the capital heightened the impression of state indecisiveness and helped to create the impression of a power vacuum. His supporters recognized that it was an unwise move, even if François Mauriac could joke oracularly: "It is true that de Gaulle's absence will be advantageous. When there is trouble we can, as before, call him back."[259] The president certainly was not afraid to inflame the situation when he defended selection on Rumanian radio: "In Rumania, you have a special entrance examination to enter the university, and you're right [to have it]. We don't, and students who cannot or will not keep up overwhelm us. It follows that they agitate. We must follow your example regarding selection."[260] His ill-timed elitism embittered the masses of egalitarian French students.

The first occupation of a Parisian university transpired on Saturday afternoon, 11 May, when several dozen students took control of Censier, the Sorbonne's annex in a back street (rue de Santeuil) of the Latin Quarter. At that time, busloads of police were guarding the Sorbonne, but Censier remained unprotected. The number of occupiers rose to two thousand during the night, perhaps in response to a radio flash.[261] Censier occupiers very quickly prohibited the news media and tourists from entering the building. Radicals distrusted the "bourgeois" press and feared media sensationalism and "recuperation," i.e., dilution and distortion of revolutionary goals. Even the revolutionary author Jean Genet was sent packing.[262]

Censier's struggle against conventional publicity had the consequence of making its occupation less well known than its counterpart at the Sorbonne. Censier's antimedia posture anticipated the occupation of the Odéon Theater, which would attract much more fame and notoriety because of its cultural and geographical centrality.

The Censier occupation quickly transcended an initial period of disorder. Although the traditional sexual division of labor persisted, the daycare center and the infirmary were efficiently run.[263] Medical students staffed the latter, which was said to have "worked perfectly." Donations were solicited to feed hundreds of participants, but workers and peasants were not particularly forthcoming, although "two girls from the rue Saint-Denis," a focal point of Parisian prostitution, gave 10,000 francs. Nevertheless, Censier was eventually unable to nourish all occupiers and was forced to give priority to its own militants. Circumstances forced even those who were hostile to the establishment of privileged elites to accept discriminatory measures. Officials asserted that well-fed occupiers prepared to defend themselves with "a basket of ... Molotov cocktails."[264]

The influence of Herbert Marcuse pervaded one of Censier's action committees, Nous sommes en marche.[265] It accused the bourgeoisie of trying to integrate French workers through "false consciousness" and racism.[266] Contemporary capitalism, it argued, doubly exploited workers as wage laborers and as consumers. Advertising fostered exploitation by promoting individualism and ignoring social needs, such as lodging, health, public transportation, and education. Despite their Marcusianism, even Censier occupiers saw their main goal as attracting workers to the movement, and one of their first tracts called for worker-student unity.[267] Sympathizers claimed that Censier militants had "created a new social form: the worker-student action committee."[268] Their members quickly stormed the gates of factories, train stations, department stores, and even cafés to distribute pamphlets and to recruit wage earners for the movement. A few workers made the trek to the occupied university in search of material aid, moral support, and militant assistance. Some returned to their firms to form their own action committees. Censier occupiers' critique of contemporary consumption influenced several tracts produced by employees at the Bazar de l'Hôtel de Ville, a major department store.[269] Various strikers at another department store, Belle Jardinière, acknowledged that they "were blinded by the race for overtime.... We are dupes. We are divided, and we are stupidly dedicated to consumption."[270] Censier radicals recommended task rotation and the limitation of the work week to thirty hours as ways to overcome alienation. They advocated making available free goods and services, such as the "occupation of empty apartments [and] distribution of supermarket goods to strikers."[271] New modes of expression of popular culture in factories and offices should replace the elitist high culture dispensed by universities and theaters.

Censier's occupiers were critical about the organization of work in capitalist society, but contrary to Marcuse or the Situationists, they preserved the core of traditional productivist rhetoric. Given most militants' fixation on the working class, it is not surprising that some of them retained respect for the labor of the proletariat. In contrast to the antiwork rhetoric of the most radical theorists of the movement, Nous sommes en marche considered work "the principal human activity ... through which man expresses his social and individual humanity."[272] The Worker-Student Action Committee at Censier argued that "workers should have power since work, not money ... creates value."[273] As with the many European Maoists who imagined Chinese workers laboring happily in their factories, Censier revolutionaries continued to award an exalted place to *travail* in worker-controlled environments. In fact, they envisaged punitive measures for workers who did not "labor for society."[274] The latter would be denied any wages beyond "subsistence," and a worker who left his job would be held responsible if "chaos" ensued.

This obsession with labor and its "authentic and historical class struggle" led to ambivalence towards feminism. University students were generally unconcerned about many women's issues.[275] Nous sommes en marche asserted that feminism was based on "an absurd and impossible war between the sexes" and resulted in "alienation" and "confusion." At the same time, Censier activists were critical of notions such as "femininity" and "virility" because they failed to raise class consciousness and helped to integrate individuals into capitalist society. Nous sommes en marche recognized that the "functions of men and women are different in the sexual act," but objected to the extrapolation of this difference into other realms, especially that of the workplace. Activists praised female sexual and economic independence and believed in the sharing of housekeeping chores. They attacked the "decadent bourgeois family," marriage, the traditional couple, and heterosexual exclusivity. Although the *gauchiste* ideologies of May did not encourage specifically female emancipation, any revolution that aimed—as '68 did—to alter everyday life had the inevitable consequence of questioning traditional sexual roles. In May, the Cité Universitaire, home of approximately six thousand foreign students on the southern edge of the fourteenth *arrondissement*, abolished sex segregation.[276] The obscure Mouvement démocratique féminin advocated complete wage equality of men and women and the establishment of daycare centers to alleviate women's double burden. On 4 June a discussion on "women in the revolution" occurred at the occupied Sorbonne.[277]

May did see the quick growth of equality in one domain: after 3 May, female demonstrators were beaten as badly as male protesters and sometimes were particularly abused and humiliated. Police undressed them forcibly, pulled their hair, kicked them in the pelvic region, and labeled them "whores" and "bitches."[278] Demonstrators claimed that police raped females. It is hardly surprising that the Odéon's Anti-Repression Committee and its counterparts at the Sorbonne and Censier investigated complaints from those attacked or raped by police; however, an unlikely individual supported the charges. Colonel X, accompanied by his victimized daughter, marched into the commissariat of the Latin Quarter and showed on-duty officers the dress and stockings that their men had torn from her during the rape attempt in the woman's apartment.[279] The angry colonel filed a formal complaint, lending credence to UNEF's charges of police abuse of females.

Inspired by the occupation of Censier, students took over the Sorbonne on Monday, 13 May. In the first days, officials reported that approximately five hundred students occupied the university.[280] *Clochards* (beggars) who "were active for prosaic reasons" and hippies, whom police termed "beatniks," joined them.[281] Occupiers generously fed and lodged them, and they returned the favor by performing odd jobs. The participation of large numbers of non-students sparked objections from traditionalist male students, three of whom complained about "undemocratic" electoral procedures to the police superintendent of the Latin Quarter.[282]

Women were active and were said to have almost equaled the number of male occupiers. Their miniskirts inspired in more than one middle-aged Frenchman sentiments other than love for the revolution.[283] As at Censier, the customary sexual division of labor persisted at the Sorbonne. Female chefs prepared food, and women "volunteers" composed the cleaning brigade, which—police reported—was at least in the early weeks of the occupation quite efficient.[284] "Girls, often with more staying power and fervor than boys, typed, cut stencils, cooked, looked after children in the nursery, made beds in the improvised communal dormitories."[285] French students—unlike the American New Leftists at, for example, Columbia University—did not challenge this partition of tasks. However, it should be mentioned that in the French context, creators of good food— whether male or female—had considerable status. Its taste and smells were so enticing that a number of militants came close to believing that the revolution had really arrived. The Situationist-inspired cooking service dreamed of "a restaurant where soup is really soup. Where there are no lines, where comrade-chefs are not overworked, where champagne corks are popping happily everywhere."[286] Feminists were more critical: "No one has declared that changes in the relations among men imply changes of the relations between men and women."[287] A young married woman with two children regretted that "the revolution remained very masculine.... Women were politically inferior."[288] A young women reported: "I knew that May was over when after 24 May, a guy tried to pick me up in a hall at Censier. The old regime had returned."[289]

Sorbonne student organizations did not fear feminist criticism but rather the possibility that they would be isolated from workers' struggles. One of their first acts was to declare, "The Sorbonne is permanently opened to workers."[290] Their *ouvriérisme* promoted dreams that students and wage earners would join to abolish the repressive bourgeois state and to construct a nonhierarchical society of *autogestion*. The Situationist-inspired Council for the Maintenance of Occupations demanded workers' councils and fantasized that the agitation would open the way for a proletarian revolution.[291] Non-Situationists on the occupation committee concurred with their rivals: "The essential task of students is to support the workers' struggle against the regime."[292] The occupation committee of the Sorbonne tried to prefigure a classless society by demanding the revocability of all elected representatives. Not everyone agreed that the occupied Sorbonne was run democratically. Traditionalist students complained that the voting procedure—raising hands in public—was intimidating and demanded a secret ballot.[293] Police noted that a dozen young people controlled entry into the occupied *faculté*.[294]

The occupation committee seized the opportunity presented by the collapse of authority to attempt to construct the longed-for "workers' university."[295] Most of the *groupuscules*—JCR, UJCml, and pro-Situationists—that were active during the Sorbonne occupation reiterated the themes voiced by Nanterre radicals: The university was a class institution dominated by the bourgeoisie. Thus, professors served as educated cops who trained future managers of capitalist society. Only a working-class revolution could liberate the university and create a nonrepressive society. On 15 May in a general assembly of sociology students, 328 voted for (compared to 85 against) a "university for workers."[296] On 20 May, in the midst of a growing strike wave, the general assembly of the Sorbonne agreed to boycott "the capitalist university" and once again insisted that students link up with workers. Others—specifically an action committee that called itself The Unknowns—went further and argued that the student movement should dissolve itself into the workers' movement. The UNEF advocated a "real union with workers' and peasants' struggles" and censorship for publications with "false information."[297] At Nanterre in early June, the commission, Culture et Contestation, declared the university open to "all workers." Its goal was to combat the consumerist "subculture" dispensed by the bourgeois media and to liberate authentic (i.e., revolutionary) working-class discourse. Nanterre students congratulated themselves for making a solid contribution to the revolution by "connecting themselves to the workers' struggle against capitalist society."[298] Widespread *ouvriérisme* became completely uncritical. For instance, students approved unanimously tracts introduced by workers who had made the pilgrimage to the Sorbonne. A Renault wage earner who came to speak to a Sorbonne assembly embarrassed his reverential audience into silence by remarking at the beginning of his talk: "What? You applaud even before I speak. You must be *cons*."[299]

Wage earners were unquestionably the most exploited group, but students also considered themselves oppressed. That examinations in May and June could only take place under police guard bolstered radicals' interpretation of the university as a coercive institution. *Gauchiste* leaders—Krivine,

Cohn-Bendit, and Sauvageot—felt that adherence to the normal exam schedule would mean the end of the movement.[300] The UNEF, Movement of 22 March, and the action committee of Censier considered exams to be the "repressive" keystone of the university system.[301] Examinations were for students what wages were for workers. Testing was part of the pleasure-denying bourgeois culture that encouraged competitive individualism. It served "only to exclude students who were victims of failed teaching."[302] Exams did not measure merit but rather class background and social conformity. By eliminating students, they aided selection and discriminated against the poor.[303] Only a social revolution could resolve the "problem" of exams. In the meantime, the solution was to strike, not to study: "To exams, respond with questions."

At the same time, the inability to administer exams in May aroused student anxieties. The disturbance of academic routine and the postponement or cancellation of examinations worried those who feared they would lose a semester's credit. This prospect was particularly troublesome for serious students from modest backgrounds who lacked the resources to repeat courses. A similar split between radicals and moderates occurred nearly simultaneously at Columbia University.[304] Activists at Nanterre and the Sorbonne were aware of this dilemma and to resolve it proposed innovative exams, which were to be administered in the fall semester, on the nature of "repression." A longer-term solution was that examinations be replaced by the "constant testing of knowledge" in seminars. These were to be staffed by massive numbers of instructors and teaching assistants who would be chosen collectively by their peers. Radicals outbid PCF demands for a more generous budget and wished to establish the seeds of a classless society within the university itself. Of course, the Sorbonne faculty did not entirely agree, but an assembly composed of full, associate, and assistant professors voted on 18 May to create new structures that would allow for student participation in university decision-making.

Professors sympathetic to the movement—such as Pierre Bourdieu, Pierre Vidal-Naquet, and Jacques Monod—supported the demand for the elimination of traditional exams. They also lamented the bourgeois and antiworker nature of higher education. Institutions needed "democratization" and concerted efforts to minimize the inheritance of social class.[305] Some professors learned the hard way that overtures to the student movement did not guarantee its sympathy. As at Nanterre, teachers became objects of derision and abuse. Given the radical analysis that *profs* acted as the management team of the bourgeois university, this lack of respect was not surprising. During a general assembly at the Sorbonne, one instructor asked the audience whether it had confidence in him. Someone in the crowd responded, "I am not your student, and I don't [have confidence]. Here you don't have the right to speak to us as inferiors."[306] Another professor engaged in a pathetic *autocritique*: "You are making a revolution that we did not have the courage to undertake." Such toadying did not protect the speaker from abuse, and a student replied, "We don't ask our teachers to be more demagogic than we are."

Some students maintained a proletarian internationalism that often held uncritical opinions toward Third World revolutions.[307] Algeria, Cuba, and China were not analyzed but admired. More positively, foreign workers and students were defended—at least verbally—from the control and repression of the bourgeois state. Proposals from action committees included the abolition of the *carte de séjour* (French green card) and the elimination of all official borders. American students present at the Sorbonne joined in condemning the "bourgeois imperialist societies" of France and the U.S. Internationalism and attacks on the nation-state encouraged regionalists from Brittany, Corsica, and the Basque country to condemn the "colonial" and centralized French state. According to police sources, the Argentine, Spanish, Overseas French, and Greek buildings at the Cité Universitaire were occupied, and their supposedly right-wing compatriots usually expelled.[308] Portuguese students took over the Cité's Maison de Portugal and then raided its director's apartment, taking paintings, records, furniture, and even a piano with them.[309] By 14 June, they had abandoned their occupation.

The challenge to the state educational system continued to spread beyond Parisian universities. According to police, in elite *lycées*—Turgot, Henri IV, Condorcet, Charlemagne, and others in the *banlieue*—rapidly growing CALs, often dominated by the JCR and usually opposed by socialist and Communist teachers, played an active role.[310] The prefect reported that on Thursday, 23 May, certain *lycées* were occupied; a strike order by the FEN followed a week later.[311] In working-class and popular *arrondissements* (10th, 11th, 18th, 20th) nearly all daycare (*école maternelle*) and elementary schools were shut down by the strike. In more bourgeois neighborhoods, almost half the schools stopped functioning. The *école maternelle* in the third was occupied by a Parents' Defense Committee that had no intention of strikebreaking but wished to assure childcare. One hundred families (out of two hundred) managed the school with the help of *lycéens*. This and other occupations passed without incident, even though Occident threatened attacks at a few *lycées*. For example, police were informed that a dozen helmeted students armed with billyclubs attempted unsuccessfully to enter the occupied Lycée Jean-Baptiste Say in the sixteenth.[312]

Protest encompassed nearly all cultural institutions, including the state-controlled mass media. On 17 May, Geismar and Sauvageot called for a march on ORTF. Communists opposed the plan, fearing that the government would use force rather than tolerate an occupation of the means of wireless communication. In any case, authorities concluded that the UNEF and SNESup changed their objective when ORTF agreed to let student leaders speak on television.[313] This branch of the state's cultural apparatus was obviously more immediately influential than the universities.[314] Communist fears were not exaggerated, and as early as 15 May police were sent to "protect"—i.e., to empty—ORTF buildings.[315] According to police, the unions of ORTF had called a meeting of their adherents and had screened 900–1,000 persons to make sure that no students or outside agitators were among them. Members then voted overwhelmingly against occupation.[316] Nevertheless, fearing the worst, authorities rushed several hundred CRS and a few plainclothes officers to the ORTF studios to ensure that the national transmission tower remained under government control.[317] Police cooperated very closely with management to screen entry into ORTF offices.[318] On 19 May, officers received orders to remove thirty-one strikers who were occupying the second floor of the Buttes Chaumont building.[319] Strikers left after police threatened force, but these heavy-handed tactics estranged many broadcasting employees. By 21 May, 70 percent of ORTF personnel at Buttes Chaumont had voted to strike, and hundreds of police remained stationed around ORTF offices.[320] Under pressure from alienated ORTF personnel and a dissatisfied public, the government allowed, for the first time, live TV coverage of the National Assembly's debate on 21–22 May.[321] Pompidou criticized radio stations not controlled by the government—RTL (Radio, Télévision Luxembourg) and Europe One—for encouraging demonstrations. According to the prime minister, private broadcasters had propagated militancy, not information.[322] Pompidou was correct that independent reporting challenged the spin of the state channels, but there was no question that their complacency needed challenging.

The most striking and enduring cultural legacy of May remains the posters produced by Parisian art students. Poster images offer insights into an ideologically complex student movement by reflecting many of its "isms": corporatism, libertarianism, internationalism, antifascism, anti-imperialism, and anticapitalism. Most importantly, they were *ouvriériste*. The faith in the transformative might of the working class became the major theme of revolutionary art. The art of the revolution lends little support to those who argue that May was fundamentally an individualist rebellion or a crisis of civilization.[323] Instead, it shows that the traditional focus on the working class by activist artists and other militants constrained individualist impulses in 1968. Artists never signed their posters; thus their identity remained hidden. In effect, students denied the uniqueness and individuality of a work of art by asserting that it merely mirrored sociological and historical reality. This basic argument of Marxist (and structuralist) cultural theory was—like the revolutionary role of the working class—uncritically accepted by poster producers. Its simplistic reductionism and exaggerated glorification of the social did not prevent students from creating powerful images. The role of the artist—and approximately three hundred of them participated, including some who were very accomplished—should be to "work in the Atelier populaire … to support the striking workers who occupy their factories against the anti-popular Gaullist government."[324] All—whether French or foreign—who wished to accept the rules of the game and put themselves at the service of the working class were welcomed. For example, the sense of design of participating Latin American artists was highly appreciated.[325]

Agitation had quickly affected Parisian art students.[326] By 8 May, the Ecole Nationale des Beaux-Arts was on strike. Art students formulated their own grievances against an institution well known in certain quarters for the inadequacy of its teaching.[327] Students complained that they no longer wanted professors "who spend fifteen minutes per week at school to evaluate student paintings.... We want teachers who are here and know how to teach."[328] On 14 May, the day after the massive demonstration of students and workers against state repression, student strikers in the lithography workshop produced the first poster, which predictably called for unity between workers and students. A general assembly of 15 May attacked the principle of selection and demanded freedom of the university from bourgeois control.[329] Painters, who occupied their studio on 16 May, wrote over its entrance "Atelier populaire: Oui. Atelier bourgeois: Non." Desiring to participate in collective struggles, they rebutted what they considered the bourgeois ideology of individual creation that fostered "aggressive and irresponsible competition."[330] "Bourgeois culture" created the illusion of artistic freedom, but, they lamented, in a capitalist society, supply and demand—not quality—determined aesthetic value. For the students, real culture was a product of group, not individual, effort: "To work on one's own personal idea, even if correct, is to remain within the narrow boundaries of bourgeois creation."[331] Their general assembly selected posters according to two questions. The first, "Is it politically correct?" was topical and communitarian. The second, "Does it convey its idea well?" was more aesthetic.[332] Every submission had to undergo a collective critique, or what we might more frankly call censorship, and was altered according to group criticism. Such tight control frightened a few but was nevertheless maintained. An important exception was made for designs produced by workers. The dominant *ouvriérisme* guaranteed their acceptance without criticism.[333] The students' stated goal of creating images that all workers could easily understand discouraged some bold and experimental ideas.

The occupation of the Beaux-Arts and the art that it produced served as a model for other Parisian institutions, such as Arts-décoratifs, and for provincial art schools at Marseilles, Caen, Strasbourg, Amiens, Grenoble, Montpellier, and Dijon.[334] Prominent activists regarded the Atelier populaire as an exemplary "active strike," where the influence of "lumpen" and Bohemian elements was kept to a minimum.[335] The Atelier's policies won the acclaim of other organizations. The Union des Arts Plastiques rejected "the formulation of the Bohemian artist" in favor of building a new society in which "art will no longer be a luxury but rather a permanent and daily reality."[336] Creation had to have a social, i.e., a useful, meaning. Citing the Soviet author Vladimir Maiakovsky, students believed that "art is not art for the masses when it is born but only after enormous efforts. We must teach understanding."[337]

Posters (and photographs) were the primary visual representation of the revolt, which—like its predecessors—fostered the development and expansion of new and old forms of expression. The poster form signaled the desire to reach the public without the mediation of the marketplace and reflected the activists' hostility toward the commodity. Like tracts and even radical newspapers such as *Action*, the *affiches* (posters) were distributed without charge.[338] A nation where universal male suffrage had been in effect throughout much of its late modern history fought its political struggles visually. The Great Revolution had seen increasing use of printed images to appeal to the crowd. Anonymous popular artists contributed disparaging portraits of the monarchy, Church, and nobility. The politicization of images motivated postrevolutionary governments to control them tightly. For instance, his caricatures of King Louis Philippe earned Honoré Daumier a prison term. The reappearance of mass suffrage at the end of the nineteenth century further stimulated the poster tradition. Progressives encouraged poster production to propagate republican ideals.[339] The persistence of democratic republics in France assured that political parties would campaign using images. In universities prior to May, militants displayed their ideas on bulletin boards or hung pictures of Trotsky, Ché, or Mao. These visual references were internationalist, not republican.[340] The right and the center would effectively monopolize the republican symbols of the tricolor, Marianne, and the "Marseillaise."[341]

There was a broad public, if not a market, for the posters. Originally, the plan was to display the works at a sympathetic gallery, but instead students and other volunteers spontaneously decided to glue them to city walls, thus bypassing the commercial network entirely.[342] Workers were sometimes responsible for distributing posters that supported strikes in their own factories. The poster regained the significance that it had once achieved in the nineteenth century because strikes disrupted the daily production and distribution of other media, particularly newspapers and television, which were sometimes unfriendly to students. The closure of national and municipal museums at the end of May and during the first week of June transformed city walls into the principal Parisian artistic forum. The spirit of protesters was hostile to conventional exhibitions and museum culture. Police sources stated that approximately fifty young people abandoned the occupied Sorbonne for the Musée d'Art Moderne in the sixteenth *arrondissement* and left tracts calling for its permanent closure and a banner reading "closed for uselessness."[343] Sympathy in the art world for the movement was considerable. On 24 May, sixty artists belonging to the Parisian Union des Arts Plastiques endorsed "student protest and working-class struggle." Twenty-four dealers, whose profession depended upon the commodification of art, nevertheless signed a petition supporting "the fight of students and workers" and promised to distribute the posters without profit for themselves.[344] Among them were some of the most prestigious galleries in France, a number of which offered donations to the student movement. So did—at least according to police—numerous architects.[345]

The most popular posters of the approximately 700 that were designed were reproduced in quantities of 2,000 to 3,000, thereby diluting the originality of the work of art.[346] By encouraging job rotation, the occupation began to breakdown the traditional—but not sexual—division of labor. Famous artists did not just design posters but also distributed them. Yet the more democratic and unsupervised organization of labor led to a situation in which an unscrupulous but shrewd poster-hanger, who believed that art as a commodity would survive the revolution, hoarded his quota of posters for sale at a later date.

An analysis of the content of the posters revealed the continuation of the customary *ouvriérisme* of the French left. In the most complete published collection, 123 posters focused on workers' issues, whereas, only 23 were concerned with students.[347] Examination of a smaller published collection showed a similar obsession with worker actions: 78 involved wage earners and only 7 concentrated on the student movement.[348] In another published collection, 56 posters centered on the workers' struggle compared to 3 that focused on university student activities.[349] Students placed themselves "at the disposal of the workers."[350] Posters with the caption "Down with Speed-Ups" were some of the first to be massively printed (figures 1 and 2). Even though artists feared that the CRS or fascists would

FIGURE 1: "Down with Speed-Ups," version 1

FIGURE 2: "Down with Speed-Ups," version 2

attack the atelier of the ex-Beaux Arts, they were told to "stop making posters about repression since good ones have already been created" and dedicate themselves to supporting the proletariat. By the end of May, individual strikers or representatives of strike committees were approaching the artists and asking them for graphic assistance. Artists gave their time and talent to support work stoppages in the major nationalized firms—Renault, PTT, ORTF, SNCF, RATP (figures 3 and 4). Reflecting the weight of large enterprises in the French economy of the 1960s, the struggles of strikers in small firms were the subject of only a tiny number of *affiches*. The call for worker-student unity (figure 5), the focus of 25 posters in the largest published collection, was treated more often than the student movement itself (22 posters).[351]

Internationalism and the encouragement of an alliance between French and foreigner inspired over two dozen *affiches*. The most famous image of internationalist solidarity was a picture of Cohn-Bendit with the caption "we are all undesirable [aliens]." The caption had originally been "We are

FIGURE 3: "Renault Flins"

FIGURE 4: "Solidarity with the Postal Workers' Strike"

FIGURE 5: "The Same Problem, the Same Struggle"

all Jews and Germans," but, according to one historian, had been changed because it seemed "too violent" (figure 6).[352] There may be another explanation for the modification. Militants were primarily interested in class, not ethnicity or religion. Thus, "undesirable alien" was an appropriate substitute for "Jew" because it evoked a venerable tradition of left internationalism and implied solidarity with foreign workers and students. To the committed, what was significant about Cohn-Bendit was not his Jewishness but that, like other foreigners who participated in demonstrations and strikes, he might be (and was) expelled. Indeed, it may be the case that activism in extreme-left movements was a way for some Jews to become assimilated into French society.[353]

FIGURE 6: "We are all Jews and Germans. We are all Undesirables"

Posters focusing on individuals were relatively rare. Cohn-Bendit was one of the few who inspired visual admiration; de Gaulle, of course, was the person who was the object of most visual attacks. He was ridiculed because he symbolized the political power of the older generation, whereas Dany was admired because he represented engaged youth. In the largest published collection, attacks against the general and his government were found in sixty posters. Artists militarized the president of the Republic by depicting him with his general's *képi* (figure 7). They equated—with the hyperbole typical of the period—the Fifth Republic with Franco's or Salazar's military dictatorships. Militant Gaullists and even the general himself were portrayed as fascists. If today this treatment seems excessive, conservatives too were guilty of rhetorical excess when they labeled the

FIGURE 7: "Be Young and Shut Up"

student rebels "left-wing fascists." Of course, the CRS were identified with the SS and seen as the epitome of the forces of darkness (figure 8). Like priests in the nineteenth century in their clerical garments, helmeted and uniformed CRS in the twentieth were easily recognized and ridiculed. A tract distributed in the Latin Quarter suggested that students make police look ludicrous and laughable.[354] Anticop drawings replaced anticlerical and antimilitarist ones.

Often, though, de Gaulle was derided more than hated. The most effective images made him appear ridiculous rather than fearsome and recalled Daumier's caricatures of Louis Philippe (figure 9). They mocked his description of the demonstrators as *chienlit*, an archaic term that made the general seem out of touch and totally unhip. At its best, there was something *bon enfant* about this revolutionary art. Posters occasionally avoided the *langue de bois* and the militant but mindless sloganeering of the French revolutionary tradition.[355] They could be witty and playful with images and words. For example, artists protested against the forced end of the Beaux-Arts occupation by producing an image captioned, "La police s'affiche aux Beaux-Arts, les Beaux-Arts affichent dans la rue" (figure 10). One poster punned, "De Henri IV à de Gaulle: 1 poulet par habitant."[356] Another played with a Rousseauian theme: "La volonté générale contre la volonté du général." Referring to the pre-May government reform of the health insurance system, which had increased the financial contribution of workers and therefore aroused the opposition of the major trade unions, one poster declared, "Les médecins peuvent faire des ordonnances, les

FIGURE 8: "CRS = SS"

FIGURE 9: "The *Chienlit* Is He"

gaullistes non!" Cows gathered at the Centre d'Intoxication Civique (a play on the name of the Gaullist paramilitary group, Service d'Action Civique) were ordered to "*veautez*" for the UDR. The posters' humor lessened some of the "belligerent realism" of much of the earlier poster art of the left.[357] Their appeal mirrored the popularity of irreverent humor magazines such as *L'Enragé* or *Le Canard Enchaîné*. Artists effectively employed irony and caricature against the class enemy. Even though they sometimes broke with a socialist realist style, the posters remained, as in the 1930s, largely fixated upon workers.

LA POLICE S'AFFICHE AUX BEAUX ARTS

LES BEAUX ARTS AFFICHENT *dans la* **RUE**

FIGURE 10: "The Police Show Up at Beaux Arts. Beaux Arts Shows in the Streets"

In terms of quantitative output, antirepression themes were second to solidarity with workers. Artists defined repression very broadly to include, in addition to selective admissions policies, the "obligation to execute and learn without discussion, the impossibility to express oneself, inhibitions and traumatisms, mutilation of creative capacity, stereotyped modes of thinking."[358] Artists also protested against government control of the mass media. The largest published collection contained more posters on the media than on the student movement itself. In an unpublished collection, the number of posters critical of the mass media equaled the number of those supporting workers.[359] Image makers challenged what they considered to be distorted coverage of events by the state-controlled channels. Posters supported the strike of unionized ORTF employees who were

protesting against government censorship and demanding a more independent and autonomous television channel (figure 11). Barbed wire
symbolized the tight state control of the official media.

Perhaps because of the reduced ascendancy of the Chamber during the
Fifth Republic, published collections have underestimated antiparliamen-
tarianism. Yet it remained virulent among militants and artists (figure 12),
especially after de Gaulle's radio speech of 30 May in which he announced
new legislative elections while threatening to unleash once again police
and even army repression.[360] Activists felt that in a capitalist society the
bourgeoisie, not the working class, would inevitably control elections.
Revolutionary artists used *détournement* to mock electoral politics. They
changed the late 1950s anti-alcoholism advertising campaign slogan from
"Quand les parents boivent, les enfants trinquent" to "Quand les parents
votent, les enfants trinquent." *Détournement* of advertising was another
example of hostility to the commodity and the marketplace.

What the posters ignored revealed as much as they depicted. They sanitized movement violence by neglecting arson and other attacks against
property. Only cobblestones reminded viewers of youth violence. Visual
attacks usually omitted Pompidou, which again reflected the frequency of
collectivist, not personal, concerns. The omission was an indication of the

FIGURE 11: "ORTF Fights"

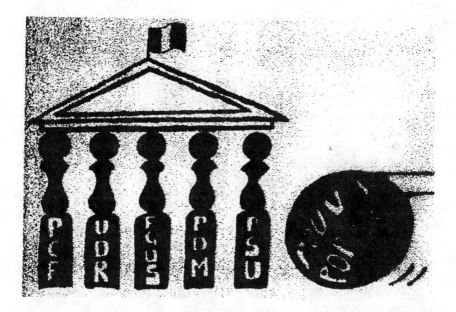

FIGURE 12: "Popular Power"

prime minister's success, which would be crucial for his political future, in avoiding identification with what many saw as government incompetence in early May. De Gaulle, not Pompidou, became the strikebreaker, the Clemenceau or Cavaignac of May. Unemployment was not a major concern for artists, who referred to it in only a handful of posters. The relative lack of anxiety about joblessness reflected the economic prosperity of the late 1960s, although two approved slogans—"Halte au chômage" and "le capitalisme c'est la planification du chômage"—echoed the fears of many humanities and female students, the most likely "victims" of unemployment. The desire for a peasant-worker alliance appeared in only a handful of pictures. The low number is not surprising given that the social movement—whether worker or student—was overwhelmingly urban and largely ignored peasant problems. As in 1848 or 1871, rurals were usually indifferent or hostile to urban disorder and resented what they perceived as student privilege.[361]

Despite nearly universal opposition to the American presence in Vietnam, anti-American sentiment appeared in only a few published posters. Antiwar demonstrations may have helped to spark the movement but were not its raison d'être. Anti-imperialism, however, continued to act as a cement among leftists. One poster asked, "What are you doing to fight hunger?" and responded earnestly to its own question, "I struggle against imperialism." The *lutte* of the *lycéens*, pictured in a handful of posters, was not of major interest to revolutionary artists. Feminist or ecologist demands, which originated early in the "long" 1960s, were completely absent.[362] Their omission showed that the May events—often assumed to be the apex of the 1960s and its most representative expression—were indifferent to some of the central developments of postwar Western culture. The political issues of May temporarily eclipsed the protection of mother earth and the glorification of mothers and daughters. No Joan of Arc or Marianne was created. Instead, creators, who were male, remained preoccupied with the virile worker and his factory. Consequently, several posters depicted strikebreakers and anti-union workers as "scabs" and not real men: "Somebody who profits from a victory without fighting for it is not worthy to be called a man." If hints of anticonformism (and revolutionary condescension) pervaded an image that depicted the mass who were returning to work as a flock of sheep (figure 13), group—not individual—struggles were the principal concern of creators. The visual production of May does not sustain the argument that the May rebellion prepared the terrain for the individualistic and hedonistic 1980s.

The reception of the posters remains a generally unexplored topic. Many on the right undoubtedly dismissed them as leftist propaganda, but some appreciated a humor that recalled the Dada movement.[363] A police official in the eighteenth *arrondissement* called three—"Flic à Flins—Flics chez Vous," "La Police à ORTF, c'est la Police chez Vous," and "La Détente s'amorce"—"posters of a new type" despite their uniformly anticop messages.[364] ORTF strikers so appreciated the poster designs that they reproduced them on pins and badges and sold them to support their strike.[365] The non-committed may have regarded posters indifferently or were as impervious to their message as they were to advertising. Sympathetic observers thought that the images made the streets more festive. They moved and inspired activists, which was exactly what their creators intended. A barricade builder who was close to the Movement of 22 March found them "ferocious and tender, so rich and clear, as amusing (and effective) as a Molotov cocktail in the yellow face of a cop. This raw art marks the end of the galleries of the left and right banks. Its slogans were poetic and as beautiful as windows that one opens after making love … [Here is] the blossoming, for the first time in this country, of revolutionary art."[366] To the appreciation of militants was added the sympathy of the great artists— Pablo Picasso, Alexander Calder, and Max Ernst—who condemned police brutality and proclaimed solidarity with students. Aesthetes appreciated the posters' creativity and vitality.

An outburst of street art accompanied poster production. *Enragés*, Situationists, anarchists, and anonymous graffiti artists spray-painted more than two thousand slogans on the Sorbonne and elsewhere in the city. They had temporarily triumphed over police in the war of walls. Their scrawling expressed the main libertarian, libertine, and antiwork themes of the French May much better than the posters. The satisfaction of libidinal desires had top priority: "The more I make love, the more I feel like

FIGURE 13: "Return to Normal"

making the Revolution; the more I make the Revolution, the more I feel like making love." "If we don't fuck, they'll fuck us." "I came in the cobblestones." "Come without obstacles." "The Revolution stops as soon as you must sacrifice for it." "Those who work are bored when they don't. Those who don't work are never bored." "Live without dead time."

The cultural agitation inevitably spread to the theater. According to police, on 15 May students of the National Conservatory of Dramatic Art (ninth *arrondissement*) formed an action committee and sequestered the school's director, who "could not leave until he promised that he would resign. They ... are planning to occupy the Comédie Française and the Odéon theaters."[367] At 11:30 P.M. that night, as spectators were leaving, a group of fifty students invaded the Odéon National Theater and occupied center stage.[368] Numerous young people quickly arrived, and by midnight four thousand were present. They raised the red flag on the pediment and placed at the entrance a banner: "The Odéon is closed to a bourgeois audience." At midnight, two to three hundred persons occupied the National Conservatory of Dramatic Art and the National Conservatory of Music.

Cultural revolutionaries wanted to take over other theaters.[369] A high-level police official reported that the CRAC (Comité révolutionnaire d'agitation culturelle) initiated a campaign against what it branded as bourgeois civilization at both the Odéon and the Sorbonne. It had disrupted three private theaters and threatened to intrude on others throughout the capital.[370] A cynical but perhaps perceptive police commissioner who dabbled as art critic commented: "On June 5 a group of mediocre artists constituted a Revolutionary Committee and occupied the Pacra Theater of the Marais. Since that time they have performed plays."[371] The forces of order were prepared to intervene if management requested them. Even though many theater professionals were hostile to the occupation, support was robust and numerous enough to halt a scheduled police operation to evacuate the Odéon.[372] General de Gaulle and other high-ranking members of the government had approved an aggressive initiative in which 870 police and firefighters, armed with high-pressure hoses, planned to empty the Odéon premises of sit-down strikers on the night of 19–20 May. However, the Syndicat des comédiens endorsed the occupation, and, it was believed, prominent celebrities—M. Piccoli, S. Frey, and R. Rouleau—intended to be present. In addition, the potential resistance of the two to three thousand persons inside gave police second thoughts. Fearing a public relations disaster— which again showed the reluctance of public opinion to tolerate overt "repression" in mid May—the government canceled the operation. The suspension showed notable patience and timing.[373] The government tried but failed to engineer an occupation by the theater's technical personnel, whom it trusted more than youthful protesters and their supporters.

Objectives at the Odéon repeated those at other occupied institutions: to link up with the working class, end capitalism, and inaugurate a classless society. Only the first of these grand designs met with any success. Occupiers almost immediately approved a motion: "The Odéon has stopped being a theater. It has become a meeting place for workers."[374] Protesters banned performances of "commodity-spectacles" and planned to develop a collective and revolutionary art. "The only theater," they argued, "was guerrilla." The only art was that of combat.[375] Jean-Jacques Lebel, whose happening had sparked unpredictable results at Nanterre, was one of those who promoted the takeover. His performances attracted hundreds, who were perhaps expecting a repetition of his well-known sexual scandals.[376] The theater was opened to everyone (except rightists, police, and other so-called representatives of the bourgeoisie).[377] The celebrated director and actor Jean-Louis Barrault, who had headed the theater before the takeover, told occupiers, "I am in complete agreement [with you]." Making his own critique of the *vedettariat* (star system) and reigning cultural hierarchy, Barrault resigned as director and proclaimed himself "an actor like others. Barrault is dead." Barrault's new role was particularly annoying to the minister of culture, André Malraux, who disliked the spread of the movement from its university base into his own cultural arena. Malraux would exact his revenge by firing him a year later. A narcissistic Italian actress told the revolutionary audience that she would no longer participate in show business and refused to become "a consumer commodity that inspires millions of viewers to masturbate."[378] Slogans conveyed the same message: "We don't linger on the spectacle of protest, but we protest the spectacle." According to one activist, "One of the primary goals of the 'cultural revolution' is the destruction of the star system.... Long live the anonymity of Gothic cathedrals and Hindu temples. Art is an expression of the most profound, essential, and cosmic forces. The individual is only an instrument.... When the instrument is exalted, what is transmitted is diminished."

Like the visual artists of the Atelier populaire, the occupiers of the Odéon adopted practices that enforced artistic anonymity. After debate, the theater's assembly agreed that bourgeois journalists would be permitted inside, but they were forbidden to request individual interviews, take photo portraits, or even to report individual names. So-called revolutionary artists who had become celebrities—even those such as Paul Taylor's troupe, which had earned accolades in New York and Havana—found that their avant-garde credentials were no protection against hostile criticism. The May strikes had left Taylor's company without funds, and he appealed to the occupiers to permit his troupe to perform. If it could not, he implored the crowd, financial problems would force it to leave France. Taylor's pleading was met with a hostile reception from a pitiless audience, a number of whom shouted back that they—unlike Taylor and his company—had always been penniless. For those who made a critique of the "commodity-spectacle," no form of show business, no matter how apparently progressive, qualified as revolutionary. Instead of regular performances and exhibitions, actors were encouraged to engage in street theater and photographers to record police repression during demonstrations. The narrowness of the assignments showed that the Odéon radicals were quite capable of formulating their own updated version of socialist realism.

Recognized bourgeois—however well intentioned and sympathetic to students—who ventured into the ex-Odéon risked insult. The fashionable author Françoise Sagan was told to leave the theater: "We absolutely refuse to greet the spy of the capitalism of the sixteenth *arrondissement*. Go back to your Ferraris, to your whiskey, and to your orgies."[379] Sagan recounted her own version of the confrontation: while in the ex-Odéon, a long-haired individual who was using a loudspeaker recognized her and sarcastically asked, "Have you come in a Ferrari, comrade Sagan?" "No," the best-selling author replied, "it's a Maserati." Police officials, who fancied themselves amateur art critics, had an even more antagonistic view of the proceedings: "A permanent debate where many tendencies are manifest continues. All kinds of artists express their resentment of a society whose principal fault seems to be to have ignored their talent."[380]

As soon as the Odéon occupation began, a newly created *service d'ordre*, who wore red armbands, controlled entry into the theater.[381] To prevent a possible assault by the extreme right, Odéon occupiers stationed armed lookouts on the roof.[382] Nevertheless, police reported that a young male threw several gas grenades that slightly injured a person leaving the theater.[383] Inside, the *service d'ordre* zealously imposed respect for health and safety regulations, such as a ban on smoking and maintenance of basic hygiene.[384] Administrators' offices were strictly off-limits, and no damages were initially reported. However, Odéon occupiers were reluctant to follow rules. Debates and discussions sometimes degenerated into disorder since many wished to speak at once. Elementary safety measures came to be ignored.[385] Prohibitions on smoking in the attractive wooden ex-theater and limitations on the number of people in the balcony met with resistance from a crowd that took the slogan "It is forbidden to forbid" more seriously than most. Those with a sense of responsibility counterattacked cleverly to achieve results: "Urination prohibited in the halls under penalty of confiscation of material." Humor, though, was ineffective against fire, and authorities stated that one had broken out in the basement the day after the occupation began.[386] Three companies of firefighters needed an hour to put out another basement conflagration.[387] Several weeks later, a third blaze, which police believed was intentional, started in a bunch of rags.[388] Again, firemen rushed to the scene.

By 1 June the occupation had largely ended, and only approximately thirty persons, whom police termed "hard-core elements," remained in the theater at night.[389] By that time, the Odéon had accumulated an "unbelievable mess."[390] Its infirmary made anti-crab lice inspections mandatory. Some of the hippies, beggars, and homeless people who found shelter in the ex-theater confiscated costumes and jewelry for their own personal use. Militants debated whether to tolerate marijuana, hashish, and LSD. One historian reported that "every night six or seven young people" were brought to the Odéon infirmary for drug abuse treatment.[391] This seems highly unlikely since the numbers of occupants declined drastically during the night. The assertion shows that the image of '68 perpetuated notions of unlimited freedom. Unconfirmed reports circulated describing free love and orgies in the basement: "In the improvised dormitories of the fourth floor, people made love in chorus, joyously, without complications. Girls, who were good housekeepers, cleaned up the rooms, which, in contrast to the rest of the building, remained immaculate until the end."[392] A graffito announced, "Aimez-vous les uns sur les autres." The "scandal" of the Odéon was that activities that were usually private or nocturnal occurred in broad daylight. Stories of orgies may have been exaggerated, but they showed that many continued to identify the supposed political-social-cultural revolution of 1968 with unrestricted sexual freedom.

The police narrative of the occupation of the Maison des Jeunes et de la Culture at Fresnes lends limited justification to this identification.[393] Antony students and a few *lycéens* had seized it on 21 May and renamed it the Maison Autonome des Jeunes. As in other occupations, daytime residents (200–300) far outnumbered night-time inhabitants. Some activities—Ping-Pong and dancing—were innocuous. However, "numerous infractions of mores occur daily. The oldest don't restrain themselves in front of minors of fifteen years." Occupiers invited speakers who were members of the Movement of 22 March or anarchists. Some of these guests might have inspired instructors to offer a course on the making of Molotov cocktails. Cinema equipment was damaged. Thefts at the Monoprix and Familprix chain stores provided free meals. The left-wing municipality did not dare to re-establish order, and even though the Maison's board of directors wanted to clear the building, they also feared calling in the police.[394] As in the early 1960s at nearby Antony, permissiveness at Fresnes expanded and profited from generalized qualms concerning police repression.

By almost all accounts, the attempt to establish a nonrepressive society at the Odéon, the Sorbonne, and other institutions encountered obstacles.[395] Ideologies of *autogestion* did not ensure efficient management of occupied institutions. As at the occupied Milan University, a happy anarchy, which some saw as a precursor of the future society, coexisted with unhealthy conditions and the threats of sabotage and violence.[396] A movement that originated in solidarity against repression found it hard to be repressive against its own supporters. At the Sorbonne, the manufacture of Molotov cocktails to oppose a possible siege by police defied "bourgeois legality."[397] Early in the morning of 20 May, a fire broke out among the old papers stored in the basement of the university.[398] Authorities reasoned, "It seems that it was set voluntarily by students who could not stop it from spreading." Firemen arrived and noted the destruction of several chairs and benches. Five companies of *pompiers* responded to another blaze that flared on the fourth floor of the university in the archives of the Academy of Paris and severely damaged its roof.[399]

Students and their followers occupied many institutions and streets of the Latin Quarter, where they held property and commodities under incendiary siege. The sympathy and tolerance of the public, which the government was loath to alienate, permitted them to control major cultural spaces. Workers too would profit from expanding permissiveness and radical audacity to take action at their workplaces or to avoid them altogether.

Notes

1. See Henri Lefebvre, *The Explosion: Marxism and the French Revolution*, trans. Alfred Ehrenfeld (New York, 1969), 117.
2. The statistics are from Pierre Bourdieu and Jean-Claude Passeron, *Les Héritiers: Les étudiants et la culture* (Paris, 1964), 73–75.
3. Jean-Philippe Legois, *La Sorbonne avant mai 68* (Mémoire de maîtrise, Paris I, 1993), 163–164.
4. Priscilla Robertson, *Revolutions of 1848: A Social History* (Princeton, 1952), 29. Mark Traugott, "The Crowd in the French Revolution of February, 1848," *American Historical Review*, vol. 93, no. 3 (June, 1988): 638–652, downgrades the student contribution.
5. John C. Gallaher, *The Students of Paris and the Revolution of 1848* (Carbondale and Edwardsville, Ill., 1980), xii; Roger Price, *The Second French Republic: A Social History* (Ithaca, 1972), 164.
6. Cf. Lewis S. Feuer, *The Conflict of Generations: The Character and Significance of Student Movements* (New York and London, 1969), 265. Feuer claims that students started the Revolution of 1848.
7. André Coutin, *Huit siècles de violence au Quartier latin* (Paris, 1969), 285.
8. René Viénet, *Enragés et Situationnistes dans le mouvement des occupations* (Paris, 1968), 41.
9. Le commissaire du 5e, 2 May 1968, Fa 278, Archives de la Préfecture de Police, Paris [henceforth APP]. Police found ax handles and a tear gas grenade in the office.
10. 3 May 1968, Fa 248, APP; La crise de mai, 24 June 1968, AN 800273/61; Union Nationale des Etudiants de France [and SNESup], *Le livre noir des journées de mai* (Paris, 1968), 8.
11. La crise de mai, 24 June 1968, AN 800273/61.
12. See Stephen J. Pyne, *World Fire: The Culture of Fire on Earth* (New York, 1995), 14–15.
13. Jean Bertolino, *Les Trublions* (Paris, 1969), 13; Jean-Raymond Tournoux, *Le mois de mai du général* (Paris, 1969), 350; Viénet, *Enragés*, 45.
14. 4 May 1968, Fa 248, APP.
15. Jean-Claude and Michelle Perrot, Madeleine Rebérioux, and Jean Maitron, *La Sorbonne par elle-même*, special issue of *Le Mouvement social*, no. 64 (July–September, 1968): 36.
16. 1 May 1968, Fa 278, APP. Lucien Rioux and René Backmann, *L'Explosion de mai* (Paris, 1968), 302, denied that Occident had any influence on events.
17. Ministère de l'Intérieur, Direction générale de la Police nationale, renseignements généraux, Bulletin mensuel, September 1968, AN 820599/89.
18. 8 May 1968, Fa 252, APP.
19. Direction générale de la Police nationale, renseignements généraux, Bulletins quotidiens, 10 May 1968, AN 820599/40.
20. 3 May 1968, Fa 278, APP.
21. 4 May 1968, Fa 248, APP.
22. Adrien Dansette, *Mai 1968* (Paris, 1971), 90. Their defenders claimed that only an old table was damaged. See UNEF, *Le livre noir*, 12.
23. 3 May 1968, Fa 278, APP.
24. Directeur-Général de la police municipale à M. le préfet de police, « Objet Manifestation au Quartier Latin, 3 mai, » 4 May 1968, Fa 248, APP.
25. Arthur Marwick, *The Sixties: Cultural Revolution in Britain, France, Italy, and the United States, c. 1958–c. 1974* (New York, 1998), 606.
26. Luisa Passerini, *Autobiography of a Generation*, trans. Lisa Erdberg (Hanover and London, 1996), 99.
27. Jacques Durandeaux, *Les journées de mai 68: Rencontres et dialogues* (Paris, 1968), 142.
28. Jean-Pierre Duteuil, *Nanterre 1965–66–67–68: Vers le Mouvement du 22 mars* (Paris, 1988), 214; Mouvement du 22 mars, *Ce n'est pas qu'un début, continuons le combat* (Paris, 1968), 23; Dansette, *Mai*, 91; Jacques Baynac, *Mai retrouvé* (Paris, 1978), 29.
29. Bertolino, *Trublions*, 33; Pierre Andro, A. Dauvergne, L. M. Lagoutte, *Le mai de la révolution* (Paris, 1968), 27; Philippe Labro, ed., *Ce n'est qu'un début* (Paris, 1968), 65.

30. 4 May 1968, Fa 248, APP; Journée du 6 mai, Fa 250, APP.
31. Quoted in Baynac, *Mai*, 33–34.
32. On the police in the Sorbonne in February 1964, see Alain Monchablon, *Histoire de l'UNEF de 1956 à 1968* (Paris, 1983), 156. Cf. Kristin Ross, *May '68 and Its Afterlives* (Chicago, 2002), 29, who states that police had "never before … violated that sanctuary."
33. Le chef du premier district, 6 May 1968, Fa 250, APP.
34. Mouvement du 22 Mars, *Début*, 57.
35. Jacques Perret, *Inquiète Sorbonne* (Paris, 1968), 27; Journée du 6 mai, Fa 250, APP.
36. "La liberté volée," *Esprit*, no. 373 (August–September, 1968): 189; Alain Schnapp and Pierre Vidal-Naquet, *Journal de la commune étudiante* (Paris, 1969), 49, 664.
37. Perrot et al., *La Sorbonne par elle-même*, 50.
38. 15 May 1968, AN 820599/75.
39. 4 May 1968, Fa 248, APP; Maurice Grimaud, *En mai, fais ce qu'il te plaît* (Paris, 1977), 83.
40. 4 May 1968, Fa 248, APP.
41. Dansette, *Mai*, 91. Figures in Tournoux, *Mois*, 351, are 596 arrested, 24 injured, including 4 policemen; Bertolino, *Trublions*, 34; Baynac, *Mai*, 33; 10 May 1968, AN 820599/40; 4 May 1968, Fa 248, APP.
42. 4 May 1968, Fa 248, APP.
43. Cited by Duteuil, *Nanterre*, 220.
44. Danielle Tartakowsky, *Le pouvoir est dans la rue* (Paris, 1998), 162.
45. Duteuil, *Nanterre*, 216; Bertolino, *Trublions*, 47; Dansette, *Mai*, 95; Marc Kravetz, ed. *L'Insurrection étudiante* (Paris, 1968), 98.
46. Labro, *Début*, 81.
47. 4 May 1968, Fa 278, APP.
48. Quoted in Kravetz, *L'Insurrection étudiante*, 85.
49. 8 May 1968, AN 820599/75.
50. David L. Schalk, *War and the Ivory Tower: Algeria and Vietnam* (New York, 1991), 174; Benjamin Stora, *Histoire de la Guerre d'Algérie 1954–1963* (Paris, 1993), 64.
51. Bulletin mensuel, August 1968, AN 820599/89.
52. 7 May 1968, AN 820599/40.
53. Quoted in Labro, *Début*, 183.
54. Bertolino, *Trublions*, 42; Hervé Hamon and Patrick Rotman, *Génération*, 2 vols. (Paris, 1987), 1: 424; Schnapp and Vidal-Naquet, *Journal*, 402; Dansette, *Mai*, 110.
55. Manifestations, 3 May 1968, Fa 248, APP.
56. 6 May 1968, Fa 249, APP.
57. Ibid.
58. Tournoux, *Mois*, 331.
59. Pierre Grappin, *L'Ile aux peupliers* (Nancy, 1993), 256; Guy Michaud, *Révolution dans l'université* (Paris, 1968), 34.
60. Duteuil, *Nanterre*, 218.
61. Tract reproduced in Viénet, *Enragés*, 260–261.
62. Cited in Duteuil, *Nanterre*, 219.
63. Tract reproduced in Viénet, *Enragés*, 262.
64. Quoted in Patrick Seale and Maureen McConville, *Red Flag Black Flag: French Revolution 1968* (New York, 1968), 65.
65. 4 May 1968, Fa 278, APP.
66. Duteuil, *Nanterre*, 220; Dansette, *Mai*, 96; 5 May 1968, Fa 249, APP; Perrot et al., *La Sorbonne par elle-même*, 39; Christian Charrière, *Le Printemps des enragés* (Paris, 1968), 89.
67. Baynac, *Mai*, 50.
68. 8 May 1968, AN 820599/75; 6 May 1968, Archives de la brigade de sapeurs-pompiers de Paris, confirms the disorder.
69. 6 May 1968, AN 820599/40.
70. Schnapp and Vidal-Naquet, *Journal*, 200; Dansette, *Mai*, 96; Viénet, *Enragés*, 53.
71. 31 May 1968, Fa 263, APP.

72. "La Faculté de Nanterre de 1964 à 1968, Entretien avec Pierre Grappin," in Geneviève Dreyfus-Armand and Laurent Gervereau, eds., *Mai 68: Les mouvements étudiants en France et dans le monde* (Nanterre, 1988), 104.

73. 5 May 1968, Fa 249, APP. During the early 1970s in Italy, this type of low-grade terrorism would take more violent forms against factory supervisors. See Robert Lumley, *States of Emergency: Cultures of Revolt in Italy from 1968 to 1978* (London and New York, 1990), 281.

74. 8 May 1968, Fa 252, APP.

75. 17 May 1968, Fa 257, APP.

76. 5 May 1968, Fa 249, APP.

77. 10 May 1968, AN 820599/40.

78. Kravetz, *L'Insurrection étudiante*, 149; see also Robert Davezies, ed. *Mai 68: La rue dans l'église* (Paris, 1968), 28; Grégory Barrau, *Le mai 68 des catholiques* (Paris, 1998), 38.

79. 18 May 1968, AN 820599/40.

80. 21 May 1968, Fa 259 APP.

81. 22 May 1968, Fa 259, APP; Yaïr Auron, *Les juifs d'extrême gauche en mai 68* (Paris, 1998), 138.

82. Perrot et al., *La Sorbonne par elle-même*, 54–57.

83. Kravetz, *L'Insurrection étudiante*, 146; Seale and McConville, *Red Flag*, 78.

84. 10 May 1968, AN 820599/40.

85. Dansette, *Mai*, 112.

86. Danielle Tartakowsky, "Le PCF en mai–juin 1968," paper presented to Colloque acteurs et terrains du mouvement social de 1968, 24–25 November 1988, Paris.

87. Perrot et al., *La Sorbonne par elle-même*, 45–47, 61.

88. Schnapp and Vidal-Naquet, *Journal*, 201–205; Perrot et al., *La Sorbonne par elle-même*, 58–66; Pierre Peuchmaurd, *Plus vivants que jamais* (Paris, 1968), 24.

89. Kravetz, *L'Insurrection étudiante*, 388.

90. 6 May 1968, AN 820599/40.

91. 7 May 1968 and 10 May 1968, AN 820599/40; 8 May 1968, AN 820599/75. Cf. Alain Touraine, *The May Movement: Revolt and Reform*, trans. Leonard F. X. Mayhew (New York, 1979), 165: "During that week [3–10 May] violence was rarely excessive."

92. 15 May 1968, Fa 263, APP.

93. 6 May 1968, Fa 250, APP.

94. 7 May 1968, Fa 250, APP.

95. Journée du 6 mai, Fa 250, APP.

96. Kravetz, *L'Insurrection étudiante*, 453.

97. 7 May 1968, Fa 250, APP.

98. 6 May 1968, Fa 250, APP. The massive use of tear gas on 6 May is confirmed in the Archives de la brigade de sapeurs-pompiers de Paris.

99. 7 May 1968, Fa 250, APP.

100. 8 May 1968, Fa 274, APP.

101. Monday, 6 May 1968, Fa 249, APP.

102. 13 May 1968, Fa 251, APP.

103. Seale and McConville, *Red Flag*, 73.

104. Baynac, *Mai*, 53.

105. Gaston Bachelard, *The Psychoanalysis of Fire*, trans. Alan C. M. Ross (Boston, 1964), 102–104; Johan Goudsblom, *Fire and Civilization* (London, 1992), 1.

106. On the denial of arson and the claim that the police set the fires, see UNEF, *Le livre noir*, 84. Grimaud, *Mai*, 156, furnishes the official response.

107. Gay L. Gullickson, *The Unruly Women of Paris: Images of the Commune* (Ithaca, 1996), chap. 5.

108. André-Jean Tudesq, "La radio, les manifestations, le pouvoir," in *Mai 68 à l'ORTF* (Paris, 1987), 140; Andro, *Mai*, 122. For an extremely insightful essay, see Evelyne Sullerot, "Transistors et barricades," in Labro, *Début*, 124–140.

109. Baynac, *Mai*, 58. Cf. the interpretation of Dansette, *Mai*, 97, which argues that the demonstrators' attitude towards the National Assembly signified the relative unimportance of the legislature in the Fifth Republic.

110. Mouvement du 22 mars, *Début*, 119; Andro, *Mai*, 47; Dansette, *Mai*, 97; Baynac, *Mai*, 59; Kravetz, *L'Insurrection étudiante*, 278; *Débats de l'Assemblée Nationale: Seconde session ordinaire de 1967–1968*, 14 May 1968 (Paris, 1969), 1769.

111. 14 June 1968, Fa 251, APP.

112. 8 May 1968, Fa 251, APP.

113. Ibid.

114. 7 May 1968, Fa 251, APP.

115. Ibid.

116. 8 May 1968, AN 820599/75.

117. Ibid. This document claims that only 22 officers were hurt. See also Journée du 7 mai, Fa 251, APP; 13 May 1968, Fa 251, APP.

118. 8 May 1968, Fa 251, APP.

119. Ibid.

120. 15 May 1968, Fa 256, APP.

121. 16 May 1968, Fa 257, APP.

122. 18 May 1968, Fa 258, APP.

123. 30 May 1968, AN 820599/40; 20 May 1968, Fa 258, APP.

124. François Duprat, *Les journées de mai 68: Les dessous d'une révolution* (Paris, 1968), 160.

125. 21 May 1968, Fa 259, APP.

126. 19 May 1968, Fa 258, APP.

127. 21 May 1968, Fa 259, APP.

128. 22 May 1968, Fa 259, APP.

129. Schnapp and Vidal-Naquet, *Journal*, 201.

130. Séguy quoted in Claude Prévost, *Les étudiants et le gauchisme* (Paris, 1969), 154.

131. Quoted in Charrière, *Printemps*, 102.

132. Schnapp and Vidal-Naquet, *Journal*, 208; Perrot et al., *La Sorbonne par elle-même*, 65.

133. Charrière, *Printemps*, 113; Schnapp and Vidal-Naquet, *Journal*, 198; Alain Monchablon, "L'UNEF et mai 1968," in Dreyfus-Armand and Gervereau, *Mai 68*, 4. For an account that differs slightly, see Baynac, *Mai*, 56.

134. Kravetz, *L'Insurrection étudiante*, 211.

135. Perrot et al., *La Sorbonne par elle-même*, 84.

136. 21 May 1968, AN 820599/40; 29 May 1968, AN 820599/40.

137. Baynac, *Mai*, 63; Juliette Minces, *Un ouvrier parle: Enquête* (Paris, 1969), 50; Peuchmaurd, *Vivants*, 33.

138. Quoted in Kravetz, *L'Insurrection étudiante*, 230, 261–262.

139. Manifestations, 8 May 1968, Fa 252, APP.

140. Dansette, *Mai*, 109. "L'Explosion de Mai," *France-Forum*, no. 89 (July–August, 1968), 14, thought that use of the word "repression" had become obsessive.

141. Préfet de Paris à Ministre de l'Education Nationale, 14 June 1968, Ministère de l'Education, Direction des collèges, AN 790793; Journée du 8 mai, Fa 252, APP.

142. 8 May 1968, Fa 252, APP.

143. Préfet de Paris à Ministre de l'Education Nationale, 14 June 1968, AN 790793.

144. Louis Astre of the FEN in *Matériaux pour l'histoire de notre temps*, no. 20 (July–September, 1990): 51; *Mai 68 par eux-mêmes: Le mouvement de Floréal, an 176* (Paris, 1989), 41. On similar Italian developments, Lumley, *States of Emergency*, 94–100.

145. 10 May 1968, AN 820599/40; 9 May 1968, Fa 252, APP.

146. Philippe Bauchard and Maurice Bruzek, *Le syndicalisme à 1'épreuve* (Paris, 1968) 71; Roger Martelli, *Mai 68* (Paris, 1988), 60.

147. Direction générale de la Police Nationale, renseignements généraux, Bulletins quotidiens, 10 May 1968, AN 820599/40.

148. 10 May 1968, AN 820599/40; 16 May 1968, AN 820599/40.

149. Kastler quoted in Labro, *Début*, 83.
150. Charrière, *Printemps*, 115–123; Andro, *Mai*, 55; Bauchard and Bruzek, *Syndicalisme*, 71; Kravetz, *L'Insurrection étudiante*, 274, 301.
151. 16 May 1968, Fa 257, APP.
152. Declaration of 11 May, cited in 16 May 1968, AN 820599/40.
153. Baynac, *Mai*, 78.
154. 29 May 1968, Fa 263, APP.
155. 16 May 1968, Fa 263, APP.
156. 11 June 1968, Fa 263, APP.
157. 7–10 May 1968, Fa 263, APP.
158. 9 May 1968, Fa 252, APP.
159. 10 May 1968, Fa 252, APP.
160. Ibid.
161. 15 May 1968, Fa 256, APP.
162. Ibid.
163. Ibid.
164. 17 May 1968, Fa 257, APP.
165. 20 May 1968, Fa 258, APP.
166. Quoted in Labro, *Début*, 103; *Débats de l'Assemblée Nationale*, 14 May 1968, 1773.
167. 15 May 1968, Fa 256, APP.
168. Letter quoted in Labro, *Début*, 115, and reproduced in Grimaud, *Mai*, 341–343.
169. Mouvement du 22 mars, *Début*, 27–29; Perrot et al., *La Sorbonne par elle-même*, 80.
170. Journée du 10 mai, Fa 253, APP.
171. In fact, the arrested demonstrators were in the Fresnes jail. See Andro, *Mai*, 61.
172. Peuchmaurd, *Vivants*, 50: "La première commune libre depuis 1871." Mouvement du 22 mars, *Début*, 67; Dansette, *Mai*, 127; Kravetz, *L'Insurrection étudiante*, 325; Baynac, *Mai*, 80.
173. Claude Raimon-Dityvon, *Mai 68* (Paris, 1988), 72.
174. Schnapp and Vidal-Naquet, *Journal*, 432; Wolfgang Ruppert, "Zur Konsumwelt der 60er Jahre," in Axel Schildt, Detlef Siegfried, and Karl Christian Lammers, eds., *Dynamische Zeiten: Die 60er Jahre in den beiden deutschen Gesellshaften* (Hamburg, 2000), 758.
175. Cf. Dansette, *Mai*, 353: "There existed among these rival sects [of *gauchistes*] no other cement than that of hatred of orthodox communism."
176. Labro, *Début*, 141; Peuchmaurd, *Vivants*, 43.
177. E. S. [Evelyne Sullerot?] in Labro, *Début*, 142.
178. Peuchmaurd, *Vivants*, 39–53; Kravetz, *L'Insurrection étudiante*, 484; Davezies, *Mai 68*, 30–42.
179. 9 May 1968, Fa 252, APP.
180. Tournoux, *Mai*, 63–64. Some of the most aggressive street fighters may have been *agents provocateurs*. See Paco Rabanne's eyewitness account in Gilles Caron, *Sous les pavés la plage* (Sèvres, 1993), 91; Perrot et al., *La Sorbonne par elle-même*, 92.
181. W. Rabinovitch, "Contribution à la sociologie des masses en mouvement," *Revue internationale de criminologie et de police technique*, no. 3 (July–September, 1968): 209.
182. Ibid.
183. Raymond Aron, *La révolution introuvable* (Paris, 1968), 87–88; Alain Corbin, "Préface," in Alain Corbin and Jean-Marie Mayeur, eds., *La barricade* (Paris, 1997), 21; Michel de Certeau, *La prise de parole: Pour une nouvelle culture* (Paris, 1968), 14; Ingrid Gilcher-Holtey, *Die 68er Bewegung: Deutschland-Westeuropa-USA* (Munich, 2001), 83.
184. 9 May 1968, AN 820599/40.
185. Price, *The Second French Republic*, 178.
186. Rupert Christiansen, *Paris Babylon: The Story of the Paris Commune* (New York, 1996), 349.
187. Mark Traugott, "Barricades as Repertoire," in Mark Traugott, ed., *Repertoires and Cycles of Collective Action* (Durham and London, 1995), 51.
188. 23 May 1968, Fa 259, APP; 28 May 1968, Fa 260, APP.
189. See 8 June 1968, Fa 271, APP. The assault never occurred.

190. Patricia O'Brien, "The Revolutionary Police of 1848," in Roger Price, ed., *Revolution and Reaction: 1848 and the Second French Republic* (London, 1975), 143; John Roach, "The French Police," in John Roach and Jürgen Thomaneck, eds., *Police and Public Order in Europe* (London, 1985), 107–142.

191. Bulletin mensuel, May–July 1968, AN 820599/89.

192. Bulletin mensuel, September 1968, AN 820599/89. Police figures vary. Other statistics posit 54 percent non-students.

193. 10 May 1968, Fa 250, APP. Police believed that "la pègre" had joined spontaneously with students. 24 June 1968, AN 800273/61.

194. 24 June 1968, AN 800273/61.

195. Première nuit des barricades, 10–11 May 1968, Fa 253, APP.

196. 11 May 1968, Fa 253, APP.

197. 17 May 1968, Compte-Rendu … dans la nuit 10–11 mai, Fa 253, APP. Firemen confirmed police charges on 11 May 1968, Archives de la brigade de sapeurs-pompiers de Paris.

198. Première nuit des barricades, 10–11 May 1968, Fa 253, APP. The Archives de la brigade de sapeurs-pompiers de Paris are silent on this issue.

199. 14 May 1968, Fa 253, APP.

200. Commissaire, 10 May 1968, Fa 253, APP.

201. 11 May 1968, Fa 253, APP.

202. The following is from 10–11 May 1968, Fa 253, APP, and 11 May 1968, Fa 256, APP.

203. 11 May 1968, Fa 253, APP.

204. Journée du vendredi 10 mai, Fa 253, APP. Figures on foreigners are somewhat different in Daniel A. Gordon, "Immigrants and the New Left in France, 1968–1971" (Ph.D. diss., University of Sussex, 2001), 116.

205. Peuchmaurd, *Vivants*, 51; Mouvement du 22 mars, *Début*, 123; Charrière, *Printemps*, 135; Perrot et al., *La Sorbonne par elle-même*, 89; Patrick Ravignant, *L'Odéon est ouvert* (Paris, 1968), 148; Kravetz, *L'Insurrection étudiante*, 411.

206. Perrot et al., *La Sorbonne par elle-même*, 89.

207. Dansette, *Mai*, 113.

208. Ch.-A. Hirsch, "La police dans la tourmente," *Revue internationale de criminologie et de police technique*, no. 3 (July–September, 1968): 220.

209. Kravetz, *L'Insurrection étudiante*, 319.

210. Tournoux, *Mois*, 109.

211. Lecanuet quoted by Jean Charlot, "The Aftermath of May 68 for Gaullism, the Right, and the Center," in D. L. Hanley and A. P. Kerr, eds., *May 68: Coming of Age* (London, 1989), 77.

212. This and the following quoted in Kravetz, *L'Insurrection étudiante*, 365–366, 420.

213. Odile Aubourg, "La presse contaminée: *France-Soir, Le Monde, L'Humanité* et *Le Figaro*," in Dreyfus-Armand and Gervereau, *Mai 68*, 243.

214. 24 June 1968, AN 800273/61.

215. Quoted in Dansette, *Mai*, 392.

216. Quoted in Alfred Willener, Catherine Gajdos, and Georges Benguigui, *Les cadres en mouvement* (Paris, 1969), 38.

217. Guy Caire, "La situation sociale," *Droit social*, no. 7–8 (July–August 1968): 453; Michel Johan, "La CGT et le mouvement de mai," *Les Temps modernes*, no. 266–267 (August–September, 1968): 329.

218. Geismar cited in Labro, *Début*, 189.

219. Perrot et al., *La Sorbonne par elle-même*, 96–101; Tartakowsky, "Le PCF."

220. Marc Goldstein, "Le Parti communiste du 3 mai au 6 juin 1968," *Les Temps modernes*, no. 269 (November, 1968): 850. Attacks against Cohn-Bendit were renewed after 13 May.

221. PCF Bureau Politique, 12 May, quoted in Prévost, *Les étudiants*, 158.

222. Hirsch, "La police," 221.

223. Quoted in Labro, *Début*, 101.

224. 13 May 1968, Fa 263, APP.

225. André Sernin, *Journal d'un bourgeois de Paris en mai 1968* (Paris, 1988), 62.

226. Cf. Rioux and Backmann, *L'Explosion*, 384.

227. *Le Monde*, 25 May 1968.

228. 14 May 1968, Fa 263, APP.

229. Labro, *Début*, 104–109; Dansette, *Mai*, 103. Gilles Martinet, *La conquête des pouvoirs* (Paris, 1968), 20, states that police, gendarmes, and CRS in the capital numbered 100,000. This seems exaggerated. Bernard Kouchner and Michel-Antoine Burnier, *La France sauvage* (Paris, 1970), 250, report that in 1970 in Paris, there were over 25,000 police officers, 2,250 of whom had been recruited since 1969.

230. Dansette, *Mai*, 130; Tournoux, *Mois*, 29.

231. De Gaulle quoted in Dansette, *Mai*, 106–107. See also Perret, *Sorbonne*, 33; Tournoux, *Mois*, 73.

232. Dansette, *Mai*, 133.

233. Grève politique du 13 mai, 3 October 1968, Groupement des Industries Métallurgiques, Neuilly [hereafter cited as GIM]. See Dansette, *Mai*, 138; see also Jean Rochet, *Cinq ans à la tête de la DST* (Paris, 1985), 70–90, which also argues that the movement was a result of Pompidou's lack of firmness.

234. 14 May 1968, AN 820599/40.

235. 14 May 1968, Fa 255, APP.

236. Henri Simon Oral History Project, 1994. I wish to thank Mr. Henri Simon for conducting these interviews with workers on my behalf.

237. Martelli, *Mai*, 56. Figures are probably exaggerated but nonetheless demonstrate growth.

238. 14 May 1968, AN 820599/40.

239. Véronique Campion-Vincent, *La légende des vols d'organes* (Paris, 1997), 220.

240. 10 May 1968, Fa 253, APP.

241. 11 May 1968, Fa 253, APP.

242. 16 May 1968, AN 820599/40.

243. 21 May 1968, AN 820599/40.

244. 20 May 1968, Fa 258, APP.

245. 8 June 1968, Fa 271, APP.

246. Campion-Vincent, *La légende*, 220.

247. Perrot et al., *La Sorbonne par elle-même*, 93.

248. 13 May 1968, Fa 255, APP; 14 May 1968, AN 820599/40. See also UNEF, *Le livre noir*, 93.

249. 13 May 1968, Fa 255, APP. Cf. Grimaud, *Mai*, 185, who gives a more favorable account of police.

250. 14 May 1968, Fa 263, APP.

251. 13 May 1968, Fa 255, APP.

252. 14 May 1968, Fa 255, APP.

253. 19 May 1968, Fa 258, APP.

254. 29 May 1968, Fa 266, APP; 25 May 1968, Fa 281, APP.

255. Sylvain Roumette, "Aide-Mémoire," *Les Temps Modernes*, no. 265 (July, 1968): 156.

256. 13 May 1968, AN 820599/40.

257. The writer was also jeered when he spoke to a crowd of four thousand on the boulevard Saint-Michel on 9 May. 9 May 1968, Fa 252, APP.

258. 14 May 1968, 1 June 1968, Archives de la brigade de sapeurs-pompiers de Paris.

259. Dansette, *Mai*, 443; François Mauriac, *Bloc-notes*, 5 vols. (Paris, 1993), 5: 76.

260. Quoted in Dansette, *Mai*, 187.

261. Kravetz, *L'Insurrection étudiante*, 406; Seale and McConville, *Red Flag*, 90; Baynac, *Mai*, 15.

262. Edmund White, *Genet: A Biography* (New York, 1993), 501–506, does not mention the incident.

263. Baynac, *Mai*, 127; R. Gregoire and F. Perlman, *Worker-Student Action Committees: France May '68* (Detroit, 1991), 44.

264. 15 May 1968, Fa 256, APP.

265. André Stéphane, *L'Univers contestationnaire* (Paris, 1969), has based much of his analysis on the writings of this group. Claire Duchen, *Women's Rights and Women's Lives in France*

1944–1968 (London, 1994), 209, states that the group met every evening at Censier. Its writings are partially reproduced in Schnapp and Vidal-Naquet, *Journal*, 626–637.

266. *Quelle université? Quelle société?* (Paris, 1968), 149.
267. Baynac, *Mai*, 119.
268. Gregoire and Perlman, *Worker-Student Action Committees*, 37.
269. Baynac, *Mai*, 122.
270. Tracts, 24–25 May 1968, Bibliothèque Nationale [hereafter BN].
271. Baynac, *Mai*, 196, 257.
272. *Quelle université? Quelle société?* 153–155.
273. Quoted in Baynac, *Mai*, 265.
274. *Quelle université? Quelle société?* 170.
275. See Noëlle Bisseret, "L'enseignement inégalitaire et la contestation étudiante," *Communications*, vol. 12 (1968): 65.
276. Seale and McConville, *Red Flag*, 117; Schnapp and Vidal-Naquet, *Journal*, 601; Gordon, "Immigrants," 48.
277. 5 June 1968, AN 820599/41.
278. UNEF, *Le livre noir*, 14–75; Rioux and Backmann, *L'Explosion*, 197, 369.
279. 14 June 1968, Fa 273, APP.
280. 16 May 1968, AN 820599/40.
281. 29 May 1968, AN 820599/40. Italian students and radicals offered similar shelter to street people.
282. 15 May 1968, Fa 256, APP.
283. Sernin, *Journal*, 25.
284. Schnapp and Vidal-Naquet, *Journal*, 50; Dansette, *Mai*, 400; Perret, *Sorbonne*, 46; 29 May 1968, AN 820599/40.
285. Seale and McConville, *Red Flag*, 105.
286. Perrot et al., *La Sorbonne par elle-même*, 114.
287. Schnapp and Vidal-Naquet, *Journal*, 604. Duchen, *Women's Rights*, agrees that May gave little attention to women's issues.
288. Durandeaux, *Les journées*, 153.
289. Quoted in Baynac, *Mai*, 164. For a similar incident, Cercle Barbara Salutati, *Longtemps je me suis souvenu de mai 68* (Bordeaux, 2002), 72.
290. Perrot et al., *La Sorbonne par elle-même*, 108.
291. Schnapp and Vidal-Naquet, *Journal*, 449; Perrot et al., *La Sorbonne par elle-même*, 119.
292. Perrot et al., *La Sorbonne par elle-même*, 125; Schnapp and Vidal-Naquet, *Journal*, 444.
293. 15 May 1968, Fa 256, APP.
294. 22 May 1968, Fa 259, APP. Anonymous students charged that plans were being concocted to blow up police buses to provoke officers into using their arms. See 25 May 1968, Fa 260, APP.
295. Schnapp and Vidal-Naquet, *Journal*, 443; Perrot et al., *La Sorbonne par elle-même*, 131, 134.
296. Schnapp and Vidal-Naquet, *Journal*, 453, 579, 667.
297. Ibid., 393, 728; Dansette, *Mai*, 415.
298. Schnapp and Vidal-Naquet, *Journal*, 737; Peuchmaurd, *Vivants*, 90.
299. Jacques Frémontier, *La forteresse ouvrière: Renault* (Paris, 1971), 360.
300. 17 May 1968, AN 820599/40.
301. *Quelle université? Quelle société?* 30–35.
302. Schnapp and Vidal-Naquet, *Journal*, 394, 633, 646, 663, 666, 679; Perrot et al., *La Sorbonne par elle-même*, 126–130; *Quelle université? Quelle société?* 37.
303. 15 May 1968, AN 820599/75.
304. Robert V. Daniels, *Year of the Heroic Guerrilla: World Revolution and Counterrevolution in 1968* (New York, 1989), 143.
305. Schnapp and Vidal-Naquet, *Journal*, 697.
306. Quoted in Dansette, *Mai*, 196.
307. Schnapp and Vidal-Naquet, *Journal*, 609–617, 625–628.

308. 22 May 1968, Fa 259, APP.
309. 6 June 1968, Fa 269, APP; 14 June 1968, Fa 273, APP.
310. 16 May 1968, AN 820599/40; 17 May 1968, Fa 257, APP.
311. Préfet de Paris à Ministre de l'Education Nationale, 14 June 1968, AN 790793. See also Nicolas Daum, *Des révolutionnaires dans un village parisien* (Paris, 1988), 140.
312. 22 May 1968, Fa 259, APP.
313. 17 May 1968, AN 829599/40.
314. René Andrieu, *Les communistes et la révolution* (Paris, 1968), 101; Tudesq, "La radio," 152.
315. 15 May 1968, Fa 256, APP.
316. 18 May 1968, Fa 257, APP.
317. Ibid.
318. 19 May 1968, Fa 258, APP.
319. 20 May 1968, Fa 258, APP.
320. 21 May 1968, Fa 259, APP.
321. Seale and McConville, *Red Flag*, 141–143; Jean-Pierre Manel and Alomée Planel, *La crise de l'ORTF* (Paris, 1968), 27.
322. Emmanuel Souchier, ed. *Mai 68* (Paris, 1988), 46.
323. Gilles Lipovetsky, "Changer la vie ou l'irruption de l'individualisme transpolitique," *Pouvoirs*, no. 39 (1986): 91–105; Luc Ferry, "Interpréter Mai 68," *Pouvoirs*, no. 39 (1986): 5–13; Luc Ferry and Alain Renaut, *68–86: Itinéraires de l'individu* (Paris, 1987).
324. *Atelier Populaire présenté par lui-même: 87 affiches de mai-juin 1968* (Paris, 1968), 10.
325. "La sérigraphie à l'Ecole des Beaux-Arts: Entretien avec Rougemont," in Dreyfus-Armand and Gervereau, *Mai 68*, 180.
326. Schnapp and Vidal-Naquet, *Journal*, 800–810; Kravetz, *L'Insurrection étudiante*, 427.
327. André Fermigier, "No More Claudels," in *Art and Confrontation: The Arts in an Age of Change*, trans. Nigel Foxell (Greenwich, Conn. 1968), 43.
328. J.-J. Léveque, "Les arts en colère," *La Galerie des arts*, no. 56 (September, 1968), 3.
329. *Atelier Populaire.*
330. *Quelle université? Quelle société?* 117.
331. Mai 68, Ecole des Beaux-Arts, documents originaux, QB mat, BN.
332. Laurent Gervereau, "L'Art au service du mouvement," in Dreyfus-Armand and Gervereau, *Mai 68*, 162.
333. Vasco Gasquet, *Les 500 affiches de mai 1968* (Paris, 1978), 8; "L'Atelier populaire de l'ex-Ecole des Beaux-Arts: L'Entretien avec Gérard Fromanger," in Dreyfus-Armand and Gervereau, *Mai 68*, 166; *Le Monde*, 25 May 1968.
334. Gervereau, "L'Art au service du mouvement," 166; Bibliothèque Nationale, *Les affiches de mai 68 ou l'imagination graphique* (Paris, 1982). Police have indicated that certain Beaux-Arts students believed the strike committee to be "extremist." See 14 June 1968, AN 820599/41.
335. Alain Geismar, Serge July, and Erlyne Morane, *Vers la guerre civile* (Paris, 1969), 174, 325.
336. Quoted in *Quelle université? Quelle société?* 132.
337. Commission Université-Culture, Faculté de Droit, Paris, May 1968, quoted in *Quelle université? Quelle société?* 139.
338. 9 May 1968, AN 820599/40.
339. Miriam Levin, "Democratic Vistas—Democratic Media: Defining a Role for Printed Images in Industrializing France," *French Historical Studies*, no. 1 (spring, 1993), 83.
340. See Robert Frank, "Imaginaire politique et figures symboliques internationales: Castro, Hô, Mao et le 'Ché,'" in Geneviève Dreyfus-Armand, Robert Frank, Marie-Françoise Lévy, and Michelle Zancarini-Fournel, eds., *Les Années 68: Le Temps de la contestation* (Brussels, 2000), 31–47.
341. See Jean Garrigues, *Images de la révolution: L'imagerie républicaine de 1789 à nos jours* (Paris, 1988), 148–149.
342. "L'Entretien avec Gérard Fromanger," in Dreyfus-Armand and Gervereau, *Mai 68*, 184; Mai 68, Ecole des Beaux-Arts, documents originaux, QB mat, BN.

343. 18 May 1968, Fa 258, APP.
344. Raymonde Moulin, "Living without Selling," in *Art and Confrontation*, 131; Léveque, "Les arts en colère," 4.
345. 18 June 1968, AN 820599/41.
346. On the technique of reproduction, see Gervereau, "L'Art au service du mouvement," 162. Pierre Gaudibert, "The Cultural World and Art Education," in *Art and Confrontation*, 145, gives figures of "350 different posters with a total of 600,000 copies." Alain Gesgon, director of Centre International de Recherche sur l'Imagerie politique, estimated that 600–700 different posters were produced during the events and that approximately 600,000 were glued to city walls. Conversation at CIRIP, Paris, 7 August 1994.
347. Gasquet, *500 affiches*.
348. Mésa, *Mai 68: Les affiches de l'atelier populaire de l'ex-Ecole des Beaux-Arts* (Paris, 1968).
349. *Atelier Populaire*.
350. Mai 68, Ecole des Beaux-Arts, documents originaux, QB mat, BN; Gasquet, *500 affiches*, 8.
351. Cf. Ross, *May '68*, 206, which repeats the error that "almost none [of the posters] … makes an allusion to the existence of a student movement."
352. See Gervereau, "L'Art au service du mouvement," 164.
353. Stéphane Courtois, "Le joli mois de mai," *Communisme*, no. 18–19 (1988): 229.
354. 29 May 1968, Fa 266, APP.
355. Cf. the Commune's posters in Christiansen, *Paris Babylon*, 305.
356. "From Henri IV to de Gaulle: A *poulet* (chicken) in every pot." *Poulet* also meant cop.
357. See Sarah Wilson, "Martyrs and Militants: Painting and Propaganda: 1944–1954," in Michael Scriven and Peter Wagstaff, eds., *War and Society in Twentieth-Century France* (New York and Oxford, 1991), 220.
358. Declaration of Beaux-Arts quoted in *Quelle université? Quelle société?* 117.
359. Musée d'histoire contemporaine, Bibliothèque de documentation internationale contemporaine [BDIC], Nanterre.
360. Mai 68, Ecole des Beaux-Arts, documents originaux, QB mat, BN.
361. Gilbert Mury, *La société de répression* (Paris, 1969), 191; Marcel Faure, "Premières réflexions sur mai 1968," *Paysans* (May, 1968): 8.
362. Gervereau, "L'Art au service du mouvement," 169; Laurent Gervereau, *La propagande par l'affiche* (Paris, 1991), 141; Antony Copley, *Sexual Moralities in France 1780–1980* (London, 1989), 225, reports that a gay liberation poster appeared on the walls of the Sorbonne.
363. Léveque, "Les arts en colère," 4.
364. 8 June 1968, Fa 271, APP.
365. Rioux and Backmann, *L'Explosion*, 548.
366. Peuchmaurd, *Vivants*, 105.
367. 15 May 1968, Fa 256, APP.
368. Ibid.
369. 16 May 1968, Fa 257, APP.
370. 10 June 1968, Fa 271, APP.
371. 26 June 1968, Fa 276, APP.
372. 20 May 1968, Fa 258, APP; 16 May 1968, Fa 257, APP.
373. Grimaud, *Mai*, 195–214. Cf. Duprat, *Les journées*, 98, which dismisses the Odéon occupation as "inconsequential."
374. Sernin, *Journal*, 34; Schnapp and Vidal-Naquet, *Journal*, 466; Charrière, *Printemps*, 174.
375. Ravignant, *L'Odéon*, 65; Schnapp and Vidal-Naquet, *Journal*, 622.
376. 21 May 1968, Fa 258, APP; Bertrand Dorléac, "Les artistes et la révolution," and Marie-Ange Rauch, "Le théatre public, lieu de contestation," in Dreyfus-Armand et al., *Les Années*, 231, 263.
377. 16 May 1968, Fa 257, APP.
378. The following citations are from Ravignant, *L'Odéon*, 43–75.
379. Quoted in Sernin, *Journal*, 66.
380. 21 May 1968, Fa 258, APP.

381. Ibid.

382. Ibid.

383. 28 May 1968, Fa 261, APP.

384. 21 May 1968, Fa 258, APP.

385. Ravignant, *L'Odéon*, 56–73. Geismar et al., *Vers*, 332, claims that the Odéon experienced the "only occupation which was entirely under the control of the lumpen-proletariat."

386. 16 May 1968, Fa 257, APP.

387. 26–27 May 1968, Fa 260, APP.

388. 13 June 1968, Fa 273, APP.

389. 1 June 1968, Fa 269, APP.

390. Ravignant, *L'Odéon*, 181, 195.

391. Dansette, *Mai*, 337.

392. Ravignant, *L'Odéon*, 183.

393. 8 June 1968, Fa 274, APP.

394. 13 June 1968, Fa 273, APP.

395. Charrière, *Printemps*, 182; Schnapp and Vidal-Naquet, *Journal*, 456, 472; Dansette, *Mai*, 154.

396. Lumley, *States of Emergency*, 89.

397. "La Sorbonne occupée: Entretien avec Madeleine Rebérioux," in Dreyfus-Armand and Gervereau, *Mai 68*, 158; *Quelle université? Quelle société?* 55; 20 May 1968, Fa 258, APP.

398. 20 May 1968, Fa 258, APP.

399. 31 May 1968, Fa 261, APP.

Chapter Four

WORKERS RESPOND

Wage earners took advantage of the momentary weakness of state power in the middle of May to initiate the largest strike wave in French history. The fact that student radicals looked to workers to make the revolution was less important in sparking strikes than the divisions among political elites. What has been called the "political opportunity structure" encouraged the extension of the unrest to wage earners.[1] Even some members of the Gaullist majority wavered in support for the government. As in 1789, 1848, and 1871, cleavages within ruling groups promoted popular revolt. Both student and worker actions were parts of "a general cycle of protest," which traversed the social system from its center to the periphery.[2] The new allies of the student movement delayed its demise and provided it with more opportunities, but these allies had their own agenda and their support for young protesters was quite conditional. Wage earners were less interested in the destruction of property and more in its acquisition. Their desire to consume ultimately became a powerful force for social cohesion.

The strike movement of 1968 confirmed and reinforced a postwar pattern that showed the difficulty of involving most workers in ambitious social or political projects based on ideologies that attracted elites and militants much more than the general public or the working class.[3] For many wage earners, immediate personal and familial concerns took precedence over broader political and social issues. The PCF-sponsored strikes of 1947 and 1948 were unsuccessful because large numbers of workers were reluctant to follow politicized and sometimes violent militants against a government that was more than willing to use force to maintain order. Neither the anti-American "peace" campaigns of 1949–1950 nor the Communist-inspired sloganeering of 1952, *Ridgway la Peste* (the PCF falsely accused the American general Matthew Ridgway of employing biological warfare in Korea), was effective in winning over the masses. The success of strikes in the public service and nationalized sectors during August 1953 contrasted sharply with previous

---

failures. The activism of the base surprised union officials and demonstrated that a rank and file that was apprehensive about bread-and-butter issues had a different appreciation than union leaders of the proper moment to protest. In 1953 millions of strikers—who had gained the backing of the CGT, FO, and Confédération française des travailleurs chrétiens (CFTC)—were able to defend their retirement and promotion benefits. Their victory encouraged a return to bread-and-butter trade unionism and ended the futile insurrectional wave of the immediate postwar period.

The 1953 work stoppage showed the effectiveness of mass action by a rank and file supported by major confederations. Given the political and religious divisions among the unions, unity could be constructed in either of two ways. Confederations could act together on the basis of concrete workplace demands endorsed by often apolitical and individualistic wage earners; or, alternatively, they could rely upon the lowest common political denominator, i.e., the defense of democracy against a military, "fascist," or anti-Republican coup d'état. On the latter foundation, at the end of the Algerian War (1958–1962), the confederations came together sporadically to defend the republic. The settlement of the Algerian question permitted the unions to focus their attention more exclusively on domestic matters. During the miners' general work stoppage of March–April 1963, a coalition was reconstituted on the basis of specific wage-and-hours goals, as in 1953. Union unity—which, as it had during the Algerian War, included the UNEF—challenged the Gaullist regime. The government acted even more aggressively than its counterpart had during the 1947–1948 strikes and forced defiant miners back to work.[4]

In addition to creating a potent union alliance, the miner's strike of 1963 anticipated the stoppages of 1968 in many other ways. First, at its inception the strike won the sympathy of the public, and three thousand students demonstrated in Paris in solidarity with the miners.[5] White-collar workers and even some engineers employed by the mining companies supported their blue-collar comrades. Encouraged by these multiple endorsements, the Lorraine miners became the first group of workers since the 1930s to organize a march to the capital.[6] Second, transistor radios permitted the actors to follow the progress of negotiations.[7] Third, the massive strike won considerable wage increases and longer vacations. Workers' militancy forced a settlement that threatened the government's anti-inflation policies. Finally, as in 1968, the rebellion baffled and disconcerted de Gaulle.

The miners' strike encouraged coalitions of the left. In the mid 1960s the PCF and the CGT became more receptive to common action with other left organizations and momentarily put aside Cold War differences. The CGT and eventually the PCF backed the candidacy of the "Atlanticist" and relatively pro-American François Mitterrand in 1965. In 1966, the two major confederations—the CGT and the CFDT—solidified their alliance by signing a common program that included demands that, at least partially, prepared the way for the May 1968 strike wave. Both unions affirmed their opposition to the regime's wage policies and emphasized their determination to increase the salaries of the lowest-paid workers, who were often female, foreign, or young. In the following years, strikes increased, causing a loss of three million working days in 1966 and four million in 1967.[8] In the first round of the legislative elections of 1967, the PCF, SFIO, and PSU all gained votes. In the second round, Gaullists emerged with only a narrow working majority.

In the period immediately preceding the general strike of May and June, a number of violent confrontations expressed worker dissatisfaction. *Gauchistes* interpreted these work stoppages as *grèves sauvages* or wildcat strikes, i.e., stoppages undertaken without union approval. In December 1967 at Lyon during a worker demonstration against management policies at Rhodiaceta—a branch of the major conglomerate Rhône-Poulenc—young strikers disobeyed union calls for moderation and battled police.[9] A month later at Caen, the Renault-owned SAVIEM factory, which employed 4,800 workers, was the scene of another violent work stoppage. A strike involving the majority of salaried personnel erupted on Tuesday, 23 January. The following day, police occupied the entrance to the plant to protect the "right to work." In Caen itself, the CRS charged a crowd of strike supporters and inundated them with tear gas. Demonstrators replied by throwing rocks, Molotov cocktails, and other objects at the gendarmes and CRS. Protesters roamed the city and deliberately broke windows at the prefecture, various banks, and the local employers' organization. Over one hundred were injured, and eighty-five persons—mostly students—were arrested. *Gauchistes* blamed the strike's failure to produce concrete results on union unwillingness to spread the work stoppage and on massive state repression in the form of seven thousand CRS, gendarmes, and *gardes mobiles*. Despite the defeat of the movement, leftists rejoiced that new sectors of the working class, in particular proletarianized Norman peasants, were developing "class consciousness." Seventy percent of SAVIEM workers were *ouvriers spécialisés* (unskilled) and uninterested in union membership. The small percentage that became involved generally joined the CFDT. On 11 March officials reported that protesting workers at Redon (Ille-et-Vilaine) flouted police and blocked train traffic.[10] When the forces of order attempted to clear the way, workers replied by tossing stones and bolts. A tear gas response followed, and a ten-minute battle ensued. Skirmishes continued in the center of town, where protesters stoned the *sub-préfecture*. Twenty-one police and ten demonstrators were injured.

Student activists found additional reasons to "rediscover the workers' movement."[11] In Paris on 1 May 1968, police estimated that 12,000 demonstrators and 4,000 sympathetic sidewalk spectators assembled during the first May Day demonstration permitted by the government since 1954.[12] Foreigners participating in the crowd included 1,800 Spaniards and 200 Algerians. Although the parade was generally peaceful, 15 people were slightly injured when scuffles erupted between the CGT marshals and a few of the 500–600 anarchists, Trotskyites, and Maoists, some of whom had ventured into the capital from Nanterre. A police specialist noted that "May Day of 1968 signals a rebirth of the large (c. 25,000) public demonstrations of the early 1950s."[13]

Without the student revolt, workers' strikes might have remained as isolated and localized as they were before May. By challenging the state and, at the same time, provoking its brutality, students precipitated the enormous wave of work stoppages during the second half of the month.[14] On Thursday, 9 May, Georges Séguy of the CGT and Eugène Descamps of the CFDT met at the headquarters of the UNEF to study the possibility of a unified demonstration against the government.[15] Descamps was born in 1922 in Lomme, a suburb of Lille, a region where a socially conscious Catholicism was influential. He became an active militant of the Jeunesse ouvrière chrétienne (JOC) in his teenage years, which coincided with the Popular Front. Several years after the German invasion, he joined the Resistance. Following the Liberation, he retrained as a metallurgist while remaining active in the JOC. In 1954 he became the secretary general of the Metallurgy Federation of the CFTC. Descamps and his friends wanted to deconfessionalize the union and transform it into the great democratic rival of the pro-Communist CGT. Gradually, the "Deconfessionalists" gained control of the organization, and in 1964 the CFTC became the CFDT. By January 1966, Descamps was negotiating unity of action with the CGT.

Georges Séguy followed a different trajectory. Born in 1927 in Toulouse, he had been too young to participate in the Popular Front. In 1942, he joined a Communist youth group and entered the Resistance. Arrested by the Gestapo in 1944, he was deported to Mauthausen. After the Liberation, he became an employee of the nationalized railroad company, the SNCF. Perhaps Séguy's formative union experience came during the insurrectional general strikes of 1947 when the interior minister, Jules Moch, employed massive force, including CRS, to end the work stoppages. The memory of this round of repression would make Séguy reluctant in 1968 to confront directly a well-organized and determined state. His selection in 1967 as secretary general at age forty revealed the CGT's fervent desire for rejuvenation.

Séguy realized that solidarity achieved results. He did not forget that in 1963 his railroad workers had benefited from the pit stoppage by gaining the same increases as striking miners. His agreement with Descamps and other union leaders for a one-day general strike on Monday, 13 May, manifested the potential of union unity. Despite the illegality of the strike (the five-day advance notice was ignored), the work stoppage was widespread. State employees proved especially receptive: the strike was largely followed at the RATP, where perhaps 60 percent of trains and buses were halted.[16] Only a few professional unions of the RATP and SNCF—*syndicats autonomes* that were not affiliated with any major confederation—refused to participate.[17] Officials estimated that 40 percent of major SNCF routes were affected, and 50 percent of suburban traffic disrupted.[18] The secretary of the CGT Railroad Workers' Union reported that SNCF strikers engaged in sit-down strikes in their depots on 13 May. Perhaps half of the *cheminots* followed the strike order. The Paris airport was paralyzed and occupied.[19] Ministry of Interior officials calculated that 70 to 90 percent of wage earners at the nationalized gas company stopped work.[20] The Monday strike won the adherence of 60 to 90 percent of elementary school teachers.[21]

The private sector was also affected. Although the "immense majority" of Parisian metallurgists reported to work, the stoppage interrupted their workday. The metallurgical employers evaluated strike participation at 19 percent of the work force. The Ministry of Labor stated that in 48 metallurgical firms, whose personnel totaled 97,000, 28 percent were strikers.[22] In 11 construction firms employing 6,500 workers, 30 percent participated. Workers in large firms were more likely to strike than their counterparts in medium or small enterprises.[23] This propensity was especially true in metallurgy, where workers in big automobile firms downed their tools for an extended period. Almost 25 percent of wage earners in large firms participated, and 78 percent of big businesses were affected by the strike. These figures were a bad omen for the government and employers since these major firms included aviation and automobile companies that were in the vanguard of industrial development and represented the new, more concentrated and competitive sectors of the French economy in the late 1960s. The following weeks would show that many wage earners in these vital sectors supported work stoppages.

Most small businesses (under fifty workers)—which employed over a third of wage earners in commerce and industry—remained untouched by the movement. Thus, small enterprises would constitute a large and significant island of stability in May. Moreover, the stoppage was often localized. For example, the railroad workers' strike was less effective nationally than it was in the Paris region.[24] Furthermore, white-collar workers seem to have been relatively uninterested in the movement. Although 35 percent of social security workers of the Paris region were absent, only between 10 and 16 percent of bank and insurance company employees participated in the work stoppage. At the Assurances Générales de France—one of the largest French insurance companies, which employed over four thousand workers at its Parisian headquarters—the Monday demonstration went nearly unnoticed even though the unions had a powerful presence in the firm.[25] Only a fraction of its employees seemed concerned with the confrontation between students and authorities. In four firms totaling 5,300 workers in the chemical and pharmaceutical industry, only 12 percent were strikers. Of course, the number of those affected by transportation stoppages and the closing of firms was, much higher. Yet the state was by no means helpless, and the Ministry of

Transport partially filled the vacuum by converting military trucks into passenger service vehicles during morning and evening rush hours.[26]

Immediately after the Monday general strike, five work stoppages continued in metallurgical plants in the Paris region, and significant strikes broke out in aviation and automobile firms in the provinces.[27] Sud-Aviation near Nantes led the way on Tuesday, 14 May, by initiating the first strike accompanied by an occupation. It should be recalled that a stoppage supported by anarchosyndicalist workers had erupted in the firm at the beginning of the month. Sud-Aviation management had wanted a reduced work week (from 48 to fewer than 47 hours). Workers agreed but insisted upon retaining pay for 48 hours.[28] By Tuesday afternoon, only 15 percent of the work force remained in the factory, and one thousand demonstrators marched from the plant to the center of town. A group of three hundred proceeded to the airport, where, according to interior officials, they shouted and shoved the firm's director, who was forced to return in a police vehicle. On the next day, two thousand strikers occupied the plant and confined the director and his personnel manager to their offices.[29]

The example of the Sud-Aviation occupation was copied by the Renault plant at Cléon (Seine-Maritime) on 15 May and Renault factories of the Paris region, including Flins and the giant Boulogne-Billancourt, on Thursday, 16 May. At the latter, according to police, five thousand workers remained inside the plant.[30] Labor ministry officials reported that strikers blocked management's exit and took over the telephone exchange.[31] Georges Séguy remarked that "workers understood that the government was put to the test and weakened by the confrontation [with students] and that the moment had come to settle accounts."[32] The head of the CGC, André Malterre, believed that the student strikes had opened the way for factory occupations "by revealing the impotence of the government."[33] The dismissal of the education minister, Alain Peyrefitte, on 14 May appeared to be another admission of weakness or incompetence. De Gaulle himself stated: "When the French are no longer afraid, they challenge the authority of the state."[34] As in other periods of French history, such as the Popular Front, workers profited from perceived indulgence to advance their own interests. The strikers of 1968 repeated the tactic of the late 1930s, when wage earners chose the sit-down because they calculated that the government would be reluctant to use force to evacuate the factories. While their hunch was correct, the government prudently called up ten thousand gendarme reservists.[35]

The growth of the movement and its support from various quarters—including that of unionized television producers—gave it access to state-controlled television. On the heels of the Renault occupation on Thursday evening, Cohn-Bendit of the Movement of 22 March, Geismar of SNESup, and Sauvageot of the UNEF debated on live television with a young journalist from *Le Figaro* and another reporter from *Paris-Presse*.[36] The journalists wanted to focus the discussion on the question of university examinations.

After ten minutes of talk, the radicals became weary of the issue and refused to answer any more questions on the subject. They switched the debate to the social situation. The young and aggressive *Le Figaro* reporter, who had the habit of thumping on the table when he disagreed, irritated Cohn-Bendit. Totally unintimidated, Dany displayed his media savvy when, in front of millions, he admonished the journalist, "Listen, that's enough. When you don't like something, you make so much noise that no one else can hear. Either stop or leave ... because we want to speak seriously to the audience." Dany's rebuke raised laughter from studio technicians. Even some hostile observers thought that Cohn-Bendit was amusing, if not intelligent.[37] Police officials, though, found his style demagogic or "Poujadist."[38] As the debate proceeded, the professional journalists were unexpectedly put on the defensive.

Pompidou appeared on the screen immediately after Cohn-Bendit and company had departed. The prime minister's rebuttal was almost as awkward as the interventions of the conservative journalists who had preceded him: "My appeal has not been heard by everyone. Some groups of *Enragés*—we have shown a few—want to propagate disorder.... Frenchmen, French women ... whatever your political preferences, whatever your social demands, you must show that you reject anarchy."[39] Pompidou's "we" was an error that needlessly reminded the audience of the government monopoly of television. Despite the misstep, the prime minister's intervention was not a total failure. He was astute enough to identify the regime with the party of order, which was struggling against the forces of chaos. Throughout the crisis, Gaullists would constantly link their political opposition to violent and destructive insurrectionaries.

In the short term, though, Pompidou's warnings had little effect, and the work stoppage continued to expand. A few strikes seem to have been undertaken spontaneously. The most important occurred at the Renault factory at Flins and the Assurances Générales de France, where workers stopped laboring "without formulating demands."[40] This indicates that some workers were rebelling against everyday routine or, as the popular expression put it, *métro, boulot, dodo ... ras le bol* (subway, work, sleep ... we're sick of it). Of course, *gauchistes* and their sympathizers have consistently emphasized the spontaneous nature of the strikes as a way of demonstrating the militancy of the base and the CGT's lack of influence on workers.[41] In fact, in most cases strikes were initiated by unions or their militants.[42]

The PTT (Postes, Télégraphes, Téléphones) provided a telling example of union weight in the public sector that—in contrast to the strike wave of 1936—was especially favorable to work stoppages. At the end of April, postal authorities believed that the CGT and CFDT were encouraging a strike of thousands of employees of both *bureaux ambulants* (mobile post offices) and of sorting centers for higher night, weekend, and holiday pay.[43] In early May, officials of the various Fédérations des fonctionnaires were—according to a police bulletin—seeking a propitious date to launch the strike: "Union leaders want to begin to strike but cannot agree on a date.... They are discussing the end of May but the strike will probably break out before then."[44] By 8 May, a strike had erupted, affecting 33 percent of postal workers at the Gare de l'Est and 74 percent at the Gare du Nord.[45] Strikers were joined by drivers of mail trucks who wanted a forty-hour week divided into five days of eight hours. At the major mail sorting center of Paris-Brune, an overwhelming majority participated. On Friday, 10 May, 214 out of 366 drivers obeyed the CGT order to stop work, and the administration reacted by employing private carriers as scabs, a practice that leftist politicians and publications had challenged even before the stoppage.[46]

In this context of labor tensions, more postal workers struck on 13 May. Drivers, maintenance workers, and carriers conformed to the general strike order. Foremen and clerks, who had previously been quiescent, also joined the stoppage. Police declared that strikers occupied and then vacated without incident a post office in the Latin Quarter (rue l'Epée de Bois).[47] On 14 May airmail delivery was halted, and during the night of 17–18 May sorting centers were occupied and picket lines established. The latter effectively discouraged individuals who wanted to return to work. On 18 May the minister of the PTT requested that police expel one hundred workers occupying a key telecommunications office near the stock exchange in the second *arrondissement*. The local police commissioner arrived to discuss the matter with CGT delegates, who consented to end the occupation peacefully. "However, young employees refused to leave. Instead of following their delegates, the youngest and most disorderly absolutely demanded that they be expelled forcibly. That was done."[48] This sort of resistance was exceptional, and major postal checking centers were usually emptied without incident.[49] Violence to people or property was not reported. Police learned that their merely symbolic appearance was nearly always sufficient to convince strikers to leave postal centers.[50] However, the forces of order confirmed instances of passive resistance to evacuation by postal workers who—like nonviolent American civil rights demonstrators—left the building only after officers pulled them up by the shoulders. As the occupiers departed, they naively shouted "the cops are with us" and "police on strike."[51] At the postal check center on the rue de Vaugirard, strikers tried to cow and pressure non-strikers, and police were summoned to separate the two groups. By 21–22 May, 50,000 of 80,000 postal workers were on strike in Paris and 66,000 of 175,000 in the provinces. Many Parisian centers were occupied, and most bureaus in the city and immediate suburbs were forced to close. Even though police commissioners were ready to intervene to protect "the right to work" at occupied post offices, a majority of workers adhered to the strike, and lack of transport prevented others from commuting.[52]

Major nationalized companies joined the movement. Air France employees occupied their offices on the boulevard Blanqui, refused to leave until police verified that they had not damaged or destroyed anything, and then departed peacefully.[53] Their concern for state property distinguished them from the most radical street demonstrators. A police commissioner confirmed that a very similar occupation occurred at Météorologie Nationale, whose thirty-five occupiers abandoned their sit-down after a police request.[54] Despite the lack of violence or sabotage, the public sector strikes constituted major defiance of the state. Transportation difficulties and a scarcity of fuel contributed to a 35–40 percent absenteeism rate among the largely loyal state employees at the Préfecture de Police.[55]

Even when the work stoppage began without union sponsorship, union militants ended up interpreting workers' demands and formulating bargaining positions. Parisian metallurgical employers claimed that in their firms the strikes that occurred immediately after 13 May were not, contrary to many accounts, "spontaneous" but caused by CGT militants.[56] Their analysis was seconded by the employers' organization, the CNPF, which was convinced that the student and worker strikes were totally distinct and believed that the latter were *grèves comme les autres* (strikes like others).[57] The Ministry of Interior largely concurred: "The strike movement is massive but… it is not always spontaneous or profound."[58] In large firms, a minority often imposed it. A statistical analysis has demonstrated that the "traditional sectors" where unions were strong—metallurgy, construction, transportation, and mining—powered the strikes.[59] An interior ministry document that was circulated to prefects in June held the CGT responsible for workplace agitation as early as 15 May.[60] According to police informers, union activists abandoned their scheduled "day of action against the attack on social security" and concentrated on stopping work:[61] "The secretariat of the CGT discreetly let it be known to its regional officials that its position was hardening and that they should encourage an extension of the strikes…. A new general strike cannot be excluded."[62]

Police sources indicated that the CGT led the occupations of twelve major enterprises and "wants to develop the movement to avoid being outbid by leftists." According to interior ministry officials, "the headquarters of the unions continue their agitation but have not ordered a formal general strike. They permit union locals to take the initiative."[63] In most branches traditional demands regarding salaries, work time, and union rights revealed CGT control and influence. "The CGT and the CFDT wanted to take advantage of student agitation to win certain demands." This argument was supported by the leader of the CGT Railroad Workers' Federation, who claimed that on 16 May CGT militants were instructed to foment work stoppages at the most strategic Parisian railway stations.[64] On that day, the union issued a statement protesting against sanctions for striking railroad workers and listing their demands. *Cheminots* were fed up with ineffective twenty-four-hour strikes, which the unions had encouraged before mid May, and were prepared to engage in a long stoppage.[65] On 17 May, wage earners at the Saint-Lazare and Achères stations walked out. On 19 May, the Censier Worker-Student Action Committee asserted that strikes no longer erupted spontaneously but rather because of union pressure.[66]

Even if in the second half of May, the CGT shared the PCF's political goal of dissolving the ruling majority, it officially rejected violence. The Confederation had planned a "National Festival of Working Youth" at Pantin for 17–19 May and expected the attendance of thirty to forty thousand young people from all over France. Police ascertained that union leaders cancelled the gathering to avoid a potentially uncontrollable protest.[67] The CGT, Interior officials admitted, wanted a change of government but without disorder or "anarchy." Instead, the Confederation pressed for higher pay and greater benefits for young people. Ministry sources portrayed a prudent Descamps who considered that "the left could not replace the current government because the PCF and the FGDS were not able to agree on a common program." His CFDT was tempted to join the CGT "to avoid the multiplication of wildcat strikes and to discipline the movement." Force Ouvrière was even more cautious than the CFDT. The unions did not want the situation to get out of hand.

De Gaulle's early return from Rumania on Friday, 17 May, showed that the social movement had wrested priority from foreign affairs, the general's favorite domain. He continued to take a hard line and recommended the storming of the Sorbonne and the Odéon, but his ministers—who were more attuned to the public mood—convinced him that the moment was not opportune for a massive assault against student occupiers.[68] Some expected the general's return to slow the spread of the movement, but strikes continued during the weekend of 18–19 May. Railroad traffic declined as SNCF workers, whose rate of unionization was relatively high, began to gain confidence that the state would be unable to punish them for participation in an illegal strike in the public sector. At the same time, union delegates cooperated with police. At the Gare d'Austerlitz, a police commissioner related that union leaders "understood" and "supported" his decision "to substitute plainclothes officers for uniformed agents to avoid any incident with 'unenlightened' strikers."[69]

Police returned the favor by serving as mediators between striking workers and the extreme right. On 20 May, the latter showed that it would not relinquish its domination of western Paris without a struggle. On that day, police reported that a crowd of right-wingers abandoned their habitual attendance at the relighting ceremony of the flame at the Tomb of the Unknown Soldier to listen to a speech by Tixier-Vignancourt.[70] A commando then broke away from the crowd and headed to the Opéra, where it tore down striking workers' banners and burned them on the grandiose stairs of the theater. The rightists entered the building, damaged interior doors, and smashed windows. They then proceeded to the Lycée Condorcet, where they tried to force doors open. Ironically enough, the *lycéens* called upon the police to protect them from the raiders. An officer tried to halt the rightists, but they challenged his authority and criticized the forces of order for tolerating the "revolutionary" occupation of the Odéon. The group next advanced to the Gare Saint-Lazare, where it demanded that strikers remove a red flag. Police negotiated with the SNCF strikers and the commando. The parties reached a compromise that stipulated that strikers would remove the red flag in return for a promise that the right-wingers would not re-enter the train station.[71] Strikers at the station and at the Opéra prepared to defend themselves against any future Occident or right-wing raid.[72] When police stopped and searched a car carrying four skilled workers from the Opéra, they discovered *matraques* (rubber truncheons) for "self-defense."[73]

Sympathetic public opinion encouraged the extension of the strike movement, which acquired increased momentum on Monday, 20 May.[74] Polls showed that 40 percent of the population favored spreading work stoppages from the universities to other sectors.[75] On the other hand, police asserted that opinion was ambivalent: "The general public is tired of student anarchy and complains about the strike in public services." "Yesterday [17 May] the sudden strike in the *banlieue* provoked such discontent among riders that the unions agreed to suspend it."[76] Unions remained sensitive to the public and cultivated its sympathy by only rarely cutting off electrical power, at least until the last week of May. Proliferating strikes among postal and telephone workers demonstrated that work stoppages were reaching sectors where female workers constituted the majority. Educational establishments, especially *lycées* and vocational schools, halted instruction well before the FEN's national strike order of 22 May. The militancy of these teachers led one concierge to refuse to admit forty children to the Ecole des Filles in the second *arrondissement* since, as she told police, "she did not wish to be assassinated by the strikers."[77] At one of the nation's largest insurance companies, white-collar workers who had ignored the 13 May demonstration stopped working on the following Monday. According to Interior statistics, 85,000 (92 percent) of 92,000 SNCF workers in the Paris region joined the work stoppage; in EDF-GDF 33,200 of 38,700 or 86 percent struck; in the RATP 29,000 of 30,300 or 96 percent walked out.[78]

The shutdown of public transport on Monday, 20 May, blocked commuters and caused one of the most massive traffic jams in Parisian history. Hitchhiking—with its promise of instant community or at least communication—overcame the customary individualism of French motorists. Drivers generously stopped to help the stranded. Evoking the tradition of *Saint Lundi*, Mondays remained pivotal in May. Throughout the decade of the 1960s, Monday continued to be the day of greatest absenteeism.[79] Striking on Monday may have been an effective way of joining wage-earning men and women since the latter—who composed, for example, about 20 percent of the work force in metallurgy—had especially high rates of absenteeism on the first workday of the week. Monday was the day when workers engaged in a general strike (13 May), stopped working in large numbers (20 May), and, as will be seen, rejected the agreement among the government, unions, and employers (27 May). Nationally, by the end of Monday, 20 May, over five million workers had stopped laboring in a wide variety of branches—transportation, energy, post office, metallurgy, education, and banks.[80] Financial establishments began to limit withdrawals, and a black market for gasoline started to develop.

In the industrial *banlieue* of Argenteuil and Bezons, the strike movement "developed massively" from 20 May onward.[81] Employers noted that on that Monday strikers became more prone to illegality. A few workers ignored the CGT's and the PCF's condemnation of sequestrations or expelled management from factories.[82] Sabotage, however, seems to have been rare. More commonly, strikers violated the "right to work of non-strikers."[83] The occupations often contested management prerogatives and industrial hierarchy.[84] Employers complained bitterly of the collapse of state power and especially of the failure of the police to come to their aid.[85] The Ministry of Interior ignored a petition from 1,200 Citroën employees who demanded that the state protect their right to work. As has been seen, police did not always play a repressive role. Nor were officials uniformly hostile to strikers. In fact, with the help of the Communist mayor of Levallois-Perret police mediated between striking Citroën workers and strike-breaking foremen to arrange to pay workers in advance.[86] All of these parties agreed that women—given their role as homemakers—would receive their advance before men. The prefect's assertion that during the strike wave his men acted "as much as justices of the peace and mediators than as policemen" was only a partial mystification.[87]

Industrialists in the western suburbs grumbled that CGT militants from Avions Marcel Dassault and other large enterprises encouraged the work stoppages while local municipalities controlled by the left aided strikers.[88] A CFDT militant reported that the CGT initiated the strike at the chemical firm Carbone Lorraine, which employed 1,200 in Gennevilliers.[89] CGT control of strikes in many firms, especially at the Imprimerie Nationale, frustrated young revolutionaries from Censier. Employers continued to attribute "responsibility" for most strikes to union militants, particularly the CGT.[90] Of the 77 metallurgical strikes listed, CGT militants were responsible for 68, CFDT for 6, and FO for 3. As a rule, militants were male. Although women in the textile and service industries were unusually active, sectors with a female work force generally struck less than male-dominated branches.[91] Metallurgical industrialists reported that older and more experienced workers provoked the stoppages.[92] Fifty-one out of 88 strikes (58 percent) were started by wage earners between 30 and 40 years old. Twenty-four (27 percent) were begun by 20- to 30-year-olds. Only 7 (8 percent) were initiated by those under twenty. Young people under 30 may have become strike leaders in firms where unions were weak, but usually activists had some seniority.[93] Workers who had been employed in their firms for more than one year were leaders of 67 percent of the strikes. Wage earners at Renault-Billancourt and at a major electronics firm, Jeumont-Schneider, in La Plaine Saint-Denis, did not remember young wage earners as particularly active in the strike.[94]

The above information is significant because it modifies the common interpretation of May 1968 as a youth revolt.[95] Even in cases, such as that of Renault-Cléon (Seine-Maritime), where young workers were said to be most committed to the movement, the major unions and their more mature trade unionists quickly gained control over the work stoppage.[96] Relatively mature, stable, and unionized French workers were largely responsible for initiating metallurgical strikes in the Paris region. The stoppages in Parisian metallurgy confirm the statistical analysis that has established that age was not a determining factor in the strike wave.[97] Maturity, though, did not exclude boldness. Metallurgical industrialists noted that in 35 out of 41 reported strikes, workers used threats to convince their colleagues to stop work. In 16 of 60 strikes, militants resorted to force; yet they did not usually insult their bosses or lock in management. In only two cases was property damaged, but the threat of sabotage certainly existed. For example, several persons entered a factory at night and set a truck on fire. A police investigation was unable to conclude if the incident was provoked by strike tensions or by a desire for "vengeance" on behalf of a worker fired before May.

In metallurgy militants were seldom revolutionaries, and the influence of *gauchistes* was quite circumscribed among the rank and file.[98] Just 2 out of 88 firms reported contact with persons belonging to Maoist, Castroist, Trotskyite, or anarchist organizations. Nor was the direct sway of revolutionary or radical students consequential. Among strikers in the western *banlieue* (Argenteuil-Bezons) that bordered on Nanterre, student radicals had contact with workers during only 9 of 88 strikes, and these were probably in larger metallurgical factories. Students did meet with personnel at the Dassault plant at Saint-Cloud, but their influence was negligible.[99] In one case, contact had been initiated not through a *groupuscule* but rather by a Christian youth organization. At the Assurances Générales de France, where the CFDT and FO were more influential than the CGT, students and leftists had little sway during the strike and were refused entry into the occupied offices. Thus, the brief fusion of the student and worker movements after 12 May was destined to unravel. The radical students' desire to merge with the working class was not to be fulfilled. Neither the Parisian *métallos* nor other wage earners were seeking the correct party or the right revolutionary ideology.[100]

When on the evening of 16 May and again in larger numbers (1,500–2,000) on 17 May, students went off to Billancourt to show support for the strikers, workers greeted them with a combination of curiosity, skepticism, and some hostility.[101] They were not permitted to enter the occupied factory. Police concluded that "most of the attempts to unite students and workers … were failures."[102] No action committee—no matter what its ideological coloration—took root at Billancourt. In fact, the establishment of certain action committees might be interpreted as a sign of the distinct minority status of the extreme left. The committee at Assurances Générales de France was created in response to the domination of the major unions during the occupation.[103]

Whether reformers or (much less likely) revolutionaries—the strike-provoking *meneurs*, as metallurgical employers called them—were largely French. Immigrants seemed somewhat marginal. Only 9 percent were foreign: three Spanish "anarchists," two "insolent" Algerians, and several Poles, Italians, and Portuguese.[104] The police noted that "the major foreign groups—Italians, Spanish, Algerians, Portuguese, Poles, Yugoslavs—obeyed strike orders of the CGT, CFDT, and FO but without enthusiasm."[105] Foreign workers often viewed the strike as a French work stoppage in which they played only a passive role.[106] Their relative tranquility was significant since they composed approximately 15 percent of the work force in Parisian metallurgy and, as in Germany and other advanced European nations, were overwhelmingly present in the lowest paid and least skilled jobs.[107] On assembly lines, they might constitute over half the work force. The beginning of the strike wave "provoked panic among foreign workers."[108] Rumors of civil war and a possible devaluation spread among them. Spanish seasonal agricultural laborers, who remembered first- or second-hand their own civil war thirty years earlier, left Ile-de-France and other French regions for Spain at the end of May. Similarly anxious, many Portuguese departed for their native country at the beginning of June. Interior ministry sources argued that only the Italians, "accustomed to major social movements" of a European democracy, did not panic. Italian emigrants were more likely to vote Communist than the Italian population as a whole.[109] Their calm showed that the Common Market may have been integrating, or more precisely, "Europeanizing" its wage earners during the late 1950s and early 1960s.

The work stoppages of May revealed that North African workers had not yet assimilated through the labor movement, as had previous generations of immigrants. Regardless of a shared class position, North African and French workers reacted differently to the strike wave. The reasons for this are complex. Some authors have pointed to political issues, such as the Algerian War, which divided French from North Africans in the early 1960s.[110] Others have seen cultural factors, or what Fernand Braudel called the "clash of civilizations," as inhibiting assimilation. Braudel cited the Islamic way of life and its special attitudes towards parental authority and the role of women: "Every year there are about 20,000 mixed marriages on average. Two-thirds end in divorce since such marriages tend to require one or the other partner (or both) to break with their background. Yet without intermarriage there can be no integration."[111]

In the French tradition of Proudhonism and decentralization, a number of working-class organizations encouraged strikers to demand *autogestion* or *cogestion*. The most vocal advocate of workers' control was the CFDT, whose secretary general, Descamps, believed that the worker and student movements shared the same democratic aspirations. He argued that administrative and industrial "monarchies" must be replaced by democratic workers' control.[112] The CFDT saw its advocacy of *autogestion* as a means of distinguishing itself from its major rival and as a way of bolstering militancy, especially among its white-collar base. The demand for workers' control meshed with the CFDT's critique of consumer society. On 11 May its Parisian federation praised students for "refusing the automobile society, television, advertising."[113] On 16 May the CFDT proclaimed that "the struggle of students to democratize the university is identical to that of workers to democratize their factories." On 20 May, CFDT-Renault urged "the first steps toward *autogestion*." The Action catholique ouvrière, which had nurtured an important number of CFDT militants, was in complete "solidarity with the workers struggling to gain power in their firms and in society." Even André Bergeron and the leadership of the FO advocated a reformist version of *autogestion* or *cogestion*.

Student radicals, such as Cohn-Bendit, also imagined that the time for *autogestion* had arrived. Dany suggested that the conflicts at Cléon and Flins resembled the struggles at Nanterre.[114] The Movement of 22 March advised workers to "engage in active strikes" and to offer free services to consumers. It continued its struggle for *autoréductions* (e.g., taking the *métro* without paying) or for what those who accepted property rights would label theft. On 25 May, the Worker-Student Action Committee at Censier urged wage earners to destroy the power of the bourgeoisie by taking over the organization of production and distribution.[115] The archbishop of Paris, François Marty, proposed a high-minded justification for democratic participation in wage labor: "Many reject today's economic and social system.... The critique of consumer society, of Eastern as well as Western materialism is not surprising.... All men must share actively and freely in decision making."[116]

The demand for *autogestion* found some echoes among middle-class professionals. During the work week of 20–25 May, a group of doctors occupied the premises of their medical association, and some architects proclaimed the dissolution of their own traditionalist corporate body.[117] On 22 May a "commando" of writers, led by Michel Butor and Natalie Sarraute, occupied the Société des Gens de Lettres and—like many others—expressed their desire to create a new society in collaboration with students and workers.[118] Unsurprisingly, Sartre, Simone de Beauvoir, and Marguerite Duras supported the initiative. From its stand at the occupied Sorbonne, the Comité de coordination des cadres contestataires demanded an industrial democracy that, it imagined, would encourage "a flowering of individuality at the workplace."[119] At the Assurances Générales de France, *cadres* were much more interested in *autogestion* than were lower-paid employees. Engineers, technicians, and scientists in organizations that had a large number of highly skilled personnel set forth demands for more professional autonomy.[120] Employees of the Commissariat à l'Enérgie Atomique, the Thomson electronics plant at Gennevilliers, and the Conseil National de Recherche Scientifique requested more internal democracy. The highly trained personnel in these organizations no longer wished to be passive executors of orders from above, and many refused to oppose occupations.[121] However, negotiations between management and salaried personnel often ignored qualitative demands for more democracy in favor of quantitative issues of pay and working hours. Performing artists who entertained occupiers found themselves more committed to "active strikes" than were their audiences.

Many analysts—for example, Alain Touraine, Cornelius Castoriadis, and the editors of *Les Temps modernes*—have seen the novelty and uniqueness of May in the generalized demand for *autogestion*. Other progressives sympathetic to the movement wanted so badly to believe that workers desired to take over their factories that they invented the story that the personnel of the CSF factory at Brest had initiated "democratic control" and were producing walkie-talkies.[122] The myth-makers—who included historians Alain Delale and Gilles Ragache, and the major newspapers *Le Monde* and *Témoignage chrétien*—proved as willing to take their desires for reality as any youthful *gauchiste*. Yet workplace democracy was seldom found in the lists of demands formulated by union militants.[123] Rather than reflecting worker sentiment, the call for *autogestion* may have served as a facile solution to the genuine and thorny problem of worker dissatisfaction with industrial discipline in particular and wage labor in general. The doctrines of self-management had little appeal to a mass of wage laborers for whom work remained *travail* and who were more enthusiastic about escaping the factory or enjoying the pleasures of consumption. Despite the rhetoric of unions and parties, including the *groupuscules*, workers never fully identified themselves as producers who wanted to take control of the means of production. American radicals—such as the League for Industrial Democracy, which greatly influenced SDS—were similarly superficial. SDS inherited the League's commitment to democracy and tried to make it "participatory."[124] Most workers, though, did not wish to participate in their own wage slavery. Todd Gitlin has argued perceptively that "participatory democracy was the ideology of a middling social group [educated radicals] caught between power and powerlessness, and soaked in ambivalence toward both."[125]

Implicit in the notion of workers' control was the demand that the individual remain subordinate to the productivist collectivity. The Movement of 22 March unmistakably advocated that "*autogestion* means the control of oneself and everything that concerns oneself, but this self refers to a collectivized self, not an individualist one. *Autogestion* is not a certain number of individuals who want to manage themselves autonomously ... but a collective totality that wishes to control itself. In the latter, the individual has no place."[126] Workers inevitably questioned whether it was really advantageous for them to run the factories.[127] Many concluded that it was not, since successful workers' control demanded a degree of professional and social commitment that they could not or would not provide.

Instead of *autogestion*, the CGT and even local CFDT affiliates recalled their agreement of January 1966, which pledged to struggle for a dramatic increase in the minimum wage, higher salaries, job security, and a reduction of the working week.[128] In metallurgy, the CGT and the CFDT demanded less work time and more pay, particularly for the lowest-paid workers, who were often foreigners, women, or young people.[129] This signaled the resolve of union activists (generally male and French) to reach out to social groups who composed the majority of industrial workers. Well before May, the CGT had made efforts to attract different categories of wage earners.[130] As early as 1965 it had called for a reduction of working hours for women. Aware of "the double and profoundly social role of female workers as both wage earners and mothers," it campaigned in 1967 for equal wages and opportunities for working females. CGT militants insisted upon "the end of any type of discrimination against women."[131] In a special edition of its women's magazine, the confederation argued that females should labor less. Its activists claimed that a work-free Saturday and reduced work time were even more necessary for women because "time-measurement and piecework has pushed them to the brink."[132] The CFDT too had appealed for equal pay for equal work, regardless of sex.

Women were not the only objects of the unions' attentions. The confederations also wanted young workers and foreigners to participate as equals in the worlds of labor and leisure. Recognizing that "one out of four workers is foreign," the CGT congratulated itself on its "long tradition of internationalism" and supported the demands of *immigrés*.[133] French Communists backed the Italian Communists' MOI (Main d'Oeuvre Immigré), which fought for equal pay and equal rights.[134] The unions urged the end to discrimination against foreigners and youth and demanded the suppression of the practice of paying lower wages to youthful wage earners. Prior to May, the CGT made special efforts to recruit young rebels who resisted factory discipline and the authority of supervisory personnel. It wanted to enlist insurgent youth who might have otherwise gravitated towards *gauchisme*.[135] Young CGT activists insisted that employers pay for educational courses, sporting activities, housing for young married couples, and a fifth week of paid vacation. Displaying their desire for a key commodity of consumer society, youthful automobile workers at Citroën pleaded for the right to discount car rentals during their vacations.[136] As in automobile firms, the formal demands of striking youth in vocational high schools—more money for scholarships and the creation of a technology teaching center—were highly materialist.[137]

On 22 May the surge of demands and strikes stimulated a major parliamentary debate. The opposition offered a motion of censure of the government's economic, social, and educational policies. It condemned the administration's "refusal of any real dialogue" and its "enormous repression."[138] The government's position was precarious since it held only a narrow majority—245 seats (including 43 critical *giscardiens*, followers of Giscard's group of Independent Republicans) against 242 for the opposition. On the floor of the chamber, Pompidou defended his ministers and attacked "anarchists" who wished to destroy state and society. He forgot his own implicit repudiation of police and praised them for defending the social order with great professionalism. He blamed the media, especially the radio, for encouraging rioters and treating them sympathetically. He confessed that the "weakness of [state] authority" had the purpose of avoiding "confrontation" with the strikers. At the same time, he hinted that the strikes were becoming "insurrectional." It was, he argued, an inappropriate time to bring down the government. He was more than willing to negotiate social and economic demands with the unions but excluded any "political" negotiations with them.

Pompidou had become a skilled debater during his long premiership, and on 14 May, he had tried to impress the Assembly with his intellectual abilities by engaging in a wide-ranging historical analysis. The former *normalien* compared the unrest of 1968 with that of the fifteenth century, which had signaled the end of the Middle Ages. He concluded that the current crisis did not truly center on the university, government, or even the nation. Instead he insisted that it was a "crisis of civilization" that challenged traditional values. He implied that a new postmodern age was dawning, a conception which—however inflated—has not yet ceased to be influential.

François Mitterrand of the FGDS was undoubtedly impressed by the Olympian quality of Pompidou's analysis: "We are listening to you, Mr. Prime Minister, and when we reflect on certain passages of your speech, we think, 'Wouldn't it be fine if he were in the government to execute his ideas.'"[139] On 22 May, not forgetting that he had the attention of a national television audience, Mitterrand displayed his own oratorical skills: "You have no more trains, no more subways, no more functioning factories, no more schools, no more banks, no more department stores, no more post offices but you [the ministers] are here, you are all here."[140] The FGDS leader suggested that the National Assembly be dissolved and new elections held.

Mitterrand and the parliamentary left wanted to use the strike wave to attain political power. Interior ministry authorities believed that the Socialist leader had astutely recognized that the government would not easily collapse.[141] Mitterrand correctly predicted that de Gaulle was prepared to make large concessions to the workers and thereby avoid a *"crise de régime."* At this time, the Socialist parliamentarian was reluctant to discuss a common program and the composition of a possible coalition with the PCF, which was urging a "popular government." Instead, Socialists insisted on new elections.[142] Criticism of the Pompidou government was not confined to the conventional left. Edgar Pisani, a *gaulliste de gauche* and a former minister, defected from the majority coalition and voted for censure. Despite earlier police predictions that the centrist parliamentary group Progrès et démocratie moderne (PDM) feared "endemic disorder" and might support the government, 34 of its 42 deputies voted for the censure of the Pompidou government.[143] Although frightened by the prospect of a new government dominated by the PCF, these centrists were nevertheless appalled both by the government's refusal to negotiate seriously and by the brutality of its police. The *giscardiens* criticized the government for its failure to encourage "dialogue," but—fearing "disorder" if the government fell—did not vote for the censure motion. The motion was lost 233 to 244, and the government survived.[144]

The debate indicated that Pompidou was willing, if necessary, to sacrifice the Gaullist left and the centrists to show that his majority gave the highest priority to the re-establishment of order. In other words, the government did not wait passively until the end of the month to encourage a return to normality. One of its first steps was to reassert tight control over the airwaves. To accomplish this, the minister of the PTT, Yves Guéna, issued an order that, in effect, forbade radio stations to use short-wave transmissions. To justify the ban, the minister made the dubious claim that police needed all frequencies. The media, including the conservative newspaper *Le Figaro*, was skeptical and criticized the government's heavy hand.[145] The intention of this prohibition was to deny radio stations a means to broadcast live reports of the confrontations in the Latin Quarter and other areas of the capital. The state aimed to censor the airwaves to prevent activists from massing at battle sites and rushing to aid their comrades in response to news conveyed by transistors. Paradoxically, the government's past policies made its own ban largely unsuccessful. The consumer society that it had encouraged multiplied the availability of public and private communications and therefore rendered censorship difficult. Thus, the prohibition on short-wave reporting was only partially effective since local residents or café owners were usually willing to let a reporter use their telephone.[146] In fact, protesters had the means to tap police communications, and a competent ham radio operator could overhear official conversations. The police reacted to this vulnerability by coding their messages.[147]

Live radio coverage continued and focused on the demonstrations of 22 May and subsequent days, which were provoked by the government's unwise decision to ban the "foreigner" Cohn-Bendit from France. Considerable numbers of radio listeners and television viewers may have found the expulsion difficult to understand since they had quickly learned that the "German anarchist" handled the French language better than many journalists, deputies, and ministers.[148] Antirepression once again brought together radicals of varying agendas. Several thousand demonstrators, backed by the UNEF, again expressed international solidarity by shouting on 22 May, "We are all German Jews."[149] By expelling Dany, the government disregarded the humanitarian traditions of French higher education and conceded to the demands of the xenophobic, if not anti-Semitic, extreme right. *Minute*, its organ, had urged that Cohn-Bendit "be taken by the scruff of the neck and carried to the frontier without any formality. And if our authorities do not have the courage to do so, we know a certain number of young Frenchmen itching to perform this task of public safety."[150]

The PCF and the CGT fractured the fragile antirepression front on 22 May by choosing not to protest against Cohn-Bendit's expulsion.[151] "Stalinists" were hostile to any public show of support for the redhead, and *L'Humanité* accused Dany of "slandering Communists and insulting our Party."[152] Likewise, the CGT termed the pro-Cohn-Bendit demonstration "a new provocation" that could aid only the government. Séguy condemned "troublemakers … whose acts have alienated workers."[153] Séguy's attacks on the student movement aroused dissension from the CGT's more radical elements, such as the Syndicat des correcteurs. This union possessed a tradition of revolutionary syndicalism stretching back to the late nineteenth century, and it disapproved of the CGT leader's "anti-unitary attitude."[154] Some PCF intellectuals—including historians Jean Bouvier, Madeleine Rebérioux, Jean Chesneaux, and Albert Soboul—publicly criticized the party for its failure to support students and Cohn-Bendit.[155]

Not surprisingly, PCF and CGT condemnations failed to dampen protest by extreme-left demonstrators. On the evening of 22 May, a student crowd of four thousand proclaimed—once again hyperbolically—"We are all aliens" at the heavily guarded National Assembly.[156] A police superintendent declared that Geismar had admitted that one of the goals of the demonstration was to influence debate on amnesty.[157] After the bulk of protesters had departed, a group of four hundred remained. These *trublions* tried to incinerate the historic headquarters of the Gaullist movement on the rue de Solférino. Inhabitants of the building quickly extinguished the flames and, in retaliation, tossed primitive missiles from the upper floors down at the demonstrators, injuring two of them. After midnight, a cooperative UNEF parade marshal warned police that some protesters were ready to bombard agents with cobblestones and other objects. According to the authorities, hundreds of these mostly very young people were *"blousons noirs et voyous* (young delinquents), who always surface during insurrections." Commanders concluded that the UNEF and SNESup were incapable of controlling "the fauna which haunt the Latin Quarter."[158]

Police were able to dialogue with UNEF militants, whom they generally considered to be reasonable and well-behaved.[159] When on the night of 23 May five hundred demonstrators attacked police headquarters in the Latin Quarter (Place du Panthéon), damaging an emergency vehicle and stealing a half-dozen truncheons, the demonstration's *service d'ordre* formed a human barrier to limit wreckage of the vehicle and to restrain "the most excited [protesters]."[160] Other demonstrators, unchecked by the UNEF, shattered café windows and launched tear gas grenades against police, which the latter claimed were more toxic than the government's own gas.[161] Protesters attempted to occupy the trash depot on the quai de la Tournelle. Authorities stated that throughout the night and early morning of 22–23 May, several hundred demonstrators—flying red and a few black flags—began blazes in the Latin Quarter and as far away as the eighteenth *arrondissement*.[162] By 2:45 A.M. "the Place Maubert had a ring of fire." Police utilized high-pressure hoses to extinguish the flames and to disperse demonstrators.

The CRS were no doubt particularly aggressive and brutal. The riot police, according to one police commissioner, acted with "special *allant* (liveliness) and needed to be restrained rather than encouraged." "The exasperation and the impatience of CRS officers and men were considerably aggravated in direct proportion to increasing fatigue."[163] Another commissioner remarked that they were "terribly tired" from working several shifts without relief.[164] The minister of interior had to employ all manpower available and to concentrate shifts during the night, adding to the exhaustion and discomfort of the men. In the wake of the growing strike wave, on 21 May the director of the municipal police had suspended all leave and vacations.[165] The decision came in the context of increasing police "*nervosité* [irritability] due to the extended wait [that was] caused by the long delay of relief forces."[166] This admission of police excitability and impatience lends additional credibility, if any more is needed, to charges of police brutality.

The number of injured was an additional reason for police violence. By 21 May, 900 officers, about 10 percent of on-duty officers, had been hurt. Cobblestones and ordinary rocks wounded the majority (525 or 58 percent).[167] These rudimentary weapons proved the most dangerous. Tear gas harmed 216. A few protesters manufactured their own gas, which officials continued to insist was more poisonous than the government brands.[168] Yet their own fumes blowing back against police undoubtedly downed many of them. They often lacked the mobility of protesters, who could disperse easily at the first smell or sign of a chemical cloud. A police commissioner reported that he had been "very affected" by the use of a "variety of gases" during the nights of 6, 10, and 25 May and on 10–11 June: "The discomfort was caused either by my prolonged stay in an atmosphere saturated with tear gas, when protesters stayed on momentarily, or certainly because the demonstrators [on 10 June] threw more noxious gases [than ours]."[169] However, none of the agents sickened by gas was hospitalized. Police statistics undermined accusations that the government used highly toxic gases pioneered by Americans in Vietnam. It would have been foolhardy for the state to endanger its own men by employing very poisonous gases in urban crowd control. Molotov cocktails hurt only two agents, demonstrating that this simple weapon, which had been invented to destroy tanks, continued to incinerate property more than people or even police. Most injuries were light: only 19 officers had to be hospitalized, even though 396 (or 44 percent) were hurt enough to obtain sick leave.

A commander reminded his men that "they should keep their cool given the current political situation [but the] the reasonableness of such arguments had little effect because of the rain of cobblestones."[170] High-ranking government officials had taken measures to limit the possibility of brutality and the consequent backlash from moderate public opinion. They ordered their forces to use tear gas only for defensive actions, i.e., against cobblestone throwers and barricade builders.[171] "Clashes which are not strictly necessary for the maintenance of order must be avoided." High-pressure hoses also defended police lines. The state shrewdly restrained its police forces from hot pursuit into student lairs, even though demonstrators infuriated them by escaping into university buildings that were off-limits to uniformed agents. Once again, calculated tolerance checked repression. Until the middle of June, the forces of order refused to invade occupied institutions where protesters could retreat, rest, eat, and occasionally manufacture Molotov cocktails or tear gas grenades.[172] Police statistics showed the increasing participation of non-students whom the UNEF was unable to discipline. During the night of 22–23 May, 65 were arrested, of whom only 20 were students and only 6 female.[173] This violence anticipated that of subsequent nights. Protests started calmly in the daylight but ended fiercely in the darkness.

During the night of 23–24 May, barricades were erected, some of which a commissioner called remarkably "formidable."[174] After midnight, five to six hundred protesters guarded one fortification on the rue des Ecoles. Burned cars, snipers casting cobblestones, and a second barricade on the rue de la Montagne Sainte-Geneviève obstructed the advance of police who tried to capture it from behind. Only after depleting their supply of gas did agents successfully remove both barricades, which had been assembled from felled trees, cobblestones, and the gratings of the Ecole Polytechnique. "The army bulldozer took more than an hour to remove them [barricades] from the streets."[175] After neutralizing the fortifications, police commanders—who had been awarded considerable autonomy—undertook negotiations with a group of professors. The result favored protesters by permitting two hundred demonstrators, among whom were an "important number of girls," to depart without arrest. Crowds attacking isolated police vehicles and agents injured nineteen CRS. Objects thrown from top floors of apartment houses hurt several of them. Demonstrators seemed more mobile and aggressive than on previous nights, and riot police remained tired and tense. The CRS were acquiring a dreadful reputation among demonstrators, some of whom authored a tract praising several municipal police who had apparently rescued them from a brutal

CRS beating.[176] Officials were aware that belonging to the municipal police, not the CRS, saved one plainclothes policeman whom five students captured near the Sorbonne.[177] A crowd of twenty-five had forced him to accompany them to the *faculté*, where they—imitating their adversary—examined his papers. When protesters learned he was a traffic cop, they released him, warning, "you're lucky not to be a CRS; otherwise, we would have lynched you."[178]

Of 186 persons arrested, 44 (24 percent) were foreigners, a relatively elevated figure. Of these 44, only 13 were students. One hundred seventeen (63 percent) were not students, a remarkably high percentage.[179] Of these 117, 86 were French and 31 foreign. Nine of the foreigners were Algerians, and 5 were Spanish. Women were not numerous, perhaps because of the sexism of the forces of order who, as has been seen, had been reluctant to haul away (but perhaps not to brutalize) female protesters. Only 12 (6 percent) of the arrested were female: 10 French and 2 foreign. Another 10 were unemployed, perhaps casting doubt on police charges that protesters were merely juvenile delinquents. The average age of the arrested was twenty. The working-class *banlieues* dispatched a relatively large contingent. Ten had journeyed from Seine-Saint-Denis and 12 from the Val-de-Marne. Only a few of those arrested were previously known to police, once again showing that protesters could not be dismissed as criminals. By one count, 102 policemen were injured, including 5 CRS who were listed "in a serious state" during the night of 23–24 May.[180] Seven barricades were built, 5 streets *dépavé* (torn up), 9 vehicles burned and 10 damaged, 30 windows broken, 6 trees felled. Firemen were summoned 60 times. The night took on devastating possibilities as dispersed protesters once again lit fires in garbage and trashcans throughout the capital.[181] Rubbish flamed in the fashionable eighth *arrondissement*, and, more ominously, in the fifteenth at the parking lot for the private garbage trucks that were being employed to replace the vehicles of striking sanitation men.[182] Firemen required two hours to put out this blaze.

To attempt to redress the situation, de Gaulle spoke briefly on television in the evening of 24 May. His effort was a disappointment to his supporters, closest aides, and himself. He asserted to an incredulous public that the state was maintaining order. Although the audience had some reason to be skeptical, the fact that the general could deliver his speech provided evidence of his position. Plainclothes police protected the radio station and its electricity plant during his address.[183] At the same time, the president attempted to preempt his adversaries by calling for a Gaullist form of *autogestion*, which he termed "participation." The general's desire to promote participation was not merely a political ploy but reflected the longstanding Gaullist search for a middle way between capitalism and socialism. This quest had attracted progressives such as Capitant, Pisani, and others to the Gaullist movement. Finally, de Gaulle proposed a referendum to be held in

June on the renovation of the university and economy and promised to resign if it were not approved.

The reaction to the speech was largely negative. The centrists rejected what they considered to be the "Bonapartist" gadget of a referendum that they claimed would kill "dialogue."[184] Opposition politicians distrusted de Gaulle's proposed referendum even more and labeled it authoritarian and anti-Republican. Mendès-France summed up their reaction: "You do not discuss a plebiscite, you fight against it." Most observers and even the general himself agreed that it was probably one of the least effective speeches of his political career.[185] A Sorbonne graffito summarized it succinctly: "He took three weeks to announce in five minutes that he would try to do something in a month that he had not succeeded in doing for ten years." Support for the government continued to suffer attrition. Two days after the speech, a poll revealed that 55 percent of the French thought less of the general than before May and only 15 percent thought better of him.[186]

The government's refusal to permit opposition politicians (Gaston Defferre and Mendès-France) to reply to the address aggravated negative reaction. The blatant censorship outraged television journalists, and most ORTF personnel eventually joined the longest work stoppage in its history.[187] Their reasons for striking varied. Some wanted additional autonomy from government control; others sought job security. Only a small percentage of filmmakers and producers possessed long-term contracts, and the CGT took up their battle for more secure posts.[188] Independent creators threatened to strike when the Gaullist management censored a popular news program, *Zoom*.

The government's failure to reassert immediate control over its radio and television and the ineffectiveness of the General's 24 May talk led some militant Gaullists to conclude that the regime was in mortal danger.[189] On the other side, activists who were engaging in various demonstrations and protests throughout Paris were emboldened. As usual, the CGT was well-behaved, engaging in two peaceful demonstrations that were intended to show its domination of the capital. The first rallied four thousand people who marched west to east from the Place Balard to the Porte de Choisy. The second gathered ten to fifteen thousand who walked in the opposite direction from the Bastille to Havre-Caumartin.[190] The Movement of 22 March, action committees, and the CAL demanded "power to the workers" and the "abolition of employers."[191] The UNEF—backed by 22 March and the SNESup—persisted in its protest against the expulsion of Cohn-Bendit and government repression.

Some dreamed of occupying the Hôtel de Ville and reviving the Commune. Others wanted to spread the struggle to the working-class suburbs north of the city. Instead, the dynamism of the Parisian movement intensified the pilgrimage of activists from the *banlieue*. Moving to the right bank, the UNEF gathered twenty-five thousand at the Gare de Lyon in the evening of Friday, 24 May.[192] As they marched west towards Les

Halles and the Bourse, police halted them. Demonstrators then built barricades between the Gare de Lyon and the Bastille and set them on fire, but police bulldozers quickly leveled them. At midnight, protesters attacked the *commissariats* of the eleventh and the twelfth *arrondissements*. Police declared that three to four thousand made their way to the Bourse, and some—perhaps 100—of them put "the temple of money" to flame.[193] According to the forces of order, "firemen, who were stoned by the demonstrators, quickly domesticated the blaze. A vast operation, using quantities of tear gas, was able to clear the Bourse and the Place de l'Opéra. The hooligans were perfectly guided and commanded."[194] Once again, radical protesters ignored the UNEF *service d'ordre*. Police maintained that the most destructive members of the crowd were over 30 years old and not students.[195]

The arson of the Bourse surpassed a symbolic attack on capital.[196] It showed the government's momentary inability to enforce its plan to confine student demonstrators to the Latin Quarter, although it must be said that the state was able to avoid protests at its designated "priority sectors—Elysée Palace, U.S. Embassy, Chamber of Deputies, and various ministries and embassies in the seventh."[197] Police in the Latin Quarter were instructed to avoid the boulevard Saint-Michel, boulevard Saint-Germain, and *quais* from the Austerlitz Bridge to the Pont Royal.[198] Their withdrawal meant that the Latin Quarter was, in effect, abandoned to students. Once again, government reaction comprised both repression and—often forgotten during those days and nights of violence—toleration. Officers were ordered not to patrol in isolation and to form groups for mutual protection.[199]

The attack on the Bourse was also part of the general attempt by protesters to dominate the urban darkness. Immediately before and after the assault on the stock exchange, street activists, waving red and black flags and armed with axes and sticks, tried to halt trucks serving the markets of Les Halles. The sanitation strike provided protesters with plenty of trash to burn, and they set garbage aflame, forcing a sally by firemen. Just before midnight, police and demonstrators clashed violently at the rue de Rivoli and the rue Saint-Denis. The battle disturbed unloading and deliveries; however, wrote the local police commissioner, "the demonstrators never tried to harass the [strikebreaking] workers nor to damage the warehoused merchandise. They were right not to bother the workers since several of them wanted only an excuse to give protesters a good pummeling."[200]

The *commissariat* on the rue Beaubourg was set aflame, and firemen evacuated 12 persons and assisted 3 who had fainted.[201] The director of the Bibliothèque Nationale worried that demonstrators might endanger the Bibliothèque de l'Arsenal by igniting police vehicles parked near the latter.[202] He requested that police leave their cars elsewhere. The many officers who lived in the *banlieue* were also afraid of fire. At an apartment complex in the northern suburb of Gonesse, inhabited by three hundred police families, rumors circulated of pending arson by youth bands.[203] A gang of sixty reportedly attacked a group of policemen.[204] Officers, with their wives and children, worried that hostile youth would burn their apartments and vehicles. At Noisy-le-Sec four Molotov cocktails were tossed at a police sergeant's house.[205] At Eaubonne an unknown person fired a shot at an off-duty policeman driving home from work.[206]

Even more dramatic incidents erupted in the Latin Quarter.[207] Early Friday night, barricades were erected at the boulevard Saint-Michel and the rue Saint-Jacques. Chain saws felled 130 trees, picks and shovels tore up streets, and construction sites were again looted for useable materials.[208] Flaming trashcans illuminated the quarter. A barricade of cars and trees at the boulevard Saint-Michel and rue des Ecoles was stacked three meters high. Once again, bulldozers proved to be the official antidote, although they and their crew suffered "a steady rain of flying objects." "It [the bulldozer] is a remarkable tool which changes totally the conditions of attack."[209] The heavy equipment made police work considerably easier, but bulldozers needed a skillful driver, special protection against Molotov cocktails, and courageous officers to protect them.[210] Fire could render impotent even the best machinery. At 3:00 A.M. on 25 May, flames jumped so high that they forced a bulldozer to await assistance from firemen. All barricades were eliminated by 6:00 A.M. on 25 May, but students returned several hours later. Only after the army cleaned up the debris late on Saturday night could the city begin to repave streets in the Latin Quarter.

During this so-called Second Night of the Barricades, demonstrators repeated their assault on police headquarters at the Place du Panthéon.[211] For one hour they pelted it with Molotov cocktails, cobblestones, and other objects. Fire entirely destroyed the command car and scorched a number of buses.[212] Protesters doused vehicles with flammable fluids and left them ablaze. They also overturned parked cars and ignited fuel spewing forth from gas tanks, provoking loud explosions. "The violence of the flames forced demonstrators to leave momentarily and gave us [police] some respite."[213] Eight *gardiens* were injured, and all of the windows of the *commissariat* were broken. Protesters set fire to the building, and the combination of smoke and tear gas caused dozens of police to vomit. Fire slowed the arrival of relief forces, and police under siege inside threatened to retaliate violently.[214] The assurance that relief was imminent helped them regain their discipline.

On the night of 24–25 May, police reported 23 barricades throughout the city, most of which (17) were in or near the Latin Quarter.[215] Nevertheless, demonstrators had been successful in breaking out of their student ghetto. Crowds had erected several fortifications on the right bank and another in the *banlieue*. Some protesters transported gasoline containers to facilitate their incendiarism, and even in the chic sixteenth *arrondissement*, a police *commissariat* was burned.[216] The boulevard Sébastopol suffered much damage, and several blocks from the Gare de Lyon demonstrators set fire to the gas of overturned cars.[217] A total of 123 officers were reported hurt—98 municipal police, 19 CRS, and 6 *gendarmes mobiles*.[218] Flying cobblestones occasioned most police injuries, but Molotov cocktails filled with metal pellets injured 4, of whom 2 were hospitalized.[219] Police arrested hundreds, although a lucky few escaped in Red Cross vehicles. The forces of order detained 727 persons at their Centre Beaujon.[220] Seventy-two (10 percent) were female; 98 (13 percent) were foreigners; 79 (11 percent) were minors. Only 280 (39 percent) were students. Police even apprehended a soldier on leave. The weeks of demonstrations prolonged their toll on men whose commander sensed that they "had reached the limit of their ability to re-establish order without resorting to extreme methods."[221]

In July, the director of the Municipal Police reflected that violence attained its acme during the Second Night of the Barricades.[222] "This was the first time the municipal police found themselves in such an exceptional situation." Only the help of the Gendarmerie Mobile and the CRS enabled them to cope. "Intervention groups" of 200 to 240 men were formed to overwhelm protesters without using firearms. Echoing the prime minister, the police director sharply faulted radio stations for "a rare mischievousness. They behaved irresponsibly" by broadcasting falsely or sensationally. "We must take measures against them." He considered cobblestones as pernicious as the media and recommended that streets be paved over in the Latin Quarter and throughout the capital.

Busy firemen responded to 350 alarms during the Second Night of the Barricades and offered first aid to twenty-five demonstrators.[223] Smoke poisoning and flying cobblestones injured twenty-five firemen. Eight fire department vehicles were damaged. Demonstrators ignored the customary public confidence in firemen by attacking and stoning *pompiers* who had tried to extinguish the Bourse fire.[224] Asserting their control over water, they opened fire hydrants.[225] These protesters wanted to see the city in flames. What many considered to be gratuitous violence began to turn sectors of public opinion, which had been tolerant or even supportive of the movement, against radicals.[226] Street fighters' attacks on property and *pompiers* alienated what Arthur Marwick has called the "measured judgment" of a generally open-minded public that shared demonstrators' doubts about unreasonable state authority.[227] Police reported that students themselves disavowed violent street action.[228] Jacques Baynac, a participant associated with the extreme left, "experienced with sadness the hostility of the population. The romance with students was ending even though the venerable anti-cop attitude of the French was still alive."[229] A café owner who had previously given students drink and refuge exploded after the danger of a police attack had passed: "You *petits cons*. You're preventing us from working. We're sick of your nonsense." The lower middle classes, important and numerous in the capital, turned on youthful revolutionaries. Concierges slammed shut the doors of their apartment houses and even betrayed demonstrators to police. Of course, the PCF repudiated the protesters.[230] Pompidou's strategy of permitting the movement to reveal its hatred of property was beginning to succeed. The astute prime minister ordered police to disperse the crowds towards the western half of the city in order to strike fear into the hearts of Parisian bourgeois.[231] Student radicals, such as Cohn-Bendit and UNEF leaders, grasped what polls confirmed—the turn of public opinion against protesters.[232]

Even after the first Night of the Barricades on 10–11 May, workers had objected to the burning of parked vehicles.[233] The second wave of car torchings during the night of 24 May compounded fears of *automobilistes*. Owners of compact cars empathized with proprietors of high-priced models, who were the major target of demonstrators' attacks. Student violence was no longer seen as a legitimate defense against a brutal state but rather as needless aggression against property. Increasing reliance on violence seemed to disclose the movement's lack of strategy and a clear vision of where it was going.[234] The Pompidou government, hoping to erode support for demonstrators, left reminders of destruction by refusing to clean up material damaged by the conflict.[235] Incinerated vehicles and abandoned barricades quickly became attractions for tourists fascinated or repulsed by the spectacle of Parisian revolution.

To many, the state still seemed supremely incompetent. Yet behind the scenes government officials were engaged in a well-organized effort to break some of the most significant strikes. The markets of Les Halles were fundamental for feeding Paris and for linking the urban and rural economies.[236] What authorities called the "economic police" of Les Halles reported daily to the ministries of Finance and Agriculture. Officials wanted to ensure that the intense nocturnal activities of the markets were not interrupted.[237] During the night of 23–24 May, students tried to invade the markets, but "they never broke through because of the vigilance and the actions of the municipal police."[238] "Very tough clashes [occurred] between police and large groups of students who blocked streets with rubbish and even burned a supply truck on the rue Renard." Another dozen or so young people set trashcans ablaze. Police detained 150. At the same time, students encountered little sympathy and even some hostility from workers. Although nearly all Les Halles manual workers approved of the CGT strike, they seemed indifferent or even hostile to student struggles.[239]

Independent truck drivers were both willing and able to bypass the SNCF strike and transport produce—especially fruits and vegetables—to the city, but they needed help to unload their vehicles. However, the *forts* (unloaders) of the CGT, an important minority, had gone on strike. *Forts* at Les Halles were public service workers who had a history of agitation. Several months prior to May, they had stopped work to gain higher wages.[240] The striking CGT unloaders were joined by members of an independent union, seafood personnel, and half of Les Halles' salespeople. Strikers' demands were traditional, involving higher wages and, given plans to transfer the market to Rungis, job security. They threatened to destroy merchandise but ultimately did not do so. However, CGT unloaders locked three buildings to prevent their bosses from gaining access.[241] Police, though, had extra keys and demonstrated that they had the markets well under control. The forces of order did not hesitate to hire strikebreakers or even to use uniformed police to load and unload commodities for nearly a week.[242] Police were assisted by *mandataires* (licensed food brokers) and a good number of their employees, who served as temporary butchers. The government, aided by food brokers, controlled prices to ensure that victuals remained affordable.

At another essential supply center, the La Villette slaughterhouse, the state secured "the right to work" and freedom of movement. With the CRS surveying, strikebreakers were able to unload meat at La Villette and seafood at the La Criée fish market.[243] Strikers at La Villette attempted to stop truck deliveries, but the police presence rendered their opposition ineffective.[244] A simple verbal warning dispersed one hundred of them. Police were ready to close the gates of the slaughterhouse as soon as students approached.[245] The power of the state, promises of higher pay, and guarantees that days lost to stoppages would be fully compensated convinced strikers to end their walkout. The result of a 23 May strike vote—conducted with a secret ballot, not raised hands—was 189 for a return to work on the following day and only 14 against. Police commanders were pleased to be able to transfer their forces from the pacified slaughterhouse to the continuing strike at ORTF. Control of the media was nearly as high a priority as feeding Paris.

Police policies were effective, and deliveries to La Villette and Les Halles remained steady. Nevertheless, the strikes changed Parisian eating habits. Consumers wanted produce with a long shelf life, such as potatoes, and rejected perishables, e.g., asparagus, even when available.[246] The price of potatoes even dropped at the height of the crisis.[247] By the end of the week of 20–27 May, the cost of dairy, fish, and poultry products had drifted lower. Thus, despite the continuation of the strike wave, police confirmed that prices remained stable at Les Halles.[248] The state effectively encouraged supply to match demand.[249]

To accomplish this, drivers and merchants had to have gasoline. The government quickly acted to ensure its supply and distribution. At a meeting on Monday, 20 May, "the prime minister and the minister of industry consider[ed] that priority must be given to solve the problems of distribution of gasoline in the Paris region."[250] On 14 May, the Municipal Police had at their disposal 17,280 *gardiens* (agents), 3,100 *brigadiers* (officers), 3,225 gendarmes, and 3,500 CRS.[251] Officials reasoned that they needed two to three thousand men to defend the gasoline depots at Gennevilliers and Nanterre and therefore shifted several thousand from guard duty at intersections, embassies, and other institutions to safeguard gas deliveries. Three essential complexes that surrounded the capital needed protection: the port of Gennevilliers (where a major pipeline terminated),

Villeneuve-le-Roi—Choisy-le-Roi, and Colombes. On 21 May the major gas depots at Gennevilliers (Mobil, Elf, Antar, SITESC) were on strike; only Esso and BP were working.[252] Workers at Total at Saint-Ouen, Antar at Villeneuve, and Desmarais at Colombes also participated in the work stoppage. On the night of 23 May, a dozen strikers assaulted non-strikers at the Shell complex at Nanterre.[253] Three persons were injured, and telephone wires were sabotaged.

In order to guarantee the "right to work" and freedom of circulation, police had to be prepared to evict strikers from the interior of these centers. However, in the face of union opposition and that of local officials (many of whom were members of the PCF) who supported the strikers, a forcible takeover risked "serious incidents."[254] An operation—labeled Dégel—was planned for 30 May to vacate the depots of Gennevilliers and Juvisy-Grigny. Officials intended to use the military, if necessary, to occupy strategic points. Soldiers would form groups of thirty-five to forty men, mostly draftees, who would be under the orders of professional officers. Like some Parisian police, they would be armed with unloaded rifles. Plans were drawn to guard tank-car vehicles from strikers who might be tempted to assail them. Officials recommended that motorcycle police accompany gas trucks. Military personnel who managed army gas stations were ready to assist the operation and were assigned to the major distribution center near Langres.[255] However, at the last minute, the prefect delayed Operation Dégel and the evacuation of the striking centers for several reasons.[256] Police feared that strikers could easily sabotage trucks parked inside depots, or, more dangerously, start an intentional or unintentional fire. Petroleum company executives also objected to the planned evacuation.[257] Authorities decided to postpone the operation until after General de Gaulle's 30 May address to the nation.

Officials responded to truck drivers' fears that they would not be able to acquire enough fuel to travel to and from Paris. The Direction des Carburants, a branch of the Ministry of Industry, established gas stations exclusively for trucks and other vehicles carrying perishable goods.[258] Despite the walkout of gasoline workers, fuel supply depots were generally well stocked. Petroleum companies, merchants, and teamsters collaborated to establish a list of functioning gas stations that was forwarded to the truckers' union (Syndicat des transporteurs) and to the grocers' association (Syndicat des épiciers détaillants).[259] Truckers were able to obtain documents attesting that their vehicles were used for provisioning. The 9,500 firms of the Parisian trucking industry—which normally supplied 70 percent of foodstuffs to the capital—found access to fuel.[260] After threatening protests and even a strike, so did grocery store employees. Authorities agreed that "the thousands of small grocers of Paris and its suburbs must be able to get whatever they need to satisfy housewives."[261] The corporatism inspired by the events of May included small as well as the large employers, labor unions, and the state. The government and the petroleum companies were able to offer privileged supplies to the still numerous lower middle classes. Even as late as 1973, small independent commerce composed 75 percent of all French distribution.[262]

Unlike in 1848 or 1871, authorities were able to feed the city and thus to prevent their adversaries from gaining the solid support of housewives.[263] Strikers' attempts to intimidate food store owners were too sporadic to be successful.[264] The owners of bakeries were willing to produce as long as they could obtain flour, which well-fueled provincial millers supplied directly to them.[265] Thus, Paris never lacked bread. Officials counted 20,000 *détaillants* and thus established four centers—two at Les Halles, one at La Villette, and another on the rue de Vaugirard—manned by 12 *fonctionnaires* to distribute gas certificates. Les Halles workers, a significant number of whom were striking, were bribed to return with awards of priority gasoline status.[266] Non-strikers at ORTF informed potential applicants over the airwaves and thereby heightened demand for gas coupons.[267] Hundreds of certificates were delivered in several hours, and telephone inquiries overwhelmed officialdom.[268] By 25 May, 518 certificates had been issued.[269] In fact, by 28 May so many certificates had been granted that the Direction des Carburants ceased accepting them and told the *détaillants* and their employees to get documentation from their own professional organizations. The *détaillants* were outraged, threatened again to strike, and were immediately issued more.[270] Ultimately, an impressive total of 10,170 certificates were delivered. On 28 May officials felt that although supplies were dwindling, they could still fill the tanks of priority vehicles for several more days.[271] The return of gasoline in large quantities on 31 May resolved the issue. Gas created a solidarity among the state, small business, and much of the working class. May 1968 saw a Popular Front at the pumps. Indeed, after the fact, union leaders wanted to take credit for the provisioning of the capital and insisted that their members had ignored the "provocations" of the "big bosses."[272]

Ministries established five priority consumers: health care personnel, vehicles with perishables, diplomats, media, and, of course, police themselves.[273] The last were encouraged to carpool and required permission from their superiors to get served at stations.[274] Authorities arranged dormitory facilities and military transport for policemen.[275] Police were assigned to guard gas stations when it became clear that "certain drivers used force to get fuel." Gasoline shortages provoked anger and violence. When the Porte-Saint-Augustins station ran out of fuel, drivers became furious and wanted to sack it.[276] Police expelled the outraged motorists without incident. Female drivers could be extremely militant when refused fuel. At the station at the Porte des Ternes, which was reserved for medical personnel, Mlle. X, 26 years old, was denied gas. She became "very agitated," and several police officers accused her of punching them in the testicles.[277] A 35-year-old dentist from Upper Volta tried to get gas at one station. When refused, he irately drove directly into an officer of the law.[278]

In the suburbs, "individuals with red armbands [had] taken over certain priority pumps" and distributed gas as they wished.[279] Officials ordered an immediate end to this practice. The violence of gas consumers did not aim to destroy property but rather to acquire it. The acquisitive individualism of drivers in May anticipated the mass exodus of early June that announced the end of the strike wave.

The state's efforts to control distribution were largely successful. At only one major depot, SITESC, was a total strike accompanied by an aggressive picket line; at Antar (Gennevilliers), Mobil (Gennevilliers), Total (Colombes), and Antar (Villeneuve) neither occupations nor picket lines transpired.[280] At Total (Saint-Ouen) the picket line was "good-natured." In fact, strikers cooperated with authorities and distributed gas to priority customers: "Fifteen trucks driven by strikers served priority clients and circulated usually with a sign, '*Laissez passez, prioritaires.*'" Indeed, the distribution of the fuel of consumer society inspired close collaboration among the union leadership, the media, and the state. The Direction Générale des Carburants planned to open the Elf station (rue de Bellefond, 9th) exclusively for union (CGT and CFDT) members.[281] Not just *Le Figaro* but also *L'Humanité* agreed to publish a list of priority stations.[282] The Ministry of Industry informed police that the Antar station (Place F. Liszt, 10th) was reserved for union delegates.[283]

Not all trade unionists were so cooperative. Police escorts had to protect some fuel truck convoys from hostile vehicles manned by strikers.[284] At least three tankers were hijacked in the *banlieue*.[285] National highway nineteen, on which nearly one hundred gas tankers traveled at night, needed police protection to ensure uninhibited circulation.[286] Strikers on this road used walkie-talkies to coordinate movements that intimidated scabbing truck drivers. The forces of order were ready to intervene at the service station on national route nine near Chevilly-Larue, where strikers refused to distribute gas to priority customers.[287] Police terminated the occupation of the BP gas depot at Vitry by forcing twenty-five strike pickets to vacate the premises.[288] Even after de Gaulle's 30 May address, the forces of order had to be prepared to safeguard the depot at Villeneuve-Saint-Georges.[289]

In the morning of 31 May, 480 tanker trucks departed while police intervened at certain depots to guarantee the "right to work."[290] Officials noted that at the end of May, a CFDT delegate, who wanted to discourage a return to motorized normality, made the rounds at the Total depots in Colombes and Nanterre and asked strike pickets to *dénaturer* (adulterate) gasoline.[291] They flatly refused. If they had imitated the pyrotechnics of youth in the Latin Quarter, the state and the oil companies would have had to confront an industrial disaster. Instead, the government received enough cooperation from gas workers to keep the liquid flowing.[292] On Saturday, 1 June, gasoline distribution was nearly normal.[293] In June, Albin Chalandon, the minister of industry and a high-ranking Gaullist, praised police work at Asnières in a letter to the local commissioner: "[The forces of order] were efficient and cannot be faulted. I especially appreciated how you re-established the right to work at the port of Gennevilliers."[294] Other officials echoed the minister's approbation: "With regard to the gasoline conflict, police interventions that occurred at Nanterre, Colombes, Saint-Denis or Saint-Ouen, etc. fortunately and necessarily contributed to a solution, which probably would not have occurred without them."[295]

On 25 May, negotiations on the national level opened among the government, employers' organizations (CNPF, CNPME), and unions (CGT, CFDT, CGT-FO, CFTC, FEN, CGC). Farmer and peasant organizations, such as the FNSEA (Fédération nationale des syndicats d'exploitants agricoles), did not participate, demonstrating the urban nature of the movement.[296] Growers did not wish to weaken the French state when it had to conduct Common Market negotiations, which were scheduled to open at Brussels on 27 May.[297] Despite opposition from *gauchistes*, the unions could hardly refuse the high-level bargaining that they had been demanding for years. In many ways, the negotiations resembled those that had culminated in the Matignon Agreements in 1936 during the Popular Front. As in 1936, the elites of labor, business, and government tried to reach a national settlement. Yet differences between the two sets of negotiations reflected changes over three decades. The presence of the CNPME (Confédération nationale des petites et moyennes entreprises) showed that the Gaullist government had no intention of completely ignoring the small and medium-sized firms that had been left out of the talks in 1936. The "petty bourgeoisie"—destined to disappear, according to Marxists—had earned a place at the corporatist bargaining table. Also, by 1968 the *cadres'* union, CGC, became a full bargaining partner. Its participation showed the rise of a new social group of university-trained middle management, whose activities sociologists had predicted and depicted. Like other participants, the CGC downplayed demands for workers' control or *autogestion*. Although its leader, André Malterre, insisted on increasing autonomy for ORTF, the CGC stressed bread-and-butter issues, such as the lowering of the retirement age and salary increases.[298] In 1968, the union movement appeared more divided than it had been in 1936. At that time, the CGT exercised a near monopoly on worker representation and garnered greater sympathy from a Socialist-led government.

All parties in the 1968 negotiations tacitly agreed to debate not the nature of the pie but rather its division. Pompidou expressed gratitude that he was able to deal with unions that could "guide" the working class.[299] His team—which included a future prime minister, Edouard Balladur, and a future president of the republic, Jacques Chirac—ignored de Gaulle's plans for participation in favor of hard bargaining over material concessions to workers. Pompidou and his aides were ready to redistribute some wealth but not to implement Gaullist ideas of a third way between capitalism and socialism. The prime minister tried to divide the unions by appealing to the anti-Americanism of the CGT leaders. He warned them that if disorder continued and Gaullism was swept from government, Atlanticism and American domination would return to France. Pompidou was quoted: "I prefer to be a low-level bureaucrat in a Communist government than prime minister in a France ruled by Americans."[300] Séguy asserted that Jacques Chirac repeated the same line of argument and tried to frighten the union into moderation by arguing that if negotiations failed and de Gaulle fell, Atlanticists would seize control of the nation. Séguy claimed that he loftily ignored the remarks and continued to fight for "the interests of the workers."[301]

On Monday, 27 May, an accord was reached. It was informally called the Grenelle Accord or officially the *projet de protocole d'accord*, i.e., an outline that was left unsigned. The employers conceded a 35 percent hike in the minimum wage. The percentage gained in 1968 thus greatly exceeded the 7 to 15 percent won during the negotiations in 1936. In the 1960s, women, youth, and foreigners would tend to profit from this dramatic increase more than other wage earners. Madeleine Colin, a prominent official of the CGT, argued that "women [who earned on the average 36 percent less than men] and young people were among the principal beneficiaries of the raises" since "they constitute the majority of workers who earn the minimum wage." Some young women, she asserted, "saw their salary double."[302] In comparison, higher-paid workers gained only a 10 percent increase. Thus, the CGT and the CFDT delivered on their 1966 promise to fight to obtain an increase in the minimum wage. Even though the raises threatened its anti-inflation policies, the government quickly conceded them because they affected small and medium-sized firms much more than the dynamic, large enterprises that the regime had continually favored.[303]

Wage concessions were also admissions that disparities had grown enormously during the Fifth Republic. Salaries of *cadres* had increased 2.5 times from 1956 to 1967, 2.2 times for employees, and only 1.8 times for those laboring at minimum wage.[304] From 1956 to 1967, *cadres* had registered a 48 percent increase in real purchasing power; employees a 39 percent increase; the average worker 31 percent; and the minimum-wage worker from 3.7 to 6 percent. Thus, some *cadres* and professionals had the luxury of demanding qualitative reforms that lower-paid workers did not.

Many ORTF journalists and technicians had engaged in an illegal strike to demand structural changes in the decision-making process.[305] However, not all journalists and technicians shared a pro-strike attitude, and some of them were concerned that the stoppage violated ORTF's public-service role and would consequently lessen public support for the state monopoly. Antistrike supervisory personnel made their presence felt in other enterprises. In a number of important factories, including SNECMA at Villaroche and Dassault at Saint-Cloud, *cadres* remained close to upper management and tended to exercise a conservative influence during strikes.[306] On the other hand, research personnel were generally more favorable to the strike than engineers and supervisory personnel. Whether white- or blue-collar, wage and hours issues dominated negotiations.

The Grenelle agreement reflected union concern that French workers labored longer than other Europeans. It guaranteed a moderate and progressive reduction of the work week—2 hours for wage earners laboring more than 48 hours and 1 hour for those laboring between 45 and 48 hours. Pompidou supported in principle a reduction of the work week but, perhaps recalling the unfortunate experience of French capitalism during the Popular Front, when the forty-hour limit restricted production, he insisted that the reduction occur in stages and not "in a brutal manner."[307] The most divisive issue might have been the extent of increases for non-minimum-wage personnel. Early Sunday morning, 26 May, unions and employers remained deadlocked over the amount of salary hikes. The CNPF was arguing for a 5 percent raise on 1 June and another 3 percent on 1 October. Séguy wanted 12 percent, but Descamps of the CFDT then proposed 7 percent on 1 June and 3 percent on 1 October, totaling 10 percent for the year. Séguy rallied to Descamps' proposal but cautioned, "if Descamps' suggestion is accepted by the CNPF, it will be brought to the attention of the workers on strike. It cannot be accepted independently of other questions." The "other questions" included guarantees for union rights and activities. On this issue, the prime minister affirmed that "the government is not hostile to the union movement. It is convinced that the *encadrement* (guiding) of the working class by unions possessing the correct formation and influence helps the smooth functioning of firms." The head of the government—who, it should be remembered, had informed the National Assembly during the debate on censure that the strikes had begun spontaneously—was more favorable to union rights than the leader of the CNPF, who blamed work stoppages on union agitation.[308] The prime minister's statement confirmed the suspicions of some *gauchistes* and others who had argued that, in the final analysis, unions were an intrinsic, if not vital, part of the capitalist system. Those with a stake in the system ultimately overcame the property haters who had initiated the movement and had given it its subversive edge.

The accord granted employers the authority to recover hours lost because of the strike but affirmed and extended union activities. It recognized the unions' right to organize members, collect dues, distribute literature, and hold meetings. The agreement provided the greatest gains for workers since the Liberation, and it opened the way for subsequent negotiations on public service employees that began on Tuesday, 28 May.[309] At that time, teachers' unions pursued discussions with the state. The teachers' presence and importance demonstrated both the demographic weight of youth and the growth of public education during the postwar era. The government was not merely a mediator, as it had been in 1936, but an active partner in negotiations.

On Monday, 27 May, when union leaders attempted to sell the Grenelle agreement to the rank and file, strikers in certain large firms reacted with considerable hostility. Many *métallos* may have felt that the greatest strike wave in French history should have produced more significant results. In the private sector, interior ministry officials asserted that metallurgy was the branch most affected by the strike wave.[310] The ineffectiveness of the limited and partial strikes prior to May had frustrated large numbers of metallurgical workers who were anxious to take advantage of opportunities created by the mass movement.[311] The momentum of the wave encouraged ambitious material demands. Wage earners sought the concessions that their unions had been demanding for years, such as an eventual return to a forty-hour week—which German metal workers had won in 1966—and no salary under 1,000 francs per month. The most famous example of the rejection of the Grenelle protocol occurred on Monday at Renault. Georges Séguy and Benoît Frachon, the veteran leader of the CGT, assisted by André Jeanson, president of the CFDT, were unable to convince the crowd of five to six thousand auto workers that the protocol should be endorsed. The rank and file—who were generally mature wage earners (the average age at Billancourt was 41 years old)—especially objected to clauses that granted employers the right to recover the hours lost because of the strike.[312] RTL and Europe One quickly conveyed the news of the workers' rejection. The Ministry of Interior believed that the rapid diffusion of the information encouraged workers in other plants to reject the agreement and thus helped to prolong the strikes.[313] Similar disapproval of the Grenelle settlement transpired at other major metallurgical firms, including Citroën and Sud-Aviation. Metallurgical workers, according to one interior ministry document, "believed that the agreement did not resolve all the problems and that many demands must be negotiated on the local level."[314] Strikes "will continue in many places," but, police concluded, the rank and file had and would continue to follow their union representatives.

Some analysts have interpreted the workers' rejection of the protocol as an indication of growing revolutionary sentiment of the working class or its desire for workers' control.[315] An American historian expressed the view that "despite the prompting of their leaders, the rank-and-file rebelled against union discipline and disavowed any settlement with the bourgeois order."[316] The *Nation*'s Daniel Singer reported that the "traditional union and Party establishment of the labor movement looks as bewildered by the sweep and significance of the new conflicts as are the rulers themselves."[317] French workers "felt rather dimly that no wage increase, no material concession, could really be big enough to match their new political power." *Les Temps modernes*—whose editorial board included Simone de Beauvoir, André Gorz, Claude Lanzmann, and Jean-Paul Sartre—argued that that the rejection of the accord showed "an unsuspected political radicalization of the working class."[318] The editorial committee of *Esprit*, which comprised

Jean-Marie Domenach, Jacques Juillard, Daniel Mothé, Paul Ricoeur, and Michel Winock, wanted to reorganize French society into a "democracy of participation."[319] Leftists of various sorts have claimed that the unions, especially the CGT, betrayed the revolutionary desires of the rank and file.[320] Trotskyite historians have blamed the failure of revolution on the reformism of the CGT and especially the PCF.[321] Likewise, Maoists accused the PCF of betraying the working class. The PSU militant Gilles Martinet believed that the rejection of Grenelle demonstrated that the CGT had lost control of the movement.[322]

Ironically enough, the Maoists, Trotskyites, and *Les Temps modernes* have rather uncritically accepted PCF claims to represent the working class. They assumed that the party controlled the workers and could have made revolution.[323] It is doubtful, though, that even a revolutionary PCF would have been able to convince wage earners to take power. As has been seen, the influence of revolutionaries—whether *gauchistes* or *autogestionnaires*—was relatively insignificant in Parisian metallurgy and other industries. Wage earners might have desired to limit the "arbitrary" authority of supervisory personnel and to slow down production rhythms, but little evidence exists to suggest that workers wanted to take over their factories.[324] Instead, they demanded higher pay (especially for lower-paid personnel), a further reduction of work time, total (and not half) payment for days lost to strikes, a nominal recuperation of strike time, and—for the activists—a union presence in the factory. The compromise among national elites did not fully satisfy many wage earners, including CGT militants, who felt that they had an unprecedented chance to get even more.[325]

The failure of the union leadership to obtain approval of the original package from the rank and file in certain large metallurgical factories has led some nonrevolutionary observers to emphasize either the weakness of French unionism or its supposed nonrepresentivity. The Catholic newspaper *La Croix* lamented that "even when they conclude an agreement, the unions are not strong enough to convince the workers to ratify it. The French economy and the employers have paid dearly for twenty years of contempt for unions."[326] Believing that only unions could control an unpredictable rank and file, some "progressive" employers—who were usually from large industries in advanced sectors—regretted postwar policies that had excluded or marginalized the major federations.

Yet the unions adjusted quickly and without much difficulty to the unpopularity of the protocol in large firms.[327] Union leaders had never signed the agreement and may have suspected that they could encounter obstacles selling it. Séguy, Descamps, and Bergeron did not consider Grenelle a final agreement but a basis for discussion.[328] Descamps requested a forty-eight-hour period of reflection before his union would respond definitively. For Séguy, "much remained to be done" to produce an acceptable settlement. In his speech to the Renault workers on 27 May, Jeanson of the CFDT congratulated strikers for refusing to return to work and hoped that other factories would follow their example.[329] At the same meeting, Séguy declared that since the CGT had not formally issued a strike order, it could not ask workers to return to their jobs. Several hours later, the CGT administrative commission endorsed the refusal of its Grenelle delegation to sign the agreement because of employers' "insufficient concessions."[330]

A police bulletin informed the Ministry of Interior of the CGT's ambivalence toward the accord: "The day after the agreement, the CGT administrative commission considers that substantial gains have been obtained [from Grenelle] especially concerning minimum wage, union rights, and collective contracts. After consultation with its rank-and-file militants, it came to the conclusion today that these gains are clearly insufficient."[331] When the "base" rejected Grenelle, police ascertained that "quickly... the CGT and the CFDT, wanting to maintain control of the rank and file, called for the struggle to continue.... Union officials are united. They reinforce picket lines so as to discourage those who wish to return to work."[332] *L'Humanité* rapidly seconded the rejection of Grenelle.

Thus, *gauchistes'* charges that the unions "broke" the movement are hard to sustain.[333] The unions' rapid adaptation to the rank-and-file rejection of Grenelle displayed their continuing ability to domesticate rapidly impulses that may have been initially outside their control. A disappointed radical in the Nord lamented that the "working class prudently acquiesced to the bureaucrats that it paid to defend it. The noise of tear gas grenades was unable to raise its consciousness after decades of prostration ... [and] of television, refrigerators, and cars."[334] To resolve continuing conflicts, the CGT recommended that negotiations be conducted by industrial branch and profession, but discussions quickly reverted to the level of the individual firms when metallurgical employers' organizations and unions could not agree on a national or even on a regional bargaining agreement. Parisian metallurgical employers especially resisted a regional accord that would have been more generous than Grenelle and preferred to negotiate on a firm-by-firm basis.[335] The Groupement des Industries Métallurgiques wished to protect the autonomy of its members, especially owners of small and medium-sized firms that were very reluctant to make further concessions.

The immediate failure of Grenelle and the continuation of the strikes emboldened radicals. The government had yet to gain control over its own television network, whose employees continued to strike to protest heavy-handed censorship of the news.[336] The UNEF organized a meeting of representatives from both the parliamentary and extreme left to be held at the Charléty stadium on the afternoon of 27 May. Talks among the UNEF, PCF, and CGT had broken down over "attitudes toward repression"—i.e., Cohn-Bendit's expulsion—and the CFDT and UNEF reacted by holding their own meeting at Charléty.[337] The PCF and the CGT refused to endorse the gathering; instead, the party recapitulated its polemic against *gauchisme*.[338] Interior Minister Fouchet, supported by Edgar Faure, was able to convince the president of the republic, who favored outlawing demonstrations, to permit the gathering.[339] Calculated toleration again prevailed at the highest levels of government.

Even so, the psychosis of fire possessed certain police officials who feared that "uncontrollable elements" might incinerate the Hôtel de Ville, Ecole Normale Supérieure, Panthéon, or Sorbonne.[340] Police Prefect Grimaud took preventative measures and ordered massive inspections of young people circulating on bicycles, motor scooters, or in cars.[341] Hundreds of youths were indiscriminately searched for weapons, including flammable materials. Although Grimaud approved most inspections and interrogations, he admitted that his men may have acted too roughly during searches and seizures and cautioned them: "I have received numerous direct testimonies of these interrogations, and I think they are often impolitic and uselessly brutal." He stressed that young people should be treated fairly, regardless of their appearance: "It is fruitless to manhandle them, tear their clothing, or bully them."[342]

Despite the obstacles, 20,000–22,000 (police estimate) to 50,000 persons showed up at the Charléty gathering, which passed without violence.[343] André Barjonet, who had been the CGT's director of economic research, spoke to the crowd about the revolutionary possibilities of the situation. Repeating the slogan of Marceau Pivert, who had led the left wing of the Socialist party during the Popular Front, an optimistic Barjonet intoned that "everything is possible." The audience rejoiced and demanded both de Gaulle's resignation and "Workers' Power." The UNEF, *groupuscules*, CFDT militants, and a few CGT and FO dissidents composed the bulk of the participants.[344] Mendès-France and members of the PSU hierarchy were also in attendance. The presence of Mendès-France—who continued, in contrast to the more obviously opportunistic François Mitterrand, to win respect from some radical students—showed that the movement possessed the potential of bringing down the government.

The Movement of 22 March suspected CFDT maneuvering (what *gauchistes* termed *récupération* by parties and unions). Like the Communists, 22 March refused to endorse the Charléty meeting and organized its own neighborhood demonstrations, which had virtually no impact. Police reasoned that 22 March was "losing steam.... At the Square Saint-Lambert there was no gathering despite the numerous appeals of the action committee of the fifteenth *arrondissement*."[345] At the Place des Vosges only twenty people came, and a mere thirty assembled at the Square des Batignolles in the seventeenth *arrondissement*.

The Charléty meeting encouraged the parliamentary left to propose alternatives to Gaullist rule. Opposition figures wanted to turn the continuing strikes to political advantage. On Tuesday, 28 May, Mitterrand declared himself ready to take charge of the republic.[346] His statement offering to serve as president reminded observers of a similar declaration by de Gaulle ten years earlier. It also struck some, including a few in his party, as unconstitutional and perhaps undemocratic. Lamenting the weakness of the state, Mitterrand attempted to reach out to those who wanted order. "Since May 3," he declared, "the state has disappeared." This was, of course, a common but erroneous perception at the time, and a prominent intellectual would repeat it later.[347] Mitterrand proposed to re-establish the state and appealed for new elections. As he offered his candidacy for president, he suggested the PSU's Mendès-France as prime minister. The unorthodox Mendès had many supporters in the CFDT, whose secretary general had suggested that the crisis could be resolved by a Mendès-led government.[348] The PSU leader's reputation for anticommunism and economic rigor was capable of garnering support from certain employers and even from the center. Jean Lecanuet called for a "government of public safety" and implied support for Mendès.[349] In an opinion piece in *Le Monde*, Alfred Fabre-Luce, a political maverick who dabbled in extreme-right politics, asked the former prime minister to take charge.

But the PCF was less than enthusiastic about Mendès. Mitterrand and others realized that for the left to take power, the split between the PCF and other parties, which was evident at Charléty, had to be healed. Overcoming division was difficult since—police analysts believed—both the Socialists of the SFIO and the left-of-center Radicals were afraid to ally with the PCF.[350] For their part, the Communists remained the strongest force on the left and desired to make a deal on their own terms by reconstructing a Popular Front style coalition. The left's strong showing in the legislative elections of March 1967 encouraged their strategy.[351] *L'Humanité* urged that the left parties formulate a minimum program that could satisfy students and workers. Throughout the strikes, the PCF was negotiating with the FGDS and trying to create a viable coalition. The CGT advocated a kind of Liberation-era government to initiate "a new policy of democracy and social change."[352]

Many Socialists and moderates, though, were frightened by the prospect of Communist domination of such a coalition. The slogan of "popular government" may have fondly evoked the Popular Front for Communists and *cégétistes*, but for others it raised the disturbing prospect of the "popular democracies" of the Soviet block. For its part, the PCF was quite suspicious of what it considered to be the neocapitalist and pro-American orientations of the non-Communist left. The divisions among the left never permitted the PCF to realize its goal of "popular government" in 1968. In twentieth-century France, only when non-Communists dominated a left-wing coalition was a Popular Front solution acceptable to the majority of the electorate. This had occurred during the depression of the late 1930s and would occur again during the recession of the early 1980s. It proved unattainable in 1968.

The economy of the consumerist 1960s made a Popular Front less urgent. Unlike the depressed 1930s, the economic policies of the right had not been discredited. Indeed, they had fostered mass consumption. Furthermore, unemployment was not the obsession that it had been during the decade of the Great Depression or that it became during the recession of the early 1980s. Although some have underlined rising unemployment as a crucial factor in fostering the movement, neither workers nor unions insisted upon complete job security in negotiations. The unemployed numbered fewer than 500,000, 40 percent of whom were under 25 years old.[353] It did not approach the millions of present-day France. In contrast to the 1930s or 1990s, workers and unions demanded a shorter work week not in order to give work to the unemployed but rather for the sake of enjoying leisure itself. A strictly imposed forty-hour week would have met much more opposition from the rank and file in 1968 than it had in 1936 since consumer society had made overtime more attractive than it had been in the past.[354]

Instead of healing the divisions among the left, the Charléty meeting aggravated them. The PCF feared that Charléty might lead to a new "Third Force," a grouping of the center-left parties whose glue would be anti-Communism.[355] The CGT was outraged by accusations from some Charléty speakers that it had betrayed the workers. In response, the confederation organized a demonstration on Wednesday, 29 May, to show its ability to out-mobilize Charléty. The CGT urged all unions to participate. The CFDT, FGDS, and UNEF turned down the invitation, and the UNEF once more demanded that the CGT protest against the government's exile of Cohn-Bendit.[356] Nevertheless, the police declared that some leftists and students attended the CGT march.[357] One hundred thousand (police estimate) to 300,000 persons—the largest crowd since 13 May—marched "without incident" from the Bastille to the Gare Saint-Lazare.[358] The multitude was led by a host of distinguished *staliniens*: Georges Séguy, Benoît Frachon, Waldeck Rochet, Jacques Duclos, Jeannette Vermeesch, and Louis Aragon. The trajectory of the demonstration passed near the Parisian political centers of the Hôtel de Ville and the Elysée, thereby frightening a few members of the government and other *bien pensants* who felt that a Communist coup d'état was in the making.[359] Many were aware that the PCF regarded de Gaulle's accession to power in 1958 as illegitimate. According to the party, the general had used the threat of civil war to blackmail his way into the presidency.[360]

Even though the state had by no means disappeared, its seeming impotence allowed all kinds of fears (and hopes) to emerge from obscurity. On the day of the CGT demonstration, Grimaud authored an unusual letter that warned his men to avoid brutal treatment of demonstrators.[361] The prefect of police may have been apprehensive about provoking the PCF into revolutionary action. If so, his worries were superfluous. The party's analysis posited that the situation was not revolutionary. The PCF correctly believed that the state had not disintegrated and wanted to avoid giving the republic an excuse to crush the "vanguard" of the workers' movement, as it had in 1848 and 1871.[362] The leading slogan of the march remained the Communist/CGT call for a "popular government" in which the party would have a strong, if not leading, voice. The *manif* showed, if any proof was needed, that the CGT remained the dominant force among organized workers.

Just as workers had profited from a perceptibly weakened state to advance their demands, so did ethnic and national groups, whose May–June activities have largely been ignored.[363] Material difficulties caused by strikes aggravated ideological and ethnic tensions. According to the forces of order, anti-imperialist West Indian protesters disrupted a gathering presided over by the "assassin" Pierre Billotte, Minister of Territories.[364] A violent fight erupted during which 7 policemen and 3 demonstrators were injured, and 7 persons arrested. In another incident, 50 persons of the Young Guiana Movement, many from Guadeloupe, occupied an apartment in the ninth *arrondissement*.[365] They confronted police, who assaulted them with tear gas. Thirty-one men and 7 women were detained. Seven agents were hurt, and the apartment was considerably damaged. Several days later at the Place Clichy, 500 supporters of the arrested protested against police actions.[366]

The most dramatic ethnic confrontations were not between a minority and police, but rather between Jews (many from Tunisia) and Arabs at Belleville, a working-class area in eastern Paris.[367] Material difficulties caused by the strikes increased tensions between the two communities, which, it should be noted, had coexisted peacefully through the 1967 Six-Day Arab-Israeli War. On 2 June, the eve of the first anniversary of that conflict, fights erupted between members of the two groups.[368] Firemen believed Arabs to be the aggressors: "North Africans—armed with clubs, bottles, and iron bars—pursued *israélites* (Jews)… Numerous hot-heads smashed shop windows. Women and children were manhandled and thrown to the ground."[369] Stone-throwing ensued, and police used tear gas to disperse threatening crowds.[370] Both sides formed commandos that looted and burned the stores and bars of its ethnic adversaries. "Hysterical" (in police parlance) Jews, who feared being outnumbered, claimed that the Arabs were incinerating their religious edifices and attacking children and pregnant women. Four Jewish stores were put to flame, and 35 boutiques (Jewish and Arab) were damaged.[371] The forces of order tried to seal the neighborhood and protect its synagogues, one of which was lightly damaged by fire. At least four policemen and an undetermined number of North Africans were injured. Six Arabs were arrested, one for throwing a Molotov cocktail at a barber shop. Arabs envied the Jews' position as French citizens, which gave the *israélites* an advantage in any legal battle.[372] Everyone knew that most Arabs could be expelled and most Jews could not. Eminent personalities—such as the prefect of police, the local rabbi, and the Tunisian ambassador—visited the scene and appealed for calm. The state was able to restore order quickly. The capital was never in danger of being lost.

At the end of May, the separate demonstrations of ethnic groups, Communists, and the non-Communist left revealed that antirepression no longer served as the antigovernment glue that it had been at the beginning of the month. The movement against repression had weakened the state, encouraged strikes, and promoted demonstrations of hundreds of thousands. Yet it could not provide a basis upon which to form a stable coalition. The evident divisions encouraged the government to retake the offensive.

Notes

1. "Political opportunities cannot make the poor conscious of grievances of which they were formerly unaware, but it can help them to detect where and how the system is most vulnerable, enabling them to overcome their habitual disunity and lack of information." Sidney Tarrow, *Struggle, Politics, and Reform: Collective Action, Social Movements, and Cycles of Protest* (Ithaca, 1991), 36.
2. Tarrow, *Struggle*, 4, 34, 46. See also Sidney Tarrow, *Power in Movement: Social Movements, Collective Action, and Politics* (New York, 1994).
3. Useful for this period are George Ross, *Workers and Communists in France* (Berkeley and Los Angeles, 1982); Jean-Pierre Rioux, *La France de la Quatrième République: L'Expansion et l'impuissance, 1952–1958* (Paris, 1983); Serge Berstein, *La France de l'expansion: La République gaullienne, 1958–1969* (Paris, 1989); Georges Lefranc, *Le Mouvement syndical de la libération aux événements de mai-juin 1968* (Paris, 1969); Noir et Rouge, *Socialisme ou Barbarie: Organe de Critique et d'Orientation Révolutionnaire Anthologie* (Mauléon, 1985).
4. Philippe Bauchard and Maurice Bruzek, *Le syndicalisme à l'épreuve* (Paris, 1968), 19.
5. Jean-Philippe Legois, *La Sorbonne avant mai 68* (Mémoire de maîtrise, Paris I, 1993), 197.
6. Danielle Tartakowsky, *Le pouvoir est dans la rue* (Paris, 1998), 153.
7. Bauchard and Bruzek, *Syndicalisme*, 21; Jacques Kergoat, "Sous la plage, la grève," in Antoine Artous, ed., *Retours sur mai* (Montreuil, 1988), 43; Michel Dreyfus, *Histoire de la CGT: Cent ans de syndicalisme en France* (Paris, 1995), 263; Jean Lacouture, *De Gaulle: The Ruler, 1945–1970*, trans. Alan Sheridan (New York and London, 1992), 2 vols., 2: 496.
8. Roger Martelli, *Mai 68* (Paris, 1988), 47.
9. Bauchard and Bruzek, *Syndicalisme*, 165; Alain Schnapp and Pierre Vidal-Naquet, *Journal de la commune étudiante* (Paris, 1969), 92–93; Adrien Dansette, *Mai 1968* (Paris, 1971), 168.
10. Ministère de l'Intérieur, Maintien de l'ordre, Manifestations et conflits sociaux, 12 March 1968, AN 860581/25.
11. Nicole de Maupeou-Abboud, *Ouverture du ghetto étudiant: La gauche étudiante à la recherche d'un nouveau mode d'intervention politique (1960–1970)* (Paris, 1974), 246; *Matériaux pour l'histoire de notre temps*, no. 20 (July–September, 1990): 7.
12. In 1967 3,500 had congregated at the Bourse du Travail. 2 May 1968, AN 820599/40; 2 May 1968, Fa 278, APP.
13. 1 May 1968, Fa 278, APP.
14. The CGT rejected the thesis that students had detonated the strike wave in favor of the more *ouvriériste* argument that the workers and their unions were the spark. See Michel Johan, "La CGT et le mouvement de mai," *Les Temps modernes*, no. 266–267 (August–September, 1968): 327. For a comparison between the student movement's weakening of the state in 1968 and 1986, see Roger Duclaud-Williams, "Student Protest: 1968 and 1986 Compared," in D. L. Hanley and A. P. Kerr, eds., *May '68: Coming of Age* (London, 1989), 52.

15. Bauchard and Bruzek, *Syndicalisme*, 71. The following biographical information is taken from this work.

16. Journée du 13 mai, Fa 255, APP; Bauchard and Bruzek, *Syndicalisme*, 75; Dansette, *Mai*, 136; André Sernin, *Journal d'un bourgeois de Paris en mai 68* (Paris, 1988), 19; "La grève des cheminots en 1968: Entretien avec Daniel Moreau," in Geneviève Dreyfus-Armand and Laurent Gervereau, eds., *Mai 68: Les mouvements étudiants en France et dans le monde* (Nanterre, 1988), 215. There is, however, no evidence that the strike was "revolutionary." Cf. Marc Kravetz, ed., *L'Insurrection étudiante* (Paris, 1968), 10.

17. 14 May 1968, AN 820599/40.

18. 13 May 1968, AN 820599/40.

19. 20 May 1968, AN 820599/40.

20. 13 May 1968, AN 820599/40.

21. Préfet de Paris à Ministre de l'Education Nationale, 14 June 1968, AN 790793.

22. Ministère du Travail, Conflits du travail, Ministère d'état chargé des affaires sociales, 14 May 1968, AN 760122.

23. Gérard Adam, "Etude statistique des grèves de mai-juin 1968," *Revue française de science politique*, no. 1 (February, 1970): 106.

24. Dansette, *Mai*, 175; Ministère d'état chargé des affaires sociales, 14 May 1968, AN 760122.

25. Henri Simon Oral History Project, interviews with workers, 1994.

26. Journée du 13 mai, Fa 255, APP.

27. On Parisian strikes, Situation sociale dans les industries des métaux de la région parisienne, 27 May 1968, GIM [Groupement des industries métallurgiques].

28. Ministère de l'Etat, 14 May 1968, AN 760122; 3 May 1968, AN 820599/40; 2 May 1968, AN 820599/40. A similar strike had occurred at Brest.

29. 15 May 1968, AN 820599/75.

30. 16 May 1968, Fa 257, APP.

31. Sous-Direction des relations professionnelles, 17 May 1968, AN 760122. A retired Renault worker claimed that in the evening of 13 May his workshop at Billancourt stopped suddenly in support of students. However, most printed sources agree that the Billancourt plant went on strike on 16 May at the earliest. See Henri Simon Oral History Project. See also Philippe Gavi, "Des ouvriers parlent," *Les Temps modernes*, no. 265 (July, 1968): 82.

32. *L'Humanité*, 18 May 1968.

33. *L'Aurore*, 21 May 1968.

34. Quoted in Lacouture, *De Gaulle*, 2: 536. On Peyrefitte, see Bauchard and Bruzek, *Syndicalisme*, 78; Christian Charrière, *Le printemps des enragés* (Paris, 1968), 220.

35. Charrière, *Printemps*, 220.

36. Daniel Cohn-Bendit, *Le Grand Bazar* (Paris, 1975), 48.

37. See Sernin, *Journal*, 35; Bulletin mensuel, May–July 1968, AN 820599/89.

38. 24 June 1968, AN 800273/61.

39. Quoted in Charrière, *Printemps*, 221; A. Belden Fields, *Student Politics in France: A Study of the Union Nationale des Etudiants de France* (New York, 1970), 120.

40. Situation sociale, 13–26 May, GIM; Henri Simon Oral History Project.

41. See Daniel Singer, *Prelude to Revolution: France in May 1968* (New York, 1970), 9: "The spontaneous forces carried the movement as far as they could against the opposition of all official establishments." Most recently, Andrew Feenberg and Jim Freedman, *When Poetry Ruled the Streets: The French May Events of 1968* (Albany, 2001), 33: "Over one hundred thousand workers in thirteen major factories went on strike and occupied their plants without a word from the unions." Cf. also Ingrid Gilcher-Holtey, *Die 68er Bewegung: Deutschland-Westeuropa-USA* (Munich, 2001), 85–86.

42. Henri Simon Oral History Project; Bulletin mensuel, May–July 1968, AN 820599/89; Lucio Magri, "Réflexions sur les événements de mai," *Les Temps modernes*, no. 277–278 (August–September, 1969): 23. This article attempts to synthesize the "spontaneous"

and "organizational" interpretations of the revolt but admits that, "faced with the first strikes and occupations, the unions were not guilty of the hesitation which characterized their reaction to the student revolt." Michelle Zancarini-Fournel, "La longue décennie des mouvements sociaux et la grève générale de mai-juin 68," in Geneviève Dreyfus-Armand, Robert Frank, Marie-Françoise Lévy, and Michelle Zancarini-Fournel, eds., *Les Années 68: Le temps de la contestation* (Brussels, 2000), 277, provides support for the argument that the CGT did not discourage the strikes but instead controlled them.

43. Préavis, 29 April 1968 and Note pour M. le Ministre, 7 May 1968, Ministère de l'Industrie, des Postes et Télécommunications, AN 810484.

44. Direction générale de la police nationale, renseignements généraux, bulletins quotidiens, 3 May 1968, AN 820599/40.

45. Note, 8 May 1968, Ministère de l'Industrie, des Postes et Télécommunications, AN 810484.

46. 10 May 1968, Ministère de l'Industrie, des Postes et Télécommunications, AN 810484.

47. 13[?] May 1968, Fa 255, APP.

48. Ministre des PTT, 18 May 1968, Fa 258, APP.

49. Réquisition, 19 May 1968, Fa 258, APP.

50. 20 May 1968, Fa 258, APP; Laurent, 20 May 1968, Fa 259, APP.

51. Le commissaire du 14e, 20 May 1968, Fa 259, APP.

52. Le commissaire du 9e, 25 May 1968, Fa 281, APP.

53. Le commissaire du 13e, 20 May 1968, Fa 258, APP.

54. Le commissaire du 1e, 21 May 1968, Fa 259, APP.

55. Le préfet de la r.p., 28 May 1968, AN 800273/61.

56. Situation sociale dans les industries des métaux de la région parisienne, 27 May 1968, GIM. Cf. Alfred Willener, Catherine Gajdos, and Georges Benguigui, *Les cadres en mouvement* (Paris, 1969), 21; Chris Howell, *Regulating Labor: The State and Industrial Relations Reform in Postwar France* (Princeton, 1992), 3; Hugues Portelli, *La Ve République* (Paris, 1994), 144. Most recently, cf. Kristin Ross, *May '68 and Its Afterlives* (Chicago, 2002), 68: "The workers' strike, by erupting outside the confines of the big French labor confederations and outside the desiderata of any of the various left parties, particularly the Communist Party, had come to threaten the very existence of those institutions and organizations."

57. Willener et al., *Les cadres*, 21. See also Michael Rose, *Servants of Post-Industrial Power? Sociologie du Travail in Modern France* (White Plains, N.Y., 1979), 140.

58. 22 May 1968, AN 820599/40.

59. Adam, "Etude statistique," 111–117.

60. Document reproduced in Jean-Raymond Tournoux, *Le mois de mai du général* (Paris, 1969), 365. A former PCF militant, turned *gauchiste*, admitted the leading role of the CGT in metallurgy of the Saint-Quentin region. See "Bilan d'une adhésion au PCF," *Informations Correspondance Ouvrières*, [hereafter *ICO*], no. 91 (March–April, 1970).

61. Direction générale de la Police Nationale, renseignements généraux, bulletins quotidiens, 16 May 1968, AN 820599/40.

62. 17 May 1968, AN 820599/40.

63. 18 May 1968, AN 820599/40.

64. "La grève des cheminots en 1968: Entretien avec Daniel Moreau," in Dreyfus-Armand and Gervereau, *Mai 68*, 216; Frank Georgi, "Vivre demain dans nos luttes d'aujourd'hui: Le syndicat, la grève et l'autogestion en France (1968–1988)," in Dreyfus-Armand et al., *Les Années 68*, 401.

65. *Matériaux*, 49; Baynac, *Mai*, 265.

66. Baynac, *Mai*, 265.

67. The following paragraph is based on daily police reports, 16 May 1968, AN 820599/40; 17 May 1968, AN 820599/40; 18 May 1968, AN 820599/40.

68. Dansette, *Mai*, 188. Several days later, the general expressed similar sentiments. See Jacques Foccart, *Le Général en mai: Journal de l'Elysée-II 1968–1969* (Paris, 1998), 118.

69. 19 May 1968, Fa 258, APP.
70. 20 May 1968, Fa 258, APP.
71. Ibid.
72. 24 May 1968, AN 820599/40.
73. 22 May 1968, Fa 259, APP.
74. Henri Simon Oral History Project; Aristede and Vera Zolberg, "The Meanings of May (Paris, 1968)," *Midway*, no. 3 (winter, 1969): 91.
75. Baynac, *Mai*, 151.
76. 18 May 1968, AN 820599/40.
77. 22 May 1968, Fa 259, APP.
78. 21 May 1968, AN 820599/40.
79. Absentéisme (1964), AN 39AS 287.
80. *Les Echos*, 21 May 1968; Charrière, *Printemps*, 232.
81. Groupement des industriels d'Argenteuil-Bezons et communes avoisinantes, "Enquête concernant les conflits sociaux" [hereafter known as Enquête], July–November 1968, GIM.
82. At Renault-Cléon, management was confined to its offices and held hostage to prevent a police raid. See *Notre arme c'est la grève* (Paris, 1968), 23; Baynac, *Mai*, 139.
83. Situation sociale, 27 May 1968, GIM.
84. Many were illegal since the five-day advance notice, which had been established by the law of 31 July 1963, was not respected. See Centre national d'information pour la productivité des entreprises, *Les événements de mai-juin 1968 vus à travers cent entreprises* (Paris, 1968), 25. Singer, *Prelude*, 234, states that the five-day notice was applicable only to the public sector.
85. Crise de mai 1968, 22 May 1968, GIM. On the pre-May history of employers' relations with strikers, see Jacques Capdevielle and René Mouriaux, *Mai 68: L'Entre-deux de la modernité: Histoire de trente ans* (Paris, 1988), 51. On the failure of Citroën management to get police to confront the occupiers, see Lucien Rioux and René Backmann, *L'Explosion de mai* (Paris, 1968), 438; also, Charrière, *Printemps*, 246.
86. 24 May 1968, Fa 260, APP.
87. Maurice Grimaud, *En mai, fais ce qu'il te plaît* (Paris, 1977), 218.
88. Enquête, GIM. See also Grimaud, *Mai*, 217, who states that the mayor of Gennevilliers threatened to have his supporters "massively occupy" a fuel distribution center if police intervened to break the strike.
89. J.-C. Davidson in *Matériaux*, 54; Baynac, *Mai*, 130.
90. Enquête, GIM. Cf. *Les événements de mai-juin 1968 vus à travers cent entreprises*, 16, 25. For the union role at Citroën, see Patrick Hassenteufel, *Citroën-Paris en mai-juin 1968: Dualités de la grève* (Mémoire de maîtrise, Paris I, 1987), 44. For the industries of the Nord, see Pierre Dubois, "Les pratiques de mobilisation et d'opposition," in Pierre Dubois, Renaud Dulong, Claude Durand, Sabine Erbès-Séguin, and Daniel Vidal, *Grèves revendicatives ou grèves politiques?* (Paris, 1971), 342–345. Jean-Philippe Talbo, ed., *La grève à Flins* (Paris, 1968), 90, underlines the role of "active minorities" in initiating strikes.
91. Adam, "Etude statistique," 109, 117.
92. Enquête, GIM.
93. Robert Davezies, ed., *Mai 68: La rue dans l'église* (Paris, 1968), 84.
94. Schnapp and Vidal-Naquet, *Journal*, 777; Henri Simon Oral History Project.
95. See Cohn-Bendit in Jean Bertolino, *Les Trublions* (Paris, 1969), 391: "Almost everyone agrees … that young workers … started the movement." Georges Pompidou also claimed that "young workers … ignoring union orders" began the occupations. See *Débats de l'Assemblée Nationale: Seconde session ordinaire de 1967–1968*, 22 May 1968 (Paris, 1969), 2039.
96. Bulletin mensuel, May–July 1968, AN 820599/89; Ronan Capitaine, *Dassault Saint-Cloud en mai-juin 1968* (Mémoire de maîtrise, Paris I, 1990), 102. See *Notre arme c'est la grève*, 14–18; cf. Dansette, *Mai*, 349: "Without these young people, Trotskyites, new industrial workers from farms, non-unionized workers influenced by students, wildcat strikes

would have never happened. These strikes worried the CGT and the PCF." Pierre Peuchmaurd, *Plus vivants que jamais* (Paris, 1968), 94, attributes the strikes to the working class itself, not to the PCF or the CGT.

97. Adam, "Etude statistique," 110.

98. Henri Simon Oral History Project; 28 June 1968, AN 820599/41.

99. See Capitaine, *Dassault*, 78; Davezies, *Mai 68*, 86; Henri Simon Oral History Project.

100. Claude Dejacques, *A toi l'angoisse, à moi la rage: Mai 68 Les fresques de Nanterre* (Paris, 1969) [not paginated].

101. Dansette, *Mai*, 200–201; Baynac, *Mai*, 134.

102. Bulletin mensuel, September 1968, AN 820599/89.

103. Henri Simon Oral History Project; Baynac, *Mai*, 133.

104. Cf. Alain Geismar, Serge July, and Erlyne Morane, *Vers la guerre civile* (Paris, 1969), 340, which claims that *immigrés* led the strike at the Citroën Javel plant in Paris; cf. also George Katsiaficas, *The Imagination of the New Left* (Boston, 1987), 104; Ross, *May '68 and Its Afterlives*, 95: "May '68, in fact, marks the emergence onto the political scene of the *travailleur immigré*." Daniel A. Gordon, "Immigrants and the New Left in France, 1968–1971" (Ph.D. diss., University of Sussex, 2001), supports Ross's view, but a study of pre-1968 immigrant strike participation—which is still lacking given the period covered by his dissertation—is necessary to confirm it.

105. 28 June 1968, AN 820599/41.

106. See Hassenteufel, *Citroën*, 108; Interview with Mr. and Mrs. Bomelle, 20 July 1990; Talbo, *Flins*, 17; Danielle Kergoat, *Bulledor ou l'histoire d'une mobilisation ouvrière* (Paris, 1973). On *immigrés* as a percentage of the metallurgical work force, La main d'oeuvre étrangère—les industries des métaux de la région parisienne, 31 December 1969, AN 39AS 287. Gordon, "Immigrants," would dispute the judgment of immigrants' passivity but admits (84) "a very low level of unionization" among immigrants.

107. On the German comparison, see Ulrich Herbert and Karin Hunn, "Gastarbeiter und Gastarbeiterpolitik in der Bundesrepublik: Vom Beginn des offiziellen Anwerbung bis zum Anwerbestopp (1955–1973)," in Axel Schildt, Detlef Siegfried, and Karl Christian Lammers, eds., *Dynamische Zeiten: Die 60er Jahre in den beiden deutschen Gesellshaften* (Hamburg, 2000), 292.

108. 28 June 1968, AN 820599/41. Gordon, "Immigrants," 146–151, greatly qualifies this judgment.

109. Gordon, "Immigrants," 163.

110. See Donald Reid, "The Politics of Immigrant Workers in Twentieth-Century France," in Camille Guerin-Gonzales and Carl Strikwerda, eds., *The Politics of Immigrant Workers* (New York, 1993), 269.

111. Fernand Braudel, *The Identity of France*, trans. Sian Reynolds (New York, 1988), 2 vols., 2: 215.

112. *Le Figaro*, 17 May 1968 and 21 May 1968.

113. Quotes from Schnapp and Vidal-Naquet, *Journal*, 777–779; Dansette, *Mai*, 199; *Le Monde*, 23 May 1968; *L'Aurore*, 21 May 1968.

114. "Le mouvement du 22 mars: Entretien avec Daniel Cohn-Bendit," in Dreyfus-Armand and Gervereau, *Mai 68*, 127; Mouvement du 22 mars, *Ce n'est qu'un début, continuons le combat* (Paris, 1968), 33, 47.

115. R. Gregoire and F. Perlman, *Worker-Student Action Committees: France May '68* (Detroit, 1991), 60.

116. Quoted in Bauchard and Bruzek, *Syndicalisme*, 95.

117. Singer, *Prelude*, 159; Jacques Julliard, "Syndicalisme révolutionnaire et révolution étudiante," *Esprit*, no. 372 (June–July, 1968): 1042.

118. Sernin, *Journal*, 50.

119. Quoted in Schnapp and Vidal-Naquet, *Journal*, 797.

120. Claude Durand, "Ouvriers et techniciens en mai 1968," in Dubois et al., *Grèves revendicatives*, 48–73.

121. Le Préfet de Paris à Ministre, 12 June 1968, AN, 800273/61.

122. Vincent Porhel, "L'autogestion à la CSF de Brest," in Dreyfus-Armand et al., *Les Années 68*, 395.

123. See the editorial in *Les Temps modernes*, no. 264 (May–June, 1968): 11; Edgar Morin, Claude Lefort, and Cornelius Castoriadis, *Mai 68: La brèche* (Paris, 1988), 95; André Gorz, "Limites et potentialités du mouvement de mai," *Les Temps modernes*, no. 266–267 (August–September, 1968): 240–241. Cf. Gianni Statera, *Death of a Utopia: The Development of Student Movements in Europe* (Oxford, 1975), 137: "On May 25 … millions of people poured into the squares and streets of every French town to demonstrate against the regime, to ask for 'revolutionary reforms,' substantial wage increases, a genuine share in power for the masses." Cf. also Katsiaficas, *Imagination*, 106: "In general, however, workers' actions against management revealed a fundamental aspiration of the general strike: *autogestion*." Feenberg and Freedman, *Poetry*, 34: "It was to the Sorbonne, to an alternative to union leadership, to advocates of the anarchistic theory of self-management, that the workers turned."

124. James Miller, *Democracy Is in the Streets: From Port Huron to the Siege of Chicago* (New York, 1987), 68.

125. Todd Gitlin, *The Sixties: Years of Hope, Days of Rage* (New York, 1987), 258.

126. Mouvement du 22 mars, *Début*, 92.

127. Sylvain Zegel, *Les idées de mai* (Paris, 1968), 43. Recent articles have questioned the importance and extent of *autogestionnaire* desires among workers. See Alexis Bonnet, "L'Autogestion et les cédétistes lyonnais," and Porhel, "L'autogestion," both in Dreyfus-Armand et al., *Les Années 68*, 363–399.

128. Guy Caire, "La situation sociale," *Droit social* (July–August 1968), 455; Capitaine, *Dassault*, 81.

129. Situation sociale, période du 13 au 26 mai, GIM.

130. For the CGT's attitude prior to May 1968, see René Mouriaux, "Le mai de la CGT," paper presented to Colloque: Acteurs et terrains du mouvement social de mai 1968, Paris, 24–25 November 1988. On the central and thus "non-marginal" role of women and immigrants, see Thierry Baudouin, Michèle Collin, and Danièle Guillerm, "Women and Immigrants: Marginal Workers?" in Colin Crouch and Alessandro Pizzorno, eds., *The Resurgence of Class Conflict in Western Europe since 1968* (New York, 1978), 2 vols., 2: 63.

131. CGT, Chemins de fer, 28 mai, Tracts de mai 1968, BN; CFDT, 23 mai, Tracts de mai 1968, BN.

132. *Antoinette*, [n.d.].

133. Mouriaux, "Le mai," in Colloque; Ross, *Workers and Communists*, 165.

134. March 1968, AN 820599/89.

135. *ICO*, April 1968, 13.

136. Citroën, 26 May 1968, Tracts de mai 1968, BN.

137. Lycée d'état Corbeil-Essonne, 20 May 1968, AN 790793; C. Michel in *Matériaux*, 71.

138. *Débats de l'Assemblée Nationale*, 21 May 1968, 1982.

139. Quoted in Dansette, *Mai*, 185. Full text of Pompidou's speech is found in Dansette, *Mai*, 407–413.

140. *Débats de l'Assemblée Nationale*, 22 May 1968, 2032.

141. 22 May 1968, AN 820599/40.

142. Caire, "Situation sociale," 454.

143. Charlot, "The Aftermath," in Hanley and Kerr, *May*, 77–78; 16 May 1968, AN 820599/40.

144. Cf. Charrière, *Printemps*, 259, on the PDM group.

145. Emmanuel Souchier, ed., *Mai 68* (Paris, 1988), 47; Charrière, *Printemps*, 274.

146. Philippe Labro, ed., *Ce n'est qu'un début* (Paris, 1968), 135; Pierre Andro, A. Dauvergne, and L. M. Lagoutte, *Le mai de la révolution* (Paris, 1968), 146.

147. 1 June 1968, Fa 269, APP.

148. Alain Touraine, *The May Movement: Revolt and Reform*, trans. Leonard F. X. Mayhew (New York, 1979), 246.

149. Singer, *Prelude*, 177. Aimé Césaire, the progressive poet-deputy from Martinique, declared: "I am quite willing to shout it, but nobody will believe me."

150. Quoted in Singer, *Prelude*, 119. For the tolerance of a large foreign presence in pre–World War I French universities, see George Weisz, *The Emergence of Modern Universities in France, 1863–1914* (Princeton, 1983), 258–259.

151. Singer, *Prelude*, 176; Johan, "La CGT et le mouvement de mai," 335; Marc Goldstein, "Le Parti communiste du 3 mai au 6 juin," *Les Temps modernes*, no. 269 (November, 1968): 860.

152. *Le Monde*, 25 May 1968.

153. Quoted in Claude Prévost, *Les étudiants et le gauchisme* (Paris, 1969), 158.

154. Yves Blondeau, *Le Syndicat des correcteurs* (Paris, 1973), 288.

155. Jean-François Sirinelli, *Intellectuels et passions françaises: Manifestes et pétitions au XXe siècle* (Paris, 1990), 386.

156. Seale and McConville, *Red Flag*, 174.

157. 23 May 1968, Fa 259, APP.

158. 24 May 1968, Fa 259, APP.

159. Grimaud, *Mai*, 137.

160. 23 May 1968, Fa 259, APP.

161. Ibid.

162. Ibid.

163. Le commissaire principal du 31e, 23 May 1968, Fa 259, APP.

164. Le commissaire du 5e, Manifestation du 22–23, Fa 259, APP.

165. Exceptions were made for family deaths or illnesses. 21 May 1968, Fa 258, APP.

166. 22 May 1968, Fa 259, APP.

167. 21 May 1968, Fa 263, APP.

168. 24 June 1968, Fa 277, APP.

169. Commissaire du 1e, 24 June 1968, Fa 277, APP.

170. Le commissaire, Manifestations du 22 mai, 23 May 1968, Fa 259, APP.

171. Note pour Etat-Majeur, 23 May 1968, Fa 259, APP.

172. 29 May 1968, Fa 266, APP; 25 May 1968, Fa 281, APP.

173. 22–23 May 1968, Fa 259, APP.

174. 24 May 1968, Fa 259, APP.

175. 24 May 1968, Fa 259, APP; 24 May 1968, Archives de la brigade de sapeurs-pompiers de Paris.

176. "Remerciements," 28 May 1968, Fa 260, APP.

177. 25 May 1968, Fa 281, APP.

178. Ibid.

179. 24 May 1968, Fa 259, APP.

180. 23–24 May 1968, Fa 259, APP. Other figures offer a total of 45 policemen injured, 27 of whom were forced to stop working; 24 May 1968, Fa 259, APP. Charrière, *Printemps*, 277, reports 78 police injured in street scuffles and 220 people arrested and then released.

181. 23 May 1968, Fa 259, APP.

182. Ibid.

183. 25 May 1968, Fa 260, APP.

184. Charlot, "The Aftermath," in Hanley and Kerr, *May*, 78.

185. Foccart, *Le Général en mai*, 127; Dansette, *Mai*, 227.

186. Bauchard and Bruzek, *Syndicalisme*, 119.

187. Jean-Pierre Filiu, "Le gouvernement et la direction face à la crise," in *Mai 68 à l'ORTF* (Paris, 1987), 169.

188. 13 May 1968, AN 820599/40.

189. Roger Gascon, *La nuit du pouvoir ou le 24 mai manqué* (Paris, 1968), 14.

190. 24–25 May 1968, Fa 260, APP.

191. Geismar et al., *Vers*, 194; Baynac, *Mai*, 188.

192. 24–25 May 1968, Fa 260, APP.

193. Ibid.; 24 June 1968, AN 800273/61.

194. 24–25 May 1968, Fa 260, APP.

195. 24 June 1968, AN 800273/61.

196. For the emphasis on the symbolic, see Henri Lefebvre, *The Explosion: Marxism and the French Revolution*, trans. Alfred Ehrenfeld (New York, 1969), 123. There were other symbolic moments of the Second Night of the Barricades. Seven employees of the Musée de l'Homme invaded the apartment of Minister of Interior Fouchet and told his wife that the premises belonged to the Museum. The invaders were arrested. See 20 June 1968, Fa 260, APP.
197. 23 May 1968, Fa 259, APP.
198. 28 May 1968, Fa 261, APP.
199. 25 May 1968, Fa 260, APP.
200. Le commissaire des Halles, 25 May 1968, Fa 260, APP.
201. 25 May 1968, Fa 260, APP. There were thirty-two *commissariats d'arrondissement* in Paris.
202. Ibid.
203. 26 May 1968, Fa 260, APP.
204. 25 May 1968, Fa 281, APP.
205. 3 June 1968, Fa 269, APP.
206. 15 June 1968, Fa 274, APP.
207. 24–25 May 1968, Fa 260, APP.
208. Journée du vendredi 24 et nuit 24–25, Fa 260, APP.
209. 26 May 1968, Fa 260, APP.
210. 27 May 1968, Fa 260, APP.
211. 24–25 May 1968, Fa 260, APP.
212. 25 May 1968, Fa 281, APP.
213. Ibid.
214. Grimaud, *Mai*, 245.
215. 24–25 May 1968, Fa 260, APP.
216. Ibid.; 25 May 1968, Fa 281, APP.
217. 24–25 May 1968, Fa 260, APP; 26 May 1968, Fa 260, APP.
218. 24–25 May 1968, Fa 260, APP.
219. 25 May 1968, Fa 260, APP.
220. Ibid. Other figures are 447 civilian and 212 police injuries, in addition to 760 arrests. Seventy-two trees were cut down, and 67 vehicles (including 8 fire trucks and 7 police cars) set on fire. See Andro et al., *Mai*, 182. Gordon, "Immigrants," 122, reports a higher percentage of foreigners arrested. Baynac, *Mai*, 189, contends that police refused to admit their responsibility for the death of a protester.
221. Maurice Grimaud, "Mai 1968, vingt ans après: L'Etat face à la crise," in Dreyfus-Armand and Gervereau, *Mai 68*, 71.
222. 9 July 1968, Fa 274, APP.
223. 24–25 May 1968, Fa 260, APP.
224. 20 June 1968, Fa 260, APP.
225. 24–25 May 1968, Archives de la brigade de sapeurs-pompiers de Paris.
226. Gilles Martinet, *La conquête des pouvoirs* (Paris, 1968), 35; Dansette, *Mai*, 283; Magri, "Réflexions," 464.
227. Arthur Marwick, *The Sixties: Cultural Revolution in Britain, France, Italy, and the United States, c. 1958–c. 1974* (New York, 1998), 594.
228. 27 May 1968, AN 820599/40.
229. Baynac, *Mai*, 191.
230. "Bilan d'une adhésion au PCF," *ICO*, no. 91 (March–April, 1970), 23.
231. Tartakowsky, *Le pouvoir*, 183; Georges Pompidou, *Pour rétablir une vérité* (Paris, 1982), 188.
232. Claude Paillat, *Archives secrètes, 1968–69: Les coulisses d'une année terrible* (Paris, 1969), 193, 204.
233. Peuchmaurd, *Vivants*, 69; Sernin, *Journal*, 59.
234. Henri Simon Oral History Project.
235. Dansette, *Mai*, 276, 423; Peuchmaurd, *Vivants*, 124.
236. 22 May 1968, Fa 259, APP.

237. 13 July 1968, Fa 277, APP.
238. 24 May 1968, Fa 259, APP.
239. J. Livi in *Matériaux*, 69.
240. 27 February 1968, Fa 282, APP.
241. 22 May 1968, Fa 259, APP.
242. 24 May 1968, Fa 259, APP; 25 May 1968, Fa 260, APP; 28 May 1968, Fa 261, APP; 30–31 May 1968, Fa 261, APP.
243. 24 May 1968, Fa 259, APP; 25 May 1968, Fa 260, APP.
244. 25 May 1968, Fa 260, APP.
245. 26 May 1968, Fa 260, APP.
246. Direction de la circulation, 22 May 1968, Fa 259, APP.
247. 28 May 1968, Fa 261, APP.
248. 28 June 1968, AN 800273/61.
249. 28 May 1968, AN 800273/61.
250. 21 May 1968, Fa 261, APP.
251. Effectifs, n.d., Fa 262, APP. Grimaud, *Mai*, 33, states that 25,000 agents were available.
252. 21 May 1968, Fa 262, APP.
253. 23 May 1968, Fa 262, APP.
254. Grimaud, *Mai*, 217.
255. 28 May 1968, Fa 262, APP.
256. Compte-rendu, 30 May 1968, AN 800237/61.
257. Ibid.
258. 23 May 1968, Fa 261, APP.
259. 24 May 1968, Fa 259, APP.
260. Dansette, *Mai*, 277–278.
261. 4 June 1968, Fa 262, APP.
262. Suzanne Berger, "Regime and interest representation: The French traditional middle classes," in Suzanne Berger, ed., *Organizing Interests in Western Europe* (Cambridge, 1981), 84.
263. On 1848, see Roger Price, *The French Second Republic: A Social History* (Ithaca, 1972), 171.
264. 25 May 1968, Fa 281, APP.
265. 28 May 1968, AN 800273/61.
266. 4 June 1968, Fa 262, APP.
267. Ibid.
268. Ibid.
269. 25 May 1968, Fa 260, APP.
270. 4 June 1968, Fa 262, APP.
271. 28 June 1968, AN 800273/61.
272. Cf. the account by J. Livi, in *Matériaux*, 69. Cf. also Feenberg, *Poetry*, 43: "No one worked. No planes, trains, mail. No gas. No trash collection."
273. 28 May 1968, Fa 261, APP; 29 May 1968, Fa 263, APP.
274. 27 May 1968, Fa 263, APP.
275. 18 May and 21 May 1968, Fa 263, APP.
276. 29 May 1968, Fa 262, APP.
277. 30 May 1968, Fa 262, APP.
278. 29 May 1968, Fa 262, APP.
279. 30 May 1968, Fa 262, APP.
280. Situation à 18:15, n.d., Fa 262, APP.
281. 26 May 1968, Fa 262, APP.
282. 28 May 1968, AN 800273/61.
283. 26 May 1968, Fa 262, APP.
284. 30 May 1968, Fa 262, APP.
285. 31 May 1968, Fa 262, APP; 29 May 1968, Fa 262, APP.
286. 29 May 1968, Fa 262, APP.

287. Ibid.
288. 31 May 1968, Fa 262, APP.
289. Ibid.
290. Ibid.; 9 July 1968, Fa 274, APP.
291. 31 May 1968, Fa 262, APP.
292. Grimaud, *Mai*, 206.
293. The Esso depot at Asnières was scheduled to return to work on Tuesday, 4 June. See 2 June 1968, Fa 262, APP.
294. 17 June 1968, Fa 262, APP.
295. 19 June 1968, Fa 262, APP.
296. Other peasant organizations, Mouvement de Défense des exploitations familiales and the CNJA (Centre national des jeunes agriculteurs), were more sympathetic to the workers and students. See Tartakowsky, *Le pouvoir*, 185–186.
297. On FNSEA corporatism, see John T. S. Keeler, *The Politics of Neocorporatism in France* (New York, 1987), 15; Rioux and Backmann, *L'Explosion*, 389; May 1968, AN 820599/75.
298. Willener et al., *Les cadres*, 42–43; Réunion tenue les 25–27 mai, AN 860561.
299. Bauchard and Bruzek, *Syndicalisme*, 102.
300. Martelli, *Mai*, 135.
301. *Matériaux*, 45.
302. *Le Peuple*, August 1968.
303. On the protests of the PME against Grenelle, see Rioux and Backmann, *L'Explosion*, 396.
304. Caire, "Situation sociale," 456. For somewhat different figures, see Jacques Kergoat, "Sous la plage, la grève," in Artous, *Retours sur mai*, 46.
305. See *Mai 68 à l'ORTF*.
306. Henri Simon Oral History Project; Capitaine, *Dassault*, 96; Magri, "Réflexions," 458.
307. The following is taken from Réunion tenue les 25–27 mai au Ministère des Affaires Sociales, AN 860561.
308. J.-M. Jeanneney in *Matériaux*, 36; Michelle Zancarini-Fournel, "Retour sur « Grenelle »: la cogestion de la crise?" in Dreyfus-Armand et al., *Les Années 68*, 452.
309. A. Prost in *Matériaux*, 5. Public service workers feared that they might not be able to win the same gains as others. 27 May 1968, AN 820599/40.
310. 21 May 1968, AN 820599/40.
311. *Ouvriers face aux appareils: Une expérience de militantisme chez Hispano-Suiza* (Paris, 1970), 107. On the isolation of the Peugeot strike of 1965, see Lefranc, *Le Mouvement syndical*, 190. See also Noir et Rouge, *Socialisme ou Barbarie* for the failures of a national strike movement and consequent frustrations among workers prior to 1968.
312. Dansette, *Mai*, 249; *Le Monde*, 28 May 1969; Alain Delale and Gilles Ragache, *La France de 68* (Paris, 1978), 111, estimated the crowd at Renault at 10,000 workers; Rioux and Backmann, *L'Explosion*, 406, put the figure at 15,000. The average age of Renault workers is cited by Laurent Salini, *Mai des prolétaires* (Paris, 1968), 34.
313. Bulletin mensuel, May–July 1968, AN 820599/89.
314. 27 May 1968, AN 820599/40.
315. Delale and Ragache, *France*, 113; Gilcher-Holtey, *Die 68er Bewegung*, 88–89. On the extreme right, François Duprat, *Les journées de mai 68: Les dessous d'une révolution* (Paris, 1968), 104–109.
316. Alain Silvera, "The French Revolution of May 1968," *The Virginia Quarterly Review*, vol. 47, no. 3 (summer, 1971): 343.
317. Singer, *Prelude*, xii, 11. A similar opinion is voiced by Gilbert Mury, *La société de répression* (Paris, 1969), 14.
318. Magri, "Réflexions," 467.
319. "Mai 68," *Esprit*, no. 372 (June–July, 1968): 970.
320. Chris Harmon, *The Fire Last Time: 1968 and After* (London, 1988), 118–119. This charge is repeated by Francis Sitel, "1968–88," in Artous, *Retours*, 22.

321. Ernest Mandel, "The Lessons of May 1968," *New Left Review*, no. 52 (November–December, 1968): 27: "May 68 has demonstrated once again the absence of adequate revolutionary leadership."

322. Martinet, *La conquête des pouvoirs*, 17.

323. See *Les Temps modernes*, no. 264 (May–June 1968) and no. 266–267 (August–September, 1968).

324. Cf. Serge Mallet, *Essays on the New Working Class*, trans. Dick Howard and Dean Savage (St. Louis, 1975), 62–67, who argues that workers' struggles against industrial discipline and hierarchy were entirely compatible with their supposed desire to manage the workplace in an efficient and modern way. For the inapplicability of Mallet's theories in Italy, see Robert Lumley, *States of Emergency: Cultures of Revolt in Italy from 1968 to 1978* (London and New York, 1990), 204.

325. For a rank-and-file view, see Juliette Minces, *Un ouvrier parle: Enquête* (Paris, 1969), 58.

326. *La Croix*, 30 May 1968.

327. For an example, see Capitaine, *Dassault*, 151; Zancarini-Fournel, "Retour," 457.

328. Bauchard and Bruzek, *Syndicalisme*, 106; Magri, "Réflexions," 466; Martelli, *Mai*, 138.

329. *Le Monde*, 28 May 1968.

330. *L'Humanité*, 26 May 1968; Bauchard and Bruzek, *Syndicalisme*, 109–112.

331. 30 May 1968, AN 820599/40. See also 24 June 1968, AN 800273/61.

332. 28 May 1968, AN 820599/40.

333. See Minces, *Un ouvrier*, 66.

334. "Bilan d'une adhésion au PCF," *ICO*, no. 91 (March–April, 1970): 22.

335. Situation sociale, 27 May–30 June 1968, GIM.

336. Andro, *Mai*, 170.

337. Singer, *Prelude*, 196; Goldstein, "Le parti communiste," 861; Schnapp and Vidal-Naquet, *Journal*, 40, 305.

338. Danielle Tartakowsky, "Le PCF en mai-juin 1968," paper presented to Colloque: Acteurs et terrains du mouvement social de 1968, Paris, 24–25 November, 1988.

339. Dansette, *Mai*, 284.

340. 26 May 1968, Fa 261, APP.

341. 28 May 1968, Fa 261, APP.

342. Cf. his more sanitized account in Grimaud, *Mai*, 269–270.

343. 28 May 1968, AN 820599/40; 9 July 1968, Fa 274, APP.

344. On the divisions of the CFDT concerning the Charléty meeting, see *Matériaux*, 43–44.

345. 30 May 1968, AN 820599/40.

346. Text of speech reproduced in Dansette, *Mai*, 427–428.

347. See Henri Lefebvre, *Le temps des méprises* (Paris, 1975), 121.

348. Andro, *Mai*, 196–199.

349. Seale and McConville, *Red Flag*, 208; Martinet, *La Conquête*, 27.

350. 28 May 1968, AN 820599/40.

351. Salini, *Mai*, 95; Bauchard and Bruzek, *Syndicalisme*, 113.

352. CGT quoted in Bauchard and Bruzek, *Syndicalisme*, 113.

353. Singer, *Prelude*, 110; Henri Weber, *Vingt ans après: Que reste-t-il de 68* (Paris, 1988), 81.

354. Minces, *Un ouvrier*, 32.

355. Salini, *Mai*, 42; Dansette, *Mai*, 289.

356. Schnapp and Vidal-Naquet, *Journal*, 307.

357. 30 May 1968, AN 820599/40.

358. 9 July 1968, Fa 274, APP.

359. Laurent Joffrin, *Mai 68: Histoire des événements* (Paris, 1988), 260–261.

360. René Andrieu, *Les communistes et la révolution* (Paris, 1968), 20, 123.

361. Text of letter in Dansette, *Mai*, 397–398.

362. Andrieu, *Les Communistes*, 173, 177; Schnapp and Vidal-Naquet, *Journal*, 40.

363. For example, Maurice Grimaud has written "that the *journées* marked by violent clashes numbered just nine," completely neglecting violence between police and ethnic communities.

See Grimaud, *Mai*, 258–259. Nevertheless, Grimaud has conserved a reputation for "honesty." See Jean-Pierre Rioux, "A propos des célébrations décennales du mai français," *Vingtième Siècle*, no. 23 (July–September, 1989): 51.

364. 4 May 1968, Fa 277, APP; Gordon, "Immigrants," 41–43.
365. 4 June 1968, Fa 269, APP.
366. 7 June 1968, Fa 270, APP.
367. Ibid. The most complete treatment of these events is found in Gordon, "Immigrants," 164–181.
368. Communication, [n.d., ? June 1968] AN 800237/61.
369. 2 June 1968, Archives de la brigade de sapeurs-pompiers de Paris.
370. 3 June 1968, Fa 277, APP.
371. 24 October 1969, Fa 277, APP.
372. 12 June 1968, Fa 277, APP.

Chapter Five

THE SPECTACLE OF ORDER

—◦／◦／◦—

With the streets disputed by his opponents and his parliamentary majority demoralized, de Gaulle deserted the capital on 29 May, the day of the CGT demonstration. Government officials affirmed that his departure "worried public opinion. The population has concluded that the crisis cannot be solved by social reforms [i.e., the Grenelle agreement] and that the country is on the brink of chaos.... The massive CGT demonstration, the efficiency of its *service d'ordre*, and the absence of police intervention impressed public opinion."[1] The general prudently abandoned the presidential residence and left what seemed to be a growing power vacuum, which, as has been seen, the opposition was trying desperately to fill.[2] Looking for the best way to bolster his authority, he decided to visit his fellow military professionals. The armed forces were the sector of state and society least affected by the agitation of May. Although the worker and especially student movement contained aspects of a youth revolt, the army—with the possible exception of a few draftees—seemed relatively impervious to agitation.[3] Communist or action-committee propaganda distributed among soldiers had little effect. Compared to the university or even to the workplace of the 1960s, the military remained too illiberal an environment to permit the development of *groupuscules*, parties, or trade unions. Despite lingering resentment over the outcome of the Algerian War, de Gaulle had much more support in his original profession than elsewhere.

The president of the republic decided to visit Germany to consult with General Jacques Massu, who was in charge of French occupation troops. During the Algerian War, Massu had been identified with the *Algérie Française* diehards and their practice of torture, but he had ultimately proved himself to be a loyal Gaullist.[4] Massu assured the president of his devotion and of the loyalty of fellow officers at the end of May. Within the army, Massu's influence helped to neutralize anti-Gaullist sentiment left over from the Algerian conflict. Outside the armed forces, his commitment to de Gaulle would frighten potential leftist insurrectionaries. The voyage of the president to Massu held the political promise of uniting the entire right, including its most extreme elements. A confident de Gaulle returned the following day with determination to reassert his control over the situation. On 30 May, Massu and his colleagues made preparations for possible "counter-terrorist" actions in urban areas.[5] The French occupation army in Germany, along with other tank and parachutist units, readied itself to defend public order and the constitution.[6] Widespread rumors that troops were being moved to Paris bolstered the authority of a president who wanted to show that the state had not lost its coercive potential. His task was to convince his adversaries and the public that he would be willing to use more massive repression if necessary.[7] The French must understand that the tolerant authoritarianism of the Fifth Republic could become less lenient.

Some of the opposition saw the German visit as de Gaulle's flight to Varennes. His supporters believed that as in 1940, the general left France so that, if necessary, he would be able to reconquer the nation from abroad.[8] His major goal was, as in 1944, to "re-establish the state."[9] Both friendly and hostile commentators have exaggerated the disarray of the regime. It may be the case that the trip to the Federal Republic was more of a public relations ploy or a *coup de théâtre* than anything else.[10] Some of his closest loyalists believed that de Gaulle planned his departure in order to create a vacuum that could only be filled by his return.[11] Whatever the case, the state had by no means completely disappeared even during the second half of May.[12] On the night of 28–29 May, police continued "Operation Zig-Zag," which was designed to handle two "dangerous" elements: first, "uncontrollable hooligans" who were not students; second, protesters who drove vehicles.[13] Police stopped and searched hundreds of automobiles and people. On the night of 30–31 May, they arrested dozens, mostly for carrying illegal weapons. In addition, police checked 333 people and searched scores of cars.[14] The prefect of police ordered plainclothesmen from the Police judiciaire and Renseignements généraux to interrogate all suspects. Occupants of automobiles with the unofficial insignia of the Red Cross or the cross of Malta were special targets because, officials claimed, "it has been proven that almost all of these cars transport material and arms."

Throughout May, the police proved able to protect the monumental government buildings—Elysée Palace, Matignon, Chamber, Senate, Hôtel de Ville—and the major embassies, including the American and North Vietnamese delegations to the Paris Peace Conference. By the end of the month, the military was strikebreaking to assure essential public services. Thousands of soldiers collected trash, buried decaying corpses, distributed emergency supplies of gasoline and diesel fuel, and secured essential communications—which strikes had disrupted—between ministers and prefects.[15] It should be noted that at least in garbage pickup, which was daily in Paris, the CGT did not officially oppose the military's strikebreaking even though union garbage workers (including CFDT and FO members) had a formidable record of strike militancy even before May.[16] A police superintendent reported that although the CGT affiliate in the Val-de-Marne was informed that the military would enter garages, it offered no resistance.[17] Overall, opposition to scabbing was minimal: strikers attacked and immobilized 10 trucks on Monday, 27 May, but police confirmed that 411 vehicles were able to pick up 75 percent of debris.[18]

PTT authorities decided to put the military to work when the massive work stoppage prevented postal officials from using private employment agencies to recruit strikebreakers. Military transport and aircraft moved official or emergency letters and packages after 20 May when the trains were shut down.[19] On 29 May the air force responded to continuing strikes and picket lines at Orly airport and instituted six regular interior routes, comprising fifteen flights per day from its base at Villacoublay.[20] The military (and nuclear) base at Creil was put at the disposition of private airlines such as Sabena and Skyways. Female auxiliaries of the Armée de Terre served as mail sorters and telephone operators. In three weeks, the armed forces moved one hundred tons of mail. Professional military personnel labored fourteen to sixteen hours per day. Lifers avoided delegating responsibility to draftees, who were technically inexperienced and perhaps politically unreliable. Thus, the state did not disappear during May. Its building blocks of army and police remained in place and adapted to new tasks.

After the second night of the barricades (24–25 May), Prime Minister Pompidou, with the approval of the prefect of police, ordered several parachutist regiments to be moved near the capital.[21] On 24 May, tank combat units and motorized brigades advanced through the *banlieue*, and news of their arrival circulated quickly throughout the Paris region. The professional violence of the police was reinforced by the presence and potential of massive military intervention. The government itched to scare would-be "troublemakers," whether Communist or *gauchiste*, but it was reluctant to use soldiers to maintain order.[22] Nor did it ever need to do so since police proved sufficiently capable. Yet PCF leaders believed that General de Gaulle would not hesitate to employ army shock troops. The Party's secretary general, Waldeck Rochet, confessed, "We had a real fear—with good reason—of a massive military intervention and repression."[23] This dread pervades Communist historiography.[24]

De Gaulle's address to the nation on 30 May did not initiate a new period in the history of the strike wave; rather, it continued the re-establishment of order that the military, police, and their civilian allies had already begun. In other words, instead of a turning point, the speech signaled the spectacular re-emergence of state power, which was already present and active.[25] As before, the government assigned hundreds of police to the ORTF to make sure that no one would disturb the airwaves during the general's address.[26] De Gaulle broadcast on the radio, thus evoking his famous appeal from London on 18 June 1940 for resistance against the Nazi invader. Although his televised speeches during the crises provoked by the Algerian War had been very effective, the radio address was testimony to the wireless's continuing influence in the purported age of television.[27] The general recognized that his televised talk of the previous week had been a failure, and he was willing to return to the medium of his youth. As *gauchistes* had themselves experienced on barricades and in demonstrations, radio exhibited more accessibility and flexibility than television—especially in mid-afternoon, when the speech was delivered.

The 30 May address contained two parts. The first claimed the tradition of republican legitimacy. The president told the nation that had elected him that he was determined to stay in office and to keep Pompidou as prime minister. Using presidential prerogative, he dissolved the National Assembly and—as his opposition had been demanding—called for new legislative elections. In this matter, the general was acting in accordance with French political tradition. After upheavals, France has often held elections to legitimize the challenged or newly established order. Such was the case in 1945–1946 when the constitution of the Fourth Republic was ratified and again in 1958 when the constitution of the Fifth Republic was approved.[28] As in previous republics, a renewal of parliament would resolve the crisis. The general's goal was to turn the parliamentary left's demand for new elections against it. He was confident that *la France profonde*—a concept that had long been a staple of Gaullist discourse—would triumph over adversaries whom he defined as decadent and selfish elites.

The second part of the address was less democratic and more polemical. He blamed the continuing agitation on "totalitarian" Communists and their allies, who used "intimidation, intoxication, and tyranny" to prevent "students from studying, teachers from teaching, and workers from working." To combat supposed Communist coercion, he urged the formation of Civic Action Committees. In terms that recalled the state's smashing of the insurrectionary strikes of 1947–1948 and even the reign of terror during the Great Revolution, he rebaptized prefects "commissars of the Republic" whose main task was to resist "subversion." De Gaulle had always believed that without a potent and effective state, France was powerless to manage its affairs at home or abroad. Only a republic of order could counter the *féodalités* or centrifugal forces that threatened the nation. The general would show that the perceived weakness of the state had been temporary and that he could resurrect it easily. On the day of the address, his minister of interior ordered all prefects to take any measures necessary to encourage a return to work: "It is your immediate duty to eliminate all obstacles to the right to work and to end the occupations in priority institutions."[29]

De Gaulle warned the nation that "washed-up" politicians (referring to but not naming Mitterrand and Mendès-France) were attempting to profit from the disorder, but, he implied, their ambitions would (as with Alexander Kerensky in Russia) encourage the triumph of "dictatorship" and "totalitarian communism." Thus, the general directly connected the PCF with subversion and disorder and used anti-Communism to unite the entire right, including its anti-Gaullists. His anti-Communism was not caused by the Soviet threat or by animosity to foreign Communist empires, with which he had recently and spectacularly established détente. Instead, it was based on the fear of Communism as an internal threat. This renewed anti-Communism recalled the first Gaullist party, Rassemblement du peuple français (RPF), founded during the Cold War when solid bourgeois and others worried that the PCF might come to power. Anti-Communist appeals had contributed to Gaullist majorities during the legislative contests of 1962 and of 1967. The general believed that new parliamentary elections would again return an enlarged anti-PCF majority. The call for elections had the added benefit of accentuating divisions between the parliamentary left and *gauchistes*.

The emphasis on the re-establishment of order led the opposition to label the address "Bonapartist." According to Mitterrand, "It is the voice of the Eighteenth Brumaire. It is the voice of December 2. It is the voice of May 13.... It is dictatorship."[30] Rather than Bonapartist—as the parliamentary left claimed, or fascist, as *gauchistes* asserted—the speech might be seen in the tradition of republican restorations of order in response to strike waves and demonstrations. Clemenceau before, during, and after World War I; Raymond Poincaré in the 1920s; Edouard Daladier and Paul Reynaud at the end of the Popular Front had all anticipated the general. It should be mentioned that de Gaulle omitted his previous demand for a referendum, thus showing himself to be more of a republican of order than a Bonapartist.[31] An interior ministry source posited that whether republican or Bonapartist, his speech disoriented his opponents: "The decisions announced by the President ... have created a psychological shock that has freed many from their feeling of abandonment. The opposition has been thrown into confusion."[32] Historically learned observers remarked that "one expected the farewells of Fontainebleau, but it was the return from Elba."[33] Firm signals of de Gaulle's intent to remain in office bolstered the morale of his loyalists and calmed growing agitation among left-wing Gaullists and many *giscardiens* who had earlier demanded Pompidou's resignation for failing to re-establish order and normal work routines.[34]

The speech had immediate repercussions for Parisian students and workers.[35] It surprised the extreme left and the extreme right, both of which had expected the general to resign. Perhaps most remarkably, the address momentarily silenced vocal Nanterre students. Cohn-Bendit noted that "fear dampens militancy, and we know that General de Gaulle's speech created a certain dread for militants."[36] Dany saw the ballot box as a trap for the extreme left. The "bourgeois elections" that de Gaulle promised would substitute politics as usual for the general strike, which radicals imagined offered the possibility of some sort of revolutionary workers' control.[37] The movement's strength had always been outside of parliament, directly attacking the employers and the state. De Gaulle effectively "discouraged" and "frightened" certain action committees. A member of the Comité révolutionnaire du CNRS offered a historical analysis of Gaullism in power: "The Gaullist regime began as a liberal empire but will finish as a Francoist authoritarian regime." A street fighter close to the Movement of 22 March characterized the address as "fascist."[38] Among the organizations that might be classified on the extreme left, only the heterogeneous PSU decided to participate in the election campaign.[39] According to a police bulletin, it had hopes of becoming a major political player since it dismissed the PCF and the SFIO as old-fashioned and "incapable of satisfying the new demands of the workers and students."[40]

Communists protested against the bullying tactics of Gaullist "mercenaries," i.e., the militants of the Civic Action Committees whom the general had encouraged to counter the "subversion" of "totalitarian communism."[41] PCF officials charged that de Gaulle was bolstering the violent forces of the extreme right, and Waldeck Rochet posited a choice between "Gaullist dictatorship and democracy."[42] Aware of the fate of the Greek Communist Party after the 1967 putsch of the colonels, French Communists were apprehensive. Gaullist rhetorical toughness also intimidated union leaders. The CFDT charged that de Gaulle "blackmailed the nation with fear and dictatorship."[43] Séguy opposed "actions which could lead to bloody confrontations with the forces of repression ... and to a military dictatorship."[44] The CGT was so frightened by the general's overture to the army and the appearance of military forces around Paris that it absolutely refused to participate in a demonstration proposed by other unions for 1 June.[45] It would later claim with considerable hyperbole that its moderation prevented the execution of a Greek- or Indonesian-style anti-Communist coup in France. The Communist press praised the prudence of the CGT, which was alert to the possibility of a "military coup carried out under the pretext of anarchy."[46] De Gaulle's speech reinforced feelings of resignation among those workers who had hoped for profound political or social change. According to police, the address placed workers "on the defensive. Union leaders prepared strategic retreats."[47] Interior officials concluded, "the CGT ... is now concerned only with professional issues. It has given up its demand for a 'popular government.' It now wants a return to work based on negotiations which result in advantages for workers."

Threats to use military intervention against strikers cowed Parisian working-class militants. At Renault, CGT activists were aware of "important troop movements, notably armored cars and parachutists who are being called to Paris. In addition, a large number of OAS officers are being freed [from prison]."[48] At Hispano, a firm employing 4,300 workers, the strike committee interpreted the speech as an attempt to "blackmail [workers] with civil war."[49] The executives of one striking Parisian firm believed that the military was on the verge of occupying Paris.[50] Several hours after the demonstration on the Champs-Elysées, police reported that one hundred cars crammed with right wingers drove to the Opéra to harass its striking workers.[51] The strikers retaliated by spraying them with high-pressure hoses. During Friday night or early Saturday morning, rightists turned fire against the left and threw five Molotov cocktails against the gates of the Meudon Observatory, which strikers were occupying. The government shut down gun shops and ordered them to secure their windows with grating or iron shutters to prevent looting.[52] The prefect of the Val-d'Oise reported that the president's speech and the ensuing Champs-Elysées demonstration produced "a deep impression on the population."[53] Farmers, of course, supported the president, but following the address, workers in small and medium-sized firms returned to their jobs. Most "spectacularly," all Shell gas stations reopened.

The impact of the address was enhanced by a huge street demonstration that immediately followed it. Perhaps 300,000 or 400,000 (police mentioned "several hundred thousand") gathered on the Champs-Elysées to support the general.[54] For the first time since the beginning of the events, the right was able to match or surpass the left in numbers on the concourses of the capital. During the demonstration, police favored Gaullists by permitting reporters to use the frequencies that had been denied them when they covered the left demonstrations. The bullies of the Civic Action Committees intimidated journalists while the government pressured editors to put a positive spin on the demonstration.[55] The massive counter-demonstration was not an entirely spontaneous expression of support for the president. Towards the end of May, Gaullist leaders, such as Roger Frey, fretted because throughout the month only extreme-right groups—e.g., Occident—had dared to contest the left's domination of Parisian streets. They decided to plan a massive march of their own to show the strength of a more respectable right. A number of veterans' groups associated with the Resistance, such as the Association des Français libres, rallied to the defense of the regime. An organizational network, which was significantly entitled Comités de Défense de la République, offered the backing of Gaullist militants. These efforts culminated at the 30 May *manif*, which encouraged a mingling of young with old, civilians with military, and workers with bourgeois.[56] As André Malraux put it, they were the *métro*. More precisely, the crowd was representative of the masses of French people who were hostile to strikes and attacks on property. Small employers with access to gasoline were present in large numbers, and shopkeepers may have been overrepresented in the crowd.[57] The massive and heterogeneous nature of the demonstrators showed that, in contrast to the Restoration and Orleanist monarchies, the regime of "King Charles" had active popular support in its period of greatest crisis. Only defeats in major wars—not street demonstrations or strikes—brought down Bonapartist and republican forms of government in nineteenth- and twentieth-century France. However, the Gaullist attempt to fashion the demonstration as a showcase of the respectable right was not entirely successful. The presence of partisans of *Algérie Française* and the cries of *"Cohn-Bendit à Dachau"* betrayed the extremist and fascist tendencies of some.[58] Their presence in the crowd prefigured the post-demonstration reconciliation of Gaullism and the extreme right. The 30 May gathering showed that the momentum and dynamism of the political spectacle had shifted to the regime's supporters. In the interests of re-establishing order and reaping an electoral harvest, the government was reluctant to denounce or disown the extreme right.

The reconciliation had been difficult, but the dynamism of the extreme left had revived the extreme right. In early May, Tixier-Vignancourt had matched *gauchistes'* own hyperbole by rebuking "a regime that is disintegrating and being overwhelmed by a young German fanatic."[59] In similar terms, Occident appealed to the public to reject "the passivity of the government that had ruined the army, the university, and will ruin France."[60] The nationalist and monarchist right managed to take to the streets of western Paris in relatively small numbers throughout May. The size of the demonstrations reflected the usual deep divisions among the extreme right. However, these anti-Marxists and anti-Gaullists represented, according to interior ministry officials, "an important fraction" of *pieds-noirs* (French refugees from Algeria) and violence-prone ex-OAS members.[61] Police declared that on 14 May, 1,500 extreme-right-wingers assembled near the Etoile to journey to the Concorde, and a few slipped away to throw stones at the Chinese embassy.[62] On 15 May, 1,000 marched from the Etoile to the Gare Saint-Lazare; on 17 May, 1,000 paraded from the Arc de Triomphe to the Madeleine; on 18 May, 3,000 repeated the same steps.[63] On 4 June a group of extreme-right youths invaded a sizable Gaullist demonstration on the Champs-Elysées and encouraged the crowd to engage in an immediate attack "to *vidanger* (flush out) the Sorbonne."[64] Its leader was arrested. Police acknowledged that the geographical confrontation between left and right continued when 250 veterans attending the ceremony of the flame at the Tomb of the Unknown Soldier scuffled with 2,000 metalworkers who were protesting at the nearby headquarters of the Automobile Manufacturers' Association.[65]

After the huge student-worker demonstration of 13 May, police indicated that some members of Tixier's ARLP began advocating a coalition with the Gaullists against the left.[66] Interior ministry officials reported that pressures were accumulating to amnesty convicted OAS leaders or sympathizers, Raoul Salan, Georges Bidault, and Jacques Soustelle.[67] For that purpose, Tixier's party formed a "Committee for Freedoms."[68] Tixier preferred "order" to "disorder" and "decided to support, at least momentarily, the Gaullist government." However, police revealed that Tixier, whose brilliant defense of Salan had helped him avoid the death penalty during his 1962 trial, "insisted on one essential condition—that the ex-General Salan be amnestied and freed."[69] Tixier's reconciliation with Gaullism alienated important members of his own party, whose *bureau politique* voted to suspend him. He fought the legitimacy of the suspension and was able to maintain control of the party newspaper, *L'Alliance*.[70] During the electoral campaign, Pierre Poujade, a pioneer of the populist right in the 1950s and still president of the Union de Défense des Commerçants et Artisans (UDCA), also appealed for a massive vote for the Gaullist UDR.[71] In return, according to police, the regime decided to recognize officially the UDCA as a "representative organization."[72] Poujade felt that small business had finally found its place in the Fifth Republic, and he became a devotee of de Gaulle's rhetorical "third way," which supposedly rejected both capitalism and Marxism. The government had successfully charmed at least part of the lower middle classes.

On Friday, 31 May, the general kept the promise of a cabinet shakeup proposed in his speech. The reshuffling favored orthodox Gaullists or Gaullists of order rather than *gaullistes de gauche*. The latter received a few ministerial posts but no major portfolio dealing with economic or social matters. The "expansionist" Albin Chalandon was placed in charge of industry, and the faithful Maurice Couve de Murville became minister of economy and finances. One of the most important changes was the appointment of the hard-line Yves Guéna as minister of information and head of the state's media monopoly. The regime was obviously determined to reassert control over the ORTF. As has been seen, the government and police had accused private radio stations of fomenting revolt. Pompidou and other high-ranking officials had repeatedly attacked RTL and Europe One for irresponsibly encouraging demonstrations. Both stations had acquired new listeners and influence because of the strike at ORTF. The government wanted to censor the airwaves to prevent activists from massing at battle sites in response to news of police movements conveyed by protesters' transistors that were tuned to Europe One.[73] In general, radio coverage of *manifs* boosted the spirits of protesters and barricade builders.

The May events remained highly mediatized in every sense of the neologism. During that month striking print workers refused to publish issues of major newspapers, thereby sparking intense debate on freedom of the press. Police ascertained that unionized printers halted the publication of the *Parisien Libéré*, which was on the verge of issuing a story with the headline, "The first sign of return to work to RATP."[74] On the weekend of 25–26 May, the Ministry of Interior reported that "police and striking printers confronted each other outside of the paper's print shop."[75] Another group of press workers prevented the Gaullist paper *La Nation* from publicizing the 30 May Champs-Elysées demonstration, which was—according to government supporters—"in favor of democracy and freedom."[76] Police confirmed that on 29 May plastic explosives had seriously damaged *La Nation*'s offices (rue de Lille).[77] Interior ministry sources stated that at the end of the month, editors at the left-leaning *Le Canard enchaîné* privately bewailed the CGT attempts to impose censorship.[78] *Le Canard* did print a communiqué from the Livre parisien CGT that authorized the press publications "when they accomplish objectively their mission of providing information."[79]

Although observers have often commented on the importance of the radio, print media may have reached the height of their influence in 1968. Indeed, during the last Night of the Barricades, on 11–12 June, one thousand demonstrators (according to police) paid a fiery homage to the press by rallying at the office of *France-Soir* to burn issues of the daily.[80] The crisis heightened the desire to laugh, and when the satirical *Canard* inserted its inset in *Combat*, the latter's circulation rose—in the estimation of police— from 70,000 to 200,000 copies.[81] At the same time, the very serious *Le Monde* reached its zenith. Its circulation broke all records even as kiosk, transportation, and PTT strikes prevented distribution in the provinces and to subscribers.[82] After the massive demonstration of 13 May, 638,000 copies of the newspaper were sold; following Mitterrand's speech (28 May) in which he offered himself as a presidential candidate, 609,000; when de Gaulle departed Paris, 688,000; when he returned to reassert control, a record of 732,100. In contrast, the issue of 16 October 1964, which followed Khruschev's resignation and the explosion of the Chinese atomic bomb, sold only 371,689. The results of the presidential election of 5 December 1965 attracted only 502,800 buyers. Thus, May 1968 was—and has remained—a best seller. Police were normally hostile to the media, including the mainstream press and even the official ORTF, which it thought exaggerated police brutality, encouraged student and worker strikes, and ignored violations of the right to work.[83] After May, police sued for libel *Combat*, *L'Enragé*, and the authors of the UNEF's anti-cop *Livre noir des journées de mai*.

Guéna seemed the right man to get the media in line. As minister of the PTT, he had used force against strikers as early as 18 May.[84] He was believed to be the boss who could efficiently implement the general's order on 19 May "to fire agitators."[85] On 23 May, Guéna had refused to permit reporters to employ radio frequencies. Immediately after the president's May 30 address, Guéna ordered all PTT functionaries to return to work the following day.[86] He expressed the hope that pickets would respect the right to work, but if they did not, he promised to encourage the formation of "Committees for a Return to Work." ORTF's security forces reasserted control over access to offices and studios, and only trusted, i.e., Gaullist, journalists were allowed to enter.[87] Guéna encouraged the formation of an antistrike committee at Issy-les-Moulineaux, composed of members who had attended the immense Champs-Elysées demonstration.[88] On 31 May–1 June, one of his first decisions in his new ministry was to order police to expel the strikers who had occupied the ORTF offices at Issy since 20 May.[89] They agreed to leave "on the condition that they were chased out by police. At that moment all that was necessary was the appearance of a commissioner and three officers, and the center fell without difficulty back into the hands of management."[90] On 3 June he ordered the CRS to surround the Maison de la Radio and threatened to use army personnel to break its strike. On June 4, the army took control of emission towers.[91] Shortly thereafter, the forces of order invaded the building. On 4 June, the antistrikers of the Television Civic Action Committee demanded the dismissal of prominent journalists—including François de Closets, Emmanuel de la Taille, Léon Zitrone, Alain de Sédouy, André Harris, and Philippe Labro—who had participated in the work stoppage.[92] With the goal of shaking up the hierarchy, Guéna quickly dismissed—perhaps, by his own admission, "unjustly"—several high-ranking officials.[93] By 7 June, the televised interview of de Gaulle by the sympathetic if not sycophantic Michel Droit was another sign that ORTF was becoming domesticated. The strike, though, continued as reporters insisted on winning greater autonomy from the government, and most personnel returned only at the end of the month.[94] The final holdouts among the journalists were back at their desks on 12 July.

The government's supporters on the streets aided its quest to control the airwaves. The Champs-Elysées demonstration awarded the right nearly uncontested control of western Paris. Three hundred vehicles driven by rightist demonstrators moved from the Champs-Elysées to protest at the nearby offices of Europe One.[95] On 31 May, police reported that groups of several dozen rightists demonstrated in front of the headquarters of Radio Luxembourg (RTL) and again at Europe One.[96] Demonstrators protested against the stations' "unfair" reporting, sang the *Marseillaise*, and waved their tricolors. Similar demonstrations were repeated during the following nights and persisted into mid June.[97] The combination of pressure from below and above was effective, and both private radio stations "became well-behaved" and more favorable towards the government. The radios became captives of their location in bourgeois neighborhoods. According to government officials, they "modified their attitude and softened the tone of their news programs. They stopped broadcasting at 1:00 A.M., using the excuse of technical difficulties. It seems that they are undergoing reorganization."[98]

Radicals tried hard to counter the effect of de Gaulle's speech during the sunny weekend that followed its delivery. On Saturday, 1 June, the UNEF, which still dreamed of uniting workers and students, organized a demonstration attended by forty thousand who shouted "*élections = trahison*" (elections = treachery).[99] This slogan further divided the left by alienating its parliamentary wing. Far more significant for the restoration of normality was the state's success at making gasoline more widely available. Traffic managers concluded, "the Pentecostal vacations were saved *in extremis* by the reappearance of fuel."[100] Alain Geismar concluded that "gas killed the Revolution." He might have added good weather and the availability of cash. Motoring during the long weekend proved much more popular than factory occupations and led to the oversaturation of the Paris-province road network. Reality resembled Jean-Luc Godard's extravagant vision of *Le Weekend*. On Tuesday, 4 June, the largest movement (and traffic jam) of June took place on the Autoroute du Sud, where five thousand vehicles per hour headed for the capital after a long week-end. Sixty-eight people died in automobile accidents on that weekend, compared to several during all the political violence of May.[101] Radical graffiti summed it up: "One non-revolutionary weekend is infinitely bloodier than a month of permanent revolution."[102] The resumption of normal leisure activities encouraged consumption. On Saturday morning, 85 of 101 Prisunics (discount department stores) reopened in the Paris region.[103] In fact, recommencement of consumption remained a priority. Several days later, police removed 55 strike pickets at the Samaritaine department store.[104] The following weekend also saw massive departures and extensive shopping.[105]

Antistrikers gained momentum after the general's address. At "numer-ous" PTT centers, police intervened to end occupations and disperse those who manned picket lines.[106] Five hundred postal workers from the *chèques postaux* (banking center) on the rue de Vaugirard marched to the PTT ministry to demand a return to work and then, waving the tricolor, marched back to their jobs.[107] According to the forces of order, they were joined by hundreds, if not thousands, of other postal employees from the rue de Vaugirard bureau.[108] On the opposite side, five hundred students counterdemonstrated to oppose the return of the postal workers. A num-ber of students, including a dozen or so from the Movement of 22 March, formed a Committee against Police at the major sorting center at Paris-Brune, but—according to authorities—"strikers refused all contact with this committee."[109]

Yet despite the pressures and threats of de Gaulle and Guéna, the return to work was not always immediate. Political and social chronologies did not always coincide, and the heads of state were ignored by a good num-ber of strikers who insisted that the work stoppages continue until their demands were satisfied. On 5 June the new minister of interior, Raymond Marcellin, felt compelled to repeat the same type of instructions that his predecessor had given to the prefects. Marcellin ordered them to respond favorably to demands from employers and others to protect the right to work.[110] Authorities revealed that it was only on 4–5 June that branches of the PTT and National Education voted to end the strike.[111] By 6 June, the return—backed by both major confederations—was general in the PTT of the Paris region.[112] Police ended the occupation of certain bureaus without noteworthy violence. Sporadic strikes over work schedules erupted among the PTT's mobile personnel on 7–8 June, but stoppages quickly ended when management renewed its practice of hiring temporary workers whom private employment agencies offered as strikebreakers.

The government's strikebreaking toughened the employers' bargaining stance. The UIMM (Union des industries métallurgiques et minières), an organization often seen as representative of heavy industry in France, demanded the removal of picket lines and renewal of work before it re-started negotiations.[113] On 7 June, the CGT denounced "the intransigence of the representatives of the big bosses in metallurgy, construction, and chemicals."[114] Not only the moderate FO but even police analysts essentially agreed with this assessment and termed the metallurgical employers' position "inflexible."[115] In metallurgy the first strikers who returned were largely workers of small firms (employing between 20 and 300 wage earners) whose union representatives had signed accords closely resembling the Grenelle settlement. These agreements were concluded during the first week of June, usually between Tuesday the fourth and Friday the seventh.[116] The relatively rapid return of small firms in metallurgy and other branches, especially in the private sector, was not surprising since their participation in the strike was much lower than in the larger concerns.[117] Seventy-eight percent of workers were affected by the strikes in large metallurgical firms (over 2,000 workers), 76 percent in medium-sized firms (300–2,000 workers), and only 33 percent in small businesses (under 200 workers). Furthermore, the intensity of the strike diminished as firms decreased in size. In big firms each striker missed, on the average, 175 hours of work (approximately 4 work weeks); in medium firms each striker averaged 117 hours (over 2.5 weeks); in small enterprises merely 27 hours were lost. An employers' organization in the eastern *banlieue*, whose members were mainly bosses of small and medium-sized firms, reported that only 17 percent of their businesses went on strike.[118] A left-wing Catholic activist concluded that "fear [of striking] affects small firms in particular since they are not organized, offer low wages, and employ large numbers of women."[119] A radical in one diminutive metallurgical factory (50 workers) noted the difficulty of organizing his fellow workers, even though the majority were under 35 years old. His work mates were reluctant to pay union dues and were skeptical of the union's effectiveness.[120] When small firms did strike, militants from larger surrounding factories often prompted them.[121]

On Tuesday, 4 June, public transport workers were sharply divided over the continuation of the strike.[122] On that day, the stoppage of public transportation (including taxis) and the consequent influx of private automobiles returning from the long weekend "paralyzed activity in the Paris region" and caused a record traffic jam in Paris.[123] Police asserted that "in certain Parisian train stations, picket lines of strikers prevented the entrance of *cheminots* who wanted to go back to work."[124] At the Gare Saint-Lazare, strikers armed with clubs and powerful hoses unsettled potential scabs; however, the return began at the Le Bourget airport.[125] By Friday, 7 June, negotiations of public service and transport workers were largely concluded, and the CGT was pressuring its members for a return to work in the *métro* and SNCF. Most train and RATP lines were beginning to function.[126] Buses and the *métro* began operating regularly, despite what police viewed as several violations of the right to work.[127] Officers dispersed and arrested students who were said to be blocking the entrance to the Monge *métro* station, and at the Gare Saint-Lazare on 7 June *cégétistes* resisted *gauchiste* demands to continue the strike.[128] Newspapers, another element of daily existence, began returning to reopening kiosks.[129] The strike of *diffuseurs* and *marchands* (newspaper vendors) was also ending, although police claimed that they would violently renew their stoppage in the middle of June.[130] At that time, distributors and kiosk merchants wanted a 20 to 25 percent discount, but most publications refused.[131] Police charged that *marchands* (distributors) violated the right to work, intimidated strikebreakers, and attacked and destroyed trucks carrying the daily press.[132] As with the ORTF and *batellerie* (Parisian river transportation), the strike of distributors ended only at the end of the month.[133] The return to work was slow in several important sectors, showing that de Gaulle's admonishments did not scare all strikers.

Daycare centers, most primary schools, and some secondary establishments reopened on 7 June after the FEN lifted its strike order.[134] In contrast, *lycées* remained occupied. Parents protested against the occupation at the Lycée Michelet in Issy-les-Moulineaux, whose headmaster arrived at a solution worthy of Solomon.[135] He divided the building, giving one part to strikers and the other to classes. Other principals were equally clever at calming protests but could not always avoid scuffles between striking and non-striking students.[136] By 13 June most Parisian *lycées* were offering instruction, even if they continued to experience high rates of absenteeism.[137] In the second week of June, officials estimated that only 50 percent of students were attending *lycées*.[138] Parents continued to pressure their children and the authorities to reopen all high schools.[139] The potential loss of a year's scholastic credit alarmed many parents. By 21 June, exams had begun in many *lycées* even though, according to police, the CALs continued to "disrupt the everyday existence" at a good number of high schools.[140] Maoists or Trotskyites often controlled the CALs, which *groupuscules* had commonly initiated in January 1968. CALs advocated the boycott of the *bac* and the end of selection, thereby winning the support of a number of progressive Catholic chaplains.[141] On 14 June, 500 of its 2,000 students occupied the Lycée Turgot, and by 19 June five more institutions were paralyzed.[142] Police claimed that extreme rightists, armed with guns and tear gas, stormed occupied *lycées* in the suburbs.[143] Students of Henri IV responded by establishing a nighttime picket line to protect against a rightist attack.[144] During the takeover of the Lycée Colbert in the tenth *arrondissement*, two fires—one of which caused serious damage—were reported. Authorities concluded that both "were unfortunately intentional," the handiwork of arsonists who took heated measures to stop exams.[145] While most occupiers remained within conventional social norms, the events of May permitted some malcontents to manifest a hatred of institutions and everyday routine. The strikes in the *lycées* were among the last to end. Police declared that on 26 June, members of the CAL "spontaneously" evacuated Henri IV.[146] The changes that May protests brought to *lycées* may have been the most substantial, and the perception that May loosened the mores of *lycéens* remains widespread. The freedoms of university students filtered into high schools and even into lower grades. In mid June, nearly fifty male middle-school students, from twelve to fourteen years old, protested against strict discipline inside their establishment.[147]

Monday, 10 June, saw a continuation of the pattern of a resolution of issues in moderate-sized enterprises and also initiated a work week (Monday, 10 June to Friday, 15 June) that witnessed a return to work by strikers in major Parisian department stores and in more than a dozen Parisian metallurgical firms employing over one thousand wage earners.[148] These settlements put pressure on the remaining strikers and especially the activists who participated in the occupations. Although militants occupied many factories—e.g., 31 out of 39 striking firms in Issy-les-Moulineaux and 20 out of 40 in Boulogne-Billancourt—the occupations revealed that the rank and file had little desire to become actively involved. Contrary to the assertions of UNEF radicals, many forms of worker struggle did not imply "a total change of society."[149] Even committed workers were skeptical about the movement's ability to take power.[150] In general, the number of workers actually engaged in the occupations remained a tiny percentage of the work force. At Sud-Aviation, the pioneer plant of the occupation wave, the overwhelming majority of workers did not wish to participate in the sit-in but rather to spend time alone or with their families. Only 3,195 of 8,000 workers voted, and just 1,699 of them wanted to occupy the factory.[151] Merely several hundred out of a work force of 5,000 occupied the Renault factory at Cléon.[152] At Flins, approximately 250 of 10,000 were occupiers. A few hundred of the 30,000 workers at Boulogne-Billancourt remained inside the flagship plant. At Citroën, both strike meetings and the occupation revealed the passivity of the rank and file, who remained content to permit those union militants who had initiated the strike to spend time at the workplace.[153] In the Citroën branch in the fifteenth *arrondissement*, usually no more than 100 occupiers out of a work force of over 20,000 were present. Leftists charged that the Citroën strike committee was more concerned with organizing Ping-Pong matches and card games than with educating workers politically. During the long weekend of Pentecost (1–3 June) when gasoline became readily available, only twelve remained in the factory. The occupations were the greatest wave since 1936, but the small number of occupiers suggested that the number of engaged militants was proportionally tiny. In contrast to 1936, when masses of workers remained in the factories to prevent unemployed scabs from entering, in 1968 the fear of scabbing was relatively weak, and workers felt less compelled to join sit-downs.

Usually, it was the same group who initiated the strikes—mature male French workers close to the CGT—that conducted the occupation. In certain white-collar firms, they forcibly excluded non-union workers.[154] CGT militants dominated the occupation at Jeumont-Schneider, an important electronics firm in the Parisian suburbs, and locked out anti-CGT and indifferent workers. At Flins, veteran wage earners normally manned picket lines.[155] Sometimes—especially in one large white-collar company that was occupied—older militants were joined by young *gauchistes*. The presence of leftists did not alter the corporatist concerns of strike committees, which were reluctant to forge links with students or even with other occupied firms. Police explained that the PCF, sure that the situation was not revolutionary, insisted that strikers fly not just the red flag but also the tricolor at the gates of their factories.[156] Foreigners usually played a minimal role, perhaps because French wage laborers in many cases regarded them as strikebreakers or as uninterested trade unionists.[157] Yet some nationalities were more willing to participate than others. For example, at Citroën-Levallois, Spanish workers were active during the work stoppage; whereas, North African workers were largely passive.[158]

Initially, women were excluded from certain sit-downs for "moral reasons," but in others they played important roles.[159] Occupations disclosed gender divisions. The 400 female workers at the Kréma chewing gum factory outnumbered the 200 males, but male domination of the strike provoked the resentment of women.[160] At a branch of the Compagnie des compteurs of Montrouge, women did participate in the occupation, yet only in their traditional roles as cleaners and cooks. Men proved reluctant to allow them to spend the night at the factory in order "to avoid that the bosses make an issue of morality."[161] Women rejected this argument and by the third night of the occupation were almost as numerous as men. Usually, the overwhelming majority of workers—female or male, foreign or French—preferred to stay away from the plant.

Large numbers displayed little commitment to the electoral process at the workplace, and participation in strike votes varied widely from 40 to 75 percent.[162] Union and non-union strikers of some of the most important Parisian firms—Otis Elevators, Sud-Aviation, Nord-Aviation, Thomson-Houston, Rhône-Poulenc—reflected on striker passivity in a pamphlet written at the beginning of June. They contended that "in order to win, a greater number of workers [must] get involved. While the strike forces everyone to make material sacrifices, many comrades rely on a minority and do not participate actively. This allows the government to divide workers by playing on the weariness of some and on the poor information of others…. There is only one response to these tactics of division: massive participation of all workers who have stayed away from the occupied factories."[163] To encourage non-committed or apathetic workers to join the movement, the pamphleteers recommended adopting the model of strike organization at Rhône-Poulenc (Vitry), where rank-and-file strikers elected strike committees that were easily revocable. Militants regarded the occupation of this firm as particularly impressive because 1,500 of a work force of 3,500, or 43 percent, were actively involved.[164]

Even in this example of relatively high participation approximately 57 percent of personnel avoided activism. Suggestions from an inter-union committee, action committees, and Nanterre students that proposed a more innovative and participatory form of striking failed to interest wage earners. Committees recommended that workers engage in "freebie strikes" to rally opinion to their side and to direct public anger against the government. For example, garbage men should collect accumulated trash, transportation workers should permit free rides, and PTT employees should allow free postage and telephone calls.[165] However, sanitation, transport, and postal workers disappointed activists by making only traditional bread-and-butter demands. The belief of the Movement of 22 March that the occupations expressed the "unconscious yearning of the working class to take over the means of production" was wishful thinking.[166] March 22's demand for the sabotage of the means of production in case of a police assault usually went unheeded.[167] Striking workers seldom damaged property, and when they did, their targets—telephone lines, vehicles, etc.—were precise and limited.

Sociologists observing the assembly at one striking factory noted that executives and supervisory personnel, not workers, almost always dominated the discussion.[168] Although the participation of *cadres* in union and strike affairs rose dramatically in certain major factories, active *cadres* never came close to forming a majority of their professional category. Union militants may have selected the occupation tactic because it permitted them to neutralize the hostility or, more usually, indifference of a large part of the base. Most wage earners were individualistic and acted according to their own needs and desires, not those of a collectivity.[169] Labor historians and other analysts have usually overemphasized the degree of workers' collective commitment and sociability at the expense of their individualism and atomization.[170]

For a number of *gauchistes*, the CSF factory at Brest (Finistère) became the mythical model of an active strike during which workers produced items, such as walkie-talkies, that were useful for the cause.[171] The overwhelming majority of uncommitted strikers, though, embarked upon a different course. Instead of serving the public, they used the free time that the strike imparted to pursue their own personal or familial interests. Husbands escaped the sometime oppressive sociability of factory and family by retreating to the shelter of their workshop or to the quiet of their garden.[172] Other wage earners engaged in moonlighting. The low level of participation in most occupied factories prefigured the post-strike atmosphere in which the overwhelming majority of workers were more concerned with thriving or surviving in consumer society than with collective action against the state or employers. The Movement of 22 March had to admit that it lacked a critical mass of workers who were ready to cooperate in its plans for workers' control.[173] Advocates of revolutionary worker-student action committees conceded that CGT control of the strikes was a result of "the capitalist consciousness prevalent among workers."[174] Performing artists who entertained factory occupiers were among the few to have engaged in active strikes. One Portuguese entertainer admonished his

audience for limiting itself to bread-and-butter demands during a potentially revolutionary situation.[175] Blue-collar occupiers were perfectly willing to be passive spectators, and at his firm at Saint-Cloud, the aviation
pioneer Marcel Dassault permitted sit-down strikers to watch television.[176]

Some wage earners became actively involved for immediately pragmatic reasons, not because of trade-union or political commitment. In a
number of factories, strike committees were responsible for distributing
pay. In others, militants rationed gasoline, a scarce commodity during the
second half of May. Insufficient supply of gas provoked "a rush, a great
demand" in a number of firms.[177] An activist remarked: "We never occupied the factory but instead used it to supply our needs.... When we
needed something we took it with or without the consent of the management.... Gas became scarce.... In order to get fuel you had to have connections with the CGT. Gas produced envy and required discipline."[178] At
Dassault Saint-Cloud, a shortage of the precious fluid produced "jealousy
and consequently abuse of power."[179] In the same aviation plant, the rule
that fuel was reserved for those who occupied the factory made it easier
to find volunteers. Some occupiers who spent only one night in the firm
took advantage of their passing presence to fill up their tank for a weekend trip. In response, strict rules and quotas were established. At Renault—
a supposed bastion of the CGT, where 20 percent of the workers were
unionized—a CGT member quit the federation because it would not provide him with gas.[180] Strikers interpreted in their own manner the 22
March Movement's anarchosyndicalist suggestion to establish direct contact between worker and peasant producers.[181] Radicals learned that
when they offered to establish a food distribution network directly with
peasants, strike committees were attracted only because of the low cost of
food, not as a step towards socialist *autogestion*.

Given desires and needs to consume, pressures continued to mount for
a return to work. Many wage earners were deep in debt before May. Their
mass consumption had been responsible for the fourfold increase in credit
purchases that had occurred during the 1960s.[182] For example, 44 percent
of the residents inhabiting a large apartment complex in the Parisian suburbs furnished their homes on credit.[183] Their petty bourgeois neighbors
were quite critical of what they considered to be workers' spendthrift
ways. Wage earners of rural origin, it appears, were especially vulnerable
to the attractions of credit. Their "letting go in the present" was often the
first step towards financial ruin.[184] By 1968, installment plans permitted
the purchase of almost all durable goods. At Renault, young workers were
often in arrears, and many older workers were burdened with mortgage
and car payments. In fact, large automobile firms encouraged their personnel to purchase cars on credit by offering them considerable discounts.
Autoworkers had the opportunity to become part-time entrepreneurs by
selling discounted cars to family and friends. Other wage earners could
purchase a vehicle with as little as 15 percent down. These liberal policies

ended "the forced asceticism" of the early twentieth century and opened new worlds of commodities to the laboring classes.[185]

Acquisitive individualism, which had been hidden during the interwar depression and delayed during the Spartan postwar period, was manifest by the 1960s. Only a fifth of workers owned their homes in 1954 compared to a third in 1968. The quip of the American housing developer, William Levitt—"no man who owns his house and lot can be a Communist. He has too much to do"—was also germane in the French context, especially if the *c* in "communist" is lower-case.[186] Twenty-three percent of households of skilled workers possessed automobiles in 1959, 40 percent had them in 1963, and 75 percent in 1972. Unskilled workers experienced a similar, although slightly smaller, increase in automobile ownership. The availability of individual automobiles (and consequent expenses) was a major change for a class whose main means of individual transportation before the Fifth Republic had been the bicycle.[187] No wonder that many wage earners reacted hostilely to students' destruction of automobiles in the Latin Quarter.

In addition to purchases of motor vehicles, a wide variety of other commodities were commonly found in working-class homes in 1968. French wage earners—like those of Germany, Italy, and other Western European countries—had become a key market for durable goods.[188] In 1959 only 22 percent of skilled workers had refrigerators; in 1963, 50 percent did; and by 1972, 91 percent.[189] Possession of refrigerators by unskilled workers' households jumped from 11 percent in 1959 to 83 percent in 1972. The expansion of ownership of washing machines was similar—74 percent of skilled workers' homes and 66 percent of unskilled workers' homes had one by 1972, a more than threefold increase since 1959. However, television was by far the most rapidly growing commodity of the Fifth Republic. Twelve percent of skilled workers' households had one in 1959; 35 percent in 1963; 85 percent in 1972. Ownership of *télés* by the unskilled jumped even more dramatically, from 7 percent in 1959 to 77 percent in 1972. In 1968, the 25 million regular television viewers outnumbered the 22 million regular readers. For example, at Renault-Cléon (Seine-Maritime), only 350 out of 5,000 wage earners regularly used the library of the *comité d'établissement*.[190] The lower the income, the more time was spent watching television.

These figures indicate important changes after 1955. In that year 40 percent of the unskilled and 28 percent of the skilled declared that they did "not want" to purchase a washing machine; 45 percent of the unskilled and 35 percent of the skilled did "not want" a refrigerator; 34 percent of the unskilled and 24 percent of the skilled did not desire an automobile; 44 percent of the unskilled and 37 percent of the skilled were uninterested in purchasing a television.[191] Therefore, consumption had to be taught, and workers had to learn to appreciate the advantages of the new goods. By 1968, with the help of advertising, most workers had been well instructed.

The Fifth Republic was special because it fostered a dramatic increase in prosperity and possessions. Yet it must be kept in mind that it did not constitute a break in twentieth-century French history. France during the Third Republic (1870–1940) and Fourth Republic (1945–1958) generated an increasing variety of products. The rapid rise of mass consumption and easy credit after World War II certainly contributed to the decline of the "traditional" working-class community.[192] Increases in consumption did not encourage community but rather egotisms.[193] Growth encouraged an individualism that was already present in the first half of the twentieth century.

As consumer debt mounted, pressures for a settlement increased. Students learned that debts worried workers. Strikers were grateful to Censier students for their help but told them, "It [the strike] is over. [We go] back to work for money as everywhere else."[194] The work stoppages caused consumerist desires to remain unfulfilled and thereby sharpened familial tensions: "Five weeks on strike has created an emotional strain between the married couple, Pierre and Nicole. They lived in two different worlds. He is a union representative, a devoted militant who is always active at the workplace. She is stuck in the housing project, dealing with personal problems, with unpaid rent, and with kids to feed. She feels abandoned. Suddenly their relationship turned sour."[195] Some trade unionists became misogynist.[196] According to one who participated in strikes in the northeastern industrial area: "We men did not suffer much. We occupied the factory and played cards. It wasn't bad at all. Trouble began when we returned home and our wives told us that the money had run out and that the children were hungry."[197]

Wives found themselves saddled with increased social and familial responsibilities during the strike wave.[198] When observers discussed the change of "public opinion" towards strikes, they often meant the opinion of women. School closings added to their child-care duties.[199] Unexpected shutdowns, lack of fuel, unavailability of cash, and runs on supplies complicated shopping. Many workers did not stop working because their "women at home did not look favorably upon the strike."[200] Militants reported divorces. Numerous wives opposed the work stoppage because it unbalanced the family budget or, in higher income households, destroyed vacation plans. A Flins worker with radical tendencies explained to a strike sympathizer that his wife did not want to see him involved in the movement. As the strikes endured, perhaps even more than males, women feared politicization, i.e., the subordination of material demands of the movement to the political goals of left parties and unions. Yet during the work stoppages they pragmatically welcomed the meals offered by left municipalities. They also appreciated the aid of priests in the working-class suburbs who "every day visited some families [of strikers] in their homes."[201]

Power failures, which the striking electricity workers sporadically imposed to display their bargaining leverage, disrupted daily routine.[202] The PTT strike halted customary means of communication. Regular television and radio programming was canceled. Workers and their families did not always react to the interruption of their favorite shows with class solidarity and sometimes exhibited individualist irritation. During the legislative election campaign, candidates recognized that the determined ORTF strikers were alienating the public. In the first half of June, opinion generally became much less sympathetic to wage earners still striking. According to a daily police bulletin, "the CGT knows this and has become less intransigent."[203]

The persistence of the ORTF and other work stoppages tested not only solidarity between men and women but also between young and older workers. Mature breadwinners seemed more anxious to end the strikes than younger wage earners.[204] It was at the end of the strikes—not the beginning, as many have assumed—that a generation gap became relevant in the workplace. By the middle of June, the PCF had recognized the unpopularity of the ORTF strike and pressured personnel to end it quickly.[205] Newspapers—such as *Le Figaro*, which had been critical of the government's management of the official news media—urged ORTF strikers to return to work. Some alleged that a Machiavellian administration did not wish to end the strike in order to remind the electorate of the movement's disorder.[206] In contrast, police argued that "a powerful minority" of strikers prevented successful negotiations.[207]

All bargaining partners were aware of divided and shifting worker sentiment. Perhaps recalling the dismal results of the general strike of 1947, the CGT avoided the formation of a national strike committee. The confederation recommended that negotiations be conducted by industrial branch and profession, but in metallurgy discussions quickly reverted to the level of individual firms when national and regional bargaining broke down. The unions tried to obtain additional concessions, whereas employers wanted to adhere as closely as possible to the Grenelle Accord.[208] In those firms where workers rejected the original agreement, the union delegation of each enterprise bargained directly with management and appealed to debtors and breadwinners by fighting to extend the gains of Grenelle. The extended duration of the strike in the biggest companies may be attributed to the power of the unions, especially the CGT. The confederation, although against revolutionary "adventurism," established picket lines and thus discouraged strikebreakers from returning to work.[209] In a number of cases, union militants violated the right to work of scabs entering the workplace. Employers cited four violations in early June, and conservative newspapers reported others.

Infractions included incidents at the Flins Renault plant, which employed 10,000 workers.[210] Flins was notorious for strains between *cadres* and workers, and the latter felt that their supervisory personnel were excessively authoritarian.[211] For their part, the *cadres* of certain firms complained of strong-arm tactics that had forced wage earners to stop work.[212] The CGT and other unions generally preferred to hold a public vote (with raised or lowered hands) to determine strike action. Employers believed that an open show of hands intimidated voters and advocated a secret ballot that would facilitate a return to work. The government sided with industrialists on this issue. The Ministry of Interior had argued at the beginning of the strikes that "numerous workers regret not being consulted concerning work stoppages," and prefects encouraged a secret ballot.[213] A spokesman for Pompidou declared that "every time a secret vote is taken, workers almost always decide to go back to work. What is certain is that the government must protect the right to work in order to fulfill its duty to the workers."[214] In fact, the government's pro-employer position was so pronounced that its labor inspectors in the Paris region raised objections.[215] They feared that their position as mediators between unions and employers would be compromised if they helped management organize votes intended to end work stoppages. They therefore refused to monitor or validate elections. Inspectors conceived of their job as encouraging dialogue between labor and management, not promoting the back-to-work movement that the authorities advocated. Except in small firms, secret votes were rare.[216] According to police, "activist minorities" opposed the secret ballot in major firms such as the Renault, Citroën, SKF, and the Société Chauvin at Ivry.[217] "In the Paris region, several police interventions were necessary to make strikers respect the right to work." For example, at the Usines Grandin at Montreuil, which employed a work force made up of large numbers of young women, police responded to a management request to stop a pro-strike demonstration outside its gates.[218] They detained three "young girls" and one young man.

The government ignored protests from its own Inspection du Travail and sent the police to intervene spectacularly and bloodily at Flins.[219] As in 1947, when the Socialist Jules Moch unleashed the newly reorganized CRS, the state wanted to demonstrate that it could domesticate workers' resistance.[220] Flins had been selected for special measures for several reasons. Its management wished to return to work; its geographical location in the plain of the Seine facilitated police mobility and allowed for easy encirclement; and the many foreign workers at the plant were made malleable by the threat of losing their work permit. The Flins factory was a key part of the automotive sector and an essential element of the Renault conglomerate, which was among the largest and most modern nationalized firms in France. Repression there would make strikers at other Renault branches reconsider their militancy. Police were apprehensive that Renault occupiers at Boulogne-Billancourt might blow up the bridge on the island (Ile Séguin) if police attacked their plant.[221]

On 4 June, the management of the Renault factory at Flins attempted to organize a vote on a return to work.[222] The Inspection du Travail felt that this was an especially unwise move given the high level of tension in the plant and the uncertain chances of success.[223] Inspectors criticized the prefect of Yvelines for pressuring them to organize the balloting and for cajoling them to enforce the right to work. Strike pickets then "sabotaged" an election that they claimed management had falsified. Management rebutted the charge and indicated that 80 percent of the personnel had been present for the vote.[224] Early in the morning of 6 June, 1,000 CRS (4,000, according to the Movement of 22 March) arrived in order to protect the right to work and to force an end to the occupation. Police claimed that at 3:00 A.M. they cleared the factory "without incident."[225] Later that morning, only 750 persons—400 of whom were supervisory personnel—returned to work. Strikers retaliated against the arrival of police reinforcements by establishing a picket line to prevent workers from entering the plant. The Movement of 22 March believed that the presence of thousands of CRS aimed to smash "the most class-conscious workers."[226] The CGT demanded the "immediate departure of police troops from Flins."[227]

Besieged Flins received immediate assistance from students devoted to the class struggle. According to author Nicolas Dubost, "Flins became the bastion of anti-authoritarian revolt … They [*gauchistes*] went to Flins, as others go to Lourdes, to witness miracles."[228] The ex-Beaux Arts became the meeting place for the Committee to Struggle for Popular Power and the Permanent Commission of Mobilization, which had close links to action committees and to the Movement of 22 March.[229] The Commission encouraged activists to join the Flins battle and urged students to act as revolutionaries whose goal was to defend the "mass movement."[230] For many young militants, Flins represented the culmination of the struggle to link up with workers. Art students collected cash for Flins strikers from the pedestrians who appreciated their display of two puppets ridiculing the president of the republic and a CRS.[231] Five hundred CFDT workers, fresh from their union's protest at the UIMM headquarters (avenue Wagram), joined youthful revolutionaries. According to police, they tried to take a train to Flins from the Gare Saint-Lazare, but railroad workers at the station—perhaps influenced by CGT-PCF campaigns against "provocateurs"—refused to cooperate. RATP employees denied the request of UNEF leaders who wanted the transport workers to bus them to large factories on strike.[232] Frustrated but nonetheless resourceful students commandeered two RATP buses near the Saint-Lazare station.[233] Police stopped one of the vehicles several blocks away, but the other reached the Renault plant at Boulogne-Billancourt. At that point, several hundred protesters tried to transfer to other buses for Flins, but police halted them. Police informers noted the license plate numbers of vehicles that gathered at Beaux-Arts so that their occupants could be apprehended as they traveled to the factory.[234] During the night of 6–7 June at the Saint-Cloud bridge on the route to Flins, the forces of order arrested 310 persons.[235] Two hundred thirty-three were male and 77 (25 percent) female, one of the highest percentages of female participation during the events, which usually hovered around 10 percent in major *journées*.[236] Only 20 (6 percent) were foreigners. Most, 167 (54 percent) were students. Very few, 26 (8 percent) of those interrogated had had previous run-ins with police; even fewer (15) possessed any weapons—including clubs or sticks—at the time of their arrest. The following day, the sub-prefect of Mantes recommended police inspection of all vehicles transporting young people from the Paris region to Flins.[237] The forces of order feared that youthful commandos might assault the Flins power station.[238] At the same time, unidentified groups—suspected of being members of Civic Action Committees, war veterans, fascists, or a *union sacrée* of reactionaries—attacked leftists on Parisian streets.[239]

On Friday, 7 June, officials estimated that four to five thousand people, including Alain Geismar and numerous members of 22 March, attended a demonstration at Flins.[240] One thousand demonstrators attempted to prevent non-strikers from entering the factory. Several hundred young strikers—with support from the Socialist/Communist municipality—began to harass and attack police.[241] In a manner reminiscent of the reactions of Latin Quarter residents to the police invasion of their neighborhood, the massive presence of the forces of order at Flins provoked the hostility of many locals.[242] Street battles ensued, and police, who now were patrolling the area en masse, detained over three hundred demonstrators and onlookers. When Brigitte Gros, a prominent politician who was both the mayor of nearby Meulan and a well-known journalist of *L'Express*, attempted to mediate, she was thrown into a police wagon and held for almost an hour. A CRS captain philosophized to his men: "When violence is measured, it is effective. It intimidates, and it disarms."[243] Confrontations continued over the weekend. The tactics of strikers and their student supporters, who numbered in the hundreds, infuriated the CRS who detained dozens. The suburban guerrillas hid behind railroad cars, tossed stones taken from the tracks, and burned hay "to smoke out the cops."[244] If police found parked and empty vehicles with Parisian plates, they punctured their tires. Helicopters and small aircraft reconnoitered demonstrators, who sometimes hid in the adjacent woods of Aubergenville and Elisabethville.[245] At a press conference on Sunday evening, Pompidou justified what was becoming known as "Operation Flins" by arguing that it was necessary to ensure the right to work.[246] The prime minister added, "the motto 'To Work' must be France's slogan at this moment."

On Monday, 10 June, officials reported that only 500 in a shift of 1,300 followed Pompidou's dictum and returned to their jobs.[247] Skirmishes continued as police battled workers and students on the streets of Flins. A member of the Movement of 22 March described the situation: "We saw what an army was. There were 10,000 men.... A railroad line and roads [were] protected militarily. Every ten meters there was a guy with a machine gun, and jeeps were everywhere. [It was] a fortified camp. I was never at Dien Bien Phu, but it reminded me a little of it."[248] The forces of order engaged in intensive manhunts for students, and all young people on the streets were in danger of being beaten or arrested.[249] They detained

457, of whom 72 percent were students.[250] Almost 13 percent had had previous confrontations with police. Flins violence involved students more than previous *journées*. Thus, the movement was returning to its student roots at a time when it should have been attracting workers who wished to display their solidarity with Flins comrades. Instead, a reverse osmosis prevailed. Young workers from the *banlieue* were attracted to the Latin Quarter, and students to the industrial suburbs. The targeting of the young indicated the increasing leverage of youth resistance at the end of the strike wave. The confrontations culminated in the drowning on 10 June of 17-year-old Gilles Tautin, who belonged to a Maoist organization. It is notable that Tautin was a *lycéen*. Fearing adverse public reaction, the police had orders during May to handle high-school students gingerly, but June seemed to bring a new climate where *lycéens* were treated as ruthlessly as university students and workers. Perhaps reports from informers that action committees and Sorbonne occupiers had or would acquire rifles and machine guns made the forces of order less lenient.[251]

The death of Tautin changed little at the plant. The overwhelming majority of supervisory personnel ignored the young Maoist's demise and came to work. Blue-collar workers continued the strike and occupied the factory late in the morning.[252] An agreement between management and the union later vacated the plant, totally disregarding Maoist demands for a new occupation.[253] Police maintained that the strike continued calmly and conventionally.[254] On 17 June, a secret vote was taken during which 4,811 voted for a return to work and 3,456 against.[255] By 20 June, it seems, Flins was functioning with the help of foreign strikebreakers.[256] The CFDT tried to unleash a new movement "to protest against the termination of two workers whom management disliked because of their behavior during the strike," but police asserted that its new picket line did not halt the return to work.[257]

On the same day that Tautin drowned, the CRS shot and killed a 24-year-old striker and mortally injured another worker at the giant Peugeot plant at Sochaux (Doubs). According to police, in early June a majority had voted to return to work, but "those who were in a minority enclosed themselves in the factory after having soldered the entrance gates. They argued that the voting was unrepresentative since a large number of strikers had not participated in it."[258] Once again, authorities were especially anxious to enforce the "freedom" to labor.[259] The forces of order offered several laconic accounts of the first Sochaux death:

[Officers] removed the strikers manning the picket line that blocked the entrance gates. This morning some refractory elements provoked skirmishes and confrontations during which a worker was killed.[260]

Between 2:45 and 6:00 A.M. police dispersed picket lines that guarded the entrance. This operation was characterized by combat between strikers and police. An officer was slightly injured. This morning two barricades remain inside the plant. Three thousand technicians, executives, and supervisors have returned to work, but workers have not. At 9:50 A.M. the situation deteriorated into barricade fighting, resulting in numerous injured. A worker died.[261]

The death enraged workers, especially youth, who stoned and trashed the elegant Hôtel Peugeot that served as police headquarters.[262] On 12 June, 136 people—of whom 101 were demonstrators and 35 police—were injured. Eighteen protesters were hospitalized, and two policemen remained in serious condition. "We [Police Nationale] regret moreover an[other] accidental death [of a worker]."[263] The union attempted—apparently successfully—to regain control of its troops, but the Sochaux strike persisted even after the Renault plants (with the exception of Flins) had returned to work.[264] That working-class and student deaths occurred at striking automobile factories once again underlined the real and symbolic importance of the car throughout the events. The destruction of automobiles marked the beginning of the student revolt in Paris and epitomized the attack on consumer society; the stoppage of car production initiated strikes in the Paris region; and the reprovisioning of gasoline at the end of May and the beginning of June inaugurated the return to normality. Finally, the deaths of automobile workers and one of their most fervent student supporters showed the government's determination to get wage earners back to work. The state wanted to demonstrate that it had controlled the streets and tamed the factories, while its radical opponents made a last-ditch effort to keep the automotive strike wave in motion.

Organizations that claimed to represent the working class reacted relatively calmly to the deaths. Fearing the adverse effects of a massive demonstration on public opinion during the electoral campaign, the CGT called for only a short and largely symbolic work stoppage.[265] The CGT's moderation after the Flins and Sochaux deaths favorably impressed authorities.[266] Police noted that even the CFDT was now willing "to play a moderating role" and would no longer try to outbid its larger rival.[267] The FO and CFTC were, as usual, quite temperate. To protest against CRS repression and the government's "attempt to impose a military dictatorship," both major unions (CGT and CFDT) decided to call a one-hour strike on Wednesday, 12 June. Police appreciated the confederations' response as "calm and destined to restrain the reaction of the base." Perhaps the rank and file sensed the tepidness of its leadership. At any rate, the strike call did not seem to be widely followed.[268] Almost everyone, including some *gauchistes*, now realized that violence profoundly alienated public opinion. The CGT made no attempt to resurrect the antirepressive coalition that had encouraged the strike wave after 13 May. The level of restraint exercised by the union was in sharp contrast to the massive protests that it had organized after the Charonne killings at the end of the Algerian War in 1962. The deaths and repression of 1968 nonetheless provoked worker-student anger and violence. The UNEF, action committees of *lycées*, SNESup, the

Movement of 22 March, and the CFDT organized a demonstration for 11 June. The police confirmed that "student organizations and especially the UNEF greatly exploited the death of G. Tautin in order to renew violent demonstrations."[269]

Police estimated that several thousand protested against the death of Tautin on the boulevard Saint-Michel on the night of 10 June.[270] During that night and the following (11–12 June), police confronted young demonstrators, who, it seems, were mainly workers, not students.[271] The deaths of Tautin and of the Sochaux workers (Henri Blanchet and Pierre Beylot) marked a change in police tactics. Before mid June, the forces of order made certain that they assigned enough men to control authorized demonstrations and to disperse unauthorized marches. Now they sought to prevent any gathering by exercising a massive police occupation of the streets.[272] To attempt to avoid the "vicious cycle of repression-protest," they adopted a waiting strategy and then intervened violently to attack and disperse the most committed demonstrators.[273]

The final Night of the Barricades in the Latin Quarter commenced on 11 June. In contrast to their predecessors of 1848, Parisian insurgents in 1968 never established a stable presence on the right bank.[274] Nor did the *banlieue* flame, as it would in the 1990s. Militant youth, who numbered perhaps 3,500, were not satisfied with chanting slogans such as "Funerals no, Revolution yes" and "Down with the police state." Police acknowledged that protesters launched numerous Molotov cocktails and other sorts of projectiles while constructing at least nine barricades.[275] Authorities noted that one of the potentially most dangerous barricades was established on the Maine-Vaugirard intersection.[276] Protesters there, directed by leaders with walkie-talkies, awaited the arrival of gendarmes and rendered police bulldozers powerless by setting fire to hundreds of liters of gasoline and fuel oil.[277] "The *carburant* (fuel) spread all over the street and continued to flame as it flowed into the sewer."[278] Street fighters harassed police with slingshots, and officers—who were still under orders not to use their firearms—returned the stones in retaliation.[279] Officers recounted that fighters tried to prevent a fire truck from extinguishing the blaze and worried that a nearby gas station would explode. The scene so troubled residents of the fourteenth *arrondissement* that they aided the forces of order, who reported that "for the first time" bystanders in the Latin Quarter criticized students and supported police.[280] A commissioner wrote that in the adjoining fifteenth, the UDR headquarters was sacked and burned: "A great fire, sustained with documents, furniture, etc. flared up in the middle of the road."[281] The incendiaries risked a combustible catastrophe, but firemen intervened effectively. The arson of the last Night of the Barricades defied public safety as well as property rights.[282]

Protesters damaged 75 automobiles, sacked 10 police vehicles, and attacked 5 police stations, 2 of which were put to flame. As usual, the main target seems to have been the strategically located commissariat of the fifth *arrondissement*, which was assaulted by hundreds who shattered its windows, injured five policemen, and burned nearly a dozen official vehicles parked in front of it.[283] Police found it "very difficult" to remove a barricade on the rue Saint-Jacques near the Sorbonne. The firemen warned the forces of order against lobbing their tear gas grenades for fear of starting a blaze in the university. A bulldozer braved the demonstrators' numerous Molotov cocktails and was finally able to level the barricade at 7:00 A.M. on 11 June. *Pétroleuses* or *pétroleurs*, who evoked the final days of the Commune, forced firemen to intervene fifteen times.[284] Police observed that a few distraught occupants of apartment houses acted as counterrevolutionary snipers, shooting and injuring two demonstrators. Protesters cut down "25 ancient and splendid trees," [285] showing that ecology never became a priority for these barricade builders. Police reported 72 officers injured (47 of whom were hospitalized) and detained nearly 1,500 demonstrators.[286] The non-students (729) slightly outnumbered students (718). Once again, young and militant wage earners were attracted to student territory. Despite an officer's assertion that many demonstrators were "bandits from poor neighborhoods and distant suburbs," very few of the arrested (36) had police records.[287] Foreigners composed 11 percent of those apprehended. First-aid posts in the refuge of the Sorbonne treated some of the nearly 200 demonstrators who were hurt.[288]

The government reinforced its strict control of the media. It forbade *reportage en continu* (live coverage), and it encouraged major radio stations to go off the air before much of the violence erupted.[289] When citizens learned about the confrontations, authorities concluded that many reacted negatively to what they considered to be gratuitous violence and revolutionary disorder.[290] The police self-servingly said that opinion blamed "troublemakers" for the violence and noted accurately that *L'Humanité* put the return to work at Dassault on page one and the Flins incidents on page eight.[291] *Gauchistes* sensed that "Paris was against us."[292] Motorists, including many wage earners, were again aghast at the destruction of vehicles. A trade-union activist believed that the burning of cars "shocked our men the most.... Each incinerated vehicle meant 10,000 votes for the general."[293] Many began to identify protesters with a primitive and destructive natural force. The police received a badly written letter from one anonymous informer who believed that "the 22 March Movement will invade the Jardin des Plantes and open the cages of the animals."[294]

Of course, this feeling was not uniformly shared. When doctors at Hôpital Beaujon examined ten demonstrators who had been injured during *interpellations* at Flins, physicians insulted police officers, calling them "SS."[295] They then surreptitiously released two of the injured. Officers, though, took their revenge by stealing 850 francs from one of the patients. Disregarding the putative protection offered by armbands worn by registered journalists, police brutalized reporters.[296] High police officials admitted that the assault on a Europe One journalist was "totally unjustified" and contrary to orders. However, they excused their men by claiming that they were being bombarded with "home-made bombs and Molotov cocktails" from roofs in the heart of the Latin Quarter (Place E. Rostand).[297]

Professors Monod and Jacob—Nobel Prize winners who had supported the demonstrators—criticized the "barricade mentality" of students.[298] Weeks of strikes and unrest had eroded the antirepressive consensus of mid May, and sectors of previously liberal public opinion were willing to accept the necessity of repression to restore order. The turn of opinion would undoubtedly contribute to the victory of the right in the elections at the end of the month. In the days preceding the final Night of the Barricades, police reported that five Molotov cocktails were thrown against the commissariat in the fourteenth; a plastic charge exploded at the offices of one of the organizers of the Champs-Elysées *manif*; and the Latin Quarter headquarters of the left-wing Gaullist Capitant were trashed. The forces of order asserted that invaders destroyed signs, ripped out telephone wires, smashed a typewriter, and damaged the door.[299]

Police officials implausibly blamed the May–June events on a conspiracy of international *groupuscules*, especially the JCR and the German SDS.[300] Police intelligence was always on the lookout for subversive groups whose discovery and capture justified its bureaucratic existence. In addition, the focus on conspiracy theory turned attention away from police behavior and tended to excuse brutality against "professional" or foreign revolutionaries. Officials stressed the leading role of Trotskyite "activist minorities" in demonstrations.[301] The JCR and FER "played a central role and provided compact, armed squads which constructed barricades and deliberately provoked police." Only Paris, not the provinces, experienced a "paroxysm of violence" because only in the capital did these *groupuscules* possess the critical mass of militants. On 14 May, four German nationals carrying dangerous chemicals destined to produce explosives and incendiary devices were arrested. On 21 May at Saulieu (Côte d'Or), six members of the Sorbonne *service d'ordre* were stopped, and their machine guns and pistols seized. Police suspected a German journalist close to the JCR of fabricating bombs and Molotov cocktails.[302]

On 11 June, *Le Monde*, which had been favorable to the student movement, denounced the "destructive blindness" of the marchers, the "*bateau-ivre*" of the Sorbonne, and the presence of the *katangais*.[303] The latter, who numbered perhaps several dozen, played the role of a *service d'ordre* at the Sorbonne. They had often been on the front lines of the rebellion, but their violence and lack of ideology alienated many students.[304] The *katangais* derived their name from their former mercenary status in Africa, even though police claimed that this was a "legend without foundation."[305] Authorities described them as "*voyous*" and identified one of their leaders, Christian Maricourt, as a deserter from the Foreign Legion.[306] *Katangais* too played with fire. Before the end of May, informers related that they had imported more than 350 liters of gasoline into the university and threatened to ignite it to combat a possible police or Gaullist assault.[307] Such defensive tactics worried the UNEF's National Bureau. On the morning of 14 June, police ascertained that fellow occupiers expelled the last 50 *katangais* (they had numbered 150) after they had threatened the head of the infirmary, Professor Francis Kahn.[308] Dr. Kahn was a well-known supporter of the movement and had publicly accused police of using highly toxic and dangerous gases.[309] Before the expulsion of the *katangais*, fights had erupted between them and their student opponents: "These scuffles became a confused fray, a chase down the halls, exchanges of grenades and Molotov cocktails which broke windows. Firemen had to put out a few fires. Finally, the last *katangais* were forcibly expelled."

The Odéon Theater also utilized a force that was roughly equivalent to the *katangais* of the Sorbonne. Authorities asserted that "About thirty men, most of whom were former convicts, formed a rapid intervention commando (CIR). They lived in isolation and … moved only at night, employing 'ambulances' which transported the falsely injured and their phony nurses."[310] The Odéon was emptied on the morning of 14 June. Given its history of conflagrations, police recommended that firemen participate in the removal.[311] In fact, fear of fire was so profound that police repeated a new version of Operation Zig-Zag in the middle of June. At that time, officials ordered the interrogation of all young people walking in groups of two or three to verify if any were transporting Molotov cocktails.[312] At 7:30 A.M. police with orders to intercept CIR or *katangais* surrounded the theater. During the ensuing negotiations, the prefect of police assured occupiers that only those carrying arms would be arrested. At 9:30 the evacuation began, and the operation continued without incident until 10:15. Police frisked occupiers, most of whom "resembled beatniks." Two hundred nine persons were removed; 132 released; 76 (68 men and 8 women) were taken in for questioning and then released.[313] Sixty of the 75 interrogated were French students and 15 were foreigners, a relatively high percentage that was perhaps a sign of police discrimination or of a growing integration of non-French into the movement. The forces of order found the main auditorium "in good shape." "Contrary to what we expected, there was no arms supply on top of the roof, except for a Molotov cocktail."[314] However, in the interior some light weapons (knives, clubs, chains, Molotov cocktails, grenades, etc.), two air rifles, hunting rifles, and numerous medications were discovered. A commissioner added: "The cashiers' desks in the entrance hall were pillaged, corridors dirtied, and actors' lodges and dressing rooms trashed."[315]

Police thought that the Odéon evacuation showed the public that the government was now firmly in charge of the situation, and officials asserted that no major street actions against the Odéon removal occurred.[316] A bomb explosion at a police office in the fifth *arrondissement* was the lone sign of protest. On Sunday afternoon, 16 June, the forces of order felt confident enough to clear the Sorbonne.[317] Authorities encountered several

Molotov cocktails on the first floor and three tear gas grenades and three offensive grenades in the university basement.[318] Occupiers left the exterior doors of the university undamaged but pocketed the keys as souvenirs.[319] Interior officials charged that they made uninhibited use of state property and worked the phones so much that university authorities and the PTT had decided to disconnect service.[320] Sorbonne buildings suffered an invasion of rats and reeked of stale urine.[321] The occupation of the Sorbonne left behind ten million francs' worth of damage. Of the 202 persons inside, 190 left of their own volition. Seven were arrested for illegal weapons possession, and 5 for identity checks. Unlike the situation at Odéon, police estimated that 2,500 persons almost immediately assembled to protest against the police operation.[322] Despite the UNEF's refusal to endorse street actions and the official ban on demonstrations, seven skirmishes involving hundreds of persons continued in the Latin Quarter in the nights following the Sorbonne evacuation.[323] Of the 236 arrested, 87 percent (205 persons) were male and 13 percent (31 persons) were female.[324] Eighty-seven percent were 21 or older. Sixty percent (148 persons) were not students, a figure nearly identical to that of the major Nights of the Barricades. A significant portion—14 percent (33 individuals)—were foreigners.[325] However, only 2 of these foreigners (6 percent) were women. Among the non-French, militancy was usually male.

Former occupants of the Sorbonne, including a few dozen of the remaining *katangais*, managed to escape police and found refuge at Censier. Interior ministry sources asserted that many of the refugees, especially ten members of the rapid intervention committee of the Odéon, were judged "undesirable" by Censier students, who had elected a committee to decide the issue of their admission.[326] Police noted that at this surviving bastion of militancy, "a control post strictly managed by young women is in operation.... However, students have not reorganized the building to prevent their expulsion by police."[327] At Beaux-Arts, "in contrast, numerous students (1,500 during the day) permanently maintained the occupation. Strict control is in place at the entrance, and only students from Beaux-Arts, with the exception of those who are politically hostile to the UNEF, can enter."[328]

At remaining occupied institutions, constantly circulating rumors of imminent police assaults solidified student support for leftists. Occupiers prepared to defend themselves against tear gas and planned escape routes on the roofs. At the law school on rue Assas, election results gave the *gauchiste* strike committee an overwhelming majority.[329] Nor was this an isolated case. At the Faculté des Sciences (Halle aux vins) the leftist strike committee won 65 percent of the more than 6,000 votes. The forces of order affirmed that moderate and right-wing tendencies garnered less than 33 percent.[330] Police planned a midnight operation (labeled *Obélix*) to empty this *faculté*.[331]

Beaux-Arts was cleared on 26 June. Early that morning police arrested 96 persons inside the building and 40 outside.[332] The percentage of women

(31 percent) was remarkably high, perhaps reflecting the relatively large number of female students enrolled in this institution. The number of non-students equaled students. Thirteen percent of the total interrogated were foreigners. The forces of order apparently took special revenge on those who had visually propagated the catchy slogan CRS = SS. Interior officials cited the Beaux-Arts strike committee, which angrily condemned the police at a press conference. The forces of order had launched "a night surprise attack," "chased [the committee] out of its offices," fired "grenades into the courtyard and gardens," administered copious "clubbings," and engaged in "the pillaging of the workshops."[333] The student committee implied that police behaved more destructively than any protester beyond UNEF control. The committee threatened to sue the authorities responsible for "abusively" detaining students at the Beaujon detention center.

Hearing the news of the fall of Beaux-Arts, Censier and the Faculté de Médicine reinforced their guard and put their armed commandos on alert. Police noted that lookouts on roofs were equipped with trashcans full of cobblestones.[334] A Yugoslav waiter informed the forces of order that arms were being transported to both institutions.[335] Sciences Po was cleared on 29 June, and its black and red flags lowered.[336] The law school of rue Assas, where anarchist influence was evident (it was one of the rare institutions where black flags outnumbered red), was vacated on 1 July.[337] Police informers (two of whom were professors at the medical school) reported that some of its occupiers and their logistical support—including light arms, Molotov cocktails, cobblestones, and homemade explosives—had found their way into the Faculté de Médicine.[338] This *faculté* housed at least thirty non-students who had taken control of the laboratory and its potentially dangerous chemicals.[339] Appropriately, Censier also became one of the last strongholds of the occupation movement. Two hundred persons, who included several prostitutes and as many beggars as students, remained inside.[340] Police remarked that they defiantly continued to fly four red flags and to lash out at rightists who ventured into their neighborhood.[341] Officials implied that Censier occupants, some of whom were armed with Molotov cocktails produced on-site, were responsible for night attacks on police vehicles.[342] Their attempts to burn a few cars parked near this *faculté* brought firemen to the scene before it finally fell on 6 July.

The most destructive university occupation may have occurred at Nanterre. Authorities declared that before its end on 2 July, "the cafeteria was ransacked (doors broken, percolators destroyed)… Lecture hall B suffered serious damage and numerous graffiti. Many volumes were stolen from the library, and several classrooms were pillaged."[343] Police were scandalized that during the occupation of Nanterre, "North-Africans from neighboring *bidonvilles* could enter [the university] freely, but Europeans have to identify themselves" to a group of helmeted *lycéens* and college students armed with iron bars.[344] Even before the occupation was over, the minister of education had decided to close all but one Nanterre dormitory.[345] The housing director, though, warned him that shutting them down would lead to "disaster": "The systematic destruction of buildings and their furniture might accompany the departure of students.... One thousand residents should not be punished because of the actions of one or two hundred loud-mouthed fanatics that we should eliminate, at least in part, when they ask for re-admission [to the dorms]." In mid May, the administration realized that the construction of Nanterre residences had been an "error" but felt powerless to close them because of fear of provoking riots and insufficient space to lodge their occupants: "The Paris housing office can provide only about 7,000 rooms. A sudden elimination of 1,000 rooms will probably produce unrest."[346]

The police abandoned Nanterre to its radical fate but were elsewhere effective in showing the state's determination to keep order. May's turbulence stiffened sentiment for increased centralization. According to one high-level administrator, "the events of May have proven that you should not question the prefect's centralized authority and undivided responsibility to maintain order."[347] Police tried hard to control the walls of the capital and attempted to enforce a ban on graffiti. At seven places in the sixth *arrondissement*, posters offensive to the state were ripped down. "CRS = SS" (figure 8) and "The police speak daily at 8:00 P.M." (the hour of the evening news broadcast; see figure 14) were quickly eliminated from public view.[348] The geographical distribution of posters was not surprising: 21 of 54 were in the fifth and sixth *arrondissements*, but 6 were found in the working-class districts of the twentieth and eighteenth *arrondissements*. Four were plastered in the industrial suburb of Asnières.[349] Thus, distributors made an effort not to preach to the converted. Two militants who glued an image of Hitler with the Gaullist symbol of the cross of Lorraine onto the commissariat of the twelfth were arrested.[350] Dozens of hawkers of the leftist *Action* were detained for questioning.[351] So were two poster hangers from the extreme-right group Action Française.[352]

From 11 June to 13 June, the government adopted stringent legal measures. It banned all street demonstrations during the weeks preceding the elections and dusted off a 1936 statute that the Popular Front government had used to outlaw extreme right-wing organizations. This time, though, the government dissolved leftist groups, including the Movement of 22 March, JCR, FER, CLER, and the Maoist organization to which Gilles Tautin had belonged.[353] It also expelled all foreigners who had been detained by police during protests. From 24 May to 6 June, police deported 183 persons "known for their active participation in demonstrations in France."[354] They included 32 Algerians, 22 Germans (including 12 members of the SDS), 20 Portuguese, 17 Spaniards, 15 Italians, 8 Britons, 5 Americans, and 5 Dutch, and 8 from "French-speaking black Africa."[355] North Africans were more conspicuous in street protests than in strikes, although it is unclear whether this was a result of assimilation or alienation. Prominent artists—Casson, Ragon, Bazaine,

FIGURE 14: "The Police Speak Every Evening at 8:00"

Soulages, Hellion—protested at the Ministry of Interior against the expulsions of foreign artists.[356] Foreign students, even nonpolitical ones, were especially victimized by the "events" since strikes delayed the arrival of their scholarship stipends and rendered many temporarily destitute.

The Movement of 22 March criticized the passive response of the parliamentary left to the prohibitions carried out by a "fascist state."[357] The CGT and the PCF refused to condemn the banning of *gauchiste* organizations, and police sources related that *L'Humanité* ignored the issue.[358] Perhaps to win Communist neutrality, the government did not prohibit its youth group, the UEC. Alain Krivine pointed out that only organizations linked to "proletarian internationalism," not student groups such as the UNEF, were outlawed.[359] Informers revealed that the PCF's refusal to protest against the interdictions infuriated Nanterre students who were members of 22 March.[360] They reacted with fire and burned the Party's posters. "Impressed by the size of the conflagration," police reported, "[Nanterre] administrative personnel intervened and finally students put out the flames themselves." Cohn-Bendit, having returned illegally, sensed the new climate and discreetly abandoned France for Germany. Priests and pastors sympathetic to radicals were among the few to protest against the outlawing of leftist movements.[361] Guy Mollet—who, as a former Socialist prime minister during the Algerian War, was no stranger to repression—believed the administration's decision unwise even as he criticized the violence of *groupuscules* that, he thought, only bolstered support for the government.

In mid-June, authorities reported that a number of *gauchiste* groups—22 March, Soutien aux Luttes du Peuple (Maoist), and several action committees—had annulled a demonstration that had been scheduled to assemble at the Place de la République.[362] However, the *groupuscules* could not widely disseminate news of the cancellation, and 364 people came to protest. Police arrested all and transported them to the Vincennes detention center "for identification." From 14 June to 16 June, interior ministry officials ordered at least fifty different requisitions at the headquarters of *gauchiste* organizations or at the homes of their leaders.[363] "Numerous documents were seized. Forty persons were held for questioning, one of whom was arrested."[364] Among the dozens detained were distributors of tracts calling for soldiers to revolt, three Beaux-Arts students who attempted to revive the Movement of 22 March, and five armed *katangais*— three of whom were incarcerated for theft and assault. On 16 June, Alain Krivine and his spouse were apprehended. She was released, and he imprisoned for trying "to reconstitute an outlawed organization."[365] From 24 May to 12 June, authorities initiated 55 *informations judiciaires* (investigations) into a variety of infractions: possession and transport of weapons, arson, use of explosives, theft, pillage, destruction, and assaulting officers. Based on these charges, prosecutors brought to trial 41 persons. The minister of interior wanted to pursue all leads and instructed prefects to provide him with names of anarchists, Maoists, Trotskyites, and Castroists.[366] Surprisingly, police saw a positive side to the protests, and they admitted that there had been "a notable decrease of the number of crimes in May where revolutionary action and demonstrations were most significant." In Paris, Lyon, Bordeaux, and Rouen, the number of offenses dropped by 10 percent, a decline that police attributed to the fact that "asocial elements were involved in demonstrations."[367]

Inversely, the regime tolerated the activities of extreme right-wing *groupuscules*, such as Occident, to consolidate the bloc of order. On 7 June,

General Massu met with Pompidou to plead for a broad amnesty of officers who had engaged in subversive activities against the republic during the Algerian War. These men, the commander of French forces in Germany argued with alarmist embellishment, might be needed for a "new civil war in the *métropole*."[368] On Saturday, 8 June, Georges Bidault—*résistant*, former foreign minister, and Christian democratic leader who had become linked to the OAS—was allowed to return to Paris. On 15 June the government freed eleven ex-OAS officers, some of whom had been involved in assassination attempts against de Gaulle himself. General Salan, a former OAS head, left the jail where he was serving his life imprisonment. *Le Canard enchaîné* joked that he sent Dany the following telegram: "Thanks Cohn-Bendit, from Salan."[369] The nationalist right was grateful for the pardons since "Free Salan" had been one of their slogans during their nearly unnoticed counterdemonstration of 13 May.

Left journals were outraged.[370] Police officials cited a *L'Humanité* headline, "Great Reconciliation between Gaullism and OAS." *Combat* wrote hyperbolically that "the release of the head of the OAS is the price that the president paid the army for maintaining him in power." According to a daily police bulletin, the liberation of lesser-known terrorists, such as Pierre Fenoglio, who had been responsible for the assassination of the Socialist mayor of Evian, raised strong protests from the entire left.[371] The government had temporarily healed the divisions that the right had inherited from the Algerian War. For some, June 1968 recalled the Gaullism of 1957–1958, when the movement was passionately attached to *Algérie Française*.[372] The Gaullist alliance with the extreme right, though, revealed the failure of one of its most ambitious goals—to overcome the traditional left-right split in French politics. *Gaullisme de gauche* would remain on the defensive.

Radicals reacted fearfully to the change of political landscape. They complained that the government had freed the "fascists, Salan and Bidault" and had given the green light to right-wing terror.[373] The Action Committee of Vincennes specifically accused the state of creating "a concentration camp" at Vincennes, where 1,500 students were being held and questioned before release.[374] Alain Geismar denounced the "appeal to fascists … which is the beginning of something new. Fascism is now an integral part of the state apparatus and the Fifth Republic."[375] Confirming this interpretation (at least in the students' minds), someone threw a grenade at a strike picket at Censier on 21 June at 2:00 A.M.[376] This attack led to a reinforcement of the *service d'ordre* at remaining occupied Parisian institutions. Students were sure Occident was the perpetrator, but the attack might have been in retaliation for the beating that ten armed *gauchistes* had given to the hawkers of the Gaullist *La Nation*.[377]

Back-to-work demonstrations gained momentum. On 11 June "several thousand workers and employees of Citroën," many of whom may have signed an antistrike petition at the beginning of the work stoppage, marched through the streets of Paris shouting slogans such as "Right to work,"

"Free our factories," and with reference to the occupiers, "Throw out the garbage," according to the right-wing *Figaro*.[378] Police estimated that five thousand of them finished their demonstration at the Ministry of Social Affairs.[379] Three thousand five hundred Renault workers and employees trekked from Paris to Flins to display their desire to return to work. Two thousand SIMCA employees demonstrated at Poissy, a stronghold of the "independent" CFT (Confédération française du travail), for an end to their strike.[380] According to police sources, by 12 June, 15,000 of the 17,000-strong SIMCA work force were back on the job.[381] On 12 June a Citroën group— which called itself Right to Work—claimed that 17,000 demonstrated against "disorder and anarchy." Police felt the group had the support of only 8,000, but it was dynamic enough to engage in daily demonstrations.[382] In a company known for its anti-unionism, Right to Work attracted nearly all its supervisory personnel and substantial numbers of French and foreign workers who had joined right-wing and company unions.[383] At ORTF, an Anti-Strike Civic Action Committee demanded the dismissal of well-known journalists, such as Sédouy, Harris, and Labro, who had become strike organizers.[384] *Cadres*—whether or not they had supported the strike in May—became a pressure group to end it in June.

Under these circumstances, the work week of 10–15 June saw an end to the work stoppage by most remaining large metallurgical firms of the Paris region. The votes on ending the strike stimulated a much greater turnout than the occupation itself.[385] At Dassault in Saint-Cloud, 2,000 of 2,800 workers attended the 10 June meeting that decided to terminate the stoppage. Authorities stated that Sud-Aviation plants at Courbevoie, Nantes, and Bordeaux were back to work by 14 June.[386] At Renault-Cléon (Seine-Maritime), at least 65 percent of workers voted on 16 June to return to work. On 18 June, Renault restarted with only a small minority insisting upon continuing the strike. The Ministry of Social Affairs thought the Renault agreement, which extended some of the gains of Grenelle, to be an appropriate model for other large firms, such as Citroën. However, the management of the latter refused to concede on monetary and union-rights issues, and workers continued the stoppage.[387] According to police, Citroën and Thomson-Houston would return the following week.[388] At Assurances Générales de France, the confederations expected significant opposition to their support for a return to work. They successfully overcame it by rapidly organizing the vote and by making certain that *cadres*, higher-paid workers, and non-strikers participated in the balloting. On 18 June, the president of the GIM reported that "almost all" strikes had ended and that a maximum of 75,000 workers out of 750,000 remained engaged in work stoppages.[389] Most of these strikes were settled by Monday, 24 June. Nationally, in forty-eight departments the return to work was total.

Almost all sources indicate that those who continued to strike were young, and the delayed resumption of production can be attributed to the combination of their combativeness and demographic weight. The propensity of youth to participate in extended strikes was not, however, unique to 1968 and occurred during other strike waves, such as the spring of 1936.[390] In the 1960s as in the 1930s, young people—who were relatively new to wage labor and unencumbered by familial responsibilities—were less accommodating to the daily grind of factory existence than their elders. The critique of work and the attack on accumulated labor that emerged from the revolt of the 1960s had, at least in part, demographic origins. The heavy weight of youth in the work force had the effect of prolonging the strike wave in 1968. Workers aged 15 to 24 constituted approximately a quarter of the working population.[391] Young malcontents were joined by CFDT activists and other trade unionists who felt that wage earners could achieve further advances. In one large nationalized insurance firm, workers were disappointed that the company would be able to "recuperate" (make up) lost strike days.

In the second half of June, the gains of wage earners in the most advanced industrial branches that had initiated the strikes—aviation, electrical construction, and automobiles—were most impressive.[392] Their willingness to continue the strike made their labor more valuable. A majority of wage earners in large metallurgical factories won a shorter work week than Grenelle had offered without a reduction of pay. At the Renault plant, conditions were somewhat improved for those assigned to the dirtiest jobs. Aviation workers at Dassault Saint-Cloud no longer had to work on Saturdays, thus restoring the labor-free weekend that the Popular Front had first established three decades before. Overtime pay rates improved, and union militants were to be compensated for devoting a limited number of hours to union duties. The pattern in nationalized railroads was similar. Workers won an 11 percent pay increase, the work week declined from 46 hours to 44.5 hours by the end of the year, and the number of days of paid vacation rose from 26 to 28.[393]

The strike wave was the most important step towards the eventual re-establishment of the forty-hour work week, a major goal of organized labor throughout the nineteenth and twentieth centuries. Workers' demands in May–June 1968 inaugurated an evolutionary decline of working hours. In the national agreement of 13 December 1968, employers and unions decided in principle to return gradually to the forty-hour week without a reduction of buying power.[394] As of 1 January 1969, most hospital employees would be working only forty hours. In the aftermath of the strike wave, the SNCF, a number of metallurgical firms, and certain big department stores committed themselves to the eventual re-establishment of the forty-hour week. Banks and the social security administration also pledged a diminution to forty hours in the near future. The post office cut back its hours, forcing clients to arrive before 7:00 (instead of 7:30) in the evenings and before noon (instead of 1:00) on Saturdays.

Workers' demands manifested from the beginning of the strike wave obliged metallurgical firms to raise the salaries of their lowest-paid personnel more than the Grenelle protocol had required. According to the

CGT, the strikes produced the greatest increase in the minimum wage since its introduction in 1950.[395] Wage disparities between higher-paid Parisian workers and their provincial counterparts were reduced, and pay differentials between young and older workers narrowed. Youth, women (who, according to the CGT, composed one-third of striking workers), and foreigners were especially helped by the salary compression. The CGT celebrated immigrants' participation in the strike and their large raises.[396] The federation also claimed that in certain cases the wages of women— who were paid on the average 36 percent less than men—and young workers nearly doubled. The PSU also lauded the "social victories" of Grenelle.[397] Salary increases of the mostly female work force in major department stores—Printemps, Galeries Lafayette, and Bon Marché— ranged from 13 to 35 percent.[398] In individual enterprises, women won special treatment. In a number of firms, pregnant women acquired one paid hour of rest per day and longer maternity leave, which had been union goals for years. In banks, females gained a shorter work schedule after six months of pregnancy. In a few companies, mothers were granted paid leave to care for a sick child and limited reimbursement for day care. Females contributed to the re-establishment of a work-free weekend since some were no longer required to labor Saturdays. Parisian nurses reported a drop in their working week from 45 to 42 hours.[399] Limited gains also spread to youth and foreigners. Certain firms lowered the voting age for union elections from 18 to 16. In several enterprises, those under eighteen won an additional two days of paid vacation. A number of employers granted immigrants additional time to spend in their native countries.

In keeping with wage earners' preference not to make up strike time, unions won partial compensation for days missed. In other words, workers in many branches wanted the work stoppages to be treated as paid vacation.[400] This was a sticking point that had prolonged the strike at major plants.[401] Interior ministry sources revealed that at Renault (Boulogne-Billancourt) on 24 June, four hundred workers in the artillery department "decided to go on strike for an unlimited time. They found out that *cadres* had obtained complete compensation for strike days. They want the same benefit."[402] On the morning of 27 June, three hundred Citroën workers stopped work in—what police termed—"an anarchical manner" to protest recuperation.[403] National negotiations legitimized workers' demand for compensation for strike days. The CGT Federation of Metallurgy claimed that "for the first time in France, strikers were compensated not by their strike fund but by their bosses."[404] At Dassault at Saint-Cloud, management was forced to pay the bills for gasoline that had been distributed during the occupation. Railroad workers objected to the official agreement with the SNCF, which required recuperation of half the time lost to the strike, but to their great satisfaction, the recovery of strike days never occurred.[405] In other sectors—the Aéroport de Paris, PTT, and perhaps Citroën—the threat of a new strike terminated managements' attempt to make up time lost.[406] Despite some exceptions, strike time was generally not redeemed in the public sector. The two holidays that had elapsed (Ascension on 23 May and Pentecost on 3 June) were paid as planned. After May, the number of compensated legal holidays increased. In the months following the events, the total of wage earners who could take advantage of an early retirement plan tripled from 50,000 to 150,000. Workers with seniority received extra paid vacation. The demand for time off was nearly insatiable, even though 85 percent of workers already had four weeks of paid vacation. In a number of branches and firms, young workers won a fifth week.

Student and other revolutionaries did not understand how significant and varied these gains were and constantly warned that inflation would devour them.[407] In the huge nationalized sector—SNCF, EDF-GDF, RATP, Charbonnages—the government was forced to abandon policies that had restrained wage hikes for five years. According to the CGT, prices for the average working family increased 3 to 4 percent in the final six months of 1968. Inflation may have eaten up a good chunk of wage increases, but international competition (France, after all, was a vital member of the Common Market) held down further increases and was responsible for augmented purchasing power. In a number of large enterprises (Renault, Chausson, Thomson-Houston, etc.), blue-collar workers won the right to be paid monthly (*mensualisation*) instead of hourly. *Mensualisation* improved benefits and working conditions, assured pregnant women of full salary and sick pay, ended time-clock punching, and offered extra days of paid vacation.

The unions emerged strengthened from their combat against employers and the government. In Parisian metallurgy the CGT had led the greatest strike wave in history.[408] The confederations achieved their long-term goal of securing union rights on the shop floor and in the office. The legislation of 27 December 1968, which was conceived during the events, protected the right to work but legalized the exercise of union rights in firms with more than fifty workers. Delegates were authorized to organize sections, meet monthly, collect dues, and distribute information. These rights had already existed for some time in many firms, but the National Assembly finally and formally confirmed them. The bargaining agreements of June had the consequence of diminishing unemployment, which dropped 18 percent from May to December. In the Post and Telephone (PTT), union pressures and demands compelled the hiring of at least 6,500 new workers.[409] These additions consequently increased union membership.

Many workers concluded that collective struggle was effective, and the unions reached the apex of their influence. In most sectors, the trade-union influx was the largest since the end of World War II. After the strikes ended, the CGT was able to enroll 300,000 to 400,000 new members nationally and to begin nearly 6,000 new sections.[410] Police asserted that the CFDT claimed 280,000 fresh adherents and the FO 100,000.[411] The rate of adhesion of recent recruits in the Paris region was higher than the national average. Many of them were young, and Séguy claimed that their average age was twenty-four. They may have been from the less remunerated categories of larger firms.[412] The CFDT also profited by enlisting some of those who felt that the settlements were insufficient and that a "real transformation" could have occurred.[413] However, CFDT radicalism should not be exaggerated. The metallurgical militants who attended its national congress at the end of April 1968 were hardly fiery revolutionaries.[414] According to the Ministry of Interior, 350 of 400 delegates responded to a poll that indicated that 16 percent (56 persons) were active in a political organization. Forty-three belonged to the PSU and 13 to the FGDS. Fifty-six percent read regional newspapers; 32 percent *Le Monde*; 22.5 percent *Témoignage Chrétien*, and 5.4 percent *L'Humanité*. Both confederations were particularly effective in attracting members, including foreigners, in big metallurgical enterprises where unions had been able to broaden the gains of the Grenelle agreement. At Flins, for example, union (CGT and CFDT) membership increased approximately 10 percent, and at Citroën, the CGT attracted four thousand new members. In the chemical firm Rhône-Poulenc at Vitry, the CFDT section claimed to have doubled its adherents.

But union power had definite limits. The CFDT recognized that the spurt in unionization provoked by the May events was relatively unimpressive in comparison to similar growth periods in 1936–1937 and 1945–1947.[415] Despite their gains, women remained particularly resistant to appeals to participate more actively in male-dominated unions. In 1969 and following years, membership gains of both major federations stagnated. The number of adherents stabilized in the more assertive unions, the CGT and CFDT, while the less aggressive FO increased much more rapidly. Union influence reached its zenith in May, when the confrontation with students briefly weakened the state, and in May's immediate aftermath, which produced substantial leisure and material gains for workers. In retrospect, May–June might be seen as a pinnacle of the influence of organized labor and not, as many have argued, a repudiation of unions by their more radical rank and file. By June, activists and their sympathizers had to confront a largely uncommitted and sometimes hostile rank and file that was experiencing increasing social and familial pressures to return to work.

Undoubtedly the seductions of consumer society were instrumental in inducing many workers to resume wage labor. With the spread of new possibilities of consumption during the Fifth Republic, blue-collar workers had entered an era where demands for commodities largely replaced any lingering revolutionary yearnings and even proved much more popular than workers' control or *autogestion*.[416] Consumption helped to make society cohere and encouraged workers to make their labor more expensive. Nevertheless, coercion was needed to supplement the consumerist appeal. A repressive state that was determined to make wage earners reenter factories was also a key factor in ending strikes in some of the most important enterprises in France.

Some analysts have neglected this coercive function of the state in favor of a focus on industrial relations in which the state mediates between organized labor and employers. Others, such as Herbert Marcuse, have dismissed labor entirely since they posited that consumer capitalism had integrated the working class. Yet the state's disciplinary role may have become even more important in contemporary consumer society. In the nineteenth and early twentieth centuries, individual enterprises and the culture of the work ethic had partially subjugated labor, but by the late twentieth the consumerist emphasis on immediate gratification had undermined the work ethic. The decline of labor Puritanism rendered obsolete the project of workers' control or *autogestion*, which was based on the identification of workers with the means of production.[417] Simultaneously, it made the state's disciplinary task even more essential. In 1968, for example, internalized work discipline proved inadequate to guarantee order and had to be supplemented by the external repression of the state. Late capitalism still needed the armed force of Leviathan to keep the workers in line. Police proved more necessary than priests.

Some social scientists have criticized de Gaulle's regime for its failure to integrate organized labor. They have argued that if the regime had integrated unions, it would have avoided the "spontaneous" strike wave.[418] Yet if organized labor, not worker spontaneity, was responsible for the massive work stoppages, the argument is less convincing. The regime may have been wise to restrain union power and influence to accomplish its ambitious modernization program. After May, the government remained reluctant to concede union demands. The Grenelle protocol had scheduled a meeting between the government, unions, and employers for March 1969. At that time, the confederations demanded increased wages to compensate for inflation but were completely unsuccessful in the face of combined government and employer opposition.[419] In sharp contrast to the Matignon Accords of 1936, employers in 1968 did not conceive of Grenelle as a great defeat.[420] With the assistance of the state, they had emerged intact and even reinvigorated from the ordeal.

ORTF provided the most publicized example of renewed management sovereignty. Its personnel proved incapable of winning the autonomy and independence from the government that they had sought. At the end of June, its journalists were informed that they would be rehired on an individual basis. On 12 July, the prime minister transformed the position of minister of information into a simple state secretary so that his office could directly control it. At the end of that month, ORTF experienced a "real purge," during which many younger journalists were dismissed. In August, 54 of them were either fired or sanctioned.[421] These dismissals gained notoriety and probably had the effect of intimidating wage earners in other, less publicized, sectors of the economy.

The elections at the end of June demonstrated the strength of the right. By that month, the political battle shifted to favor the parties of order.[422]

Despite the best efforts of the parliamentary left, many voters identified it with what they considered to be the gratuitous destruction and violence of demonstrators. According to official statistics, the most militant had torn up 6,400 square meters of streets, damaged 130 trees, removed 540 tree gratings, destroyed 63 street lights, trashed 450 street signs, broken 35 emergency alarms, burned 125 private cars, marred 80 more, incinerated 6 police vehicles and damaged 137 more.[423] The prefect calculated that five persons had died, and 1,910 police and 1,439 young people were injured during the protests of May and June.[424]

Just as U.S. citizens came to reject an American liberalism that failed to protect property against rioters, the French public similarly abandoned the left. Realizing its political problem, the PCF tried to sell itself as the party of order, a difficult task given its support of both student and worker strikes. Its attempt to turn the tables on de Gaulle by calling him the head of the "party of disorder and totalitarianism" was unconvincing.[425] Interior ministry officials concluded that the events of May ruined temporarily the good relations with sectors of the middle classes that the party had tried to build since the beginning of the Fifth Republic.[426] The right's capacity to unify contrasted sharply with divisions among the PCF, FGDS, and PSU and their predictable inability to govern as a unit. Following the model created by Thiers immediately after the Commune of 1871, de Gaulle and Pompidou projected their republic as one of unity and discipline. Accordingly, they renamed their party the Union for the Defense of the Republic (UDR). In the aftermath of May, Gaullism shared the tradition of law-and-order parliamentarianism that had characterized the Third Republic after the victory of the Bloc National in 1919 and the smashing of the general strike that terminated the Popular Front in November 1938. Gaullism was therefore not an antiparliamentary Bonapartist revival that had been fashioned to end the "stalemate between a revolutionary working class and a relatively backward capitalism."[427] Instead, it repeated the strikebreaking activities of the neo-Jacobins of the Third Republic, such as Clemenceau and Daladier. De Gaulle had proven himself not to be a "fascist" or a dictator, as *marxisant* analysis would have it, but rather a tough republican who conceded a rise in the price of labor while defending property and production.[428]

Resentments over the effects and consequences of the strikes aided the right. Car owners and motorists—who were one of the fastest growing segments of the population—were outraged by the destruction of vehicles, gas shortage, and the largest traffic jams in the history of the Paris region. *Téléspectateurs* resented missing their favorite programs. Many mothers (and fathers) objected to the closing of schools. These reactions allowed Gaullists to bring together the two conflicting parts of their constituency: small employers (peasants and shopkeepers) and big business (senior and junior executives). Furthermore, Gaullists were able to reach out to sectors of opinion previously alienated by the abandonment of Algeria.

The extreme right appreciated the pardons of OAS members and sympathizers. Alliance Républicaine—the party of Salan's lawyer, Tixier-Vignancourt—abstained from presenting its own legislative candidates. Civic Action Committees (SAC) adopted with relative impunity the bullying model made notorious by supporters of *Algérie Française*.

At the end of May, police toleration of SAC activities constituted a significant change from early and mid May, when the forces of order routinely arrested SAC and CDR militants who were distributing tracts, scrawling graffiti on walls, or circulating in automobiles with loudspeakers blasting propaganda.[429] By June, some police officers seemed sympathetic or even actively partisan on behalf of the Gaullist right, even though their prefect had tried to enforce a policy of political neutrality.[430] Young CDR militants, armed with sticks and Molotov cocktails, drove cockily around the city.[431] Police noted that armed "Gaullists" were bold enough to attack SNCF workers at Clichy, three of whom had to be hospitalized.[432] In response, the CGT called an afternoon strike that paralyzed all traffic at the Gare Saint-Lazare. Some CDR militants were even foolhardy enough to deliver pamphlets at Nanterre where, predictably, leftists assaulted them.[433] Others, wiser and safer, painted slogans on the walls of buildings in the sixteenth *arrondissement* or toured the eighteenth in a motorcade. Police asserted that Occident tried to extend its influence throughout the capital during the electoral campaign and threatened to disrupt electoral gatherings.[434] Incidents involving gunfire were reported in Orléans, Rouen, and La Rochelle. In Arras on 29 June, on the eve of the final round of elections, an 18-year-old Communist election worker was shot dead by government supporters.[435]

In the first round on 23 June, the UDR won nearly 44 percent of the votes, up 6 percent from the Gaullist total in previous elections.[436] Mitterrand's Fédération dropped from 19 to 16.5 percent, whereas the Communists slipped from 22.5 to 20 percent. The PSU, which ran more candidates than previously, witnessed their complete defeat but increased from 2 to 4 percent. The center lost ground compared to the previous legislative contest. In Paris, the losses of the left—with the exception of the PSU—were even greater than the national results: the PCF vote dropped from 22.3 percent in 1967 to 18.8 percent, the FGDS from 11.4 percent to 7.6 percent. The PSU vote rose from 4.7 percent to 7.4 percent, but this gain was not large enough to compensate for the decline of the left as a whole. The second round on 30 June gave the Gaullists an even clearer victory, despite the electoral discipline of both the Communists and *fédérés*, who united around the best-placed candidate of the left. Gaullist gains in the Paris region, capturing all seats in the capital except one, were more spectacular than in the rest of the nation. The unrest of May had been primarily an urban phenomenon, and the powerful reaction against it was also urban.

For the first time in the history of the Fifth Republic, a party gained an absolute majority in the National Assembly. The UDR possessed 294 deputies in an assembly of 485 members. The loss of 100 seats by the

Communists and Socialists may have represented the largest defeat in the history of the parliamentary left. The results vindicated the PCF analysis—which was rather obvious to everyone except the ultra-left—that the moment was not ripe for revolution. After the second round, Georges Marchais was reported to have complained, "It's all Cohn-Bendit's fault."[437] Even Mendès-France, seemingly so close to power the previous month, lost his Grenoble race because, it was said, he had participated in the "revolutionary" Charléty meeting.[438] The editorial board of *Les Temps modernes* had written on 6 June that "the re-election of the present majority would justify PCF politics."[439] The journal, however, continued to criticize the PCF line after May and, as with other publications favorable to *gauchisme*, would persistently overestimate the revolutionary potential of the agitation and underestimate the solidity of both the state and consumer society.

Notes

1. 30 May 1968, AN 820599/40.
2. Jean-Raymond Tournoux, *Le mois du mai du général* (Paris, 1969), 254–255; Adrien Dansette, *Mai 1968* (Paris, 1971), 314.
3. Jacques Baynac, *Mai retrouvé* (Paris, 1978), 155; [General] Jacques Massu, *Baden 68: Souvenirs d'une fidélité gaulliste* (Paris, 1983), 21; 28 May 1968, AN 820599/40.
4. On Massu's reputation, see David L. Schalk, *War and the Ivory Tower: Algeria and Vietnam* (New York, 1991), 17.
5. Massu, *Baden*, 119.
6. Dansette, *Mai*, 299; Christian Charrière, *Le Printemps des enragés* (Paris, 1968), 344; Jean Lacouture, *De Gaulle: The Ruler 1945–1970*, trans. Alan Sheridan (New York and London, 1992), 541.
7. François Bourricaud, "Une reprise en main difficile," *Preuves*, no. 218 (May–June 1969): 44.
8. The episode is complex, and may reflect the general's confusion. The best account is Lacouture, *De Gaulle*, 544–554. See also Dansette, *Mai*, 304; Tournoux, *Mois*, 290.
9. Jean Touchard, *Le Gaullisme, 1940–1969* (Paris, 1978), 67.
10. Frank Georgi, "Le Pouvoir est dans la rue: La manifestation gaulliste des Champs-Elysées (30 mai 1968)," *Vingtième Siècle*, no. 48 (1995): 50; Claude Paillat, *Archives secrètes, 1968–69: Les coulisses d'une année terrible* (Paris, 1969), 215–220; Julian Jackson, "DeGaulle and May 1968," in Hugh Gough and John Horne, eds., *DeGaulle and Twentieth-Century France* (London, 1994), 138.
11. Alain de Boissieu, *Pour Servir le général 1946–1970* (Paris, 1982), 193.
12. Cf. Raymond Aron, *La révolution introuvable* (Paris, 1968), 144 and Alain Touraine, *The May Movement: Revolt and Reform*, trans. Leonard F. X. Mayhew (New York, 1979), 229.
13. 29 May 1968, Fa 261, APP; 25 May 1968, Fa 275, APP.
14. 25 May 1968, Fa 275, APP; 31 May 1968, Fa 261, APP.
15. Dansette, *Mai*, 277, 291, 297.
16. 29 February 1968, Fa 282, APP.
17. 27 May 1968, Fa 259, APP.
18. 28 June 1968, AN 800273/61.
19. See reports on PTT strikes, Ministère de l'Industrie, May–August 1968, AN 810484.

20. 31 May 1968, AN 829599/40; 6 June 1968, AN 820599/41.
21. Dansette, *Mai*, 299; Maurice Grimaud, "Mai 1968, vingt ans après: L'Etat face à la crise," in Geneviève Dreyfus-Armand and Laurent Gervereau, *Mai 68: Les mouvements étudiants en France et dans le monde* (Nanterre, 1988), 73, 300.
22. Maurice Grimaud, *En mai, fais ce qu'il te plaît* (Paris, 1977), 253.
23. Quoted in Tournoux, *Mois*, 307.
24. See Roger Martelli, *Mai 68* (Paris, 1988), 159; Laurent Salini, *Mai des prolétaires* (Paris, 1968), 122.
25. Cf. Gilles Le Béguec, "L'Etat dans tous ses états," in Geneviève Dreyfus-Armand, Robert Frank, Marie-Françoise Lévy, Michelle Zancarini-Fournel, eds., *Les Années 68: Le Temps de la contestation* (Brussels, 2000), 469.
26. 30 May 1968, Fa 261, APP.
27. Konrad Dussel, "Vom Radio- zum Fernsehzeitalter: Medienumbrüche in sozialgeschichtlicher Perspektive," in Axel Schildt, Detlef Siegfried, and Karl Christian Lammers, eds., *Dynamische Zeiten: Die 60er Jahre in den beiden deutschen Gesellshaften* (Hamburg, 2000), 673.
28. René Rémond, *La règle et le consentement* (Paris, 1979), 370.
29. 30 May 1968, AN 800273/61.
30. Quoted in Charrière, *Printemps*, 350.
31. On de Gaulle's "Bonapartism," see Robert Gildea, *The Past in French History* (New Haven and London, 1994), 82–86, 108–109.
32. 31 May 1968, AN 820599/40.
33. Philippe Bauchard and Maurice Bruzek, *Le syndicalisme à l'épreuve* (Paris, 1968), 116.
34. Tournoux, *Mois*, 271.
35. *Aujourd'hui*, no. 2, 31 May 1968; *Ouvriers face aux appareils: Une expérience de militantisme chez Hispano-Suiza* (Paris 1970), 183; F. de Massot, *La grève générale (mai-juin 1968)* (Paris, 1968), 216–217; Pierre Grappin, *L'Ile aux peupliers* (Nancy, 1993), 260.
36. Quoted in Jean Bertolino, *Les Trublions* (Paris, 1969), 395.
37. Alain Schnapp and Pierre Vidal-Naquet, *Journal de la commune étudiante* (Paris, 1969), 408, 411, 501.
38. Pierre Peuchmaurd, *Plus vivants que jamais* (Paris, 1968), 132.
39. Roland Biard, *Dictionnaire de l'extrême-gauche de 1945 à nos jours* (Paris, 1978), 294.
40. 5 June 1968, AN 820599/41.
41. PCF Saint-Cloud; Comités d'action Meudon, Chaville, Sèvres, Tracts de mai 1968, Bibliothèque Nationale [BN].
42. Quoted in Martelli, *Mai*, 227; René Andrieu, *Les communistes et la révolution* (Paris, 1968), 131.
43. Quoted in Bauchard and Bruzek, *Syndicalisme*, 118.
44. Quoted in ibid., 305.
45. L. Astre (member of the Bureau national de la Fédération de l'Education nationale) in "Témoignages," *Matériaux pour l'histoire de notre temps*, no. 20 (July–September 1990): 52; Jacques Frémontier, *La forteresse ouvrière: Renault* (Paris, 1971), 366.
46. *France Nouvelle* quoted in Bauchard and Bruzek, *Syndicalisme*, 292.
47. 31 May 1968, AN 820599/40.
48. Confédération Générale du Travail de la R.N.U.R. [Régie Nationale des Usines Renault], *33 jours 34 nuits* (Paris, n.d.), 12.
49. "Comité de grève Hispano-Suiza," Tracts de mai 1968, BN.
50. Alfred Willener, Catherine Gajdos, and Georges Benguigui, *Les cadres en mouvement* (Paris, 1969), 89; Charrière, *Printemps*, 356; Henri Simon Oral History Project, interviews with workers, 1994.
51. 30 May 1968, Fa 261, APP.
52. Ibid.
53. 31 May 1968, AN 800273/61.
54. 300,000 is the figure provided by the Préfecture de Police. See Dansette, *Mai*, 292–326; Emmanuel Souchier, ed., *Mai 68* (Paris, 1988), 47; 30 May 1968, Fa 261, APP.

55. On the other hand, it should be recalled that in the second half of May, the CGT had tried to censor conservative newspapers. See below.

56. Pierre Andro, A. Dauvergne, and L. M. Lagoutte, *Le mai de la révolution* (Paris, 1968), 205.

57. Lucien Rioux and René Backmann, *L'Explosion de mai* (Paris, 1968), 467–470.

58. Georgi, "Le Pouvoir est dans la rue," 59.

59. Cited in police report of 9 May 1968, AN 820599/40.

60. Cited in police report of 18 May 1968, AN 820599/40.

61. 30 May 1968, AN 820599/40.

62. 14 May 1968, Fa 255, APP.

63. 30 May 1968, AN 820599/40.

64. 4 June 1968, Fa 269, APP; 9 July 1968, Fa 274, APP.

65. 6 June 1968, Fa 270, APP.

66. 22 May 1968, AN 820599/40.

67. 14 May 1968, AN 820599/40.

68. 31 May 1968, AN 820599/40. At the end of May, Roger Holeindre created a new nationalist organization whose slogan was "Order and Fatherland."

69. 5 June 1968, AN 820599/41. On Salan's trial, Alistair Horne, *A Savage War of Peace: Algeria 1954–1962* (New York, 1987), 542.

70. 11 June 1968, AN 820599/41.

71. 14 June 1968, AN 820599/41.

72. 24 June 1968, AN 820599/41.

73. 14 June 1968, AN 820599/41.

74. 24 May 1968, AN 820599/40.

75. 27 May 1968, AN 820599/40.

76. 30 May 1968, AN 820599/40.

77. 29 May 1968, Fa 266, APP.

78. 4 June 1968, AN 820599/41.

79. *Le Canard enchaîné,* May 22 1968.

80. 19 June 1968, Fa 274, APP.

81. 30 May 1968, AN 820599/40.

82. The following figures are taken from the police bulletin of 5 June 1968, AN 820599/41.

83. 24 June 1968, AN 800273/61.

84. Jean-Pierre Filiu, "Le gouvernement et la direction face à la crise," in *Mai 68 à l'ORTF* (Paris, 1987), 176.

85. Quoted by André-Jean Tudesq, "La radio, les manifestations, le pouvoir," in *Mai 68 à l'ORTF,* 154.

86. Instruction générale, Ministre des Postes et Télécommunications, 30 May 1968, AN 810484.

87. 31 May 1968, AN 820599/40.

88. Ibid.

89. Jean-Pierre Filiu, "L'Intersyndicale durant le conflit," in *Mai 68 à l'ORTF,* 47; 4 June 1968, AN 820599/41.

90. 4 June 1968, AN 820599/41.

91. Souchier, *Mai 68,* 40; 6 June 1968, AN 820599/41.

92. Jean-Pierre Manel and Alomée Planel, *La crise de l'ORTF* (Paris, 1968), 93.

93. Christine Manigand and Isabelle Veyrat-Masson, "Les journalistes et la crise," in *Mai 68 à l'ORTF,* 83.

94. 11 June 1968, AN 820599/41; 26 June 1968, AN 820599/41.

95. 30 May 1968, Fa 261, APP.

96. 31 May 1968, AN 820599/40.

97. 1 June 1968, Fa 269, APP; 21 June 1968, Fa 275, APP.

98. Direction générale de la Police Nationale, renseignements généraux, bulletin quotidien, 14 June 1968, AN 820599/41.

99. Schnapp and Vidal-Naquet, *Journal,* 499. Police estimated the crowd at half this number. See 1 June 1968, Fa 269, APP.

100. Circulation Générale, 3 June 1968, Fa 269, APP.
101. Philippe Labro, ed., *Ce n'est qu'un début* (Paris, 1968), 142. Figures on deaths vary from one or two to nineteen. See Keith Reader, *The May 1968 Events in France: Reproductions and Interpretations* (London, 1993), 171.
102. Dansette, *Mai*, 149.
103. Andro, *Mai*, 213.
104. 6 June 1968, Fa 270, APP.
105. 15 June 1968, Fa 274 APP.
106. 31 May 1968, Fa 262, APP.
107. 31 May 1968, Fa 262, APP.
108. 31 May 1968, AN 820599/40.
109. 1 June 1968, Fa 269, APP.
110. 5 June 1968, AN 800273/61.
111. Grève poste, Direction des services ambulants, 23 July 1968, AN 810484; Grève Paris, 2 August 1968, AN 810484; 5 June 1968, Fa 269, APP.
112. 6 June 1968, AN 820599/41.
113. Bauchard and Bruzek, *Syndicalisme*, 124.
114. Quoted in ibid., 125.
115. 6 June 1968, AN 820599/41.
116. The following is based upon reports, Situation sociale, 6 June–7 June, GIM. Cf. Daniel Singer, *Prelude to Revolution: France in May 1968* (New York, 1970), 211: "Many small factories in all branches of industry went on resisting for a time."
117. 28 May 1968, AN 820599/40; 5 June 1968, AN 820599/41.
118. *Revue d'informations interprofessionnelles des industries de la région est de Paris*, no. 304 (July–August 1969).
119. Jean-Marie Leuwers, *Un peuple se dresse: Luttes ouvrières mai 1968* (Paris, 1969), 149.
120. *Informations Correspondance Ouvrières* [hereafter *ICO*], May 1968, 18–19.
121. Ronan Capitaine, *Dassault Saint-Cloud en mai-juin 1968* (Mémoire de maîtrise, Université de Paris I, 1990), 131–132.
122. Bauchard and Bruzek, *Syndicalisme*, 123; Baynac, *Mai*, 227; Prost in "Table Ronde," *Matériaux pour l'histoire de notre temps*, no. 20 (July–September 1990), 5.
123. 5 June 1968, Fa 269, APP.
124. 4 June 1968, AN 820599/41.
125. 5 June 1968, Fa 269, APP.
126. 6 June 1968, Fa 270, APP.
127. 6 June 1968, AN 820599/41.
128. 6 June 1968, Fa 270, APP; 7 June 1968, Fa 270, APP.
129. 4 June 1968, AN 820599/41.
130. Direction générale de la Police Nationale, renseignements généraux, bulletin quotidien, 19 June 1968, AN 820599/41.
131. 18 June 1968, Fa 274, APP.
132. 20 June 1968, Fa 275, APP.
133. 24 June 1968, AN 820599/41.
134. Préfet de Paris à Ministre de l'Education Nationale, 14 June 1968, AN 790793; 6 June 1968, AN 820599/41; D. Pouzache in "Témoignages," *Matériaux pour l'histoire de notre temps*, no. 20 (July–September 1990), 72.
135. 2 June 1968, Fa 269, APP.
136. 4 June 1968, Fa 269, APP; 20 June 1968, Fa 274, APP.
137. 13 and 14 June 1968, AN 820599/41.
138. 11 June 1968, Fa 271, APP.
139. 13 June 1968, Fa 273, APP.
140. 21 June 1968, AN 820599/41.
141. 17 June 1968, AN 820599/41; Bulletin mensuel, August 1968, AN 820599/89.
142. 19 June 1968, AN 820599/41.

143. 11 June 1968, Fa 271, APP.
144. 20 June 1968, Fa 275, APP.
145. 19 June 1968, Fa 275, APP; 22 June 1968, Fa 275, APP.
146. 26 June 1968, AN 820599/41.
147. 14 June 1968, Fa 273, APP.
148. Situation sociale au 18 juin, GIM; 11 June 1968, AN 820599/41; 13 June 1968, AN 820599/41.
149. UNEF militants quoted in Schnapp and Vidal-Naquet, *Journal*, 302. This *gauchisant* orthodoxy is repeated in many other analyses.
150. Juliette Minces, *Un ouvrier parle: Enquête* (Paris, 1969), 78; "Histoire et leçons d'une grève," *Esprit*, no. 373 (August–September, 1968): 114. Cf. George Katsiaficas, *The Imagination of the New Left* (Boston, 1987), 102.
151. Yannick Guin, *La commune de Nantes* (Paris, 1969), 17; Claude Poperen, *Renault: Regards de l'intérieur* (Paris, 1983), 167: "Ce n'était pas toujours la bousculade pour 'occuper' l'usine."
152. *Le Monde*, 17 May 1968; Labro, *Début*, 71. Cf. Kristin Ross, *May '68 and Its Afterlives* (Chicago, 2002), 68: "The workers [were] enclosed, for the most part, in occupied factories."
153. Patrick Hassenteufel, *Citroën-Paris en mai-juin 1968: Dualités de la grève* (Mémoire de maîtrise, Université de Paris I, 1987), 49–101. For a different perspective, see Pierre Dubois, "Les pratiques de mobilisation et d'opposition," in Pierre Dubois, Renaud Dulong, Claude Durand, Sabine Erbès-Séguin, and Daniel Vidal, *Grèves revendicatives ou grèves politiques?* (Paris, 1971), 361.
154. Henri Simon Oral History Project, 1994.
155. Jean-Claude Kerbourc'h, *Le Piéton de Mai* (Paris, 1968), 46.
156. 27 May 1968, AN 820599/40.
157. *Lutte socialiste*, 20 October 1968; Hassenteufel, *Citroën*, 36; *Ouvriers face aux appareils*, 93. Cf. CGT, *33 jours*, 31, 181; *La Vie ouvrière*, 29 May 1968; *L'Anti-Mythe*, 21 August 1968; Frémontier, *Renault*, 344; Nicolas Hatzfeld, "Les ouvriers de l'automobile: Des vitrines sociales à la condition des OS, le changement des regards," in Dreyfus-Armand et al., *Les Années 68*, 355. Cf. Daniel A. Gordon, "Immigrants and the New Left in France, 1968–1971," (Ph.D. diss., University of Sussex, 2001), 107, which argues—contrary to some of his own research—that "immigrants joined the strike movement *en masse* and to an unprecedented extent."
158. Leuwers, *Peuple*, 185. Gordon, "Immigrants," 160, disputes this by accusing Leuwers of anti-Arab and pro-Catholic bias.
159. *Le Nouvel Observateur*, 30 May 1968; "CGT aux femmes," Tracts de mai 1968, BN.
160. *Le Nouvel Observateur*, 30 May 1968.
161. Ibid.
162. Situation sociale, 6 June, GIM. Fifty-five percent of French industrial workers surveyed in 1969 declared that they had never participated in a union meeting. See Gérard Adam, Frédéric Bon, Jacques Capdevielle, and René Mouriaux, *L'Ouvrier français en 1970* (Paris, 1970), 21.
163. "Défendons notre grève," Tracts de mai 1968, BN.
164. *Lutte Socialiste*, December 1968; Gilles Martinet, *La conquête des pouvoirs* (Paris, 1968), 69, which sees Rhône-Poulenc at Vitry as a model of "*tendances gestionnaires*." See also "Histoire et leçons d'une grève," 101, which claims that 1,500 to 1,600 workers occupied the factory. Police report that on 12 June only 300 out of a work force of 3,700 favored a return to work. See 12 June 1968, AN 820599/41. Censier militants wanted to popularize the Rhône-Poulenc example. See Baynac, *Mai*, 226. Trotskyites of the *Voix ouvrière* claimed to have greatly influenced the strike committee of this plant. See 18 July 1968, AN 820599/41.
165. Groupes inter-syndicaux des salariés, Tracts de mai 1968, BN; Patrick Ravignant, *L'Odéon est ouvert* (Paris, 1968), 217; Schnapp and Vidal-Naquet, *Journal*, 311; Baynac, *Mai*, 176; Dansette, *Mai*, 275.
166. Mouvement du 22 mars, *Ce n'est pas qu'un début, continuons le combat* (Paris, 1968), 99. Cf. also Lucio Magri, "Réflexions sur les événements de mai," *Les Temps modernes*, no.

277–278 (August–September, 1969): 32: "Because of its spontaneous origin and the consequent occupation tactic, the workers' struggle profoundly upset the traditional relations between masses and leaders." Similar views are found in Alain Geismar, Serge July, and Erlyne Morane, *Vers la guerre civile* (Paris, 1969), 258.

167. Cohn-Bendit during 1 June press conference in Bertolino, *Trublions*, 38.

168. Willener et al., *Les cadres en mouvement*, 87, 95.

169. On indifferent, passive, and resigned workers, see Andrée Andrieux and Jean Lignon, *L'Ouvrier d'aujourd'hui* (Paris, 1966).

170. For an interesting critique, see Olivier Schwartz, "Zones d'instabilité dans la culture ouvrière," in Guy-Patrick Azémar, ed., *Ouvriers ouvrières: Un continent morcelé et silencieux* (Paris, 1992), 124–125.

171. See chap. 4, 176, in this volume.

172. Schwartz, "Zones d'instabilité," 127.

173. Mouvement du 22 mars, *Début*, 87–89.

174. R. Gregoire and F. Perlman, *Worker-Student Action Committees: France May '68* (Detroit, 1991), 83.

175. Henri Simon Oral History Project, 1994; Marc Bergère, "Les grèves en France: Le cas du Maine-et-Loire," in Dreyfus-Armand et al., *Les Années 68*, 323, describes a serious effort to both entertain and to educate workers politically during occupations in this department.

176. Capitaine, *Dassault*, 141.

177. *Syndicalisme*, 6 July 1968.

178. Leuwers, *Peuple*, [not paginated]. At Renault-Cléon (Seine-Maritime), the strike committee controlled gasoline distribution. See *Notre arme c'est la grève* (Paris, 1968), 35. In the revolutionary "Commune" of Nantes, the strike committee ended gasoline rationing because it was unpopular with motorists. See Patrick Seale and Maureen McConville, *Red Flag Black Flag: French Revolution 1968* (New York, 1968), 169; 29 May 1968, AN 820599/40. At the Odéon, sympathetic physicians helped militants get fuel. See Ravignant, *L'Odéon*, 149.

179. Capitaine, *Dassault*, 105.

180. Frémontier, *Renault*, 225; Schnapp and Vidal-Naquet, *Journal*, 777.

181. Mouvement du 22 mars, *Début*, 106.

182. Bruno Moschetto and André Plagnol, *Le crédit à la consommation* (Paris, 1973); Victor Scardigli, "Les grèves dans l'économie française," *Consommation*, no. 3 (July–September, 1974): 99; Frémontier, *Renault*, 115–133. In 1969 three out of four workers considered credit positively. See Adam et al., *L'Ouvrier français*, 95. On ownership of automobiles and other durable goods, see Fernand Pascaud, "La consommation des ménages de 1959–1972," *Collections de L'I.N.S.E.E.* (June, 1974): 27.

183. Jean-Claude Chamboredon and Madeleine Lemaire, "Proximité spatiale et distance sociale: Les grands ensembles et leur peuplement," *Revue française de sociologie*, vol. 11 (1970): 22.

184. Gérard Noiriel, *Les ouvriers dans la société française* (Paris, 1986), 232.

185. On asceticism and its end, see Schwartz, "Zones d'instabilité," 133–134; Martelli, *Mai*, 55.

186. Levitt quoted in Maurice Isserman and Michael Kazin, *America Divided: The Civil War of the 1960s* (New York, 2000), 12.

187. A similar transformation occurred in Germany. See Axel Schildt, "Materieller Wohlstand—pragmatische Politik—kulturelle Umbrüche: Die 60er Jahre in der Bundesrepublik," in Schildt et al., *Dynamische Zeiten*, 26–27.

188. Paul Ginsborg, *A History of Contemporary Italy: Society and Politics 1943–1988* (London, 1990), 342.

189. The following information is from Pascaud, "La consommation," 27. A similar pattern occurred in Germany. See Schildt, "Materieller Wohlstand," 29.

190. *Notre arme c'est la grève*, 46.

191. Richard Hamilton, *Affluence and the French Worker in the Fourth Republic* (Princeton, 1967), 84: "Since the workers might simply be adjusting realistically to lower income

and less job stability, we compared persons having equivalent earning situations.... We find that on every item white-collar ownership is nearly twice that of workers."

192. Noiriel, *Les ouvriers*, chap. 6.
193. Cf. the provocative analysis of Daniel Boorstin, *The Decline of Radicalism: Reflections on America Today* (New York, 1969), 22.
194. Baynac, *Mai*, 204.
195. *Le Nouvel Observateur*, 15–21 July 1968; see also *La vie ouvrière*, 10 July 1968. For familial tensions in northern France, Pierre Burel, *La crise économique dans les événements de mai 1968* (Caudry, 1970), 130.
196. *Le Nouvel Observateur*, 30 May 1968.
197. Burel, *La crise économique*, 130.
198. Schwartz, "Zones d'instabilité," 126–127.
199. Leuwers, *Peuple*, 319.
200. Ibid., 64; *L'Anti-Mythe*, 9–10 June 1968; *Cahiers de mai*, August–September 1968; Georges Lefranc, *Le Mouvement syndical de la libération aux événements de mai-juin 1968* (Paris, 1969), 252, which argues that wives of workers reacted against the strike wave by voting for the right in elections at the end of June. Cf. Bertolino, *Trublions*, 288: "Les travailleurs un instant grisés par la furie des enragés, par les barricades qui rappelaient tant la Commune, luttèrent pour la chute d'un régime, et non de la société qui leur assure le travail et la vie." Cf. also *Mai 68 par eux-mêmes: Le mouvement de Floréal An 176* (Paris, 1989), 20.
201. 14 June 1968, AN 820599/41.
202. Rioux and Backmann, *L'Explosion*, 328.
203. 4 June 1968, AN 820599/41.
204. *Ouvriers face aux appareils*, 198.
205. Jean-Pierre Filiu, "l'Intersyndicale," 60.
206. 19 June 1968, AN 820599/41.
207. 24 June 1968, AN 820599/41.
208. Situation sociale, 11–18 June 1968, AN 760122.
209. Situation sociale, 6 June, GIM.
210. See situation sociale, 6–7 June, GIM; *Le Figaro*, 5 June 1968.
211. "Histoire et leçons d'une grève," 99–100. See also Xavier Vigna, "La figure ouvrière à Flins (1968–1973)," in Dreyfus-Armand et al., *Les Années 68*, 329–343.
212. Willener et al., *Les cadres en mouvement*, 72.
213. 21 May 1968, AN 820599/40; [n.d.? June] 1968, AN 800237/61.
214. Cited in *L'Aurore*, 6 June 1968.
215. Ministre d'Etat chargé des Affaires Sociales, 5 June 1968, AN 760122.
216. 29 May 1968, AN 820599/40.
217. 5 June 1968, AN 820599/41.
218. 13 June 1968, Fa 273, APP.
219. Ministre d'Etat chargé des Affaires Sociales, 5 June 1968, AN 760122.
220. Geismar in Labro, *Début*, 198; see also *Notre arme c'est la grève*, 60.
221. 8 June 1968, Fa 274, APP.
222. Situation sociale, 6 June 1968, GIM. Cf. Alain Delale and Gilles Ragache, *La France de 68* (Paris, 1978), 147, which states that the vote occurred on 5 June. See also "Histoire et leçons d'une grève," 108.
223. Ministre d'Etat chargé des Affaires Sociales, 5 June 1968, AN 760122.
224. Situation sociale journalière, 6 June, GIM. Union militants later argued that they were justified in violating the right to work since strikebreakers had not pledged in writing that they would refuse any increases in salary and benefits that resulted from the strikes. See *Combat*, 12 June 1968.
225. 6 June 1968, AN 820599/41.
226. Tract of 7 June quoted in Schnapp and Vidal-Naquet, *Journal*, 516.
227. CGT quoted in Martelli, *Mai*, 173.

228. Nicolas Dubost, *Flins sans fin* (Paris, 1979), 23.
229. 5 June 1968, Fa 269, APP.
230. Geismar et al., *Vers*, 296, 352; 6 June 1968, Fa 270, APP; 8 June 1968, Fa 270, APP.
231. 8 June 1968, Fa 271, APP.
232. 6 June 1968, AN 820599/41.
233. 7 June 1968, Fa 270, APP.
234. 7 June 1968, AN 820599/41.
235. 7 June 1968, Fa 270, APP. Other figures are 350 students detained; see 6 June 1968, AN 820599/41.
236. Cf. Khursheed Wadia, "Women and the Events of 1968," in Reader, *The May 1968 Events*, 150, who calls female participation in May "massive" and "unprecedented."
237. 8 June 1968, Fa 274, APP.
238. 8 June 1968, Fa 271, APP.
239. Peuchmaurd, *Vivants*, 147.
240. 7 June 1968, AN 820599/41.
241. *Le Monde*, 8 June 1968; Delale and Ragache, *France*, 147.
242. Kerbourc'h, *Le piéton*, 147.
243. Charrière, *Printemps*, 374–375.
244. Mouvement du 22 mars, *Début*, 121. On the participation of art students, see "L'Atelier des Arts-décoratifs: Entretien avec François Miehe et Gérard Paris-Clavel," in Dreyfus-Armand and Gervereau, *Mai 68*, 193.
245. 8 June 1968, Fa 271, APP.
246. *L'Aurore*, 10 June 1968.
247. 10 June 1968, AN 820599/41.
248. "Un militant du 22 mars raconte," in Labro, *Début*, 73.
249. Schnapp and Vidal-Naquet, *Journal*, 521; Robert Davezies, ed., *Mai 68: La rue dans l'église* (Paris, 1968), 131.
250. 10 June 1968, Fa 271, APP. Police arrested "80 youths foreign to the region." 10 June 1968, AN 820599/41.
251. 10 and 11 June 1968, Fa 271, APP.
252. 11 June 1968, AN 820599/41.
253. 12 June 1968, AN 820599/41.
254. 13 June 1968, AN 820599/41.
255. 17 June 1968, AN 820599/41.
256. Gordon, "Immigrants," 100.
257. 20 June 1968, AN 820599/41.
258. 5 June 1968, AN 820599/41.
259. Rioux and Backmann, *L'Explosion*, 575.
260. 11 June 1968, AN 820599/41.
261. Ibid.
262. 12 June 1968, AN 820599/41.
263. Ibid.
264. 18 June 1968, AN 820599/41.
265. Michel Johan, "La CGT et le mouvement de mai," *Les Temps modernes*, no. 266–267 (August–September, 1968): 348; Baynac, *Mai*, 243.
266. 24 June 1968, AN 800273/61.
267. 11 June 1968, AN 820599/41.
268. *Le Monde*, 11 June 1968, 13 June 1968; CGT, 11 June 1968, Tracts de mai, BN.
269. 11 June 1968, AN 820599/41.
270. 10 June 1968, Fa 271, APP.
271. *Le Monde*, 13 June 1968; Delale and Ragache, *France*, 153.
272. Dansette, *Mai*, 335; Peuchmaurd, *Vivants*, 151; 24 June 1968, AN 800273/61.
273. 24 June 1968, AN 800273/61.
274. On 1848, see Roger Price, *The French Second Republic: A Social History* (Ithaca, 1972), 170.

275. 11 June 1968, AN 820599/41.
276. 20 June 1968, Fa 274, APP.
277. 18 June 1968, Fa 263, APP; Commissaire du 22, 20 June 1968, Fa 274, APP.
278. 20 June 1968, Fa 274, APP.
279. 18 June 1968, Fa 263, APP; 11 June 1968, Fa 271, APP.
280. 11 June 1968, Fa 271, APP.
281. Commissaire du 22, 20 June 1968, Fa 274, APP.
282. Stephen J. Pyne, *World Fire: The Culture of Fire on Earth* (New York, 1995), 230.
283. 19 June 1968, Fa 271, APP; 10 June 1968, Fa 271, APP.
284. 12 June 1968, AN 820599/41.
285. Seale and McConville, *Red Flag*, 222.
286. 11–12 June 1968, Fa 272, APP.
287. 18 June 1968, Fa 274, APP.
288. 13 June 1968, AN 820599/41.
289. Labro, *Début*, 136.
290. 24 June 1968, AN 800273/61. For the negative reactions among rural voters, see Georges Chaffard, *Les orages de mai: Histoire exemplaire d'une élection* (Paris, 1968), 93.
291. 11 June 1968, AN 820599/41; *L'Humanité*, 11 June 1968.
292. Peuchmaurd, *Vivants*, 155.
293. Quoted in Rioux and Backmann, *L'Explosion*, 580. This reaction against car burnings was also found among foreign workers. See Gordon, "Immigrants," 154.
294. 15 June 1968, Fa 274, APP.
295. Commissaire, 11 June 1968, Fa 271, APP.
296. 19 June 1968, Fa 271, APP.
297. Ibid. and 13 June 1968, Fa 273, APP.
298. Souchier, *Mai 68*, 39.
299. 5 June 1968, Fa 269, APP; 5 and 6 June 1968, AN 820599/41.
300. 24 June 1968, AN 800273/61. Maurice Grimaud dissented from this line, which Raymond Marcellin would advocate.
301. 10 May 1968, AN 820599/40. Cf. Touraine, *The May Movement*, 182.
302. Bulletin mensuel, May–July 1968, AN 820599/89.
303. Schnapp and Vidal-Naquet, *Journal*, 523.
304. Baynac, *Mai*, 243; 13 June 1968, Fa 273, APP.
305. Bulletin mensuel, September 1968, AN 820599/89.
306. 30 May 1968, Fa 261, APP.
307. Ibid.
308. 14 June 1968, AN 820599/41.
309. For his accusations, see Union Nationale des Etudiants de France [and SNESup], *Le livre noir des journées de mai* (Paris, 1968), 86–91.
310. 13 June 1968, Fa 273, APP.
311. 14 June 1968, Fa 273, APP.
312. 14 June 1968, Fa 273, APP.
313. Ibid. Cf. 14 June 1968, AN 820599/41: "According to a prior agreement, 113 occupiers left without being arrested. Thirty young people who were outside were taken in for questioning."
314. 14 June 1968, Fa 273, APP.
315. Ibid.
316. Ibid.
317. 17 June 1968, AN 820599/41.
318. 20 June 1968, Fa 274, APP; 19 June 1968, Fa 275, APP.
319. 2 July 1968, Fa 265, APP.
320. 12 June 1968, AN 820599/41.
321. Jacques Perret, *Inquiète Sorbonne* (Paris, 1968), 43–44; Seale and McConville, *Red Flag*, 109.
322. 17 June 1968, AN 820599/41.

323. 18 June 1968, AN 820599/41; 25 June 1968, AN 820599/41.
324. Figures from Bulletin mensuel, September 1968, AN 820599/89.
325. Police recorded that a number of Algerians were involved in provincial demonstrations "for doubtful reasons."
326. Direction générale de la Police Nationale, renseignements généraux, bulletin quotidien, 18 June 1968, AN 820599/41; 18 June 1968, Fa 275, APP. According to police, during the summer a gang, including Christian Maricourt, would execute one of the escapees, "Jimmy le Katangais," who had received asylum at Censier. See Bulletin mensuel, September 1968, AN 820599/89.
327. 18 June 1968, AN 820599/41.
328. Ibid.
329. 19 June 1968, AN 820599/41.
330. 1 July 1968, AN 820599/41.
331. 4–5 July 1968, Fa 275, APP.
332. 27 June 1968, AN 820599/41. Other figures state that 68 men and 30 women were interrogated by police. See 27 June 1968, Fa 276, APP.
333. 1 July 1968, AN 820599/41.
334. 13 June 1968, Fa 273, APP.
335. 22 June 1968, Fa 275, APP.
336. 1 July 1968, AN 820599/41; 20 June 1968, Fa 275, APP.
337. 2 July 1968, AN 820599/41; 20 June 1968, Fa 275, APP.
338. 2 July 1968, AN 820599/41.
339. 2 July 1968, AN 800273/61.
340. 26 June 1968, AN 820599/41.
341. 20 June 1968, Fa 275, APP; 21 June 1968, Fa 275, APP.
342. 19 June 1968, AN 820599/41; 29 May 1968, Fa 266, APP.
343. 3 July 1968, AN 820599/41.
344. 4 June 1968, Fa 269, APP.
345. Résidence, 7 May 1968, 1208W, art. 115–117, ADHS [Archives départementales des Hauts-de-Seine].
346. CROUS, 16 May 1968, 1208W, art. 115–117, ADHS.
347. Observations sur la note du Préfet de Paris [n.d., ? June 1968], AN 800273/61.
348. 20 June 1968, Fa 275, APP.
349. 5 June 1968, Fa 269, APP.
350. 18 [?] June 1968, Fa 274, APP.
351. 26 June 1968, Fa 263, APP.
352. 5 June 1968, Fa 269, APP.
353. A list of the banned groups can be found in Souchier, *Mai 68*, 39. Eleven organizations were outlawed.
354. Bulletin mensuel, May–July 1968, AN 820599/89.
355. 25 June 1968, AN 820599/41.
356. 20 June 1968, Fa 275, APP.
357. Mouvement du 22 mars, *Début*, 133–135; Charrière, *Printemps*, 389.
358. 13 June 1968, AN 820599/41.
359. Krivine quoted in Bertolino, *Trublions*, 386; Dansette, *Mai*, 336.
360. 14 June 1968, Fa 273, APP.
361. Grégory Barrau, *Le mai 68 des catholiques* (Paris, 1998), 75.
362. 13 June 1968, AN 820599/41.
363. Bulletin mensuel, May–July 1968, AN 820599/89.
364. Ibid.
365. Bulletin mensuel, August 1968, AN 820599/89.
366. 26 June 1968, AN 800273/61.
367. Bulletin mensuel, August 1968, AN 820599/89.
368. Massu, *Baden*, 131.

369. Cited in Dansette, *Mai*, 341; Marc Kravetz, ed., *L'Insurrection étudiante* (Paris, 1968), 413.
370. 14 June 1968, AN 820599/41.
371. 26 June 1968, AN 820599/41.
372. Touchard, *Gaullisme*, 145.
373. Schnapp and Vidal-Naquet, *Journal*, 537–538.
374. 14 June 1968, Fa 273, APP.
375. Quoted in Labro, *Début*, 201.
376. 21 June 1968, AN 820599/41.
377. 10 June 1968, AN 820599/41.
378. *Le Figaro*, 12 June 1968. Crowd estimates vary according to source.
379. 11 June 1968, AN 820599/41.
380. Ibid.
381. 12 June 1968, AN 820599/41.
382. Ibid.
383. On *cadres*, see Willener et al., *Les cadres en mouvement*, 129.
384. Sylvain Roumette, "Aide-Mémoire," *Les Temps modernes*, no. 265 (July, 1968): 155.
385. Capitaine, *Dassault*, 167. See also *Notre arme c'est la grève*, 99; Henri Simon Oral History Project, 1994.
386. 14 June 1968, AN 820599/41.
387. Situation sociale, 11–18 June 1968, AN 760122.
388. 25 June 1968, AN 820599/41.
389. Procès-verbal, Conseil d'administration, 18 June 1968, GIM; Grandes entreprises en grève, 24 June 1968, GIM; Ministère d'Etat, 26 June–2 July 1968, AN 760122.
390. Jules Verger, a leader of small businessmen against the Popular Front and a supporter of Vichy, used the same pro-family strategy, i.e., the employment of mature breadwinners, to insulate his firm from the great strike waves of 1936 and 1968. On Verger, see *ICO*, April, May, and November 1968; *Anti-Mythe*, 26 July 1968.
391. Martelli, *Mai*, 54; Capitaine, *Dassault*, 182; Henri Simon Oral History Project, 1994.
392. Situation sociale dans les industries des métaux de la région parisienne, période 27 May–30 June, GIM; Situation sociale, 30 January 1969, GIM; Henri Simon Oral History Project, 1994; Capitaine, *Dassault*, 178–201.
393. "La grève des cheminots en 1968: Entretien avec Daniel Moreau," in Dreyfus-Armand and Gervereau, *Mai 68*, 220.
394. The following information is from Maurice Cohen, ed., *Le bilan social de l'année 1968* (Paris, 1969), 105–122, 387, 414. See also Accord du 13 décembre 1968, AN 860561. Cf. Chris Howell, *Regulating Labor: The State and Industrial Relations Reform in Postwar France* (Princeton, 1992), 27: "The strike wave of 1968 was not even translated into sustainable material gains for workers."
395. Cohen, *Bilan social*, 12, 128, 179, 310; cf. Schnapp and Vidal-Naquet, *Journal*, 796, which charges the CGT with cooperating with the CGC to maintain the salary hierarchy.
396. Gordon, "Immigrants," 64, 226.
397. Biard, *Dictionnaire*, 294.
398. Cohen, *Bilan social*, 97.
399. *Mai 68 par eux-mêmes*, 20.
400. Henri Simon Oral History Project, 1994; Capitaine, *Dassault*, 178; Cohen, *Bilan social*, 185; 30 May 1968, AN 820599/40.
401. 18 June 1968, AN 820599/41.
402. 25 June 1968, AN 820599/41; 26 June 1968, AN 820599/41.
403. 28 June 1968, AN 820599/41.
404. CGT quoted in *Notre arme c'est la grève*, 67; Capitaine, *Dassault*, 105.
405. "Entretien avec Daniel Moreau," in Dreyfus-Armand and Gervereau, *Mai 68*, 220.
406. The following is from Cohen, *Bilan social*; 26 June 1968, AN 820599/41.
407. See, for example, statements by the Comité d'Action Etudiants-Ouvriers, Sorbonne, June 1968, in *Quelle université? Quelle société?* (Paris, 1968), 129.

408. In 1950, the most strike-prone year of the period from 1950 to 1969, 2,400,000 days of work were lost; in 1968, 6,420,000 days. See Situation sociale, 30 January 1969, GIM.
409. Le projet de budget des PTT pour 1969, n.d., AN 810484.
410. Michel Dreyfus, *Histoire de la CGT: Cent ans de syndicalisme en France* (Paris, 1995), 274; Michel Johan, "La CGT et le mouvement de mai," 368; Cohen, *Bilan social*, 363; Bauchard and Bruzek, *Syndicalisme*, 307.
411. Bulletin mensuel, August 1968, AN 820599/89.
412. *Le Peuple*, 1–15 October 1968; *Cahiers de Mai*, August–September 1968. On the tendency of women and immigrants to join unions after strikes, see Thierry Baudouin, Michèle Collin, and Danièle Guillerm, "Women and Immigrants: Marginal Workers?" in Colin Crouch and Alessandro Pizzorno, eds., *The Resurgence of Class Conflict in Western Europe since 1968* (New York, 1978), 2 vols., 2:89. Cf. Pierre Dubois, Claude Durand, and Sabine Erbès-Seguin, "The Contradictions of French Trade Unionism," in Crouch and Alessandro Pizzorno, *Resurgence*, 2: 88–89. The 1969 survey of Adam et al., *L'Ouvrier français*, 111, contrasts the sympathy towards unions in large firms with the hostility towards them found in small ones. Bauchard and Bruzek, *Syndicalisme*, argues that strikes in 1968 showed that the unions had more influence within individual enterprises than at the national level. See also Cohen, *Bilan social*, 100; "Histoire et leçons d'une grève," 106.
413. 31 May 1968, AN 820599/40.
414. 25 June 1968, AN 820599/41.
415. Howell, *Regulating Labor*, 99; "Le syndicalisme, suite ou fin," in Azémar, *Ouvriers, ouvrières*, 180.
416. The following works emphasize the *autogestionnaire* impulse: Andrew Feenberg and Jim Freedman, *When Poetry Ruled the Streets: The French May Events of 1968* (Albany, 2001), 58: "Tangible demands had proved a liability to the CGT. The intangible notion of democratization, now adopted by the workers, gave rise to a concept of a new society." David Caute, *The Year of the Barricades: A Journey through 1968* (New York, 1988), 235: "Everywhere the workers were keen to display their capacity to administer the means of production." Touraine, *The May Movement*, chapter 5; Laurent Joffrin, *Mai 68: Histoire des événements* (Paris, 1988), which stresses the desire for "individual participation" during May. Willener et al., *Les cadres en mouvement*, 23: "One of the most important points of workers' demands during the strikes was the demand for control of the firm." Rioux and Backmann, *L'Explosion*, 615: "This will to participate in decisions and the desire to be able to question them … will not be forgotten." Bertolino, *Trublions*, 290: "Pouvoir ouvrier, autogestion voilà les mots qui vont droit au coeur des travailleurs." Jean-Jacques Servan-Schreiber, *The Spirit of May*, trans. Ronald Steel (New York, 1969), 29–33: "The movement of students and workers that erupted in Paris in May 1968 was not a movement primarily designed to win material benefits…. The simple and sometimes violent dispute quickly turned into a natural demand for responsibility." Stephen Spender, *The Year of the Young Rebels* (New York, 1969), 149–150, equates French worker occupations with the desire for worker control that supposedly characterized the Russian revolution. Robert V. Daniels, *Year of the Heroic Guerrilla: World Revolution and Counterrevolution in 1968* (New York, 1989), 157: "The workers' revolt in France thus shared with all the other movements of the 1960s the basic drive to achieve equality and humanity in face-to-face social relationships."
417. See Zygmunt Bauman, "The Left as the Counter-Culture of Modernity," in Sanford M. Lyman, ed., *Social Movements: Critiques, Concepts, Case-Studies* (New York, 1995), 356–370.
418. Cf. Howell, *Regulating Labor*, 67; cf. also the industrial sociologists of the "Groupe Sociologie du Travail," who see union weakness as a reason for industrial unrest.
419. Cohen, *Bilan social*, 184.
420. Michele Salvati, "May 1968 and the Hot Autumn of 1969: The Response of Two Ruling Classes," in Suzanne Berger, ed., *Organizing Interests in Western Europe* (Cambridge, 1981), 348.

421. Filiu, "L'Intersyndicale," 52–66; André-Jean Tudesq, "La radio, les manifestations, le pouvoir," in *Mai 68 à l'ORTF*, 156; 19 July 1968, AN 820599/41.

422. Hubert Belon, "Les élections des 23 et 30 juin," *Revue politique et parlementaire*, no. 790 (June–July, 1968): 122; Seale and McConville, *Red Flag*, 219; Jean-Jacques Becker, *Histoire politique de la France depuis 1945* (Paris, 1988), 126.

423. Conclusions, Directeur-Général de la Police Municipale, 9 July 1968, Fa 274, APP.

424. Grimaud quoted in *France-Soir*, 10 July 1968 in Fa 263, APP.

425. Danielle Tartakowsky, "Le PCF en mai-juin 1968," paper presented to Colloque: Acteurs et terrains du mouvement social de mai 1968, Paris, 24–25 November 1988.

426. 3 July 1968, AN 820599/41.

427. Cf. Singer, *Prelude*, 98.

428. Cf. Angelo Quattrocchi and Tom Nairn, *The Beginning of the End: France, May 1968* (London and New York, 1998), 122: "[De Gaulle] saw the need to erect a republican façade around his personal rule. This was to be a 'constitutional dictatorship.'"

429. 16 May 1968, Fa 257, APP; 18 May 1968, Fa 258, APP; 19 May 1968, Fa 257, APP.

430. 2 June 1968, Fa 269, APP; Grimaud, *Mai*, 54.

431. 14 June 1968, Fa 273, APP.

432. 25 June 1968, AN 820599/41.

433. 19 May 1968, Fa 257, APP.

434. 19 June 1968, Fa 275, APP.

435. Seale and McConville, *Red Flag*, 223.

436. Becker, *Histoire politique*, 120–126; Belon, "Elections," 126; "Notes sur une carte de France," *Esprit*, no. 373 (August–September, 1968): 193.

437. Seale and McConville, *Red Flag*, 224.

438. He had been in the audience but had not spoken. See Dansette, *Mai*, 285; Jean Lacouture, *Pierre Mendès-France*, trans. George Holoch (New York, 1984), 416–421.

439. *Les Temps modernes*, no. 264 (May–June, 1968): vii.

CONCLUSION

A Modest or Mythical May?

—⟨⟨⟨⟨⟨⟨—

After the revolts of May and June, Marxists and anarchists of various stripes continued to believe that agitation would persist and that the working class was on the road to revolution.[1] Radicals, confident of their dynamism and bolstered by the youthful demographic bulge, were hopeful about the future. Like their counterparts throughout the world, they felt that morality and history were on their side. Revolutionary artists reflected this sentiment in posters, such as "May 68: The Beginning of a Long Struggle" (see figure 15). Several books published at the end of 1968 carried the title *It Is Only a Beginning*. Another volume, *Vers la guerre civile*, announced that violent class war would erupt in 1970 or 1972.[2] For leading Communists and CGT trade unionists, the revolts of 1968 were the beginning of the crisis of "state monopoly capitalism" and represented the initial confrontation between the great mass of workers and the monopolies.[3] Some CFDT officials saw May as the rebirth of direct action and anarchosyndicalism.[4] PSU activists thought that the demand for *autogestion*, which they saw as the most exciting aspect of the strike movement, would grow and develop. They projected that the events of 1968 would initiate the slow conquest of power by workers, peasants, and students.[5] On the radio on 24 June, PSU leader Michel Rocard declared that "the revolution was possible."[6] PSU activists expected that progressive Christians were ready to join workers to create a radical social democracy. Some Christian democrats thought that they were living in a time analogous to 1788.[7] Regardless of the accuracy of their revolutionary predictions, Christian (both Catholic and Protestant) participation in the movement showed that long-standing religious schisms—which had separated clerical from anticlerical during much of French republican history—had largely been transcended by developments of the 1960s.

These prophecies of revolution were obviously erroneous. The "new working class" proved to be more like the group described by the British

---

Notes for this chapter begin on page 283.

FIGURE 15: "May 68: The Beginning of a Long Struggle"

sociologists Goldthorpe and Lockwood than that imagined by the French sociologist Serge Mallet.[8] Goldthorpe and Lockwood's workers had an instrumental attitude towards their jobs, unions, and political parties.[9] They were more interested in consumption than in *autogestion* and more concerned with private life than communal existence. The most dynamic members wanted to leave the class. As an exit strategy, parents encouraged sons and daughters to enter the universities, which they did in much greater numbers after 1968. This meant, in effect, that becoming a worker was increasingly linked to failure at school.[10]

The decline of class solidarity allowed employers to stage a counteroffensive. Following the strike wave, French management, assisted by a powerful state, quickly regained its dominance in the factory. Thus, the greatest strike wave in European history probably only marginally altered the authoritarian atmosphere that reigned on the shop floor and in the office.[11] In contrast, after 1968 in Italy—where both workers and employers shared a disdain for a weak and ineffective state—wage earners continued their struggles against wage labor.[12] Indeed, "the strong growth of [French] productivity after May was due in large part to profound restructuring within firms, accentuating worker mobility and intensifying work rhythms, the very processes under negotiation and challenge by the Italian unions."[13] In other words, French foremen once again became "wardens" who tried—with varied results—to increase production speed.[14] In comparison, Italian workers used either established unions or *comitati* (independent grassroots organizations) to conduct successful struggles against the authority of foremen, against linking pay to productivity, and against work time and space. According to a famous fictional character who represented Northern Italy's unskilled proletariat of 1969, happiness meant working less for more pay.[15] In the years immediately following 1968, Italian employers could not lower wages nor dismiss unruly workers.[16]

In France, the momentary corporatism that had resulted in the Grenelle agreement dissolved, and managers in the immediate post-June period acted quickly to limit the influence of militants—whether trade-union or *gauchiste*—by reinstating the authority of the supervisory personnel over both activists and rank and file.[17] In August 1968, the CFDT reported dismissals of dozens of its delegates.[18] Although the number of strikes increased in 1969 and 1970 compared to 1967 and 1966, the number of days lost and the number of strike participants declined significantly.[19] The unions' attempts to make post-May strikes relatively painless were unsuccessful. They failed to win agreements to force employers to compensate workers for time lost or to eliminate antistrike bonuses that rewarded wage earners for not participating in work stoppages. Struggles over work speed persisted, but bosses effectively combated *grèves perlées* (slowdowns).[20] Backed by the state, they challenged working-class practices of pilfering. For example, after a major payroll theft at a factory in the *banlieue*, police decided to search all wage earners.[21] They did not find the missing payroll but instead parts stolen from the firm. Apparently, theft was common practice in this enterprise where 1,000 *sangles* (straps) disappeared every year. An unfortunate worker who had been caught was asked to resign, but an important solidarity strike broke out in his defense.

Séguy admitted that the new adherents who joined the CGT after May "had only the most rudimentary knowledge of trade unionism.... To educate them is an enormous job."[22] The unions did not have sufficient influence or "pull" to retain many of the newly enrolled.[23] The rejuvenation of the CGT did little to reverse the long-term decline of French heavy industry (including metallurgy) or the eventual decay of the PCF itself. The CFDT remained committed to *autogestion*, but the lack of interest in workers' control among metallurgists and other wage earners in 1968 prefigured its gradual ideological descent in the 1970s and 1980s. A desire for wage increases and less work time largely motivated strikers both before and after 1968. Although some—like Mallet—have insisted upon the originality and innovative quality of the strikes and their demands, a basic continuity persisted before and after May.[24] Ideologies of work-centered *autogestion* may have been based on the mistaken assumption that wage earners really wanted to take over the workplace. Notions of workers' control that synthesized the desires for simultaneous personal and political emancipation ultimately failed to accomplish either. The global revolutionary projects of the *gauchistes*—Trotskyite, Maoist, Castroist, Situationist—suffered a similar fate of decline.

Those who bet on youth or students instead of workers were equally deceived. Young people were demographically weighty and biologically dynamic, but "youth" was not politically revolutionary.[25] The action committees, which young activists had hoped would be the soviets of 1968 and which numbered 460 in the Paris region at the end of May, survived into June but then either quickly faded from view or came under the ultimately stifling control of *groupuscules*.[26] In the summer, plainclothes police felt confident enough to challenge young protesters' control of the streets of the Latin Quarter.[27] Nor did the UNEF's efforts have much staying power. After an initial period of optimism, during which student activists thought that they could avoid the seasonal demobilization of summer holidays by creating courses that would attract workers, "popular universities" ended the summer with—in the opinion of police—"discouraging results" for students.[28] The UNEF's radicalism and its refusal to participate in reformist projects did not translate into an influx of new members.[29] In fact, UNEF's membership decreased from 50,000 prior to May 1968 to 30,000 by 1970. Its descent was one more example of the disintegration of the radical hopes of the 1960s.

Cycles of protest and repression are, paradoxically enough, often accompanied by attempts at reform.[30] De Gaulle's dismissal of Pompidou in July 1968 showed that their electoral victory had not resolved their differences. The general continued to believe that the prime minister's decision to concede to students by reopening the Sorbonne and releasing the arrested had helped to spread the "contagion" to workers whose demands had consequently pushed the French economy "to the limit."[31] After June, though, the president was more open to reforms than his former prime minister, who was closer to the conservative *versaillais* in his own party. The general refused to abandon his social-Catholic dream of participatory association of labor and capital.[32] Even at the height of the crisis, de Gaulle reportedly said to his ministers, "Reforms yes; disorder no." The introduction of participation—"the greatest French reform of our century"—would respond to "profound causes" of the May crisis.[33] Soon after the elections, de Gaulle appointed the *gaulliste de gauche*, René Capitant, a critic of the free market and of Pompidou, as minister of justice. During May, prior to the vote on censure, Capitant had resigned his position as deputy to protest against Pompidou's policies. On 17 June, the new minister of justice declared on the radio that if the National Assembly failed to enact Gaullist *participation*, the general would take the matter directly to the people in the form of a referendum. Capitant evoked a harmonious future where workers would be shareholders and cooperate enthusiastically in the management of an enterprise.

Employers reacted negatively to power sharing.[34] The *patrons* believed that tampering with management prerogatives and weakening the chain of command would destroy the economy. "Participation is inseparable from efficiency, which must rest on management authority."[35] Even at the height of the crisis, on 28 May, immediately after workers rejected the Grenelle protocol, the Chambers of Commerce condemned the proposed law on participation. According to their spokesperson, the authority of management should be strengthened, not questioned. Léon Gingembre of the CGPME commented sourly that "the structural upheaval recommended by Mr. Capitant can only lead to the ruin of the economy."[36] For different reasons, the unions also rejected participation. The CGT feared that the government's plan would make the workers "collaborate in their own exploitation."[37] The CFDT lamented the lack of further material concessions by the government and employers. Imposing participation in the firm created a united trade-union front against the project. At the same time, it sparked an unwinnable two-front war for reformers, who had to struggle against both unions and employers.

The culmination of the failure of participation occurred in 1969. The general had intended to make it the centerpiece of the referendum scheduled for April of that year, and he promised to resign if voters rejected it. However, the opposition of employers and of Gaullists who were sympathetic to them convinced de Gaulle not to commit his political fate to the popularity of participation, and he decided to exclude it from the referendum. Like the *gauchistes* and others on the left, the 78-year-old head of state had unwisely trusted in *autogestionnaire* desires, which had an appeal perhaps only to those—like some students and *cadres*—who either loved or identified with their jobs. The proposal for participation was replaced by a plan to reform the Senate and a program for decentralization. Both were grouped together in the 27 April referendum, which was repudiated by an electorate (52.4 percent voted no) little interested in these issues. The general resigned as he had promised. His replacement, Georges Pompidou, represented a "more conventional form of conservative rule," which persisted in its hostility towards workplace democracy.[38]

Economic vitality bolstered conservative control. From 1968 to 1974 the French economy experienced one of its greatest historical booms.[39] A post-May climate of business confidence and an upsurge in demand were largely responsible. Under Pompidou and his successors, the Fifth Republic continued to promote the development of the seductive forces. Gross disposable household income increased 7 percent per year from 1960 to 1974, when it declined to almost 3 percent annually.[40] Automobile purchases expanded at a phenomenal pace: 4.7 million in 1960 to 11.9 million in 1970. In 1967 only 27 percent used an automobile to commute to work; by 1974, 42 percent did. Almost 50 percent of working-class families owned their own homes or apartments. Residences had more space, and almost all were equipped with televisions, refrigerators, vacuum cleaners, and washing machines.

University reform fared better than participation because Edgar Faure's Law of Orientation restructured higher education. After May, Faure—twice Radical Socialist premier during the Fourth Republic—was named minister of education. Faure was ideologically close to left-wing Gaullists like Capitant, but unlike the latter, he skillfully constructed legislation that enabled his reform to pass both houses of Parliament with overwhelming majorities by 7 November, only four months after he took office.[41] His law had multiple goals. It promoted decentralization and strengthened the autonomy of each university, encouraged multidisciplinary endeavors and a core curriculum, and supported participation. Departments were replaced by new administrative units named *Unités d'enseignement et de recherche* (UER) whose organization tended to dilute the individual authority of the professor.[42] The law established procedures that allowed not only faculty but also students and staff to participate in the election of councils. Prior to the enactment of the reform, elections had occurred on French campuses, but senior professors had dominated them. They selected their incoming colleagues of junior rank and chose the dean. Junior professors and students possessed almost no voice. The Faure reform mandated that each group—senior professors, junior professors, staff, and students—elect representatives to the university senate. A precedent for student participation had been established immediately after the Liberation, but this right, it seems, had fallen into disuse. In the long term, the same fate awaited the Faure reform, even if some progressive changes did stick.[43] Students gained *parité* (participation), which in some measure integrated them into university decision-making.[44] The agitation among students in a number of disciplines, including the fine arts, led to a greater emphasis on research and interdisciplinary training.[45] The experimental university of Paris at Vincennes might have never have been built without the revolutionary/reform cycle of 1968.

In the short term, Faure's institution of elections and the broadening of the suffrage captured informed public opinion.[46] As in the U.S., reformists had a numerical majority on even radical campuses.[47] Polls showed that 65 percent of students wished to participate in university governance. A survey taken in September 1968 concluded that 54 percent of students desired to reform the university, 31 percent were concerned mainly with passing their examinations, and only 12 percent wanted to change society radically.[48] Given the 160,000 students in Paris, 19,000 could be classified as revolutionaries, 50,000 as indifferent or apathetic, and 86,400 as reformers. The May events had motivated many of the latter to act. Fifty-two percent (83,200) said they had "participated" in the movement.[49] Participation varied widely according to discipline. Thirty-seven percent of art students and 67 percent of humanities students claimed to have been engaged.

Thus, it was not surprising that the exam issue remained divisive in the fall of 1968. Police observed that "in different disciplines, examinations are taking place normally. The activists of the extreme left, fearful of being disavowed by almost all students if they recommend a boycott, have not done so."[50] Although Geismar, Sauvageot, and their organizations had refused to negotiate with the government, the UNEF adopted what police called a "prudent" position, letting the "base" decide about exams.[51] To protest against selection, a few students continued to boycott exams and wished to grade themselves.[52]

Post-May reforms possessed a less democratic, non-electoral side. They required that the dean (called university president after 1971) be master in his own house. This meant that student support services—such as dormitories, restaurants, libraries, and sporting facilities, which had their own separate administration in Paris—would now come under the authority of, for instance, Nanterre officials. University administration was unified and rationalized. For example, the Nanterre dean had not directly controlled the residence halls where students had protested against sexual segregation in 1967 and 1968. Instead, the Parisian chancellor and the organization that managed university housing (CROUS) were in charge of dormitories. A number of officials had shared responsibilities for calling police on campus to evict occupiers or to stop demonstrators. In 1970, the dean or president was given exclusive authority to maintain order throughout the campus, including its residences, restaurants, and sporting facilities. No one else was authorized to summon police. The new president of Nanterre, René Rémond, welcomed the strengthening of the powers of his office. It protected him, he claimed, from thoughtless initiatives by directors of housing or other officials and thus encouraged the normalization of the university.

After the agitation of May–June, the Parisian housing administration had wished to clean up the Nanterre "mess" by closing down most of its dorms and limiting residents to athletes, future *fonctionnaires*, and women under twenty-one:[53] "To protest against that policy, on 4 September a group of *enragés* occupied one of the buildings even though the decision to be more inclusive [about admissions] had been taken the day before."[54] Student protest was effective in guaranteeing liberalized admission policies in university dorms and restaurants. Even non-students benefited from reduced prices for meals. A ministerial memorandum of 6 November 1968 formalized freedom of visitation, which had existed in practice since the spring of 1968 despite the minister's wishes. Squatting (i.e., when a legitimate renter lodged another person without authorization) coexisted with this freedom. Squatting's "most dangerous form for peace and order on the campus" was the lodging of "activists" who had been banned from the residences. As with workers' pilfering, squatting could never be entirely stopped. Nor could pillaging, and some youths displayed their anger by trashing telephone booths. Others attacked right-wing or centrist students and continued to vilify the dean as a "fascist."[55]

One proposed solution was to shut down the sociology department and exclude its majors from the residences, but authorities felt that they could not justify "this sort of discrimination." Nor could they stop squatting by "a nightly inspection of individual rooms" since students would consider this procedure "inquisitorial and dictatorial." Furthermore, inspectors who carried out such checks risked physical assaults. Officials feared that such attacks would lead to the kind of counterproductive police interventions that had already occurred at Nanterre in 1967 and Antony in 1965. Authorities concluded that the "liberalism" of newly appointed housing directors at Antony and Nanterre had been effective in calming the dormitories and isolating the most violent *enragés*.[56] The minister of education decided to suspend restrictions on visitation rights in order to establish a "dialogue" with students. Officials knew that any controls—whether by night watchmen or police—would destroy this attempt to win the confidence of students. To avoid provoking protest, they even postponed rent increases.

Similarly, strikes in *lycées* furthered "a real and durable change in relations of students with instructors" who became more tolerant of debates on pedagogical and sexual matters.[57] Those who emphasize the significance of post-May "repression" neglect the importance of the long-term growth of tolerance.[58] They also ignore the many instances of cooperation between the authorities and protesting students and workers in the universities, factories, and streets. This type of give and take—which, as has been seen, occurred even during the most violent events of May—may have helped to prevent in France the kind of post-1968 terrorism that erupted in both Germany and Italy.

The post-May reforms stimulated an attempt at *autogestion* in one dormitory.[59] A residence of three hundred rooms was designated for a three-month, renewable "experiment" that would house both male and female volunteers of all ages. The residents themselves would manage the building and exert administrative and financial control. Housing officials and student representatives would determine admissions. Squatting was to be strictly forbidden, and a democratically elected residents' council would be established to judge disciplinary violations and expulsions. In the three other traditional (*non-autogéré*) dorms, liberalized visitation rights were envisaged. The Nanterre housing director affirmed that student victories in the domain of personal freedom were "inescapable." The Ministry of Education stood its ground at least until July but then conceded liberalization to the three dorms in August.[60] Female minors whose parents did not agree to a policy of controlled freedom would be assigned to other dormitory complexes in the Paris region.

Available sources do not indicate the results of this experiment in dormitory self-rule, but it is unquestionable that personal freedoms expanded in France and in other nations during the long 1960s.[61] The events of May did not inaugurate a new period in the history of mores but continued to reinforce cultural and social trends already present in French society for at least a decade. Secure in its control of the state, the government was able to tolerate student protest and lifestyles. Gaullism in power was hardly an inflexible old regime that constantly sought to impose an outdated moral order. France was not a "blocked" or "stagnant" society in the early Fifth Republic. The supposed "Bonapartist," "authoritarian," and "paternalist" bureaucracy of the regime proved surprisingly elastic during crises.

The French administration and those of other democracies throughout Europe and America participated in the expansion of tolerance. The constant victories of forbearance during the 1960s make some of the authorities' disciplinary actions at Antony and Nanterre unfathomable in retrospect. Likewise in the U.S., when a Barnard College sophomore publicly announced in 1968 that she was living with her boyfriend (a Columbia College junior), a major scandal erupted.[62] She became the subject of dozens of newspaper articles and was threatened with expulsion from Barnard. The incident now seems, like the police invasions of Parisian-area dorms, nearly incomprehensible. Yet the reaction of a strong segment of opinion against the punishment of the woman showed the increasing acceptance of cohabitation. In France and the U.S., attacks on property—not morality—provoked the most substantial limitations on the growth of tolerance.

Media spinmeisters sympathetic to May have furnished the events with a generally positive image.[63] One popular explanation for this tender obsession with 1968 is that veterans of the movement are now occupying command positions in the media and other bureaucracies. Like any other group of old warriors, they wish to glorify their battle experience. They tend to exaggerate the power of the social movement in which they participated and to see it as a creative rupture with the past. A "generation" continues to justify itself to its youth and elders.[64] These veterans from the middle classes have shown that they were much more capable of capturing the social imagination than workers who embarked upon the greatest strike wave in French history. *Soixante-huitards,* who sparked the events, continue to re-create their own images. This age cohort wants itself and others to acknowledge the world-shaking importance of its activities.

Yet this explanation for the perceived importance of 1968 is not totally convincing. While it may be the case that self-justification motivates some journalists and editors, the frequency and popularity of May commemorations shows that interest in the events has been much broader and wider than just its *anciens combattants.* Newspapers, magazines, movies, and television need an audience, and media moguls could not persistently re-sell May if they felt that the public would not buy it. Furthermore, generations or groups cohere not only because of common experiences but through collective imagination or the ability to use history to invent a collective identity.[65] This is demonstrated by a poll that revealed that for those who were 18 to 29 years old in 1979, May became the "beginning of a new value system" and the most important historical event of their lives. Those between 30 and 34 years old in 1979 found 1968 relatively insignificant. In other words, a generation that was much less likely to participate in May (the youngest of the group was seven in 1968) considered the events more consequential than its older brothers and sisters. Apparently, the public continues to believe that 1968 was "the most important event in France since the Second World War."[66]

What may be significant about the memory of May is not the self-justification of its veterans who have climbed the careerist ladders of the establishment, but how May continually connects itself with youth. The interpretation of May as a youth revolt is historically imprecise, especially with regard to workers' strikes, where young wage earners were often incorrectly seen as catalysts. Nevertheless, it has been widely accepted. After May, new generations remained fascinated by the powerful but ultimately unstable mixture of hedonism and altruism inherited from 1968. When there is no formidable social movement—as during the tenth, twentieth, twenty-fifth, and thirtieth anniversaries of 1968—even the sanitized memory of that year may serve as a surrogate and a reminder that popular unrest could unexpectedly erupt, as it did in France in 1986 and 1995. The antiglobalization protests of today locate their roots in the combination of anti-imperialism and anticapitalism found in the revolts of 1968.

Interest in the May events and their legacy are reminders of the grip of the revolutionary tradition on the French imagination. The Great Revolution's grand years—1789, 1792, 1794—were conceived as a radical break with the past, which became known as the *ancien régime.* As we know, 1792 was denoted Year I in the new calendar. The political, legislative, and social changes produced by the Revolution inspired it to initiate a new chronology. The "revolution" of 1968 was not potent enough to produce an officially recognized *tabula rasa,* but many of its participants and their followers retained the sense of starting from scratch that defines the revolutionary tradition. Since the insurrectionaries of 1968 never came close to capturing the state, their perception of rupture could never take the political form that it did in 1789. Instead, they imagined Year I as a cultural and personal recommencement. Thus, many see 1968 as a revolution that profoundly altered personal destinies.[67] The events of May and June—however ineffective politically—conserved the power to change individual lives.

This desire for a rupture is reflected in the popularity of *Reprise*. This late 1990s film, which was then made into a book on the thirtieth anniversary of May, shows the filmmaker, Hervé Le Roux, attempting to locate a woman who had been the subject of a short (nine-minute) documentary movie, *La reprise du travail aux usines Wonder*, in 1968.[68] In June of that year, this female wage laborer, known only as Jocelyne, was captured on film as she defiantly refused to return to work as the strike at her metallurgical factory was being settled. The popularity of antiwork ideologies quickly transformed the young woman into a rebellious heroine of the May revolt. Her refusal to labor (*ne pas perdre sa vie à la gagner* as the slogan went) pithily expressed the specific 1960s synthesis of personal, social, and political concerns. Being both female and a worker further heightened her status as a symbol of an ideology that had been articulated largely by male intellectuals. Her complete disappearance from the media spectacle enhanced her mystique. Yet ultimately neither she nor any other individual or group could solve the problem of wage labor. Thus, ideologists of the 1960s proposed contradictory solutions that ranged from the abolition of work to its internalization in a democratic workplace.

Opinion makers and opinion itself often consider the May events epochal as well as beneficial. Certainly, the activities of that month are easier to celebrate than other major events of post–World War II French history. Indochina and Algeria were major defeats, and the latter conflagration nearly led to civil war. The only real contemporary competitor for celebration is the Normandy Invasion, whose fiftieth anniversary in 1994 occasionally inspired media coverage equivalent to the thirtieth of May.[69] A comparison between the two events may be instructive: The Normandy assault was the largest amphibious operation in history and a major step in the defeat of Nazi Germany. It was as "world historical" as any event can be. May 1968, although linked to the international wave of 1960s agitation, was basically a French episode with modest consequences. The publicity surrounding it reveals the poverty of occasions suitable for celebration in recent French history. More opportunities abound for commiseration.

May 1968 fills a void in French social consciousness but may not deserve its prominence. The events did not mark a rupture but instead showed the continuity of social and political trends. No crisis of civilization suddenly erupted, and no significant attempt at workers' control emerged. On the contrary, the May–June events demonstrated the power of the centralized state and the attractions of a consumer society that had effectively smothered revolution while integrating hedonism.

Notes

1. Alain Schnapp and Pierre Vidal-Naquet, *Journal de la commune étudiante* (Paris, 1969), 10–12.
2. Alain Geismar, Serge July, and Erlyne Morane, *Vers la guerre civile* (Paris, 1969), 16.
3. Danielle Tartakowsky, "Le PCF en mai-juin 1968," paper presented to Colloque: Acteurs et terrains du mouvement social de mai 1968, Paris, 24–25 November 1988; Maurice Cohen, ed. *Le bilan social de l'année 1968* (Paris, 1969), 368; Roger Martelli, *Mai 68* (Paris, 1988), 207.
4. "Histoire et leçons d'une grève," *Esprit*, no. 373 (August–September, 1968): 118–119.
5. Gilles Martinet, *La conquête des pouvoirs* (Paris, 1968), 149.
6. Quoted in Jean-Raymond Tournoux, *Le mois de mai du général* (Paris, 1969), 298.
7. Robert Davezies, ed., *Mai 68: La rue dans l'église* (Paris, 1968), 137. See Nicolas Daum, *Des révolutionnaires dans un village parisien* (Paris, 1988), for the post-1968 history of a Parisian action committee.
8. Jean-Daniel Reynaud, "La nouvelle classe ouvrière, la technologie et l'histoire," *Revue française de science politique* (1972–1973): 533.
9. John H. Goldthorpe, David Lockwood, Frank Bechhofer, and Jennifer Platt, *The Affluent Worker: Political Attitudes and Behaviour* (Cambridge, 1968), 76.
10. See François Dubet, "Comment devient-on ouvrier," and Jean-Paul Molinari, "De la ferme à l'usine, de l'usine à la fac," in Guy-Patrick Azémar, ed., *Ouvriers, ouvrières: Un continent morcelé et silencieux* (Paris, 1992), 114, 141.
11. Henri Simon Oral History Project, interviews with workers, 1994.
12. Robert Lumley, *States of Emergency: Cultures of Revolt in Italy from 1968 to 1978* (London and New York, 1990), 10, 182–183, 250; Paul Ginsborg, *A History of Contemporary Italy: Society and Politics 1943–1988* (London, 1990), 314–319; Nanni Balestrini, *Queremos todo*, trans. Herman Mario Cueva (Buenos Aires, 1974), 76, 116, 126.
13. Michele Salvati, "May 1968 and the Hot Autumn of 1969: The Response of Two Ruling Classes," in Suzanne Berger, ed., *Organizing Interests in Western Europe* (Cambridge, 1981), 351.
14. Nicolas Hatzfeld, "Les ouvriers de l'automobile: Des vitrines sociales à la condition des OS, le changement des regards," in Geneviève Dreyfus-Armand, Robert Frank, Marie-Françoise Lévy, and Michelle Zancarini-Fournel, eds., *Les Années 68: Le Temps de la contestation* (Brussels, 2000), 358–361.
15. Balestrini, *Queremos todo*, 165.
16. Martin Clark, *Modern Italy, 1871–1995* (London, 1996), 378; Lumley, *States of Emergency*, 251–252.
17. Georges Carrot, *Le maintien de l'ordre en France au XXe siècle* (Paris, 1990), 336; cf. Chris Howell, *Regulating Labor: The State and Industrial Relations Reform in Postwar France* (Princeton, 1992), 72, who asserts that industrialists of large, modern firms had little to fear from unions and wanted to cooperate with them. See also Alfred Willener, Catherine Gajdos, and Georges Benguigui, *Les cadres en mouvement* (Paris, 1969), 110; "Histoire et leçons d'une grève," 109.
18. *Syndicalisme*, 8 August 1968; Jacques Capdevielle and René Mouriaux, *Mai 68: L'Entre-deux de la modernité, Histoire de trente ans* (Paris, 1988), 233.
19. Jeff Bridgford, "The Events of May: Consequences for Industrial Relations in France," in D. L. Hanley and A. P. Kerr, eds., *May 68: Coming of Age* (London, 1989), 107. Contrasting statistics are found in Michael Rose, *Servants of Post-Industrial Power? Sociologie du Travail in Modern France* (White Plains, N.Y., 1979), 148.
20. *Notre arme c'est la grève* (Paris, 1968), 73–74, 89.
21. La Cellophane à Mantes, 29 October 1968, Ministère d'état chargé des affaires sociales, Conflits du travail, Ministère du Travail, AN 760122.
22. Quoted in Philippe Bauchard and Maurice Bruzek, *Le syndicalisme à l'épreuve* (Paris, 1968), 307.

23. Antoine Bevort, "Le syndicalisme français et la logique du recrutement sélectif: Le cas de la CFTC-CFDT," *Le Mouvement social*, no. 169 (October–December, 1994): 135.

24. Serge Mallet, *Essays on the New Working Class*, trans. Dick Howard and Dean Savage (St. Louis, 1975), 87–106. Cf. S. Erbès-Seguin, C. Casassus, and O. Kourchid, *Les conditions de développement du conflit industriel* (Paris, 1977); Bridgford, "The Events," in Hanley, *May 68*, 116; Ingrid Gilcher-Holtey, *Die 68er Bewegung: Deutschland-Westeuropa-USA* (Munich, 2001), 86.

25. See Jacques Ellul, "La jeunesse force révolutionnaire?" *La Table ronde*, no. 251–252 (December–January, 1968–1969): 158.

26. Jean-Claude and Michelle Perrot, Madeleine Rebérioux, and Jean Maitron, eds., *La Sorbonne par elle-même*, special issue of *Le Mouvement social*, no. 64 (July–September, 1968): 12–13; 14 June 1968, AN 820599/41; 3 July 1968, AN 820599/41.

27. 4 August 1968, Fa 275, APP.

28. 24 June 1968, AN 820599/41; 4 September 1968, AN 820599/41.

29. Alain Monchablon, "L'UNEF et mai 1968," paper presented to Colloque: Acteurs et terrains du mouvement social du mai 1968, Paris, 24–25 November 1988, 11.

30. Sidney Tarrow, *Struggle, Politics, and Reform: Collective Action, Social Movements, and Cycles of Protest* (Ithaca, 1991), 92.

31. Quoted in Tournoux, *Le mois de mai*, 318.

32. Jean Lacouture, *De Gaulle: The Ruler, 1945–1970*, trans. Alan Sheridan (New York and London, 1992), 561.

33. De Gaulle quoted in Jean Touchard, *Le Gaullisme, 1940–1969* (Paris, 1978), 286–287.

34. Bauchard and Bruzek, *Syndicalisme*, 134.

35. Quoted in Christian Charrière, *Le Printemps des enragés* (Paris, 1968), 411.

36. Quoted in Guy Caire, "La situation sociale," *Droit social* (July–August, 1968): 465.

37. CGT in *Le Peuple*, no. 819 (1–15 April 1969) cited in Howell, *Regulating Labor*, 78.

38. Daniel Singer, *Prelude to Revolution: France in May 1968* (New York, 1970), ix.

39. Salvati, "May 1968," 329; Serge Berstein and Jean-Pierre Rioux, *La France de l'expansion: L'apogée Pompidou, 1969–1974* (Paris, 1995), 133–134.

40. The following is derived from *Recent Social Trends in France (1960–1990)*, trans. Liam Gavin (Frankfurt am Main, 1993). Average purchasing power rose until 1982.

41. Sidney Tarrow, "Social Protest and Policy Reform: May 1968 and the *Loi d'orientation* in France," *Comparative Political Studies*, vol. 25, no. 4 (January, 1993), 593.

42. "Comments by Philip E. Moseley," in Stephen D. Kertesz, ed., *The Task of Universities in a Changing World* (Notre Dame, Indiana, 1971), 303.

43. Tarrow, "Social Protest and Policy Reform," 599: "If the universities that emerged from the Faure reform were less autonomous, less pluridisciplinary, and less participatory than the reformers had hoped, they were an advance on the situation they replaced." "La Sorbonne occupée: Entretien avec Madeleine Rebérioux," in Geneviève Dreyfus-Armand and Laurent Gervereau, eds., *Mai 68: Les mouvements étudiants en France et dans le monde* (Nanterre, 1988), 156. Jean-Philippe Legois, Alain Monchablon, and Robi Morder, "Le mouvement étudiant et l'Université: Entre réforme et révolution (1964–1976)," in Dreyfus-Armand et al., *Les Années 68*, 291.

44. Legois, "Le mouvement étudiant," 291.

45. "L'Atelier des Arts-décoratifs: Entretien avec François Miehe et Gérard Paris-Clavel," in Dreyfus-Armand and Gervereau, *Mai 68*, 194.

46. René Rémond, *La Règle et le consentement* (Paris, 1979), 365; Louise Weiss, "Télémaque 1969," *Guerres et Paix*, no. 14–15 (1969–1970): 55.

47. David Caute, *The Year of the Barricades: A Journey through 1968* (New York, 1988), 170–173; Seymour Martin Lipset, "Introduction," in Seymour Martin Lipset and Philip G. Altbach, eds., *Students in Revolt* (Boston, 1970), xvii.

48. Three percent did not respond. See Adrien Dansette, *Mai 68* (Paris, 1971), 190.

49. However, police put the figure at 50,000 in Bulletin mensuel, August 1968, AN 820599/89.

50. Direction générale de la Police Nationale, renseignements généraux, bulletin quotidien, 4 September 1968, AN 820599/41.

51. 6 and 7 June 1968, AN 820599/41; 4 September 1968, AN 820599/41.

52. Contre, March [1969?], 1208W, art. 256, ADHS.

53. CROUS, 25 December 1968, 1208W, art. 115–117, ADHS.

54. Ibid.

55. Letter from Prof. B., 25 to 27 September 1968, 1208W, art. 180, ADHS.

56. CROUS, 25 December 1968, 1208W, art. 115–117, ADHS.

57. Louis Astre of the FEN in *Matériaux pour l'histoire de notre temps*, no. 20 (July–September, 1990): 51; *Mai 68 par eux-mêmes: Le mouvement de Floréal, an 176* (Paris, 1989), 41.

58. Maurice Rajsfus, *Mai 68: Sous les pavés, la répression (mai 1968–mars 1974)* (Paris, 1998); Kristin Ross, *May '68 and Its Afterlives* (Chicago, 2002). For an intelligent overview of this question, Arthur Marwick, "Die 68er Revolution," in Peter Wende, ed., *Grosse Revolutionen des Geschichte* (Munich, 2000), 330, and Arthur Marwick, "Introduction: Locating Key Texts and the Distinctive Landscape of the Sixties," in Anthony Aldgate, James Chapman, and Arthur Marwick, eds., *Windows on the Sixties* (London, 2000), xiii.

59. CROUS, 26 September 1968 and Projet, n.d., 1208W, art. 115–117, ADHS.

60. Procès-verbal, 5 July 1968, 1208W, art. 115–117, ADHS; CROUS, 26 September 1968, 1208W, art. 115–117, ADHS.

61. Caute, *The Year*, 108; Lumley, *States of Emergency*, 91; Detlef Siegfried, "Vom Teenager zur Pop-Revolution: Politisierungstendenzen in der westdeutschen Jugendkultur 1959 bis 1968," in Axel Schildt, Detlef Siegfried, and Karl Christian Lammers, eds., *Dynamische Zeiten: Die 60er Jahre in den beiden deutschen Gesellshaften* (Hamburg, 2000), 615.

62. Charles Kaiser, *1968 in America: Music, Politics, Chaos, Counterculture and the Shaping of a Generation* (New York, 1988), 255.

63. A glance at *Le Monde*'s and *Libération*'s thirtieth-anniversary Web sites on 1968 demonstrated this point.

64. On the formation of "generation," see Pierre Nora, "Generation," in Pierre Nora, ed., *The Realms of Memory*, trans. Arthur Goldhammer, 3 vols. (New York, 1996), 1: 499–531.

65. Marie-Claire Lavabre, "Génération et Mémoire," paper presented to the meeting of the *Association Française de Science Politique*, 22–24 October 1981, 9.

66. Michelle Zancarini-Fournel, "Introduction," in Dreyfus-Armand et al., *Les Années 68*, 21.

67. *Mai 68 par eux-mêmes*. Cercle Barbara Salutati, *Longtemps je me suis souvenu de mai 68* (Bordeaux, 2002).

68. Hervé Le Roux, *Reprise: Récit* (Paris, 1998); Ross, *May '68*, 139.

69. See *Le Figaro* of June 1994. However, cf. the international edition of *L'Express*, 1 April 1993 and 1–30 June 1994, which gave much more coverage to the twenty-fifth anniversary of May than to the fiftieth anniversary of the Normandy Invasion.

CHRONOLOGY

1955–1957	Construction of the student dormitory complex at Antony.
1962	Defiance of dormitory rules at Antony.
1963	Construction of future Faculté des Lettres et des Sciences humaines at Nanterre. Miners' strike in March and April.
1963–1964	Rent strikes at Antony and continuing protests against dormitory rules.
1965	Massive student resistance to construction of observation lodges at Antony.

1966
January   CGT-CFDT agreement.
May   Pro-Situationists take over UNEF bureau at Strasbourg.

1966–1967   De facto liberalization of visitation rights at Antony.

1967
March   Sleep-in at Nanterre's female dormitory. Strike of Rhodiaceta workers.
November   Student strike at Nanterre.

1968
January   Police/student confrontations at Nanterre. Renault-Saviem strike at Caen.
February   Valentine's Day occupation of women's residence at Nanterre.
March   Disruptions of classes and invasion of administration building at Nanterre.
April   Nanterre professors approve the creation of a university police force.
1 May   First authorized May Day demonstration since 1954.

3 May	Student protests at the Sorbonne.
6 May	University discipline council meets at the Sorbonne. First barricades built.
10 May	First Night of the Barricades.
11 May	Pompidou reopens the Sorbonne and grants amnesty to arrested students. Censier occupied.
13 May	Large worker-student demonstration and one-day solidarity strike against government "repression." The Sorbonne occupied.
14 May	Striking art students create posters. Strike at Sud-Aviation (Nantes).
15 May	The Odéon Theater occupied.
20 May	Workers' strikes expand massively.
22 May	Major debate in the National Assembly, and rejection of censure motion against the government.
24 May	Ineffective address by de Gaulle. Second Night of the Barricades follows. Government assures gasoline supplies to priority consumers.
25 May	Opening of formal national negotiations among government, employers, and unions.
27 May	Grenelle Accord issued and rejected by workers in large firms. Charléty meeting.
29 May	Large CGT demonstration. De Gaulle departs.
30 May	De Gaulle returns to Paris and addresses nation. Massive Gaullist demonstration follows.
4 June	Return from long weekend provokes huge traffic jams in Paris region.
7 June	Confrontations at the Flins Renault factory.
8 June	Amnesty issued for ex-OAS officials.
10 June	Deaths of a student at Flins and of a worker at Sochaux Peugeot factory. Back-to-work movement expands.
11 June	Final Night of the Barricades.
14 June	Police empty the Odéon Theater.
16 June	Police evacuate the Sorbonne.
26 June	Police terminate the Beaux-Arts occupation.
30 June	Gaullist victory in second round of legislative elections.
6 July	Censier occupation ended.
6 November	Formalization of freedom of visitation at Nanterre.
7 November	University reform bill (Faure law) passed.

GLOSSARY

affiche	poster
agrégé	title indicating the successful completion of the highly competitive examination called the *agrégation*, which allows university or *lycée* professors to teach at advanced levels
Algérie Française	slogan of partisans of a French Algeria, as opposed to an independent Algeria
arrondissement	one of the twenty administrative districts of Paris
autogestion	self-management or workers' control
baccalauréat	rigorous series of national examinations required of all high-school students who wish to enter the university
banlieue	suburbs, often referring to areas surrounding Paris
blousons noirs	young delinquents
cadres	executives and supervisory personnel
cégétistes	members of the CGT
cheminots	railroad workers
chienlit	disorder; literally, *chier en lit* or shit in bed
comités paritaires	committees having both student and faculty participation
curé	priest
détournement	a reversal of conventional meanings
fédérés	members of the FGDS
Enragés	pro-Situationists at Nanterre and other French institutions of higher learning
faculté	major administrative and teaching division of the French university. Typical *facultés* include humanities (*lettres*), sciences, law, medicine, engineering, and pharmacy.
flics	cops

gauchistes	members of revolutionary *groupuscules* of the extreme left
grèves sauvages	wildcat strikes
groupuscule	small political group, usually on the extreme left
katangais	self-appointed security force during occupation of the Sorbonne
licence	equivalent to a Bachelor of Arts degree
lycée	an institution comparable to better American high schools. *Lycées* are part of a national system of higher education.
manifs	*manifestations* or demonstrations
meneurs	agitators
métro	subway
normalien	graduate of the prestigious Ecole Normale Supérieure
ordre moral	traditional Catholic or conservative republican morality
ouvriérisme	the belief that only the working class can make the revolution
pétroleuses	women said to have started fires during the Paris Commune
pompiers	firemen
service d'ordre	parade marshals or a nonuniformed political paramilitary force
situationnistes (situs)	influential thinkers of the 1950s and 1960s who combined a Marxist/anarchist councilism with a cultural critique of contemporary capitalism
soixante-huitards	those who participated in student and youth protests in 1968
tiersmondiste	a supporter of Third World revolutionary movements
trublions	troublemakers, usually referring to young protesters

BIBLIOGRAPHY

Archival Sources

Archives de la brigade de sapeurs-pompiers de Paris, Paris.
Archives départementales des Hauts-de-Seine [ADHS], Nanterre.
Archives Nationales [AN], Fontainebleau and Paris.
    Ministère de l'Intérieur, cabinet du ministre, cabinet de Raymond Marcellin:
        événements de mai 1968, 800273, art. 61.
    Ministère de l'Intérieur, Direction générale de la Police nationale, renseignements
        généraux, bulletins quotidiens d'information, 820599, art. 36–44.
    Ministère de l'Intérieur, Direction générale de la Police nationale, renseignements
        généraux, bulletins hebdomadaires d'information, 820599, art. 75.
    Ministère de l'Intérieur, Direction générale de la Police nationale, renseignements
        généraux, bulletins mensuels d'information, 820599, art. 89.
    Ministère de l'Intérieur, Maintien de l'ordre, Manifestations et conflits sociaux,
        860581, art. 25.
    Ministère du Travail, Direction générale du travail et de l'emploi, Accords
        de Grenelle, 860561.
    Ministère du Travail, Conflits du travail, Ministère d'état chargé des affaires
        sociales, 760122.
    Ministère de l'Education, Direction des collèges, 790793.
    Ministère de l'Industrie, des Postes et Télécommunications, 810484.
Archives de la Préfecture de Police [APP], Paris.
Bibliothèque Nationale [BN], Paris.
    Ecole des Beaux-Arts, documents originaux.
    Tracts de mai 1968.
Groupement des Industries Métallurgiques, [GIM], Neuilly.
Musée d'histoire contemporaine, Bibliothèque de documentation internationale
    contemporaine [BDIC], Nanterre.
Rectorat de Paris, Paris.
Henri Simon Oral History Project, interviews with workers (1994), Paris.

Printed Primary Sources

1. Periodicals

Aujourd'hui
L'Anti-Mythe
Antoinette

L'Aurore
Cahiers de Mai
Le Canard enchaîné
Combat
La Croix
Les Echos
Esprit
L'Express
Le Figaro
France-Forum
L'Humanité
Informations Correspondance Ouvrières [ICO]
L'Internationale situationniste [IS].
Lutte Socialiste
Matériaux pour l'histoire de notre temps
Le Mnefomane
Le Monde
Le Nouvel Observateur
Paris Match
Le Peuple
Planning Familial
La Vie ouvrière

2. Books

Atelier Populaire présenté par lui-même: 87 affiches de mai–juin 1968. Paris, 1968.
Bibliothèque Nationale. *Les affiches de mai 68 ou l'imagination graphique*. Paris, 1982.
Comité étudiant pour les libertés universitaires. *Pour rebâtir l'université*. Paris, 1969.
Débats de l'Assemblée Nationale: Seconde session ordinaire de 1967–1968. Paris, 1969.
Gasquet, Vasco. *Les 500 affiches de mai 1968*. Paris, 1978.
Kravetz, Marc, ed. *L'Insurrection étudiante*. Paris, 1968.
Liaison des Etudiants Anarchistes. *Anarchistes en 1968 à Nanterre*. Vauchrétien, 1998.
Mésa. *Mai 68: Les affiches de l'atelier populaire de 1'ex-Ecole des Beaux-Arts*. Paris, 1968.
Mouvement du 22 Mars. *Ce n'est qu'un début, continuons le combat*. Paris, 1968.
Mouvement du 22 mars. *Mai 68 Tracts et Textes*. Vauchrétien, 1998.
Noir et Rouge. *Socialisme ou Barbarie: Organe de Critique et d'Orientation Révolutionnaire Anthologie*. Mauléon, 1985.
Perrot, Jean-Claude, Michelle Perrot, Madeleine Rebérioux, and Jean Maitron, eds. *La Sorbonne par elle-même*. Special issue of *Le Mouvement social*, no. 64 (July–September, 1968).
Quelle université? Quelle société? Paris, 1968.
Schnapp, Alain, and Pierre Vidal-Naquet. *Journal de la commune étudiante*. Paris, 1969.
Sernin, André. *Journal d'un bourgeois de Paris en mai 1968*. Paris, 1988.
Union Nationale des Etudiants de France [and SNESup]. *Le livre noir des journées de mai*. Paris, 1968.

Secondary Sources

Adam, Gérard. "Etude statistique des grèves de mai–juin 1968." *Revue française de science politique*, no. 1 (February, 1970): 105–119.
Adam, Gérard, Frédéric Bon, Jacques Capdevielle, and René Mouriaux. *L'Ouvrier français en 1970*. Paris, 1970.

Agulhon, Maurice. *La République: Nouveaux drames et nouveaux espoirs (1932 à nos jours)*. 2 vols. Paris, 1990.

Andrieu, René. *Les communistes et la révolution*. Paris, 1968.

Andrieux, Andrée, and Jean Lignon. *L'Ouvrier d'aujourd'hui*. Paris, 1966.

Andro, Pierre, A. Dauvergne, and L. M. Lagoutte. *Le mai de la révolution*. Paris, 1968.

Aron, Raymond. *La révolution introuvable*. Paris, 1968.

Artous, Antoine, ed. *Retours sur mai*. Montreuil, 1988.

Auron, Yaïr. *Les juifs d'extrême gauche en mai 68*. Paris, 1998.

Azémar, Guy-Patrick, ed. *Ouvriers ouvrières: Un continent morcelé et silencieux*. Paris, 1992.

Bachelard, Gaston. *The Psychoanalysis of Fire*. Trans. Alan C. M. Ross. Boston, 1964.

Baecque, Antoine de. *La nouvelle vague: Portrait d'une jeunesse*. Paris, 1998.

Bailey, Beth. "Sexual Revolution(s)." In *The Sixties: From Memory to History*, ed. David Farber. Chapel Hill and London, 1994: 235–262.

Balestrini, Nanni. *Queremos todo*. Trans. Herman Mario Cueva. Buenos Aires, 1974.

Balestrini, Nanni. *Vogliamo tutto*. Milan, 1988.

Barrau, Grégory. *Le Mai 68 des catholiques*. Paris, 1998.

Bauchard, Philippe, and Maurice Bruzek. *Le syndicalisme à l'épreuve*. Paris, 1968.

Bauman, Zygmunt. "The Left as the Counter-Culture of Modernity." In *Social Movements: Critiques, Concepts, Case-Studies*, ed. Sanford M. Lyman. New York, 1995: 356–370.

Baynac, Jacques. *Mai retrouvé*. Paris, 1978.

Becker, Jean-Jacques. *Histoire politique de la France depuis 1945*. Paris, 1988.

Belon, Hubert. "Les élections des 23 et 30 juin." *Revue politique et parlementaire*, no. 790 (June–July, 1968): 119–128.

Berger, Suzanne, ed. *Organizing Interests in Western Europe*. Cambridge, 1981.

Berstein, Serge. *La France de l'expansion: La République gaullienne, 1958–1969*. Paris, 1989.

Berstein, Serge, and Jean-Pierre Rioux, *La France de l'expansion: L'apogée Pompidou, 1969–1974*. Paris, 1995.

Bertaux, Daniel, Danièle Linhart, and Beatrix Le Wita, "Mai 1968 et la formation de générations politiques en France," *Le Mouvement social*, no. 143 (April–June, 1988): 75–89.

Bertolino, Jean. *Les Trublions*. Paris, 1969.

Bevort, Antoine. "Le syndicalisme français et la logique du recrutement sélectif: Le cas de la CFTC-CFDT." *Le Mouvement social*, no. 169 (October–December, 1994): 109–136.

Biard, Roland. *Dictionnaire de l'extrême gauche de 1945 à nos jours*. Paris, 1978.

Bisseret, Noëlle. "L'enseignement inégalitaire et la contestation étudiante." *Communications*, vol. 12 (1968): 54–65.

Blondeau, Yves. *Le Syndicat des correcteurs*. Paris, 1973.

Boissieu, Alain de. *Pour Servir le général 1946–1970*. Paris, 1982.

Boorstin, Daniel. *The Decline of Radicalism: Reflections on America Today*. New York, 1969.

Bosc, Serge, and Jean-Marcel Bouguereau. "Le mouvement des étudiants berlinois." *Les Temps modernes*, no. 265 (July, 1968): 1–69.

Boudon, Raymond. "La crise universitaire française: Essai de diagnostic sociologique." *Annales E.S.C.*, vol. 24, no. 3 (May–June, 1969): 738–764.

———. "Quelques causes de la révolte estudiantine." *La Table ronde*, no. 251–252 (December–January, 1968–1969): 169–183.

Bourdieu, Pierre. *Homo Academicus*. Trans. Peter Collier. Stanford, 1988.

Bourdieu, Pierre, and Jean-Claude Passeron. *Les Héritiers: Les étudiants et la culture*. Paris, 1964.

Bourricaud, François. "Une reprise en main difficile." *Preuves*, no. 218 (May–June, 1969): 38–48.

———. *Universités à la dérive*. Paris, 1971.

Braudel, Fernand. *The Identity of France*. Trans. Sian Reynolds. 2 vols. New York, 1988.

Burel, Pierre. *La crise économique dans les événements de mai 1968*. Caudry, 1970.

Caire, Guy. "La situation sociale." *Droit social* (July–August 1968): 451–467.

Campion-Vincent, Véronique. *La légende des vols d'organes*. Paris, 1997.

Capdevielle, Jacques, and René Mouriaux. *Mai 68: L'Entre-deux de la modernité, Histoire de trente ans*. Paris, 1988.

Capitaine, Ronan. *Dassault Saint-Cloud en mai–juin 1968*. Mémoire de maîtrise, Université de Paris I, 1990.

Caron, Gilles. *Sous les pavés la plage*. Sèvres, 1993.

Carrot, Georges, *Le maintien de l'ordre en France au XXe siècle*. Paris, 1970.

Caute, David. *The Year of the Barricades: A Journey through 1968*. New York, 1988.

Centre national d'information pour la productivité des entreprises. *Les événements de mai–juin 1968 vus à travers cent entreprises*. Paris, 1968.

Cercle Barbara Salutati. *Longtemps je me suis souvenu de mai 68*. Bordeaux, 2002.

Certeau, Michel de. *La prise de parole: Pour une nouvelle culture*. Paris, 1968.

Chaffard, Georges. *Les orages de mai: Histoire exemplaire d'une élection*. Paris, 1968.

Chamboredon, Jean-Claude, and Madeleine Lemaire. "Proximité spatiale et distance sociale: Les grands ensembles et leur peuplement." *Revue française de sociologie*, vol. 11 (1970): 3–33.

Charrière, Christian. *Le Printemps des enragés*. Paris, 1968.

Christiansen, Rupert. *Paris Babylon: The Story of the Paris Commune*. New York, 1996.

Clark, Martin. *Modern Italy: 1871–1995*. London, 1996.

Confédération Générale du Travail de la R.N.U.R. [Régie Nationale des Usines Renault]. *33 jours 34 nuits*. Paris, n.d.

Cohen, Maurice, ed. *Le bilan social de l'année 1968*. Paris, 1969.

Cohn-Bendit, Daniel. *Le Grand Bazar*. Paris, 1975.

Copley, Antony. *Sexual Moralities in France 1780–1980*. London, 1989.

Corbin, Alain, and Jean-Marie Mayeur, eds. *La barricade*. Paris, 1997.

Courtois, Stéphane. "Le joli mois de mai." *Communisme*, no. 18–19 (1988): 224–235.

Coutin, André. *Huit siècles de violence au Quartier latin*. Paris, 1969.

Crouch, Colin, and Alessandro Pizzorno, eds. *The Resurgence of Class Conflict in Western Europe since 1968*. 2 vols. New York, 1978.

Daniels, Robert V. *Year of the Heroic Guerrilla: World Revolution and Counterrevolution in 1968*. New York, 1989.

Dansette, Adrien. *Mai 1968*. Paris, 1971.

Daum, Nicolas. *Des révolutionnaires dans un village parisien*. Paris, 1988.

Davezies, Robert, ed. *Mai 68: La rue dans l'église*. Paris, 1968.

Debray, Régis. "A Modest Contribution to the Rites and Ceremonies of the Tenth Anniversary." *New Left Review*, no. 115 (May–June 1979): 45–71.

Dejacques, Claude. *A toi l'angoisse, à moi la rage: Mai 68 Les fresques de Nanterre*. Paris, 1969.

Delale, Alain, and Gilles Ragache. *La France de 68*. Paris, 1978.

Dreyfus, Michel. *Histoire de la CGT: Cent ans de syndicalisme en France*. Paris, 1995.

Dreyfus-Armand, Geneviève, and Laurent Gervereau, eds. *Mai 68: Les mouvements étudiants en France et dans le monde*. Nanterre, 1988.

Dreyfus-Armand, Geneviève, Robert Frank, Marie-Françoise Lévy, and Michelle Zancarini-Fournel, eds. *Les Années 68: Le temps de la contestation*. Brussels, 2000.

Droz, Bernard, and Evelyne Lever. *Histoire de la guerre d'Algérie*. Paris, 1982.

Dubois, Pierre, Renaud Dulong, Claude Durand, Sabine Erbès-Séguin, and Daniel Vidal. *Grèves revendicatives ou grèves politiques?* Paris, 1971.

Dubost, Nicolas. *Flins sans fin*. Paris, 1979.

Duchen, Claire. *Women's Rights and Women's Lives in France 1944–1968*. London, 1994.

Dumontier, Pascal. *Les Situationnistes et mai 68: Théorie et pratique de la révolution (1966–1972)*. Paris, 1990.

Duprat, François. *Les journées de mai 68: Les dessous d'une révolution*. Paris, 1968.

Durandeaux, Jacques. *Les journées de mai 68: Rencontres et dialogues*. Paris, 1968.

Duteuil, Jean-Pierre. *Nanterre 1965–66–67–68: Vers le Mouvement du 22 mars*. Paris, 1988.

Ellul, Jacques. "La jeunesse force révolutionnaire?" *La Table ronde*, no. 251–252 (December–January, 1968–1969): 150–168.

"Enquête: Télémaque 1969." *Guerres et Paix*, no. 14–15 (1969/4–1970/1).

Epistémon [Didier Anzieu]. *Ces idées qui ont ébranlé la France*. Paris, 1968.

Erbès-Seguin, S., C. Casassus, and O. Kourchid. *Les conditions de développement du conflit industriel*. Paris, 1977.

Faure, Marcel. "Premières réflexions sur mai 1968." *Paysans* (May, 1968): 6–14.

Feenberg, Andrew, and Jim Freedman. *When Poetry Ruled the Streets: The French May Events of 1968*. Albany, 2001.

Fermigier, André. "No More Claudels." In *Art and Confrontation: The Arts in an Age of Change*. Trans. Nigel Foxell. Greenwich, Conn., 1968: 41–62.

Ferrand, Jérôme. *La jeunesse nouveau tiers état*. Paris, 1968.

Ferry, Luc. "Interpréter Mai 68." *Pouvoirs*, no. 39 (1986): 5–13.

Ferry, Luc, and Alain Renaut. *68–86: Itinéraires de l'individu*. Paris, 1987.

Feuer, Lewis S. *The Conflict of Generations: The Character and Significance of Student Movements*. New York and London, 1969.

Fields, A. Belden. *Student Politics in France: A Study of the Union Nationale des Etudiants de France*. New York, 1970.

Filiu, Jean-Pierre. "Le gouvernement et la direction face à la crise." In *Mai 68 à l'ORTF*. Paris, 1987: 161–194.

Filiu, Jean-Pierre. "L'Intersyndicale durant le conflit." In *Mai 68 à l'ORTF*. Paris, 1987: 37–67.

Fink, Carole, Philipp Gassert, and Detlef Junker, eds. *1968: The World Transformed*. Cambridge, 1998.

Foccart, Jacques. *Le Général en mai: Journal de l'Elysée-II 1968–1969*. Paris, 1998.

Fourastié, Jean. *Les 40,000 heures*. Paris, 1965.

Frémontier, Jacques. *La forteresse ouvrière: Renault*. Paris, 1971.

Fukuyama, Francis. *The End of History and the Last Man*. New York, 1992.

Gallaher, John C. *The Students of Paris and the Revolution of 1848*. Carbondale and Edwardsville, Ill., 1980.

Garrigues, Jean. *Images de la révolution: L'imagerie républicaine de 1789 à nos jours*. Paris, 1988.

Gascon, Roger. *La nuit du pouvoir ou le 24 mai manqué*. Paris, 1968.

Geismar, Alain, Serge July, and Erlyne Morane. *Vers la guerre civile*. Paris, 1969.

Georgi, Frank. "Le Pouvoir est dans la rue: La manifestation gaulliste des Champs Elysées (30 mai 1968)." *Vingtième Siècle*, no. 48 (1995): 46–60.

Gervereau, Laurent. *La propagande par l'affiche*. Paris, 1991.

Gilcher-Holtey, Ingrid. *Die 68er Bewegung: Deutschland-Westeuropa-USA*. Munich, 2001.

Gildea, Robert. *The Past in French History*. New Haven and London, 1994.

Gillis, John R. *Youth and History*. New York and London, 1974.

Ginsborg, Paul. *A History of Contemporary Italy: Society and Politics 1943–1988*. London, 1990.

Gitlin, Todd. *The Sixties: Years of Hope, Days of Rage*. New York, 1987.

Goldstein, Marc. "Le Parti communiste du 3 mai au 6 juin 1968." *Les Temps modernes*, no. 269 (November, 1968): 827–894.

Goldthorpe, John H., David Lockwood, Frank Bechhofer, and Jennifer Platt. *The Affluent Worker: Political Attitudes and Behaviour*. Cambridge, 1968.

Gomez, Michel. *Mai 68 au jour le jour*. Paris, 1998.

Gordon, Daniel A. "Immigrants and the New Left in France, 1968–1971." Ph.D. diss., University of Sussex, 2001.

Gorz, André. "Limites et potentialités du mouvement de mai." *Les Temps modernes*, no. 266–267 (August–September, 1968): 231–264.

Goudsblom, Johan. *Fire and Civilization*. London, 1992.

Grappin, Pierre. *L'Ile aux peupliers*. Nancy, 1993.

Gregoire, R., and F. Perlman. *Worker-Student Action Committees: France May '68*. Detroit, 1991.

Grimaud, Maurice. *En mai, fais ce qu'il te plaît*. Paris, 1977.

Guerin-Gonzales, Camille, and Carl Strikwerda, eds. *The Politics of Immigrant Workers*. New York, 1993.

Guin, Yannick. *La commune de Nantes*. Paris, 1969.

Gullickson, Gay L. *The Unruly Women of Paris: Images of the Commune*. Ithaca, 1996.

Habermas, Jürgen. *Toward a Rational Society: Student Protest, Science, and Politics.* Trans. Jeremy J. Shapiro. Boston, 1971.

Hamilton, Richard. *Affluence and the French Worker in the Fourth Republic.* Princeton, 1967.

Hamon, Hervé, and Patrick Rotman. *Génération.* 2 vols. Paris, 1987.

Hanley, D. L., and A. P. Kerr, eds. *May 68: Coming of Age.* London, 1989.

Harmon, Chris. *The Fire Last Time: 1968 and After.* London, 1988.

Hassenteufel, Patrick. *Citroën-Paris en mai–juin 1968: Dualités de la grève.* Mémoire de maîtrise, Paris I, 1987.

Hirsch, Ch.-A. "La police dans la tourmente." *Revue internationale de criminologie et de police technique,* no. 3 (July–September, 1968): 219–222.

Horne, Alistair. *A Savage War of Peace: Algeria 1954–1962.* New York, 1987.

Horvath-Peterson, Sandra. *Victor Duruy and French Education.* Baton Rouge and London, 1984.

Howell, Chris. *Regulating Labor: The State and Industrial Relations Reform in Postwar France.* Princeton, 1992.

Isserman, Maurice, and Michael Kazin. *America Divided: The Civil War of the 1960s.* New York, 2000.

Jackson, Julian. "De Gaulle and May 1968." In *De Gaulle and Twentieth-Century France,* ed. Hugh Gough and John Horne. London, 1994: 125–146.

Jappe, Anselm. *Guy Debord.* Trans. Donald Nicholson-Smith. Berkeley, 1999.

Joffrin, Laurent. *Mai 68: Histoire des événements.* Paris, 1988.

Johan, Michel. "La CGT et le mouvement de mai." *Les Temps modernes,* no. 266–267 (August–September, 1968): 326–375.

Julliard, Jacques. "Syndicalisme révolutionnaire et révolution étudiante." *Esprit,* no. 372 (June–July, 1968): 1037–1045.

Kaiser, Charles. *1968 in America: Music, Politics, Chaos, Counterculture and the Shaping of a Generation.* New York, 1988.

Katsiaficas, George. *The Imagination of the New Left.* Boston, 1987.

Keeler, John T. S. *The Politics of Neocorportatism in France.* New York, 1987.

Kerbourc'h, Jean-Claude. *Le Piéton de Mai.* Paris, 1968.

Kergoat, Danielle. *Bulledor ou l'histoire d'une mobilisation ouvrière.* Paris, 1973.

Kertesz, Stephen D., ed. *The Task of Universities in a Changing World.* Notre Dame, Ind. 1971.

Kouchner, Bernard, and Michel-Antoine Burnier. *La France sauvage.* Paris, 1970.

Labro, Philippe, ed. *Ce n'est qu'un début.* Paris, 1968.

Lacouture, Jean. *De Gaulle: The Ruler 1945–1970.* Trans. Alan Sheridan. New York and London, 1992.

———, *Pierre Mendès-France.* Trans. George Holoch. New York, 1984.

Lacroix, Bernard. "A contre-courant: Le parti pris du réalisme." *Pouvoirs,* no. 39 (1986): 117–127.

Lavabre, Marie-Claire. "Génération et Mémoire." Paper presented to the meeting of the Association Française de Science Politique (22–24 October 1981).

———, and Henri Rey, *Les Mouvements de 1968.* Florence, 1998.

Lefebvre, Henri. *The Explosion: Marxism and the French Revolution.* Trans. Alfred Ehrenfeld. New York, 1969.

———. *Le temps des méprises.* Paris, 1975.

Lefranc, Georges. *Le Mouvement syndical de la Libération aux événements de mai–juin 1968.* Paris, 1969.

Le Goff, Jean-Pierre. *Mai 68, l'héritage impossible.* Paris, 1998.

Legois, Jean-Philippe. *La Sorbonne avant mai 68.* Mémoire de maîtrise, Paris I, 1993.

Lemire, Laurent. *Cohn-Bendit.* Paris, 1998.

Le Roux, Hervé. *Reprise: Récit.* Paris, 1998.

Leuwers, Jean-Marie. *Un peuple se dresse: Luttes ouvrières mai 1968.* Paris, 1969.

Léveque, J.-J. "Les arts en colère." *La Galerie des arts,* no. 56 (September, 1968): 3–4.

Levin, Miriam. "Democratic Vistas—Democratic Media: Defining a Role for Printed Images in Industrializing France." *French Historical Studies,* no. 1 (spring, 1993): 82–108.

Lipovetsky, Gilles. "Changer la vie ou l'irruption de l'individualisme transpolitique." *Pouvoirs*, no. 39 (1986): 91–105.

———. *L'Ere du vide: Essais sur l'individualisme contemporain*. Paris, 1983.

Lipset, Seymour Martin, and Sheldon S. Wolin, eds. *The Berkeley Student Revolt: Facts and Interpretations*. New York, 1965.

Lipset, Seymour Martin, and Philip G. Altbach, eds. *Students in Revolt*. Boston, 1970.

Lumley, Robert. *States of Emergency: Cultures of Revolt in Italy from 1968 to 1978*. London and New York, 1990.

Magri, Lucio. "Réflexions sur les événements de mai." *Les Temps modernes*, no. 277–278 (August–September, 1969): 1–45.

Magri, Lucio. "Réflexions sur les événements de mai." *Les Temps modernes*, no. 279 (October, 1969): 455–492.

Mai 68 à l'ORTF. Paris, 1987.

Mai 68 par eux-mêmes: Le mouvement de Floréal, an 176. Paris, 1989.

Mallet, Serge. *Essays on the New Working Class*. Trans. Dick Howard and Dean Savage. St. Louis, 1975.

Mandel, Ernest. "The Lessons of May 1968." *New Left Review*, no. 52 (November–December, 1968): 9–32.

Manel, Jean-Pierre, and Alomée Planel. *La crise de l'ORTF*. Paris, 1968.

Marcus, Greil. *Lipstick Traces: A Secret History of the Twentieth Century*. Cambridge, Mass., 1989.

Marcuse, Herbert. *An Essay on Liberation*. Boston, 1969.

Martelli, Roger. *Mai 68*. Paris, 1988.

Martinet, Gilles. *La conquête des pouvoirs*. Paris, 1968.

Martinotti, Guido. "Notes on Italian Students in Periods of Political Mobilization." In *Students in Revolt*, ed. Seymour Martin Lipset and Philip G. Altbach. Boston, 1970: 167–201.

Martos, Jean-François. *Histoire de l'Internationale Situationniste*. Paris, 1989.

Marwick, Arthur. *British Society since 1945*. New York, 1982.

———. *The Sixties: Cultural Revolution in Britain, France, Italy, and the United States, c. 1958–c. 1974*. New York, 1998.

———. "Introduction: Locating Key Texts and the Distinctive Landscape of the Sixties." In *Windows on the Sixties*, ed. Anthony Aldgate, James Chapman, and Arthur Marwick. London, 2000: xi–xxi.

———. "Die 68er Revolution." In *Grosse Revolutionen des Geschichte*, ed. Peter Wende. Munich, 2000: 312–332.

Massot, F. de. *La grève générale (mai–juin 1968)*. Paris, 1968.

Massu, Jacques. *Baden 68: Souvenirs d'une fidélité gaulliste*. Paris, 1983.

Maupeou-Abboud, Nicole de. *Ouverture du ghetto étudiant: La gauche étudiante à la recherche d'un nouveau mode d'intervention politique (1960–1970)*. Paris, 1974.

Mauriac, François. *Bloc-notes*. 5 vols. Paris, 1993.

Michaud, Guy. *Révolution dans l'université*. Paris, 1968.

Miller, James. *Democracy Is in the Streets: From Port Huron to the Siege of Chicago*. New York, 1987.

Minces, Juliette. *Un ouvrier parle: Enquête*. Paris, 1969.

Monchablon, Alain. *Histoire de l'UNEF de 1956 à 1968*. Paris, 1983.

———. "L'UNEF et mai 1968." Paper presented to Colloque: Acteurs et terrains du mouvement social de 1968. Paris (24–25 November 1988).

Monneret, Jules. *Sociologie de la révolution*. Paris, 1969.

Morin, Edgar, Claude Lefort, and Cornelius Castoriadis. *Mai 68: La brèche*. Paris, 1988.

Moschetto, Bruno, and André Plagnol. *Le crédit à la consommation*. Paris, 1973.

Mouriaux, René. "Le mai de la CGT." Paper presented to Colloque: Acteurs et terrains du mouvement social de mai 1968. Paris (24–25 November 1988).

Mury, Gilbert. *La société de répression*. Paris, 1969.

Noiriel, Gérard. *Les ouvriers dans la société française*. Paris, 1986.

Nora, Pierre, ed. *The Realms of Memory*. Trans. Arthur Goldhammer. 3 vols. New York, 1996.

Notre arme c'est la grève. Paris, 1968.
Ouvriers face aux appareils: Une expérience de militantisme chez Hispano-Suiza. Paris, 1970.
Paillat, Claude. *Archives secrètes, 1968–69: Les coulisses d'une année terrible.* Paris, 1969.
Pascaud, Fernand. "La consommation des ménages de 1959–1972." *Collections de L'I.N.S.E.E* (June, 1974): 20–33.
Passerini, Luisa. *Autobiography of a Generation.* Trans. Lisa Erdberg. Hanover and London, 1996.
Perret, Jacques. *Inquiète Sorbonne.* Paris, 1968.
Peuchmaurd, Pierre. *Plus vivants que jamais.* Paris, 1968.
Pinner, Frank A. "Western European Student Movements through Changing Times." In *Students in Revolt,* ed. Seymour Martin Lipset and Philip G. Altbach. Boston, 1970: 60–95.
Pompidou, Georges. *Pour rétablir une vérité.* Paris, 1982.
Poperen, Claude. *Renault: Regards de l'intérieur.* Paris, 1983.
Portelli, Hugues. *La Ve République.* Paris, 1994.
Preuss, Ulrich K. "The Legacy of 1968 in Domestic Politics." Paper presented to "1968: The World Transformed." Conference of the German Historical Institute. Berlin (May, 1996).
Prévost, Claude. *Les étudiants et le gauchisme.* Paris, 1969.
Price, Roger. *The Second French Republic: A Social History.* Ithaca, 1972.
————, ed. *Revolution and Reaction: 1848 and the Second French Republic.* London, 1975.
Prost, Antoine. "Quoi de neuf sur le mai français." *Le Mouvement social,* no. 143 (April–June, 1988): 91–97.
————. "Les grèves de mai–juin 1968." *L'Histoire,* no. 110 (April, 1988): 34–46.
Pyne, Stephen J. *World Fire: The Culture of Fire on Earth.* New York, 1995.
Quattrocchi, Angelo, and Tom Nairn. *The Beginning of the End: France, May 1968.* London and New York, 1998.
Rabinovitch, W. "Contribution à la sociologie des masses en mouvement." *Revue internationale de criminologie et de police technique,* no. 3 (July–September, 1968): 199–218.
Raimon-Dityvon, Claude. *Mai 68.* Paris, 1988.
Rajsfus, Maurice. *Mai 68: Sous les pavés, la répression (mai 1968–mars 1974).* Paris, 1998.
Ravignant, Patrick. *L'Odéon est ouvert.* Paris, 1968.
Raynaud, Philippe. "Mai 68." In *Les Révolutions françaises,* ed. Frédéric Bluche and Stéphane Rials. Paris, 1989: 435–454.
Reader, Keith. *The May 1968 Events in France: Reproductions and Interpretations.* London, 1993.
Recent Social Trends in France (1960–1990). Trans. Liam Gavin. Frankfurt am Main, 1993.
Rémond, René. *La règle et le consentement.* Paris, 1979.
Reynaud, Jean-Daniel. "La nouvelle classe ouvrière, la technologie et l'histoire," *Revue française de science politique* (1972–1973): 529–542.
Rioux, Jean-Pierre. "A propos des célébrations décennales du mai français." *Vingtième siècle,* no. 23 (July–September, 1989): 49–58.
————. *La France de la Quatrième République: L'Expansion et l'impuissance, 1952–1958.* Paris, 1983.
Rioux, Lucien, and René Backmann. *L'Explosion de mai.* Paris, 1968.
Roach, John, and Jürgen Thomaneck, eds. *Police and Public Order in Europe.* London, 1985.
Robertson, Priscilla. *Revolutions of 1848: A Social History.* Princeton, 1952.
Rochet, Jean. *Cinq ans à la tête de la DST.* Paris, 1985.
Rose, Michael. *Servants of Post-Industrial Power? Sociologie du Travail in Modern France.* White Plains, N.Y., 1979.
Ross, George. *Workers and Communists in France.* Berkeley and Los Angeles, 1982.
Ross, Kristin. *May '68 and Its Afterlives.* Chicago, 2002.
Roszak, Theodore. *The Making of a Counter Culture.* New York, 1968.
Roumette, Sylvain. "Aide-Mémoire." *Les Temps modernes,* no. 265 (July, 1968): 153–160.
Salini, Laurent. *Mai des prolétaires.* Paris, 1968.
Salvati, Michele. "May 1968 and the Hot Autumn of 1969: The Response of Two Ruling Classes." In *Organizing Interests in Western Europe,* ed. Suzanne Berger. Cambridge, 1981: 331–366.

Savon, Hervé. "Les événements de mai 1968 et leurs interprètes." *Guerres et Paix*, no. 14–15 (1969–1970): 68–84.

Scardigli, Victor. "Les grèves dans l'économie française." *Consommation*, no. 3 (July–September, 1974): 81–122.

Schalk, David L. *War and the Ivory Tower: Algeria and Vietnam*. New York, 1991.

Schildt, Axel, Detlef Siegfried, and Karl Christian Lammers, eds. *Dynamische Zeiten: Die 60er Jahre in den beiden deutschen Gesellshaften*. Hamburg, 2000.

Seale, Patrick, and Maureen McConville. *Red Flag Black Flag: French Revolution 1968*. New York, 1968.

Servan-Schreiber, Jean-Jacques. *The Spirit of May*. Trans. Ronald Steel. New York, 1969.

Shils, Edward. "Dreams of Plentitude, Nightmares of Scarcity." In *Students in Revolt*, ed. Seymour Martin Lipset and Philip G. Altbach. Boston, 1970: 1–31.

Silvera, Alain. "The French Revolution of May 1968." *The Virginia Quarterly Review*, vol. 47, no. 3 (summer, 1971): 336–354.

Singer, Daniel. *Prelude to Revolution: France in May 1968*. New York, 1970.

Sirinelli, Jean-François. *Intellectuels et passions françaises: Manifestes et pétitions au XXe siècle*. Paris, 1990.

Souchier, Emmanuel, ed. *Mai 68*. Paris, 1988.

Spender, Stephen. *The Year of the Young Rebels*. New York, 1969.

Statera, Gianni. *Death of a Utopia: The Development of Student Movements in Europe*. Oxford, 1975.

Stéphane, André. *L'Univers contestationnaire*. Paris, 1969.

Stora, Benjamin. *Histoire de la Guerre d'Algérie 1954–1963*. Paris, 1993.

Sussman, Elisabeth, ed. *On the Passage of a Few People through a Rather Brief Moment in Time: The Situationist International, 1957–72*. Cambridge and London, 1989.

Suzzoni, Monique. "Chronologie des événements à Nanterre en 1967–1968." In *Mai 68: Les mouvements étudiants en France et dans le monde*, ed. Geneviève Dreyfus-Armand and Laurent Gervereau. Nanterre, 1988: 284–303.

Talbo, Jean-Philippe, ed. *La grève à Flins*. Paris, 1968.

Tarrow, Sidney. "Modular Collective Action and the Rise of the Social Movement." *Politics and Society*, vol. 21, no. 1 (March, 1993): 69–90.

———. *Power in Movement: Social Movements, Collective Action, and Politics*. New York, 1994.

———. "Social Protest and Policy Reform: May 1968 and the *Loi d'orientation* in France." *Comparative Political Studies*, vol. 25, no. 4 (January, 1993): 579–607.

———. *Struggle, Politics, and Reform: Collective Action, Social Movements, and Cycles of Protest*. Ithaca, 1991.

Tartakowsky, Danielle. "Le PCF en mai–juin 1968." Paper presented to Colloque: Acteurs et terrains du mouvement social de 1968. Paris (24–25 November 1988).

———. *Le pouvoir est dans la rue*. Paris, 1998.

Touchard, Jean. *Le Gaullisme, 1940–1969*. Paris, 1978.

Touraine, Alain. *The May Movement: Revolt and Reform*. Trans. Leonard F. X. Mayhew. New York, 1979.

Tournoux, Jean-Raymond. *Le mois de mai du général*. Paris, 1969.

Traugott, Mark. "The Crowd in the French Revolution of February, 1848." *American Historical Review*, vol. 93, no. 3 (June, 1988): 638–652.

———, ed. *Repertoires and Cycles of Collective Action*. Durham and London, 1995.

Tudesq, André-Jean. "La radio, les manifestations, le pouvoir." In *Mai 68 à l'ORTF*, Paris, 1987: 137–160.

Vaneigem, Raoul. *Traité de savoir vivre à l'usage des jeunes générations*. Paris, 1967.

Viénet, René. *Enragés et Situationnistes dans le mouvement des occupations*. Paris, 1968.

Vincent, Jean-Marie. "Pour continuer mai 1968." *Les Temps modernes*, no. 266–267 (August–September, 1968): 265–295.

Weber, Henri. *Vingt ans après: Que reste-t-il de 68*. Paris, 1988.

Weiss, Louise. "Télémaque 1969." *Guerres et Paix*, no. 14–15 (1969–1970).

Weisz, George. *The Emergence of Modern Universities in France, 1863–1914*. Princeton, 1983.

White, Edmund. *Genet: A Biography*. New York, 1993.

Willener, Alfred, Catherine Gajdos, and Georges Benguigui. *Les cadres en mouvement*. Paris, 1969.

Wilson, Sarah. "Martyrs and Militants: Painting and Propaganda: 1944–1954." In *War and Society in Twentieth-Century France*, ed. Michael Scriven and Peter Wagstaff. New York and Oxford, 1991: 219–246.

Winock, Michel. "Années 60: La poussée des jeunes." In *Etudes sur la France de 1939 à nos jours*. Paris, 1985: 304–322.

Wylie, Laurence, Franklin D. Chu, and Mary Terrall. *France: The Events of May–June 1968: A Critical Bibliography*. New York, 1973.

Yonnet, Paul. *Jeux, Modes et Masses: La société française et le moderne, 1945–1985*. Paris, 1985.

Zancarini-Fournel, Michelle. "Genre et Politique: Les Années 1968," *Vingtième Siècle* (July–September, 2002): 133–143.

Zegel, Sylvain. *Les idées de mai*. Paris, 1968.

Zolberg, Aristede, and Vera Zolberg. "The Meanings of May (Paris, 1968)." *Midway*, vol. 9, no. 3 (winter, 1969): 91–109.

INDEX